THE PLEBEIAN EXPERIENCE

COLUMBIA STUDIES IN POLITICAL THOUGHT / POLITICAL HISTORY

COLUMBIA STUDIES IN POLITICAL THOUGHT/POLITICAL HISTORY

DICK HOWARD, GENERAL EDITOR

Columbia Studies in Political Thought/Political History is a series dedicated to exploring the possibilities for democratic initiative and the revitalization of politics in the wake of the exhaustion of twentieth-century ideological "isms." By taking a historical approach to the politics of ideas about power, governance, and the just society, this series seeks to foster and illuminate new political spaces for human action and choice.

Pierre Rosanvallon, *Democracy Past and Future*, edited by Samuel Moyn (2006)

Claude Lefort, *Complications: Communism and the Dilemmas of Democracy*, translated by Julian Bourg (2007)

Benjamin R. Barber, *The Truth of Power: Intellectual Affairs in the Clinton White House* (2008)

Andrew Arato, *Constitution Making Under Occupation: The Politics of Imposed Revolution in Iraq* (2009)

Dick Howard, *The Primacy of the Political: A History of Political Thought from the Greeks to the French and American Revolution* (2010)

Robert Meister, *After Evil: Human Rights Discourse in the Twenty-first Century* (2011)

Paul W. Kahn, *Political Theology: Four New Chapters on the Concept of Sovereignty* (2011)

Stephen Eric Bronner, *Socialism Unbound: Principles, Practices, and Prospects* (2011)

David William Bates, *States of War: Enlightenment Origins of the Political* (2011)

Warren Breckman, *Adventures of the Symbolic: Post-Marxism and Radical Democracy* (2013)

THE PLEBEIAN EXPERIENCE

A DISCONTINUOUS HISTORY
OF POLITICAL FREEDOM

MARTIN BREAUGH

TRANSLATED BY LAZER LEDERHENDLER

COLUMBIA UNIVERSITY PRESS / NEW YORK

COLUMBIA UNIVERSITY PRESS

PUBLISHERS SINCE 1893

NEW YORK   CHICHESTER, WEST SUSSEX

cup.columbia.edu

Copyright © 2007 Editions Payot & Rivages

Translation copyright © 2013 Columbia University Press

This work is published with support from the French Ministry of
Culture / Centre national du livre.

Library of Congress Cataloging-in-Publication Data

Breaugh, Martin.

[Expérience plébéienne. English.]

The Plebeian Experience : A Discontinuous History of Political Freedom / Martin Breaugh ;
translated by Lazer Lederhendler.

pages cm. — (Columbia studies in political thought/political history)

Includes bibliographical references and index.

ISBN 978-0-231-15618-9 (cloth: alk. paper)   ISBN 978-0-231-52081-2 (e-book)

1. Democracy—History.   2. Political science—History.   3. Liberty—History.   4. Plebs
(Rome)   5. Jacobins—France—History—18th century   6. Jacobins—Great Britian—
History.   7. Sansculottes.   8. Paris (France)—History—Commune, 1871–   I. Title.

JC421.B78313   2013

320.01—DC23

2013013654

c 10 9 8 7 6 5 4 3 2 1

BOOK & COVER DESIGN: CHANG JAE LEE

COVER IMAGE: PARIS COMMUNE, MAY 16, 1871 © ADOC-PHOTOS / CORBIS

For André Vachet, *homme libre*

All that people have at birth is the potential to be free.
Actual freedom begins with acts of liberation.
—Oskar Negt

While I understand that the word "people" seems to have been appropriated by
populism, I see no reason to be intimidated by this. Why desist from reappropriating the
word "people," not in the sense of an identity but in the concrete sense of the plebs?
The plebs demanding their rights.
—Jean-Luc Nancy

If history is to be creative, to anticipate a possible future without denying the past,
it should, I believe, emphasize new possibilities by disclosing those hidden episodes of
the past when, even if in brief flashes, people showed their ability to resist,
to join together, occasionally to win. I am supposing, or perhaps only hoping,
that our future may be found in the past's fugitive movements of compassion
rather than in its solid centuries of warfare.
—Howard Zinn

CONTENTS

Foreword DICK HOWARD xi

Preface xv

Acknowledgments xxv

PART I: WHAT IS "THE PLEBS"?

1. Historical Genesis of the Plebeian Principle 3
    The Roman Republic: The First Plebeian Secession (494 BCE) 4
    Florence: The Ciompi Revolt (1378) 11
    Romans: Carnival and Revolt (1580) 18
        Excursus 1: On the "Originary Division of the Social" 25
    Naples: The Revolt of Masaniello (1647) 31
        Excursus 2: On the "Intractable" 36

2. Philosophical Genesis of the Plebeian Principle 44
    Machiavelli: The Plebs, Conflict, and Freedom 46
    Montesquieu: In Praise of Division 52
    Vico: The Plebs and the "History of All the Cities of the World" 60
    Ballanche: The Plebeian Principle 66
    De Leon: The Leaders of the Plebs 73
    Foucault: The Plebs—Baseness or Resistance? 81
    Rancière: The Plebeian Disagreement 91
    Answer to the Question, "What Is 'the Plebs'?" 98

PART II: THE QUESTION OF THE FORMS OF
POLITICAL ORGANIZATION

    Prologue: On the Dominant Political Configuration of Modernity 105

3. Sectional Societies and the Sans-Culottes of Paris 112
    Origin and Action of the Sectional Societies 114
    First Exemplary Political Struggle: Against Centralization 121

Second Exemplary Political Struggle: Against the Great Specialists 127
A Practice of Insurrection 130
    The Insurrection Against the Girondins 132
    The Insurrection Against the Thermidoreans 136

4. The London Corresponding Society and the English Jacobins 142
    On the Plebs: Thinking with Thompson Against Thompson 143
    On the English Jacobins 144
    Eighteenth-Century England and the French Revolution 146
    "That the Number of Our Members Be Unlimited" 151
    "The Liberty Tree" 155
    A Heritage Without a Testament? 164
        Plurality 165
        Political Capacity 167
        Otherness 168
        New Political Spaces 169
        Active Citizenship 170

5. The Paris Commune of 1871 and the Communards 173
    What Is a Communard? 173
    Toward the Paris Commune: A Political Apprenticeship 174
    Political Clubs Under the Commune: A Radical Democracy 182
    The Communalist Contribution: Critique of Politics, Practice of
    Freedom 191

PART III: THE NATURE OF THE HUMAN BOND

Prologue: Social Bond, Political Bond, and Modernity 201

6. The Sans-Culottes: A Political Bond of Fraternity 205
    The Sans-Culottes: A Political Bond 206
    Fraternity in Action 206
    Fraternization as Political Practice 209
    Politics, Violence, and Fraternity: A Tenuous Political Bond 211
    Rousseau's Legacy? On Undividedness Among the Sans-Culottes 213

7. The English Jacobins: A Political Bond of Plurality 218
    The Industrial Revolution in England 219
    The Break-Up of the Traditional Social Bond 222
    Rebonding: The London Corresponding Society 224
    "Unlimited Number": Plurality as Political Bond 226
    A Political Bond of Division? 227

8. The Communards: A Political Bond of Association 230
   The Political Situation in France Before the Commune 231
   A Core Principle of Communal Action: Association 234
   Association as Political Bond 236
   Dividedness or Undividedness Among the Communards? 239

Conclusion 241
Notes 245
Bibliography 283
Index 301

FOREWORD

IN OCTOBER 2012, THE CONSERVATIVE PARTY CHIEF WHIP, Andrew Mitchell, was forced to resign because he apparently called a Downing Street policeman a "plebeian." The uproar was surprising, as was the usage. Those upper-class British who traditionally studied Roman history seem to have forgotten that the distinctive nature of the plebs was not their economic class but the fact that they were denied political rights. But the spontaneous public reaction to the disdainful put-down shows that the public understood instinctively the antidemocratic weight of that slur. It was as if the trace of an inherited memory had been awakened, activated, and, for a brief moment, become a public value. This political moment in however a minor key is what Martin Breaugh's historical tableau illuminates.

The Plebeian Experience reconstructs the discontinuous history of a "hidden tradition" that underlies the always renewed democratic imperative that first took form in 494 BCE when the Roman plebs withdrew to the Aventine Hill to protest their political exclusion. But this was not only a protest or a withdrawal; it was a positive self-affirmation. It was the first step in a complicated process, marked by "ruptures" that left "traces" that were later activated by "memories" that emerged unexpectedly. It began a process that recurred in recognizable patterns, for example, in the revolt of the Ciompi in Florence, the Carnival at Romans, and the revolt of Masaniello in Naples. "Different times, different region, same struggle," says Breaugh, suggesting that there is some deeper structure or tension underlying the similar appearances. And in effect, he skillfully introduces two excurses into his discontinuous history: the first explicates Claude Lefort's theory of the "originary division of the social," and the second introduces Jean-François Lyotard's account of the way in which there is always an "intractable" or irreducible element that prevents the achievement of a completely transparent society. These two excurses explain why politics can never be reduced to socioeconomic relations, however weighty they appear. By the same token, and for the same reasons, politics cannot overcome social division.

This historical introduction of philosophical reflection sets the tone for what follows by showing how historical description acquires its richness, and its ambiguity, as the result of—and as an incitation to—theoretical reflection. Breaugh illustrates this interdependence by means of vivid and concise accounts of the way the simple picture of the emergence of the Roman plebs was reinterpreted, first, in the classical period by Machiavelli, Montesquieu, and Vico; then, in the light of the revolutionary experience by Ballanche and De Leon; and, once again, in our own times by Foucault and Rancière. Because they are less well known today, the presentation of the middle group, Ballanche and De Leon, is most illustrative of Breaugh's approach. Their return to Roman history is guided by their quest to understand the "plebeians" of their time whose demands could not be reduced to economic wealth or social status. De Leon, for example, noted that although they were politically excluded, the economic divisions between the wealthy and the poor plebs was exploited by the patricians, who formed a self-serving alliance with the wealthier plebs. What else, asked De Leon, was the refusal of the skilled craft workers led by the AFL of Samuel Gompers to support their unskilled exploited brethren against their real enemy, who ensured economic power by controlling the levers of political power?

What is the plebeian *experience*? What unites this discontinuous path of rupture and rekindled memory? The plebs is not a sociological entity; it is not Marx's revolutionary proletarian agent whose revolution will bring human history to its fulfillment. Breaugh rejects the linear and progressive theory of a history of progress—even a dialectical variant—that brings humanity ever closer to its ultimate self-realization. Instead, he reconstructs a *political experience* that not only does not promise a happy end but also is repetitive and (as is particularly clear in Vico) cyclical. Political breakthroughs are followed, sooner or later, by antipolitical collapses as the fear of disorder and the uncertainty of merely human laws become too much to bear. The sequence is not fixed;

the problem of leadership, for example, was faced differently by the Ciompi and by Masaniello. As the book proceeds to the period of revolution, where the sans-culottes, then the London Corresponding Society, and then the Paris Commune face the dilemmas of the plebeian experience, it might appear that these cycles are in fact developing an upward, spiral movement. That, however, is only the effect of the still-powerful presence of the teleological myth of progressive social history. Breaugh's claim is more radical. The ontological problems that result from the "originary division of the social" and the "intractable" that were skillfully introduced by the history of the Roman plebs recur in the experience of the modern revolutions. Society *is* divided; all problems can *not* be solved. That's why politics remains necessary.

Breaugh rejects the revolutionary tradition in favor of the traces of a richer plebeian experience that he associates with democracy—which he identifies with politics *tout court*. He rejects the way in which Marx "proletarianized" the plebs by reducing its experience to economic relations; and he joins Foucault (and Nietzsche) in their opposition to theories of progress whose universality necessarily misunderstands the singularity of events. The three terms that characterize Breaugh's democratic political vision are *agoraphilia*, *isonomy*, and *association*. They suggest the foundations for a reconstruction of the bonds of community as he illustrates in another set of historical reconstructions. The human bond is articulated in the experience of fraternity of the sans-culottes; the social bond emerges in the way in which plurality is accepted in the experience of the English Jacobins; and the political bond begins— only tentatively— to take shape in the mere seventy-two days of the Paris Commune (which Breaugh does *not* interpret with Marx—and Lenin—as "the finally discovered form" in which the revolution will occur).

The Plebeian Experience offers the reader a reconstruction of memories and traces of a recurring experience of political rupture. Although he leaves us at the beginning of the twentieth century, Breaugh is aware that history—his kind of history, a discontinuous history, marked by upsurges but threatened by diverse forms of depoliticization[1]—has continued and will continue. He is aware that the opposition of a historical, sociopolitical revolution to a political "rupture" was proposed convincingly as an account of what the French call "the events" of May 1968.[2] Although his book was written before the Arab Spring of 2011 and before the great economic implosion of 2008, these could well fit into the historical scheme that guided the first part of his book: "Different times, different region, same struggle." Is it the "same struggle" in the lands of Islam and the space of global finance? That will remain for the reader to judge.

In the meantime, the reaction of the British public to the outburst of Andrew Mitchell, the former chief whip, suggests that at least a "trace" of the plebeian experience remains alive.

NOTES

1. Breaugh recalls the experience of totalitarianism, particularly as analyzed by Claude Lefort. He owes a debt as well to Miguel Abensour, whose work is too little known among Anglo-Saxon readers. He also makes wise detours that apply Hannah Arendt's distinction of the political from the social and the economic spheres.
2. Cf. Claude Lefort, J-M Coudray (i.e., Cornelius Castoriadis), and Edgar Morin, *La brèche* (Paris: Fayard, 1968). This volume was republished by Fayard, with the essay "Vingt ans après" in 1988 and was reprinted most recently in 2008.

PREFACE

The meaning of politics is freedom.
—Hannah Arendt, *The Promise of Politics*

"THE PLEBS" IS THE NAME OF AN EXPERIENCE, THAT OF ACHIEVING human dignity through political agency. The plebs designates neither a social category nor an identity but rather a fundamental political event: the passage from a subpolitical status to one of a full-fledged political subject. The plebeian experience signifies the metamorphosis of *animal laborans* into *zoon politikon*.[1] The term *animal laborans* must be understood here in a way that goes beyond the figures of the worker, the laborer, or the proletarian; it refers to those whose existence remains subjected to the order of biology, to the imperatives of the human body. Their subpolitical status results from their being denied public speech (*logos*) and reduced to the basic animal expression of pleasure and pain (*phoné*).

To forestall any attempt to equate the plebs with an objectively constituted actor proceeding from the "for-itself" to the "in-itself," this study is centered on the notion of "experience." Georges Bataille provides a valuable description of the concept of experience as it will be used here:

I call experience a voyage to the end of the possible of man. Anyone may not embark on this voyage, but if he does embark on it, this supposes the negation of the authorities, the existing values which limit the possible. By virtue of the fact that it is negation of other values, other authorities, experience, having a positive existence, becomes itself positively value *and authority*.[2]

Thus, the plebeian experience refers to a disposition that refuses the limits of the possible present of the dominant order and whose goal is to bring about a collective existence other than that which holds sway in a specific political community.

The refusal to submit to political domination is the impulse at the core of the plebeian experience, and it opens onto the expression of a desire for liberty. "Liberty" must be comprehended here in its political sense, that is, the possibility for all to take part in the life of the city. Plebeian struggles are aimed at breathing life into political freedom through an assault on the monolithic rule of domination.

This study of the plebeian experience is situated within the Machiavellian constellation. It testifies to what the Florentine Secretary calls the division of "humors" between the desire to dominate of the "nobles" and the desire not to be dominated, that is, the desire for freedom of the "people" (or "plebs"). According to Machiavelli, the division of the humors is both universal, because it is found in all political communities, and impossible to transcend, because it remains a primal fact of the human political condition.[3] At the same time, Machiavelli uses the division of the humors to classify regimes.[4] We thus find ourselves endowed with a new form of political intelligibility since the nature of a political community is revealed through the manner in which the conflict between the humors is played out.

For Machiavelli, thinker of the "effective truth," an understanding of political phenomena must necessarily derive from an analysis of the effects or consequences of political action. In other words, there is nothing to be gained from dwelling on first principles or the intentions guiding political action; all that matters are their effects. Hence, Machiavelli contends, the public expression of the division of the dispositions between the nobles and the people entails fundamental political consequences for freedom. In book 1, chapter 4 of the *Discourses on Livy*, titled "That the disunion of the Plebs and the Roman Senate made that Republic free and powerful," Machiavelli writes, "I say that to me it appears that those who damn the tumults between the nobles and the plebs blame those things that were the first cause of keeping Rome free, they consider the noises and the cries that would arise in such tumults more than the good effects that they engendered."[5] Order can emerge from disorder.[6] This, above all, is why one must not condemn the disturbances and conflicts in Rome. The surface effects resulting from these political struggles are not worthy of attention; only their political consequence matters. For Machiavelli, conflict enables a broadening of freedom within the political community:

> That in every republic are two diverse humors, that of the people and that of the great, and that all the laws that are made in favour of freedom arise from their disunion. . . . Nor can one in any mode, with reason, call a republic disordered where there are so many examples of virtue; for good examples arise from good education, good education from good laws, and good laws from those tumults that many inconsiderately damn. For whoever examines their end well will find that they have engendered not any exile or violence unfavourable to the common good, but laws and orders in benefit of public freedom.[7]

Machiavelli perceives the opposition of the two dispositions of the city to be at the root of "good laws." Whereas the nobles seek to gratify their *libido dominandi*, the plebs strive to express their desire not to be subjected to this domination. The plebeian experience is thus the affirmation of a desire for liberty that ultimately engenders the conflict necessary for the broadening of political freedom. In asserting themselves, the plebs declare their full participation in the human political condition. In a word, they become political subjects.

The plebeian desire for political freedom, however, is not immune to a relapse into domination since, paradoxical as this may seem, the desire for freedom can turn into its opposite: the desire for servitude. Indeed, a genuine political comprehension of the plebeian experience cannot dispense with an inquiry into the enigma of "voluntary servitude" as elaborated by Étienne de La Boétie in *The Discourse on Voluntary Servitude*. The hypothesis of voluntary servitude, a veritable "nuclear weapon" of political thought, must not lead to an unequivocal reduction of politics to domination. On the contrary, it obliges us to incorporate a new element of complexity—the desire for servitude—in our understanding of the relationship between politics and freedom. Especially as there exists no "ironclad law" of freedom that would make servitude an unavoidable outcome. For La Boétie, the "voluntary servitude" hypothesis is rooted in an elementary yet disturbing question: Why do people accept the rule of a single individual who holds power only because they have granted it to him?[8] Framed this way, the terms of the traditional understanding of political domination are reversed. Henceforward, the origins of domination must be sought among the dominated and not only among the masters. Furthermore, neither the fear of death ("cowardice") nor even habit (or "custom") can account for voluntary servitude.[9] It is caused, rather, by an enchantment brought about "by the name of one man alone." And it is precisely this enchantment that denatures people by distancing them from liberty.[10] In the context of the plebeian experience it is therefore necessary to take heed of the phenomena that turn struggles for emancipation into struggles for servitude.

In sum, the plebeian experience is a passage from a subpolitical to a political status and represents an experiment in the transgression of the political order of domination whose initial impulse is born of a desire for freedom. Yet any mollifying, one-dimensional vision of the plebeian experience must be dismissed at the outset since the desire for freedom does not preclude the potential for a return to domination by virtue of the desire for servitude. Still, while the overall scope of this experience comes into sharper focus, its name nevertheless continues to raise questions: Why the "plebs"? What does the term refer to?

The choice of "plebs" to designate these struggles for freedom is based essentially on two lines of reasoning. First, it seems possible to write a dual history of the politics of the "people" or, to use a more neutral expression, the "many." This possibility derives from a simple but significant observation: whenever one names or mentions the many, a twofold linguistic resource is available in the form of paired terms. A great deal can be learned from examining the names given to the many at three crucial democratic moments in Western political history: Athenian democracy, the Roman Republic, and the modern revolutions. At the birth of democracy in Greece there were two terms for the many: *demos* and *hoi polloi*. Similarly, the Latin words *populus* and *plebs* served to identify the many during the Roman Republic. Finally, at the dawn of the modern revolutions the terms used were "people" and "multitude" (or "populace"). However, even though these terms all refer to the many, their effects are not the same since the connotations of "*hoi polloi*," "*plebs*," and "multitude" are rather more pejorative than those of "*demos*," "*populus*," and "people." And it is precisely at this level that the dual history of the many can be delineated. The history of the political advent of the *demos*, the *populus*, and the people can generally be said to involve a series of institutional reforms designed to integrate gradually the political demands of social categories excluded from political decision making. In Athens, for example, the *demos* came to power thanks to political reforms initiated by aristocrats (Draco, Solon, Cleisthenes, et al.), who were motivated by the common good and desirous of freeing Athens from the perpetual conflicts between the old dominant families and the *demos*. This history contrasts sharply with the political emergence of the *hoi polloi*, the *plebs*, and the multitude, which came about as part of a movement more revolutionary than reformist, more "insurgent" than institutional, and which has certainly remained a more hidden and unfamiliar history. Thus, the choice of the term *plebs* results from a desire to understand the many through the lens of this second history, whose high points and defining features need to be brought to light.

More importantly, the term *plebs* refers directly to the Roman Republic, an all too neglected period in the history of freedom. At the heart of this book is the idea that the plebeian experience was born precisely at the time of the Roman plebs' first secession in 494 BCE. With that first secession a *recurrent political configuration* was introduced, for when the plebs seceded in Rome they inaugurated a *discontinuous* tradition of political freedom whose traces can be perceived at various epochs of Western history. This does not mean that the plebeian secession was merely "repeated" but rather that the plebs deployed political strategies that are helpful for a better understanding of various struggles for freedom and emancipation. The task, therefore, is to examine the political experience of the Roman plebs as a "founding" or "paradigmatic" moment, or even an "inaugural scene"[11] of an underground and little-known tradition of the politics of the many. But before detailing more fully the features or particulars of this founding moment, it may be useful to provide a political and historical outline of the first plebeian secession in Rome. And to do this, we must turn to the account given by Livy in book 2 of his *History of Rome*.

It is worth noting at the outset that in ancient Rome, "plebs" referred to individuals who had neither names nor the right to speak in public. They were people "deprived of both symbolic inscription and the power of speech,"[12] whose existence was subhuman because they could not take part in the life of the city. The first years of the Roman Republic witnessed political disturbances sparked by the economic situation of the plebs.[13] Crushed by debt, the plebeians were at risk of being reduced to slavery because of insolvency. The oppression was further aggravated by the plebeians' obligation to defend the Republic as conscripts in the army. The plebs thus found themselves in the paradoxical situation of having to defend Rome's freedom abroad while being threatened with subjugation at home. This, according to Livy, engendered ever-increasing "discontent" between patricians and plebeians out of which a major conflict of the orders in the Republic developed and culminated when the plebs withdrew to the Aventine Hill.[14] There they formed a camp "without any officer to direct them,"[15] but they did not launch an assault against Rome nor undergo one at the hands of the patricians. The secession created enormous difficulties for the patricians because the labor shortage undermined the Eternal City and exposed it to barbarian invasions.

To overcome the plebeian insurrection, the Senate dispatched Menenius Agrippa to the Aventine Hill. His mission was to restore the unity of the Republic by bringing the plebs back to Rome, and to achieve this, Agrippa, addressing them directly, recounted the fable of the belly and the parts. The parable describes a conflict between the various parts of the human body and the belly. The parts rebel against the idea of having to supply food to the belly, "with nothing to do but enjoy the pleasant things they gave it."[16] To protest against this inequity, the parts secede and refuse to feed the belly. The problem with this action is that it weakens not only the belly but the parts as well since the belly cannot be separated from the parts. For Agrippa, the patricians personified the belly of Rome, its vital principle, and the plebeians, its parts or members. Consequently, a secession of the plebs penalizes the plebs as well. For society to function smoothly, the orders must cooperate. The fable of the belly and the parts ensured the success of Agrippa's mission: the plebeians agreed to abandon their camp "without any officer to direct them" and returned to Rome.

Menenius Agrippa's achievement did not, however, bring about a return to the status quo. Instead it led to the appointment of specifically plebeian magistrates. Henceforward, two "tribunes" would defend the plebeians' cause within the framework of the Republic's political institutions. The tribunes were given the protection of the Sacred Law, making them inviolate on religious grounds.[17] Thus, the plebeians, deprived until then of symbolic inscription in the city, gained both political and religious status in Rome.

Two noteworthy features emerge from this first plebeian insurrection: the *political* nature of the conflict and the affirmation of a *radical equality*. Although the primary root of the secession was the economic situation, the dispute was resolved through a *political* mission and on the basis of a *political* integration. To put it another way, having acted from economic discontent, the plebs gained political status, thereby advancing from a subpolitical position to that of a full-fledged political subject. Furthermore, the political events in Rome involved a singular phenomenon. As previously mentioned, Livy notes that the plebeian military camp on the Aventine Hill was formed without an officer to direct them.[18] This amounted to rejecting the division between the "few" and the "many," in other words, between those who dominate and those subjected to domination. By the same token, the plebs' refusal to reproduce this hierarchy affirmed a radical equality among political subjects.

To grasp the genuine political meaning of the plebeian experience, it would also be useful to examine Jacques Rancière's discussion of an interpretation articulated by the nineteenth-century philosopher Pierre-Simon Ballanche.

According to Rancière, the originality of Ballanche's interpretation lies in his "restaging of the conflict in which the entire issue at stake involves finding out whether there exists a common stage where plebeians and patricians can debate anything."[19] Whereas Livy attributes no particular meaning to Menenius Agrippa's mission, Ballanche ascribes to it a great deal of symbolic weight, pointing out that from the patrician viewpoint the plebs had no voice. There could be no common ground between patricians and plebs. The plebeian was deprived of speech because he lacked both a name and a filiation, leaving him indeed "without a name, deprived of logos . . . , of symbolic enrollment in the city."[20] Consequently, the plebs were relegated to subhuman status, incapable of expressing anything but noise (*phoné*), that is, the manifestation of pleasure and pain, thereby substantiating the idea that the Roman plebs were reduced to the order of biology. Yet during his mission to the Aventine Hill, Agrippa committed an error with disastrous repercussions for patrician domination. In telling his tale, he postulated the ability of the plebs *to understand* and *to speak*, thus opening a gap in the reign of the few. The effect was to ruin an order of domination that "recognizes no *logos* capable of being articulated by beings deprived of *logos*, no *speech* capable of being proffered by nameless beings."[21]

On top of Aventine Hill, the plebeians constituted an order uniquely their own. Refusing to accept subhuman status, they seized the opportunity to gain symbolic enrollment in the city by acting as though they bore proper names. To quote Rancière's reading of Ballanche, the plebeians "thereby execute a series of speech acts that mimic those of the patricians: they pronounce imprecations and apotheoses; they delegate one of their number to go and consult *their* oracles; they give themselves representatives by rebaptizing them."[22] Through this transgression of the order of domination the plebeians appropriated the right to speak beyond merely grunting. And it is Agrippa who bears responsibility for having opened up an egalitarian political space: his address to the plebeians presupposed their capacity to rise above the imperatives of the biological order.

This "inaugural scene" of the plebeian experience displays three major features that are specific to this little-known, underground, and discontinuous history of the politics of the many, which this study proposes to extract from the Western political tradition. The progression from a subpolitical to a political status was at the outset the product of the plebs' will to emancipate themselves. They sought to assert their own desire for freedom without being compelled to act by a tutelary power intent on bending them to its aims of political domination. To put it another way, the plebeian experience shares in a "communalist" or "councilist" revolutionary tradition, that is, an approach based on the direct agency of subjects in action. While it may seem somewhat anachronistic to identify an event of the ancient world as "communalist,"[23] the term helps distinguish between revolutions "from above" and those "from below." Moreover, the actions of the Roman plebeians can justifiably be viewed, to quote Oskar Anweiler, a historian of the Soviets, as "the first historical instance of the council idea."[24] Anweiler establishes three criteria for determining whether or not a revolution can be considered councilist or communalist, in sum, a revolution "from below": "1. its connection with a particular dependent or oppressed social stratum; 2. radical democracy as its form; 3. a revolutionary origin."[25] As an "inaugural scene" of a discontinuous tradition of political freedom, the first plebeian secession enacted a will to self-emancipation that meets Anweiler's three criteria. The plebeians were dominated by the Roman patricians; they set up an egalitarian political space on the Aventine Hill; and they seceded, that is, withdrew altogether "illegally"[26] from the Roman order. In addition, the plebeian experience testifies to the persistence of a genuine "politics of the people,"[27] taken in the sense of the direct action of the many.

Anweiler also affirms that "the tendency of such councils . . . is the striving toward the most direct, far-reaching, and unrestricted participation of the individual in public life."[28] Given that the plebeian experience shares this political aspiration, its second defining feature can therefore be identified as its participation in an "agoraphilic" political tradition. The notions of "agoraphilia" and its opposite, "agoraphobia," have been developed by the political scientist Francis Dupuis-Déri to draw a fundamental distinction between different political institutions and practices.[29] Dupuis-Déri borrows from the lexicon of psychology in order to map out two possible attitudes toward the idea of a politically active people, both of which underpin modern as well as ancient political institutions and practices. He explains that "agoraphobia [is] the distrust of people governing themselves, without having their wishes filtered through representatives. [The agoraphobe] fears the 'chaos' or 'tyranny of the majority' of direct democracy. Political agoraphobia is the fear of seeing the people in power as well as contempt for the political capacities of the people."[30] Conversely, "agoraphilia" is displayed by a political regime or practice that enables the many to participate in political life. Politics then becomes decidedly democratic because it is instituted in and through the political action of the many. The plebeian experience, as inaugurated by the first Roman secession, fully partakes of the agoraphilic tradition inasmuch as it emerged through the political affirmation of an actor long banned from the stage of Roman politics, an affirmation that brought political freedom to life in the face of domination.

In addition to communalism and agoraphilia, there is a final characteristic of the plebeian experience relating to the temporal specificity of plebeian action. Plebeian temporality can generally be understood in terms of what Hannah Arendt refers to as the "gap," that is, an irruptive event that temporarily fractures the order of domination. The plebeian experience per se cannot be sustained for any length of time. Nevertheless, while this "gap" in the history of domination is destined to be sealed up, it cannot be regarded as an inheritance with "no testament."[31] For in spite of its relative brevity, the plebeian experience leaves *traces*. In the words of the historian Boris Porchnev, "The repercussions of each plebeian uprising extended not only through space but through time as well; . . . a movement never disappears without leaving traces: it continues to live for many years in the minds of the masses and guides their future behavior."[32] Oskar Negt furthermore points out that the revolutionary impact of popular movements "derives mainly from the memory of *the original democratic equality and self-government* being put into living practice, even though the actors are aware . . . of their foreseeable failure." Negt adds, "This collective memory is not restricted to certain ancient historical regimes. . . . In this case, the collective memory is at the same time a memory of the history of individual domination."[33] It is precisely the temporality of the gap and its subsequent traces that explain why the plebeian experience inaugurates a "discontinuous" history of political freedom. While its impermanence accounts for the discontinuity of this experience, its traces have made it detectable at various moments in Western history.

To recapitulate: The plebeian experience, that transition from a subpolitical to a political status, remains an experiment in the transgression of the order of political domination, a transgression born of a desire for liberty that may incorporate a desire for servitude. As for the name "plebeian," it alludes to a little-known, occulted history of the political affirmation of the many. But the use of the term "plebs" also, and even more significantly, points to the foundational or inaugural nature of the first plebeian secession in Rome. The criterion for determining whether something constitutes a plebeian experience is the observation of three defining features: communalism, agoraphilia, and a temporality of the gap that leaves traces.

What still needs to be articulated is how this analysis of the plebs' political action can be carried out. For one of this study's ambitions is to demonstrate that the plebeian experience opens onto a new political understanding that brings to light a tradition whereby collective existence is centered on freedom rather than domination. To gain access to this "plebeian experience," a three-pronged historical corpus will serve to blaze a trail: the Parisian sans-culottes during the French Revolution (years II and III), the English Jacobins during the making of the English working class (1792–1799), and the communards during the insurrection of the Paris Commune in 1871. Two major questions will guide this analysis: What form of political organization did the plebeians establish? What is the nature of the human bonds engendered through these political experiences? The aim will be to show that it is possible to read these events so as to illuminate the plebeian contribution to a discontinuous history of political freedom.

Before undertaking such a demonstration, however, two prior questions need to be addressed. On the one hand, is it possible to write a political history of the plebs? This implies that an attempt must be made to identify within various historical episodes (the Ciompi of Florence; the carnival of Romans, France; the Neapolitan revolt of Masaniello; and so on) the construction of a "plebeian principle" through the political affirmation of the plebs. On the other hand, is it possible to extract from the history of political thought a "theory of the plebs"? Through the works of Machiavelli, Montesquieu, Vico, Ballanche, De Leon, Foucault, and Rancière, can one observe the philosophical inception of the "plebeian principle," that is to say, a heterogeneous approach that casts the plebs in a predominant, even salutary, role in political affairs?

For it is in the light of such an analysis that we can assess the relevance of the plebeian experience to our understanding of politics. This said, there are already grounds for asserting that the value of such an investigation will depend as well on the enactment of a practice of political philosophy that today has been forsaken or at least marginalized. Our goal will be to carry out "an exercise in political thought" (Arendt), to show *in actu* that political thought need not be inescapably reduced to a necessary history of ideas and doctrines but, with its categories and concepts, can provide a space where the social-historical can be interpreted and made intelligible.

ACKNOWLEDGMENTS

THE PLEBEIAN EXPERIENCE WAS ORIGINALLY PUBLISHED IN PARIS by Éditions Payot-Rivages as part of the series Critique de la politique, edited by Miguel Abensour. I thank him warmly for his generosity and stimulating contribution to political theory. Marie-Martine Serrano, the foreign rights editor at Payot-Rivages, was a strong supporter of this project, which could not have been realized without her excellent work.

I am grateful to former political science editor Peter Dimock at Columbia University Press and to senior executive editor Wendy Lochner, ably assisted by Christine Mortlock and Christine A. Dunbar. They played an essential part in getting this project off the ground and taking the manuscript through the final stages of preparation. Special thanks go to Dick Howard, who welcomed this book into his prestigious new series while providing sage advice and unwavering support. His contribution to political thought is exemplary.

My colleagues and friends at the Department of Political Science at York University, especially Professors David McNally, Asher Horowitz, Shannon Bell, Stephen Newman, and Terry Maley, helped create an inspiring and gratifying work environment. At the Université du Québec à Montréal, my colleagues and friends Francis Dupuis-Déri, Yves Couture, André Corten, and Ricardo Peñafiel engaged with me in a fruitful (and often dialectical) exchange. I thank them for their passionate practice of emancipatory thinking.

Lazer Lederhendler, an award-wining translator, accepted the challenge of translating this work. Without his competent and scrupulous approach, the project would not have seen the light of day.

I wish to express my gratitude to my excellent graduate assistants at York for their much needed help: Hugo Bonin, Gabrielle Gérin, Maryann Raby, Anna Muraski, and Sarah Leblanc.

Finally, I want to thank my wife, Chiara Piazzesi, for making my life happier and more beautiful.

This translation was made possible by grants from the Centre National du Livre (France), the vice president for research and innovation at York University, and a Faculty of Arts Research Grant (York University).

THE PLEBEIAN EXPERIENCE

PART I

WHAT IS "THE PLEBS"?

1
HISTORICAL GENESIS OF THE PLEBEIAN PRINCIPLE

Besides, how shall the people, if it cannot form true judgments,
be able rightly to direct the state?
—Euripides, *The Suppliants*

WHAT DO THE TERMS "PLEBS" AND "PLEBEIANS" SIGNIFY? THE
choice of a term specific to Roman antiquity may in some ways appear anachronistic or even quaint, especially when one seeks, as we do, to characterize a
modern political actor. Yet it is possible to delineate a "political history of the
plebs" from the Roman Republic to nineteenth-century Europe that coincides
with those moments when revolt and freedom manifested themselves. The political history of the West thus includes events where the plebs demonstrated its
strength and political capacities in order to transform the dominant political
order. A "plebeian principle" has thus been asserted within our political tradition. The phrase "plebeian principle" should be understood in the general sense
ascribed to it by Pierre-Simon Ballanche, that is, a principle of action that offers human beings an emancipatory goal and serves as a principle of historical
intelligibility.[1]

Through a study of these historical manifestations it is possible to outline a
political history of the plebs and to highlight its distinguishing features. In the
course of its many struggles, the plebs indeed advocated social and political
approaches and aspirations. The feeling of revolt, which was often the initial
force driving plebeian demands, seems to have worked in tandem with a will
to broaden the public sphere through the adoption of a more inclusive politics.
It is here that the plebs set in motion an experience whereby political freedom

came to the community. Through certain eminently plebeian political experiences, we will more specifically explore the relationship between the plebs and the communalist (i.e., relating to a politics of the people) and agoraphile (i.e., relating to political freedom) traditions.

By examining four plebeian political experiences, we will be able to situate the establishment of a plebeian principle in Western history. The necessary point of departure is ancient Rome, more exactly the Roman Republic (509–27 BCE). We will then discuss the Ciompi revolt in Florence (1378) and the revolt of the carnival—the plebeian festival par excellence—in Romans, France (1580). Finally, we will consider Masaniello's Neapolitan rebellion (1647). Our intention, however, is not to circumscribe and exhaustively investigate every plebeian political experience; it is, rather, to analyze the historical construction of the plebeian principle. The selected experiences will make it possible to see how a plebeian political practice was instituted through the rejection of domination and the attempt to set up, by means of concerted action, an alternative power.

If this chronology stops on the eve of the eighteenth century, it is not because the plebeian principle disappeared at that moment. We hope to demonstrate, quite to the contrary, that the many experiences of the plebs continued until the nineteenth century and perhaps have done so even to this day. Consequently, we propose to analyze the resurgence of the plebeian principle at three key moments in modern history: the French Revolution, the making of the English working class, and the Paris Commune of 1871. Our project involves bringing to light the presence of the plebeian principle in each of these events. For now, however, we will begin by delineating the main features of these experiences so as to elucidate the historical genesis of the plebeian principle, starting with the birth of the plebeian experience in Rome.

THE ROMAN REPUBLIC: THE FIRST PLEBEIAN SECESSION (494 BCE)

The Roman Republic spanned a tumultuous period at the cusp of two major eras of Roman civilization: the Kingdom and the Empire. The conflictual nature of the Republic arose in particular from the political division of Roman society between the patricians, who controlled the levers of political and economic power and enjoyed religious status, and the plebeians, who had neither political and economic power nor any religious recognition. However, as noted by the historian Jean-Claude Richard, the patrician-plebeian duality did not exist from the very beginnings of Rome,[2] even though this notion was firmly implanted in the Roman imaginary, especially during the Empire.[3] The reason was that when Rome was founded the plebs did not constitute a political actor but would become one only under the Republic. It came into being, in other words, through a political *experience*. Thus, the plebs was not an objectively constituted actor within the political and economic reality of Rome.

Richard defines the plebs as a "heterogeneous mass comprised of elements exterior to the [patrician] elite and which emerged from non-being in the early years of the 5th century."[4] The plebs was characterized by the great diversity of its makeup. These disparate elements, united in miscellany, alterity, and plurality, came from *outside* Rome's dominant elite. The heterogeneity here was twofold, applying to both the plebs' constitution and its relationship to power. The distinction and the opposition between plebs and patricians remained in some ways irreducible and marked out a definite separation between the two orders. Significantly, Richard stresses that the plebs "*emerged* from non-being," thereby underscoring the plebs' constructedness and, hence, its creativity, since it took an active part in its own emergence as a political subject. Furthermore, the plebs asserted itself politically, moving from the category of nonbeing to that of full-fledged human being. Its existence thus grew out of its active participation in political life. By divorcing itself from the physical imperatives of the species, the plebs took on the political condition specific to humankind. Max Weber confirms the hypothesis of the political character of the plebs: "The conflict of orders in the Early Republic was a social struggle only in so far as it concerned debt law . . . *otherwise* it was a political struggle."[5]

"Heterogeneous," "exterior," emergence from "nonbeing": these are among the constitutive elements that a preliminary definition of the plebs brings to light. But before going any further, it would be appropriate to determine the ideological and material conditions that allowed the plebs to appear precisely at the time of the Roman Republic.

On the ideological level, Roman political practice during the Republic was structured by *libertas*. This notion, characterized by a degree of ideological elasticity, may refer to a number of things: political rights, equality among citizens, a fairer distribution of wealth, etc. But *libertas* can be summed up as the capacity to have rights and the absence of political subjugation.[6] The importance of *libertas* was such that it shaped not only political practice but also the other core political ideas of Rome, such as *civitas* and *res publica*. Indeed, it represents one of the founding concepts of Roman political institutions.[7] In Rome, *libertas* did not have the status of a natural right; it was an acquired right that could be lost, particularly through enslavement. On the other hand, it was possible for everyone, including slaves and excluded individuals, to acquire *libertas* and thereafter enjoy political rights;[8] hence the importance of such a notion, which, by its very nature, was subject to fluctuations within the Roman political sphere. The conventionality of *libertas* enabled its extension within the Republic.

Libertas indicated, in sum, a person's status in Rome. It overlapped—and to some extent blended with—the notion of *civitas*, which designated a person's rank according to his relationship to the political community.[9] *Libertas* and *civitas* were interrelated inasmuch as the range and scope of *libertas* varied in accordance with the political structure prevailing in Rome.[10] The Roman who enjoyed maximum *libertas* was necessarily endowed with the status of *civitas*. At the same time, for there to be *civitas*, free political institutions were needed. *Libertas* granted the right to act within inclusive political structures.[11] It was therefore linked to the citizen's autonomy, which was realized thanks to political institutions that were free and able to accommodate the citizens' participation. The political conditions for freedom had to prevail in order for *libertas* actually to take shape. That is why *libertas* appeared in Rome after the fall of the monarchies, once the Republic was established.

The *res publica*, another key concept of Roman political practice, designates a regime granting everyone an active share in political life. It was premised on the participation of the people in public affairs but without affirming the principle of government by the people.[12] In fact, ordinary citizens made up only one component of the Roman Republic's political sphere, in which patricians and others invested with authority and dignity always played a predominant role.[13] Concerning the *res publica*, *libertas* guaranteed that Roman political institutions were truly free and republican. The *res publica* could not truly be the "public thing" without *libertas*, that is, without the enjoyment of certain political rights and the absence of different forms of subjugation.

Yet the advent of the plebs did not result exclusively from an ideological mutation that placed *libertas* at the heart of politics. It was also the product of a particular economic situation. It must be stressed at the outset that, as noted by the historian H. Mouritsen, the thesis of the preponderance of the *clientela* system—a network of plebeian economic dependence on the patricians—has today been put in doubt by scholars of the Roman world.[14] The lack of empirical evidence for the existence of a system of economic and political subordination of the lower to the upper class renders such a view of Rome untenable.[15] Already in the nineteenth century, the historian Fustel de Coulanges stated, "the plebeians were not the clients; the historians of antiquity do not confound these two classes. . . . In Dionysius of Halicarnassus we read, 'the plebeians left Rome and retired to Mons Sacer; the patricians remained alone in the city with their clients.'"[16] Max Weber also underscores the difficulties concerning the distinction between plebs and clients in Rome.[17] Without claiming to resolve this interpretive issue, one can nevertheless posit that the *clientela* network did indeed exist in Rome but did not affect the majority of plebeians.

The secondary nature of the *clientela* does not, however, imply that the plebs enjoyed an enviable economic position. On the contrary, deprivation, famine, housing shortages, and high mortality rates were, among other ordeals, the plebs' daily lot.[18] Extremely harsh living conditions within a more open political context than had been the case under the monarchy, led to the "birth" of the plebs as a political subject.[19] *Libertas*, "precisely because it was such a fundamental tenet of the identity of the Roman state," allowed "all political agents [to] draw moral capital from it and exploit it for their own purposes."[20] Ideology and the economic juncture opened a gap in the political domination prevailing until then in Rome. The plebs constituted itself by exploiting that gap. The first plebeian secession (494 BCE) paralyzed the economic life of the Eternal City.

There were three plebeian secessions in Rome. The first, however, stands out as the founding event because this was the moment of the plebs' advent as a political subject. Its significance can also be attributed to its becoming a point of reference for certain political ideas and practices that followed.[21] This, at least, is what remains to be assessed at the conclusion of our investigation.

Regarding the background to the first plebeian secession in Rome, the debt problem, according to Livy, was the root cause of major political upheavals in the early years of the Roman Republic.[22] The destitute were liable to lose their status as free men and become slaves because of unpaid debts. This state of affairs seemed all the more unjust because plebeians were required to defend the Roman Republic by serving in the army. This paradoxical situation—defense of Rome's liberty against exterior threats but domestic subjection—engendered "internal dissension" between patricians and plebeians that made conflict between the orders inevitable. The plebeians, Livy writes, "complained loudly that after fighting foreign wars for liberty and empire, at home they were oppressed and made prisoners by their own fellow citizens; and that the freedom of the plebs was more secure in war among the enemy than among their own countrymen."[23]

One incident that was especially scandalous from the plebs' perspective sparked off a riot in Rome. At the forum, an old man living in misery recounted how he had been forced to sell the family's land and all his possessions. Despite having served heroically (he had been a brilliant commander of a Roman century), "he had been dragged by his creditor not just into slavery, but into a place of punishment and torture."[24] This old man embodied the plebs' intolerable situation, and the treatment he received provoked violent disturbances.

When the Volsci launched a surprise attack against Rome, the patricians were terror-stricken. To fight simultaneously on two fronts, external and internal, would no doubt mean the ruin of Rome. The plebeians, on the other hand, greeted the news of the aggression with joy: "For them, it seemed like an intervention of providence to crush the pride of the Senate." Taking advantage of the situation to apply pressure against the patricians, the plebs encouraged its members to refrain from joining the army, a tactic that forced the Senate to prohibit penalties against Roman citizens who were unable to pay their debts. Livy suggests that this was a compromise aimed at alleviating domestic strife and thus ensuring Rome's victory against its external enemies.[25]

Rome's ensuing victory emboldened the patricians, who immediately clamped down on debtors, including veterans. "Men previously bound over, were in consequence of judgements, abandoned to the mercy of their creditors, and others, previously free, were bound over in their turn." The veterans tried to avoid these stringent decrees by appealing to the consul who had issued the recent edict against imprisonment for indebtedness. But the antidebtor furor was overwhelming, and the consuls could do no better than to adopt a position of neutrality. Livy explains that because "they knew now that it was idle to look to the consuls or the Senate for relief," the plebs resorted to direct action aimed at disrupting the legal proceedings against debtors. By drowning out the consul's pronouncements with their shouts, they enabled the debtor to claim ignorance of his sentence.[26]

The threat of a new attack against Rome forced the patricians to press the plebeians into taking up arms in defense of the Republic. But the plebs refused to serve in what they perceived to be a patrician cause. "Rioting continued," and "groups of malcontents began to confer in secret," shaking the patrician regime. The appointment of new consuls did nothing to lessen the people's determination. According to Livy, "The crowd swarmed round the tribunal, and voices were raised saying that the people refused to be fobbed off any longer: the consuls would never get a single soldier without a public guarantee of redress for their grievances; every man must be given liberty again before arms were put into his hands—for if they were to fight, they were determined to do so not for their masters, but for the country and their fellow-citizens." The senate, caught off guard by the plebs' resolve, considered various solutions to the crisis. One of them was debt relief for veterans only, but the difficulty was that all of the plebeians were grappling with indebtedness. Senator Titus Largius contended that "the situation could not be remedied without general relief;

any sort of preferential treatment, far from allaying, would only aggravate their sense of grievance." The patricians ultimately rallied to the idea that in order to break the deadlock and ensure the defense of Rome they needed to name a dictator, one sympathetic to the plebeian cause.[27]

But the plebs would not be fooled. They knew perfectly well that the dictator Marius Valerius had been designated in order to halt their actions. Nevertheless, his good reputation and favorable inclination toward the plebeians convinced them to end their agitation and to engage in the defense of the Republic. The plebs' enthusiasm was such that Rome was the scene of an unprecedented mobilization. The Roman army was confronted with three foes: the Aequi, the Volsci, and the Sabines, but thanks to the great number of men under arms, Rome was able to win a triple victory. The military successes, however, were once again followed by internal strife. The reason, writes Livy, was that "the money-lenders had used all their influence and employed every device to produce a situation which was not only unfavourable to the commons, but tied the hands of the Dictator himself." Indeed, the moneylenders had the full support of the patricians, who rejected outright Marius Valerius's attempt to put the debt issue on the agenda. The patricians' opposition to his dictatorial prerogatives prompted Marius Valerius to resign, and the plebs seemed to understand his motives. "The reason for his resignation," Livy notes, "was anger at the unfair treatment they had received."[28]

At this point the plebs withdrew to the Aventine Hill, where it established a camp, as previously mentioned, "without any officer to direct them," and stayed there, neither launching an offensive against Rome nor facing an attack from the patricians. This was the beginning of the plebeian secession. Meanwhile, terror prevailed in Rome. The few remaining plebs feared the reprisals of the senators, who in turn dreaded plebeian violence. The plebs' absence was all the more problematic for the patricians, as the city could not function properly without the plebeian workforce. Rome's immediate future was considerably jeopardized. There was, for example, no one to take care of harvesting and thus ensure that the Romans would receive their daily supply of food.[29] The patricians were "supported generally by their clients."[30]

To put an end to the Republic's untenable situation, the senate dispatched to the Aventine Hill Menenius Agrippa, a parliamentarian of plebeian origins known for his oratorical skills. The purpose of Agrippa's mission was to restore Rome's lost unity by bringing the plebs back to the city. To this end he addressed the plebs directly and told them the fable of the belly and the parts. In this allegory, the various parts of the human body were indignant at having to mobilize collectively in order to supply the belly with food, unlike "the belly, which remained idle, surrounded by its ministers, with nothing to do but enjoy the pleasant things they gave it."[31] The difference of work and effort between the belly and the parts gave rise to such resentment among the latter that, by way of protest, they refused to feed the former. But by abandoning their responsibilities, the parts were weakened as much as the belly. In sum, it was impossible to isolate the belly from the body as a whole. Thus, writes Livy,

> By this it was apparent that the belly, too, has no mean service to perform: it receives food, indeed; but it also nourishes in its turn the other members, giving back to all parts of the body, through all its vein, the blood it has made by the process of digestion. . . . This fable of the revolt of the body's members Menenius applied to the political situation, pointing out the its resemblance to the anger the populace against the governing class.[32]

Following Agrippa's reasoning, the patricians represented the Republic's belly, its vital principle, whereas the plebeians were like the body parts, that is, the executants. Consequently the plebeians could not penalize the patricians without penalizing themselves. Society could not function correctly without the cooperation of the two orders, hence the importance of bringing the plebs down from the Aventine Hill and ending the first plebeian secession. Agrippa's fable convinced the plebs to abandon the camp "without any officer to direct them" and return to Rome.

The success of Menenius Agrippa's mission did not, however, mean a return to the political status quo. To achieve a lasting solution to Rome's internal problems, the patricians agreed to create specifically plebeian magistracies. The raison d'être of the plebs' "tribunes" was to defend the plebeian cause within Roman political institutions, in particular against the consuls. The new tribunals were "inviolable," and patricians could not, of course, hold office there. The two tribunes of the plebs were granted the Sacred Law and thereby became "inviolable" in religious terms.[33] The plebs thus emerged from "nonbeing" and acceded to a double status in Rome: political and religious.

Certain significant features of the plebeian principle can be derived from the first secession. Clearly, as a social category, the plebs predated the first secession. But through their "insurrectional commune"[34] a veritable plebeian *experience* occurred. By rejecting patrician political domination, the plebs asserted themselves as political subjects. They succeeded in putting forward a plebeian principle grounded in a people's politics (communalism) and in the exercise of political freedom (agoraphilia). In that founding moment of the plebs' political experience, what can be regarded as a plebeian "emergence" took place whereby the plebs transcended the biological order of *animal laborans* and transformed themselves into *zoon politikon*, publically demonstrating their political capacities.

Although the primary cause of plebeian discontent was the economic situation of the Roman plebs, it was because of a *political* mission, that of Agrippa, and the plebs' *political* integration through the creation of the tribunes that they agreed to abandon their fortified camp on the Aventine Hill. So, while their motivations were economic and social in nature, what was needed to end the crisis was a political approach on the part of the Roman patricians, one that involved establishing specifically plebeian political institutions. Here, the "wrong" done to the plebs was part of a total social fact: the struggle for recognition. In a context of widespread discontent, the plebs gained a political status amounting to the recognition of its participation in the human political condition. In sum, the political presence of the people manifested itself in the first plebeian secession.

Furthermore, a curious phenomenon arose in the midst of these events. Livy notes in his account that atop the Aventine Hill, the plebeians formed a military camp "without any officer to direct them."[35] For the plebs, this represented a refusal to create a new split between the "grandees" and the "people." By rejecting hierarchy, the plebs was able to assert the radical equality of its members and to forestall the problems stemming from the rise of a leader or a leading few. Appointing a leader could have caused as many problems as it solved, if not more. Nevertheless, the establishment of tribunes by the patrician order obliged the plebs to accept a certain differentiation within their ranks, thereby introducing a hierarchy within plebeian practice, a political inequality that might possibly weaken the democratic quality of their movement.

FLORENCE: THE CIOMPI REVOLT (1378)

Different times, different region, same struggle. The Ciompi revolt in 1378 partakes of the history of plebeian political practices inasmuch as it was a revolt of the politically excluded working people of Florence. It thus represent a "supreme effort" of "democracy" that enabled "workers [to occupy] a place in government."[36] On a historical level, this event is imprinted on the Western political imagination: "This insurrection," writes Simone Weil in 1934, "known as the insurrection of the Ciompi, is without doubt the earliest of the proletarian insurrections; and it is the more worthy of study from this point of view because it exhibits already in a remarkably pure form the specific features which appear later on in the great working-class movements."[37]

The fourteenth century was particularly affected by "popular" agitation, revolts, and revolutions.[38] The term "popular" refers to the common people, the lower classes, and the destitute. The political upheavals resulted from an economic and political conjuncture rooted in the previous century. Late thirteenth-century Europe had experienced a major surge in economic development. The advent of new forms of production and economic concentration had given rise to social tensions and conflicts. The effects were sharply felt in the major cities of Europe, where certain families settled and became extremely wealthy by profiting from the situation.[39] Such families went on to constitute dynasties whose financial power was matched only by their political influence.

Fiscal inequality, among other issues, engendered social friction in the large cities. Although in the thirteenth century "no one questioned the principle of equality in regard to taxation . . . it was far from being respected."[40] The wealthy managed to elude the principle of equal contributions to the treasury, leaving to the poor the burden of financing political initiatives, in particular the medieval political initiative par excellence, war.

The social and political conflict in Florence was partly attributable to this problem. In the thirteenth century, the social makeup of the city was characterized by a sharp division between the nobles (the *magnati*) and the commoners (the *popolani* or *popolo*). The nobility's contempt for the members of the lower class, whom they considered "more stupid than donkeys," was mutual, since the common people regarded the magnates as "rapacious wolves." However, the lower class was not homogeneous but rather split into two camps. "The popolo was first of all, the ensemble of the organized crafts." Within this group, there were, on one hand, "the merchants who managed the principle crafts, or major 'Arts' as they were called, [who] formed a sort of well-to-do aristocracy."[41] It was their commercial interests more than their political ambitions that opposed this bourgeoisie, called *popolani grassi* to the magnati, the true aristocracy of the major Italian cities. On the other hand, there was the *popolani minuti*, comprising the artisans of the middle and minor arts as well as the indigent. It was this poorest element that mediated the conflicts between the grassi and the magnati or, to use more a modern terminology, between the Florentine bourgeoisie and its aristocracy.

To round out this depiction of Florence's social divisions, one must include the power held by the supporters of the Guelph faction, who backed the Pope. Historically, the Guelphs opposed the Ghibellines, who were faithful to the emperor of the Germanic Holy Roman Empire. But at the time of Ciompi, the Guelphs had already prevailed over the Ghibellines and had grown rich and powerful in Florence by confiscating their adversaries' property. The Guelph faction, having "become the political organ of the upper bourgeoisie, . . . dominated the city, . . . abusing the ballots and taking advantage of an obsolete but unrepealed law of exclusion . . . to keep [its enemies] out of public office."[42] Moreover, the Guelph faction made it possible for the magnati to form an alliance with the great bourgeois families of Florence.

The economic domination of Florence's wealthy citizens thus went hand in hand with their political domination. They formed "a patrician class, that is, a group of families which perpetuated its control of municipal government."[43] Consequently, "far from being a democracy, the Florentine state was directly controlled by financial, commercial, and industrial capital."[44] A number of political devices enabled the patricians to maintain their monopoly over public affairs: the practice of cooptation, restrictions on the number of electors, etc. The patrician's hegemony seems to have been tolerated until the latter half of the thirteenth century.

As of 1284, Florence's municipal government enunciated "the principle that every decision should be debated in the presence of the *magnati*, the *popolani*, and the artisans."[45] This meant, at least in theory, that all levels of society could take part in civic affairs. But it was the upper stratum of the popolani, the so-called grassi, who gained the most from the new political practice. This bourgeoisie wanted at all cost to keep the popolani minuti from having a share of political power, even though they had very often supported the grassi in their struggles against the nobility.

Theoretically, then, the popolani grassi acceded to power. In reality, however, the control of Guelph supporters was so strong that power remained in the hands of the wealthiest Florentine families. This "parallel power" of the Guelph faction sapped the inclusive nature of Florence's political structures. The city's political system continued to be a patrician regime in which the upper strata of the popolani could take part but where important decisions were made under the overwhelming influence of the great patrician families, a situation that aggravated the dissatisfaction of the lower-class group known as the Ciompi, that is, the wool carders.

Yet it would be wrong to overstate the role of economic motives in triggering the events of 1378. The Ciompi revolt coincided with a period of intense political repression, even terror, launched and directed by the Guelph faction. The repression involved a policy of proscriptions (*ammonizone*) that the Guelphs applied across the board to all members of Florentine society who were considered supporters of the defunct Ghibelline faction. The condemnation was particularly harsh, as "it included the loss of social 'status,' thus depriving the victim of any influence or possibility of access to office; and it was hereditary."[46]

The Ciompi's primary motivation was therefore political. More specifically, their revolt expressed the wish of the popolani minuti to no longer bear the yoke of a Florentine patriciate subservient to the Guelph faction.

The arrival at the Florence seigniory of Salvestro de' Medici, a gonfaloniere of justice (a high civic magistrate) sympathetic to the popolani minuti, temporarily halted the Guelphist proscriptions. De' Medici attempted "to correct the insolence of the powerful,"[47] but attacks against him by Guelph supporters as well as the resumption of proscriptions against the popolani generated a political climate conducive to revolt. Salvestro de' Medici's resignation on June 18 sparked off a riot during which several palaces were set on fire throughout the city. This was the start of the Ciompi revolt.

To calm the situation, the municipal government took steps to curb the power of the magnates: the Ghibellines were exonerated, and barred individuals were granted the right to appeal their proscription. But even with these few political concessions, tension remained high to the point that some of the great patrician families hired personal guards. In spite of the government's maneuvers, the revolt "fell" under the leadership of "the working people."[48] Commenting on Salvestro's actions at the beginning of the Ciompi revolt, Machiavelli writes in his *Florentine Histories*, "No one should make a change in a city believing that he can stop it at his convenience or regulate it in his mode."[49]

The Ciompi refrained from violence and immediately decreed that pillaging would be punished by death. Hence, for Weil they prefigured the proletarian uprisings "in the French and Russian Revolutions."[50] The Ciompi also drew up a petition aimed at democratizing the political system and the operation of the trade guilds by making the treatment of Florence's various social strata more egalitarian. They demanded, for example, the creation of a trade guild for the lower classes and the reduction of the plebs' tax burden. But the seigniory's slowness in responding to these demands aroused the Ciompi's fury.

Four centers of agitation erupted simultaneously. The seigniory retaliated by arresting a number of suspects, including Simoncino, presumed to be one of the leaders of the insurrection. The revolt was further inflamed by the news of his ill treatment and torture at the hands of the authorities. On July 20, a large Ciompi rally called for the prisoner's release, and fires were set throughout the city. In the words of one eyewitness, Florence was a scene of "the most incredible disorder."[51] The next day, the fires were still burning. The city's torturer was killed and hung up by the feet, and Florence's standard, an important symbol, was seized by the rioters. The Ciompi thus forcefully demonstrated their insurrectional power.

In the wake of the riots, the Ciompi allied themselves with the Minor Arts with the aim of developing a political program. The program, articulated in two petitions, called for practical measures to end inequality and put a stop to the terror perpetrated by the Florentine patriciate. These moderate and timely demands included amnesty for the rioters and a halt to imprisonment for unpaid debts. "Most of their claims were for reforms rather than innovations," and the way in which program was applied "revealed not only a change in the kind of people involved, but also definite political resolution and a social transformation of those who were in possession of political power."[52]

The mutation took the shape of a democratic revolution, with the plebs supplanting the political authorities in order to effectuate the program of the Ciompi and the Minor Arts. On July 21, 1378, despite their futile delaying tactics, the members of Florence's municipal government handed over power to the crowd assembled at the gates of the seigniory. At this point, the popolani minuti took hold of the reins of power and proceeded to enact symbolic and practical reforms aimed at establishing a radically democratic regime in Florence.

A new *balia*, that is, a council exercising all legislative and executive powers, was elected by acclamation "under the leadership of Michele di Lando, a foreman wool carder,"[53] who was named gonfaloniere of justice. With the exception of five members whose families had political backgrounds in Florence, the balia was entirely renewed. It comprised members of the popolani groups, minuti as well as grassi, thereby ensuring its inclusive and democratic quality. What's more, to symbolize the return to democracy "and to give a beginning to the reform of the city, he dismissed the syndics of the guilds and appointed new ones; deprived the Signori and the Collegi of their magistracies; and he burned the bags of offices."[54] He thereby emblematically effaced the oligarchic tendencies of the political system.

Nevertheless, the Ciompi's support for M. di Lando and the new balia was short-lived. In order to reestablish civil peace in Florence, the gonfaloniere distributed titles and public offices evenly among the aristocracy, the bourgeoisie, and the plebs. His approach was designed to make plebeian policy acceptable to the magnates by diluting the people's victory, in keeping with the "basic idea that the more humbly the revolution deals with its adversaries, the more apt it is to assuage their rancor."[55] But these reforms discredited the seigniory in the eyes of the Ciompi. Toward the end of August, a measure considered unacceptable provided them with a pretext to demonstrate their disappointment and to revolt against the new balia. The measure involved compensating members of the balia for their public service. Di Lando awarded himself a stipend, gave Salvestro de' Medici "the income of the shops on the Ponte Vecchio,"[56] and "to the citizens who had assisted the plebeians he gave many favors."[57]

The outraged Ciompi assembled in front of the seigniory and demanded that the new officials step down immediately. But di Lando clung to power and made a speech designed to appease the plebs. It had the opposite effect. The Ciompi rejected any compromise with the man incarnating the "usurper and traitor"[58] to the plebeian cause. They gathered at the Santa Maria Novella church and elected new representatives, who were "were men 'elect' in the full sense of the word, since they were called 'The Eight Saints of the People of God.'"[59] Their mission was to replace the balia and eliminate the privileges of its members. The Ciompi moreover wanted the "Eight Saints" to become a permanent political institution. "Thus the city had two seats and was governed by two different princes,"[60] writes Machiavelli. In the opinion of Simone Weil, the "extra-legal government singularly resembled a soviet,"[61] that is, the type of workers' council that was formed during the Russian Revolution of 1905.

To make known their new demands, the Ciompi sent two messengers to the seigniory of Florence. There, they accused di Lando of betraying the plebeian cause. The gonfaloniere of justice, "unable to contain his indignation on hearing these charges,"[62] set upon the messengers and had them imprisoned. At the same time, some of the balia leaders launched a smear campaign against the Ciompi rebels, accusing them of "wanting to put power in the hands of a popular tyrant."[63] Rumors to this effect spread throughout the city, which only heightened the Ciompi's feeling of revolt.

Michele di Lando tried at all cost to check the Ciompi's actions by neutralizing the members of the balia sympathetic to the new demands. He took up and successfully propagated the rumor that the Ciompi were favorable to the installation of a tyrant. A powerful alliance of convenience was formed between di Lando and "numerous Guelphist bourgeois . . . , who called him their savior."[64] The ploys of the former Ciompi leader precipitated a wave of violence in the working-class neighborhoods that culminated on August 31, 1378: "The passion and the mutual hatred of the 'haves' and the 'have-nots' made this day one of the bloodiest in Florentine history."[65]

August 31 marked the defeat of the Ciompi revolt. However, the "liquidation" of the political and social gains of the Ciompi would take a number of years. The government of Florence created a sort of political police to flush out democratic activity. Ultimately, this episode in the history of Florence brought about a reconciliation between the magnati and the popolani grasssi.[66] Slowly but inexorably, the patricians took back political control and tightened their grip on the city: "The haunting fear of the social subversion strengthened an oligarchical form of democracy."[67]

In his *Florentine Histories*, Machiavelli claims that Michele di Lando, the former leader of the plebs, "deserves to be numbered among the few who have benefited their fatherland" because he was able to make the better class of artisans see "what ignominy it was for those who had overcome the pride of the great to have to bear the stench of the plebs."[68] This passage, which places Machiavelli among the supporters of the established order in Florence,[69] has the merit nonetheless of identifying the central issue of this plebeian experience: the problem of the leader. For it appears that the lesson of the Ciompi revolt resides precisely in what it teaches about the paradoxical, even deleterious, presence of a leader in the development of the plebs' political action.

Edgar Quinet, in *Les révolutions d'Italie*, offers an incisive analysis of di Lando's accomplishment as leader of the Ciompi. In his view, di Lando belongs not to "those exceptional men who have conferred benefits on their fatherland" but rather to the many leaders who are "surprised at their success and can think only of being forgiven for it." Indeed, di Lando spared no effort to neutralize the plebeian forces when the revolt occurred, as evidenced by his desire to gain support among the magnati and the popolani grassi, the enemies of the Ciompi. This abdication of his legitimate authority as leader, an authority conferred on him by the Ciompi when they took over the seigniory and appointed a new balia, undermined the initial successes of the insurgents and subverted the plebeian experience. The enemies of the Ciompi benefited "[from di Lando's] magnanimity, [which] may have concealed a certain lack of courage."[70]

The naming of a leader split the plebeian movement in two: on one hand, the leader with his imperatives and, on the other, the insurgents with their imperatives. From that moment, the plebeian action moved in two contrary directions, both in the name of the same revolt. Deprived of part of their resources, the plebeian forces were diminished in the face of their natural adversaries, the patricians in particular. In the case of the Ciompi, it was at exactly the moment when they diverted their efforts away from the struggle against the magnati and the popolani grassi in order to fight more effectively against Michele di Lando that they embarked on the road to ruin: "The attacks against [di Lando] grew so relentless that the minor guilds were soon directing all the energy born of their victory toward destroying their leader, without at the same time considering whether they were not in jeopardy of destroying themselves."[71] Hence, the question of the leader of the plebs becomes problematic since it raises the possibility of the many attacking their own movement. For the Ciompi, this internal strife largely contributed to the failure of their revolt.

Simone Weil contends that di Lando's behavior is understandable, as he "did what any good social-democratic president would have done in his place: he turned against his former fellow workers."[72] In drawing a parallel between the plebeian leader and the social-democratic leaders of the twentieth century, Weil demonstrates that the problem of the plebeian leader is recurrent. She seems to indicate that this issue arises periodically in the political history of the many. And isn't this also what Quinet asserts in the conclusion of his account of the Ciompi revolt? "A terrifying light spilled out from the burnt palaces of Florence. The Ciompi revolution travelled around Italy. The workers of Sienna, the Lazzares of Naples, the Capette of Genoa all had their day as well; for analogous reasons, these victories of the people all eventually ended with the destruction of the people."[73]

What may be at work here are the effects of the "voluntary servitude" enigma as conceptualized by La Boétie. The emergence of the leader represents precisely the moment when the plebeian desire for freedom turns into its opposite—servitude. Thus, an analysis of the revolt of the Ciompi leads to an initial encounter with what appears to be a central issue of the plebeian experience, the problem of the leader, to which we shall return.

ROMANS: CARNIVAL AND REVOLT (1580)

At center stage of the Romans carnival were the working people of that mid-sized city of southern France in 1580. The term "stage" is particularly apt here because the carnival was akin to both theater and art while at the same time being an occasion for play and an experience of transgression. Indeed, the carnival, which was a central event in the life of the Middle Ages and the Renaissance, is located at the intersection of art and life. To quote Mikhail Bakhtin, the theorist of the "carnivalesque," the carnival "is life itself, but shaped according to a certain pattern of play."[74]

The carnival, the plebeian festival par excellence in the Middle Ages and the Renaissance, enabled the people to experience a "second life" based on laughter and on the calling into question of the principles underlying political, social, and economic domination. Yet the carnival cannot be reduced to a game—it was a concrete experience, which, though fleeting, remained significant because through it the many entered "a special condition of the entire world, of the world's revival and renewal, in which all take part." That "special condition"—utopian relative to the existing political context—involved "community, freedom, equality and abundance."[75]

The festival played a vital role in the Middle Ages. Official festivals were legion and served to strengthen and consolidate the relationships of domination that were the framework of daily life. They celebrated the permanence and persistence of the established order together with the values of inequality and hierarchy so essential for the medieval theological-political nexus. This, writes Bakhtin, explains "why the tone of the official feast was monolithically serious and why the element of laughter was alien to it." Because of their seriousness, the official festivals were at odds with the playful nature of the festival itself. They constituted a substitute whose austerity bespoke complicity with the patrician order. The carnival and its characteristic plebeian laughter challenged the official festival, presenting themselves as its antithesis by rejecting its earnest and solemn tone. They inaugurated a different space and time out of which emerged a singular experience of freedom that called into question the order of domination prevailing in the Middle Ages. This is why the carnival was tantamount to a moment of transgression, that is, of disobedience to existing laws and norms, all in the name of liberty, equality, and fraternity, "the highest aims of human existence."[76] In sum, the carnival as a transgression against domination embodied an experience of freedom.

Transgression was thus at the heart of the carnivalesque experience and made it possible to reconnect with the festival's authentic temporality, that of "becoming, change, and renewal,"[77] where the future was radically open-ended and resolutely indeterminate. For the duration of the carnival, the plebs suppressed hierarchical distinctions and established an egalitarian space. They opened a gap in a historical period when inequalities were of the most extreme kind. The essence of this "second life" resided in the experience of properly human relations with others, regardless of differences in birth and fortune. Alienation was replaced by genuine human contact in the form of spontaneous relationships and socializing freed from the usual restraints of the Middle Ages. Hence, the carnival gave rise to a social bond realized in and through the collective laughter of the plebs in opposition to the pomposity and sanctimony of the theological-political authorities.

Bakhtin attributes the force of carnivalesque laughter to three features. First, this laughter is collective rather than individual. It is a sort of "laughing together," a laughter that appears when people amuse themselves together. Moreover, plebeian laughter is universal in that it is directed at all human things and phenomena. Consequently, this laughter not only targets the mechanisms of patrician domination but can also be aimed at the plebs themselves. The collective plebeian laughter therefore involves an element of self-derision stemming from the plebs' view of itself as a full participant in the playfulness of the world and human affairs. Finally, "this laughter is ambivalent: it is gay, triumphant, and at the same time mocking, deriding. It asserts and denies, it buries and revives." Plebeian laughter, by virtue of its ambivalence, is utopian since it ridicules the predominant forms of "superiority."[78] By scoffing at domination, this laughter's power of negation opens onto its opposite—emancipation—and frees up a "no-place place" (*lieu non lieu*), that of the carnival per se. The carnival's laughter therefore cannot be reduced to a simple negation or even to an expression of joy. Its goal was an opening up that would enable the advent of a space of freedom and equality at the very heart of the apparently "permanent" theological-political reality of the Middle Ages.

The relationship to utopia and a world where emancipation displaces domination is where festival and revolt interconnect. Their alliance is rooted especially in the possibility of setting collective life on a freer and more egalitarian footing.[79] However, the particular form of the festival represented by the carnival did not often turn into a revolt. The revolt in 1580 of the Romans carnival was an exception in the long history of the carnival in Europe.[80] The fact remains, however, that this exception was an exemplary manifestation of the features specific to plebeian political practice.[81]

The carnival in Romans involved a conflict between the notables dominating the political and economic scene and the midlevel owner-artisans. This intermediate group, while monopolizing the direction of the revolt, was able to rally the lower class to its cause. Emmanuel Le Roy Ladurie contends that, in spite of this class distinction, a proper understanding of the Romans revolt requires an "overall concept [that] takes in all the urban craftsman and peasants who were once the masses and the popular movements." The global concept that Le Roy Ladurie identifies is the idea of "the common folk," which, as in the time of the Ciompi in Tuscany, stood in opposition to "an uncommon folk, an elite minority above it: merchants, lawyers, and bourgeois patricians sometimes pretending to be nobility."[82] To put this another way, the revolt of the Romans carnival of 1580 opposed workers and nobles or, to adopt the terminology implicit in Ladurie's analysis, plebeians and patricians.

The political power of the patricians in Romans appeared to be shared but was in fact exclusive. First, the royal governor, who ordinarily would have been in charge of political life in Romans, actually carried very little political weight in the city. The power of the French crown's representative was scarcely perceptible. The reins of power were actually held by a group of four consuls and Antoine Guérin, who acted as royal judge. In his capacity as magistrate of the French monarchy, Guérin exercised both legal and executive power. In other words, he held real power and controlled the actions of the consuls. This quasi-monopoly of power by an omnipotent patrician was the result of a municipal "putsch" that, in 1542, had allowed the rich to take political control of the city. This unequal and antidemocratic distribution of power is significant for an understanding of the 1580 revolt of the carnival, because "the whole philosophy of the revolution of 1579–1580 was basically an attempt to undo the consequence of the 1542 takeover."[83]

The events of 1580 can also be traced back to a plebeian protest at the previous carnival. On the occasion of Saint Blaise's feast at the start of the carnival in 1579, the plebs of Romans decided to resort to an unusual means of expressing their political dissatisfaction: they named a leader able to speak and provide coherent direction for the advancement their demands.[84] This "plebeian leader" was Jean Serve, known as Paumier, a tradesman from the countryside. Despite the biased testimony left behind by Judge Guérin,[85] it seems that Paumier was not a violent, bloodthirsty barbarian but rather a leader capable of restraint and thoughtfulness. He put forward a set of demands centered on correcting fiscal inequities and suppressing tax concessions for the nobles. Beyond these demands, however, the election of a political representative of the plebs in a city governed by the patrician order was the inceptive act of the revolt in Romans.

Thus, as of 1579 a "*dual power*" existed in Romans.[86] The plebs' leader, Paumier, held sway over the city's ramparts and gates and a few working-class neighborhoods. In addition, he could count on the support of a political faction, referred to as "extraordinary-supernumerary," within the city council. In the face of the limited power of the plebs, Guérin and his four consuls, who retained the real power in Romans, continued to exercise effective control over the city. Paumier's presence and the fact he had a partial grip on the political sovereignty of Romans hindered Guérin's work. Consequently, the master of Romans was under pressure not only from the plebs but also the peasantry, who saw in Paumier a leader capable of articulating their demands and even acting upon them. Yet plebeian power in Romans remained parallel and limited. Paumier was unable to oust Judge Guérin and the other patrician masters from public office, so, in spite of the institutional arrangements of 1579, Romans remained under patrician rule. Still, being parallel and limited did not prevent plebeian power from being recognized, as demonstrated when the Queen Mother, Catherine de Médicis, on her way through Romans, agreed to meet Paumier, who, in a show of plebeian pride, refused to kneel before her.

In keeping with tradition, preparations for the 1580 carnival, to be held during the first week of February, began in late January. That year, however, the celebrations were imbued with new and heightened significance, since they would mark the first anniversary of the election of a plebeian leader invested with real, albeit limited, power. To signal the beginning of the carnival period, the drapers of Romans held their traditional parade with Paumier at the head of the procession, and they issued a call for the people to take up arms. Wielding lashes and other "weapons," the drapers "shouted very loudly that within three days the flesh of Christians would be selling for six deniers a pound."[87] These carnivalesque pronouncements spread terror among the patricians, who took the drapers' taunts literally. Then, on Candlemas (February 2), another feast day leading up to the celebrations, Paumier, again in keeping with tradition, dressed in a bearskin and, breaking with convention, occupied a position and seat that did not belong to him in the city council of Romans. The supporters of Judge Guérin saw this affront to patrician power as an intolerable provocation. In the mind of the judge, the plebs were preparing to massacre those holding political and economic power in Romans, something that must be prevented at all costs.

The carnival in Romans, as everywhere else, was twofold, that is, plebeian and patrician. In the patricians' pageants (more subdued than the plebeian ones), they could react and respond to the affronts of the plebs. This was precisely what they did. The patricians dressed up in "faded finery, symbolizing their striving for order, power, ostentation, intimidation, and for an alliance with the brutal forces of virile repression, against the 'Scythian' barbarity of the insurgents."[88] Thus, two groups confronted each other during the carnival: the "barbaric" plebs, who hoped to see the advent of a new politics, and the patricians, with their "virile" mobilization aimed at recovering and preserving the medieval political order.

The confrontation between the magnates and the many took place just after Sunday Mass. The patricians' parade crossed paths with that of the plebs. The insurgents' pageant was composed of plebeians dressed in red and blue, the colors of mourning, and reiterating that they would sell the flesh of their oppressors for "six deniers." The patricians "believed that the crowd of artisans and peasants had the horrible intention of the killing them all . . . on Mardi Gras, in order to wed their women and divide up their properties among themselves."[89] Perceiving this carnival conspiracy as something that would turn "the world upside down," those holding real power in Romans were gripped by fear and hatred, which would culminate in an antiplebeian massacre on Mardi Gras.

The plebeian revolt in Romans entered its final phase when the henchmen of Judge Guérin went to Paumier's house and slew him in cold blood. The fear of the magnates was succeeded by the fear of the many, who, having learned of Paumier's death, dreaded what was to follow. And, in fact, Paumier's assassination set off a kind of "civil war, it was at any rate more intense than simple street fighting in a town." The patrician forces attempted to seize a gate located in one of the city's poorest districts, a plebeian stronghold. The inhabitants of the neighborhood were sympathetic to Paumier's cause and "were likely to furnish the grass roots support for the popular faction."[90] Therefore, in order to consolidate his hold on Romans, Guérin sought to establish patrician ascendancy over that part of the city.

Indeed, the entire strategy of Judge Guérin involved strengthening the patrician neighborhoods in the city center and taking back the few neighborhoods and gates under plebeian control. District by district, the patrician troops attacked the plebeians, whose forces were disorganized and unprepared for combat. Although the plebeians did put up strong resistance in certain neighborhoods, they were no match for either Guérin's men or the judge's subterfuges. He eventually regained dominance over the city and, more especially, prevented the peasants of the surrounding countryside from coming to reinforce the plebeian forces of Romans. A coalition of the urban plebs and the rural peasantry would no doubt have confronted Judge Guérin with a formidable adversary. But Guérin never allowed this alliance to take shape and tightened his hold on the city.

Having thwarted the plebeian revolt and presided over the "premature" death of the carnival, Guérin's remaining task was to institute the repressive measures needed to squash the plebs' political hopes permanently. Since the leaders of the plebeian insurrection had all been killed in the Mardi Gras battles, Guérin saw no point in launching a bloody reign of terror in Romans. But this did not preclude his using the numerous medieval instruments of punishment against the city's plebeian population. However, it was mainly in the neighboring countryside that Judge Guérin vented his fury as conquering patrician. A veritable "slaughter of peasants" took place during the months after the plebeian uprising. The repression had the desired effect: the "Romans Carnival, and the subsequent disasters, had given them a distaste for insurrection."[91]

Le Roy Ladurie's meticulous analysis of the Romans carnival allows him to revisit the question of the plebs as a political and historical subject. For him, the revolt of 1580 confirms the views of Boris Porchnev, a historian of popular uprisings: "urban revolts [express] the resentment, grievance, and desires of a *plebeian* group of craftsmen." In other words, Porchnev and Le Roy Ladurie reject the notion that such revolts resulted from the magnates' manipulative efforts to inflame the plebeians for selfish political reasons. Those who defend the hypothesis of a conspiracy of the notables (based on the assumption that the plebs were incapable of participating in political life) are proven wrong by the plebeian insurrection. "As far as Romans in 1580 is concerned, Porchnev is right—or perhaps Rosa Luxemburg, since she theorized on the spontaneity of the masses."[92] In support of his position, Le Roy Ladurie cites, among other things, the fact that only one of the rebel leaders was a notable.

Concerning the existence of a series of plebeian political experiences throughout Western history, Le Roy Ladurie underscores the kinship of the demands of the Romans plebs with those of the Ciompi of Florence. And, in fact, the parallels between them can be readily drawn. Looking toward events yet to come, Le Roy Ladurie furthermore argues that the historical actor responsible for the "micro-revolution" of 1580 coincides with the one identified in E. P. Thompson's opus on the making of the English working class: "The British historian . . . discusses a plebeian group of self-employed craftsmen and shopkeepers in England up to and including the eighteenth century." And, because Thompson associates his concept of the many with that of Albert Soboul as articulated in his work on the sans-culottes of the French Revolution, Le Roy Ladurie contends that the plebs of Romans represents the "'sansculottes' . . . a group always to be found in traditional towns." Le Roy Ladurie recognizes, however, that, unlike the sans-culottes, the plebeians of Romans did not formulate "new egalitarian *values*."[93] These values, according to him, were developed through the plebs' many political experiences. The fact remains that from the Ciompi to the plebs of Romans and of England, right through to the sans-culottes, there emerges a political filiation constituted in and through a democratic, egalitarian political experience.

The plebeian experience of the Romans carnival of 1580 also demonstrates that the many have political capacities. Despite the ultimate failure of the Romans revolt, the plebs were able to organize themselves and designate a political leader whose real, albeit limited, authority was recognized in the poorest districts of the city. Even the patricians holding political power had to acknowledge the plebs' authority, being obliged to deal with their spokesman. By establishing a parallel political structure in the city, the oppressed of Romans displayed a political outlook that could be harnessed in a specific political action, one potentially decisive for their emancipation.[94]

Ultimately, the plebeian experience of the carnival in Romans remains a living critique of the principles of patrician domination, a fortiori because the carnival represented an ideal opportunity to carry out such a criticism. The disorder characteristic of the carnival was an excellent parody of the disorder caused by the patricians' tendentious and abusive rule.[95] The Romans plebs showed that it wanted to shoulder political responsibilities in the face of the unjust government of those holding power. In addition, inasmuch as spaces of freedom could be opened up unbeknownst to the masters of the city, the plebeian festival illustrated the limited and at times ineffectual nature of the magnates' domination. As a form of resistance, the carnival enabled the plebs, while the festivities lasted, to keep the authority of the powerful at bay.

Yet it seems to us that the primary lesson of the plebeian experience in Romans is that it both staged and gave meaning to the *originary division of the social*, as theorized by Claude Lefort. But before specifying how the Romans carnival testifies to this division, a closer examination is needed of what this obscure but fundamental concept signifies for Lefort.

EXCURSUS 1: ON THE "ORIGINARY DIVISION OF THE SOCIAL"

It would be useful at the outset to circumscribe the ambit of our analysis and to delineate our relationship to the ideas of Claude Lefort. We do not intend here to elucidate the "three-fold originary division."[96] Among the three types of divisions discussed in Lefort's work—the temporal split, the split between the outside and the inside of the city, and the social split—we will focus on the third, as this is the one most germane to an understanding of the plebeian experience. Furthermore, rather than speculate on the possible psychoanalytic origins of this division, an avenue of research suggested by Marcel Gauchet,[97] we will leave aside this difficult and delicate subject, given that Lefort himself remained quite discreet about his relationship with psychoanalysis, especially the Lacanian variant. Instead, we will examine the degree to which the "originary social division" makes it possible to rethink the political. In other words, does it open onto a new interpretation of political phenomena? To answer this question, we will test this concept against the plebeian experience.

The "originary division of the social" informs all of Lefort's thinking, but it is developed more specifically in his *Machiavelli in the Making*. The concept is grounded in the premise that in every political community there is a split that enables the social to be constituted. Lefort also elaborates on the "originary" status of the social division in "Sur la démocratie: le politique et l'institution du social" ("On democracy: The political and the institution of the social"), written in collaboration with Marcel Gauchet and published in the journal *Textures* in 1971.[98] Finally, to grasp firmly the ontological status of the originary division, it should be made clear, through an examination of his mentor, Maurice Merleau-Ponty, what Lefort's relationship is to the tradition of French phenomenology.[99] First, let us look at the substance of the "division" in Machiavelli's thinking before determining in what sense it can be considered "originary" and "ontological."

Lefort draws the theoretical underpinnings of his concept in particular from chapter 9 of *The Prince* and from chapter 4, book 1, of *Discourses on Livy*. In chapter 9, "Of the Civil Principality," Machiavelli asserts, "For in every city these two diverse humors are found, which arises from this: that the people desire neither to be commanded nor oppressed by the great, and the great desire to command and oppress the people." Machiavelli furthermore contends, "one can satisfy the people; for the end of the people is more decent than that of the great, since the great want to oppress and the people want not to be oppressed." He adds that the people ask "only that they not be oppressed."[100]

In chapter 4 of *Discourses*, titled "That the Disunion of the Plebs and the Roman Senate Made That Republic Free and Powerful," Machiavelli writes, "I say that to me it appears that those who damn the tumults between the nobles and the plebs blame those things that were the first cause of keeping Rome free, and that they consider the noises and the cries that would arise in such tumults more than the good effects that they engendered."[101] Here, rather than condemning the tumultuousness of the Roman Republic, the Florentine Secretary claims that order can come out of the disorder engendered by the struggle between the senate and the plebs.[102] Therefore, one should not fret about its superficial effects. The important thing is to grasp its political consequences, which seem to be an extension of freedom within the republic. Machiavelli states that there exists a universal composition of political communities:

> They do not consider that in every republic are two diverse humors; that of the people and that of the great, and that all the laws that are made in favor of freedom arise from their disunion, as they can easily be seen to have occurred in Rome. . . . Nor can one in any mode, with reason, call a republic disordered where there are so many examples of virtue; for good examples arise from good education, good education from good laws, and good laws from those tumults that many inconsiderably damn. For whoever examines their end well will find that they have engendered not any exile or violence unfavorable to the common good but laws and orders in benefit of public freedom. [103]

Thus, at the root of "good laws," Machiavelli discovers the antagonism between the two humors of the city. For Claude Lefort, what Machiavelli perceives here is perhaps one of the rare invariables structuring human communities: "the originary division of the social."[104]

But what is the dispute at the heart of this division? In addition to identifying in Machiavelli's work what underpins the idea of the division between the *libido dominandi* of the grandees and the people's desire for liberty, Lefort discerns in his thinking the idea of an ultimate indetermination bearing on the foundations of the legitimate exercise of political power. Because modern society cannot set down the Law once and for all—the Law understood here as the symbolic institution of the political community and not as the totality of positive laws—there is a dispute or conflict surrounding its enunciation.[105] The stakes of this enunciation are high since the Law defines, for example, what is just and unjust. If the grandees systematically oppose the people, it is essentially because its members have an interest in occupying the space of the Law, in "pronouncing" it in order to preserve their hegemony. The people, as bearers of certain negativity expressed in the desire not to be dominated, question the Law and challenge the "pronouncement" of the grandees.

The constitutive division of the social implies the risk of the dissolution of the social. Fundamentally divided, a society can collapse under the weight of that very division and the conflicts it comprises. As soon as it appears, the social bears within it the perpetual risk of implosion. In other words, from the outset the social is threatened by its own annihilation. That is why the recognition of the division involves a risk that some contemporary societies have tried to avert. To accept the division and make it public would signify a society's prior acknowledgment of the risk of being absorbed by the division and disappearing. For Claude Lefort, the two types of society—those *against* the division and those *for* it—have had a lasting impact on the political history of the twentieth century.

Before considering these two types of society, it must also be understood that the originary social division represents a *new form of political intelligibility*. The effect of this is to enable an examination of political regimes in terms of their attitude toward this division.[106] For example, a political regime is free to the extent that it allows the conflict arising from the division to be acknowledged openly. According to Lefort, Machiavelli's work teaches us that conflict acts as a motor force with regard to liberty. This is why the Florentine contends that "the desires of free peoples are rarely pernicious to freedom."[107] The active presence of the "originary social division," which presupposes the existence of a conflict between the grandees and the people, ensures the freedom of a political community.

The extreme opposite of the political regime of freedom is totalitarianism. Without going into the intricacies of Lefort's interpretation of total domination,[108] a brief look at this question will be helpful for our understanding of how the notion of the originary division of the social enables a renewed intelligibility of the political. As we have seen, the originary social division points to the idea that society is permeated by an ultimate indetermination as to its foundations. Consequently, society remains opaque; one cannot solve the enigma of its existence. For us, beings who search for meaning and are in the grip of a desire for unity and intelligibility, such indetermination represents a scandal that totalitarianism tries to quell. Through the image of the Egocrat, totalitarian regimes "embody" the idea that society has overcome division and lives in harmony and peace because the enigma of the social sphere has been solved.[109] Human beings can thus feel as One through the image of the tyrant.[110] The imaginary unity of the social is hence assured, and social division, camouflaged. But this transparency of the social comes at a high price: for nondivision to live, freedom and autonomy must perish.

In the work of Claude Lefort, "totalitarian domination" invariably brings us back to "the democratic invention."[111] For him, totalitarianism is a postdemocratic phenomenon because it arose to put an end to the indetermination and division characteristic of democratic life.[112] A regime of freedom is therefore based on the acceptance of division and of the conflict stemming from it. Democracy is the institution of the social that introduces a dynamic favorable to the development of liberty. By welcoming radical indetermination, democracy thrives on conflict and on the endless questioning of the law. In fact, it could not exist without the presence of a multiplicity of conflictual discursive sources incapable of exhausting its meaning and its orientations. Thus, "democracy is nourished by its incompletion."[113] The lesson of democracy is this: the active presence of conflict between two desires within a political space is what makes the extension of freedom possible.

There remains, however, an essential question: In what way is this division "originary"? The article in *Textures* provides invaluable though enigmatic clues on this subject. In it, Lefort and Gauchet impugn the idea that the political is an "*essentially* derivative phenomenon," in other words, that it may be "intelligible only with reference to the prior disclosure of the secret architecture of the capitalist system, which is supposed to underpin it and bestow on it its internal necessity." To derive the political from the economic is a way of occulting the fact that the institution of the political is what enables the social to emerge. In a democratic regime, for instance, the social appears necessarily divided since democracy rests on "recognition of the legitimacy of conflict."[114]

The question of the originary does not point to a chronology of events that could be followed back to an observable moment when the division had been inaugurated. To succumb to the notion of an identifiable point of origin in space and time would mean taking a "high-altitude" position, which would "have the effect of hiding the *distortion* that governs . . . our posture with regard to the originary." Rather, to explore the originary implies opening up to an experiential limit, because to understand the originary, one must be rid of the wish "to grasp *something* and, in particular, an a priori."[115] Dealing with the originary presupposes a twofold limit: the recognition of our inability to name the origin *and* our inability to assert the absence of origin.

It is within a "logic" that the originary is revealed. This logic is deployed in a paradoxical revelatory movement of the presence and absence of the origin. But the logic of the presence-absence never arrives at the end of its movement: it is forever in the nonfulfillment and incompleteness of its own trajectory. It therefore appears as something "constantly putting itself at stake, almost erasing itself, turning back, to the extent of finding itself at the point where it *would be* the risk of its disappearance."[116]

Moreover, the originary division does not have the effect of fragmenting the social into components that are mutually unaware of one another. The movement of presence-absence enables the social to know itself and to acquire its own identity. In other words, the originary character of the division stems from the fact that the social, in its twofold movement of occultation and revelation, succeeds in saying something about itself. This explains why Lefort and Gauchet write, "*the social is donation and the continued institution of itself.*"[117] It is precisely for this reason that the originary division of the social is a principle of political intelligibility: we can understand the political nature of a regime from the way it deals with division.

These reflections on the "originary" status of social division do not, however, succeed in determining the ontological nature of the division. Are we, in other words, in the presence of an "ontology of the social"? The answer may be found in Lefort's relationship to phenomenology as practiced by Merleau-Ponty in *The Visible and the Invisible*.[118] In this posthumous work, edited by Lefort, Merleau-Ponty's thinking turns away from the philosophy of consciousness as developed in *Phenomenology of Perception*,[119] which leads to "the restoration of an I whose assurance is all the greater as nothing can happen or result because of it that may disturb it."[120] In *The Visible and the Invisible*, rather than conceptualizing an "I" capable of occupying the site of the origin, Merleau-Ponty turns toward a questioning of the origin that opens onto a radical indetermination: "Investigating the origin henceforth involves investigating the distance that forever separates us from it, one that language cannot traverse; investigating the movement of the question, a movement that carries us toward that origin but where the origin is constantly hidden from us."[121]

It is the investigation itself that, for Merleau-Ponty, opens the way to Being. What is at stake is the attempt to articulate a "new ontology"[122] that would be an indirect ontology, that is, one that aims to apprehend Being obliquely. An indirect ontological approach is needed precisely because of the absence of an ultimate origin. Here is how Merleau-Ponty summarizes his new political project:

> The "originating" [originaire] is not of one sole type, it is not all behind us; the restoration of the true past, of the pre-existence is not all of philosophy; the lived experience is not flat, without depth, without dimension, it is not an opaque stratum with which we would have to merge. The appeal to the originating goes in several directions: *the originating breaks up* [éclate], *and philosophy must accompany this break-up, this noncoincidence, this differentiation.*[123]

The originating [elsewhere referred to as "the originary" —Trans.] is therefore necessarily fragmented, and philosophical thought must follow the movement of fragmentation and the gap between the self and the self of the origin.

Claude Lefort's "originary social division" seems to be located within the framework of the desire expressed by Merleau-Ponty to conceptualize a new, indirect ontology that seeks to "accompany" the breakup and the "noncoincidence" of the originary. The remarks made by Lefort and Gauchet in "Sur la démocratie" concerning a present-absent origin that is affirmed within a logic of revelation and occultation enabling the social to say something about itself must be understood in light of Merleau-Ponty's new philosophical project. The "originary division of the social" is, hence, an "ontology of the social," so long as "ontology" is understood in the sense used by Merleau-Ponty—not an "ontology" in the traditional sense (a Hegelian type of "onto-theology") but rather a "new" and indirect ontology that strives to apprehend Being obliquely and recognizes the impossibility of both locating and denying the origin.

To return to the carnival of Romans, accounts of the event seem to point to a city split between two "desires." The patricians, under the leadership of Judge Guérin, clearly wished to dominate, while the plebeians, represented by Paumier, wished to be free. A veritable "staging" of the originary division took shape in Romans. But what is the meaning of this staging?

To recapitulate, the originary division of the social represents a new "form of political intelligibility" because it allows one to assess a community on the basis of its handling of the division.[124] A community that, for example, is ready to be exposed to the effects of division can be called "democratic." The conflict of humors as explored by Machiavelli gives rise to an *expansion* of freedom within the body politic.[125] In Romans, the conflict born of the originary social division made possible an increase in liberty. Through the creation of a political structure specific to the plebs and the naming of Paumier as spokesman, the experience of the Romans plebs produced a space of freedom that, despite its inability to last, opened a "gap" in the Western history of domination. In the neighborhoods under plebeian control, the many enjoyed an absence of grandee domination and, hence, greater freedom. The situation of "dual power" was obviously conducive to liberty; "the desires of free peoples are rarely pernicious to freedom," writes Machiavelli.[126]

The originary division is grounded in a dispute concerning the possibility of *articulating* the Law. The stakes of the social division are therefore considerable. Indeed, it was because the patricians of Romans feared that the Law, as they had articulated it, was being challenged by the plebeians that their hatred for the plebs drove them to perpetrate a massacre. The threat was all the more real given that the few had already lost the power to pronounce the Law in the districts under plebeian control. The symbolic institution of the social, in this case, was on the side of the many. Such an attack on the hegemony of the grandees certainly amplified their aversion to the plebs.

The Romans carnival thus testifies to a twofold revolutionary and democratic tradition operating in plebeian political practice. On the level of both communalism and agoraphilia, the Romans experience demonstrates that the plebs' political action engendered at once a people's politics *and* the return of political freedom to the community. And it is precisely the originary division of the social that makes this plebeian political experience intelligible.

NAPLES: THE REVOLT OF MASANIELLO (1647)

As we have observed with the carnival of Romans, festivals were often an opportunity for the many to express their wish to escape from the domination of the few. And it was precisely in the context of a religious festival that the Neapolitan revolt of Masaniello took shape. But before going to the core of this plebeian experience, it would be useful to set out the historical circumstances under which it arose.

Naples had been ruled by the Spanish crown since 1559, and the 1647 revolt of Masaniello, one of the most spectacular events of the seventeenth century, was directed against that domination.[127] This attempted revolution was to reverberate strongly throughout the revolutionary history of Europe. In the Western revolutionary tradition, there are recurrent references to Masaniello, the charismatic fisherman who became the leader of a plebeian uprising.[128]

In the seventeenth century, Naples was one of the most important European cities, with over three hundred thousand inhabitants, a bustling port, a thriving silk industry, and a university. It was also the seat of a kingdom with a population of more than three million. The local representative of the Spanish crown, the duke of Arcos, lived in Naples surrounded by aristocrats and occupying a luxurious palace maintained by a small army of servants. In addition, the city was home to a large contingent of civil servants and lawyers charged with administering the kingdom on behalf of Spain. The aristocracy, made up of nobles, and the bourgeoisie, made up of civil servants and administrators, comprised a sort of patrician order exercising political and economic control over Naples. Alongside this patriciate were considerable numbers of Lazzari, whose ranks were filled by immigrants and the most underprivileged members of Neapolitan society. Unemployed for the most part, the Lazzari lived in the overcrowded lower-class neighborhoods and represented a constant source of anxiety for the patricians of Naples.

Since ancient Roman times, Naples was known to be a city given to political disorder and upheaval. In the particular context of the summer of 1647, the city found itself in the grip of acute political and social tensions provoked by the levying of a new tax—a *gabella*—on fruit. The effect of this measure, designed to help finance Spain's war against France, was more severe for the poor than for the members of the patriciate.[129] By applying a gabella, the duke of Arcos sought to shift the burden of the war onto the people rather than the wealthy patricians.

In May 1647, in Palermo, also under Spanish control and saddled with the same tax, a popular rebellion against the foreign crown and its tax on fruit forced the authorities to back down. News of this success arrived in Naples in June, eliciting admiration among the Lazzari and prompting them to rebel. An attack was launched against the tax office, and placards denouncing the viceroy's policy were posted throughout the city.[130] But the people's disgruntlement lacked a leadership capable of galvanizing the opposition forces and of focusing their revolutionary energy.

Against the background of a religious festival, a hitherto unknown individual was transformed into a leader of the popular movement. During a tournament opposing two component groups of Neapolitan society, the Alabres and the Lazzari, Masaniello distinguished himself by arming the Lazzari with poles that were "larger than usual."[131] In doing so, the fisherman challenged the authority of the duke of Arcos, the viceroy, and emerged as the people's leader and spokesman for their discontent. Masaniello's strength was that he proposed a direction for the plebeian revolt and a strategy whose goal was the advent of a free and independent regime in Naples.[132] But, while agreeing to lead the insurrection, Masaniello stubbornly rejected conspicuous displays of power and continued to dress like a fisherman, even when he was performing his new duties.

The tax collector's office was attacked once again, and a rally was held against the policies of the duke of Arcos. The patricians of Naples were dismayed, and the viceroy, frightened by the plebs' resolve and strength, fled the city, abandoning his palace to the people's fury. Thus, Masaniello and the insurgents won a first victory. Now installed in his fortress, the viceroy, together with eminent patricians and clergymen, tried to restore order in the city by enlisting the aid of politicians known to sympathize with the plebs and by resorting to religious symbols. They were, however, unable to appease the rebels. On the contrary, the insurgents, convinced that God was on their side, were outraged to see Jesuits and Dominicans invoking Catholic symbols in the name of the Spanish political order.[133]

In light of these many swift triumphs, Masaniello decided to shape the more or less spontaneous unrest into an organized revolt. He ordered the release of all prisoners except murderers,[134] called on the civil guard, and assembled a people's militia, which even included women.[135] He announced that the goal of this military force was to strike at the property (but not the individual members) of the great patrician families responsible for the ongoing crisis and for the subjugation of the many. The militia sacked and burned the palaces of the collaborators with the Spanish crown as well as the mansions of Naples' major financiers. However, looting for the personal benefit of the insurgents was strictly forbidden and severely punished. While sparing religious icons and pictures, the rebels destroyed whatever they found or distributed the plunder to the inhabitants of the poorest neighborhoods. The plebeian militias also disarmed the patrician troops sent as reinforcements by the duke of Arcos to put down the revolt. Seeing how orderly and efficient the plebeian offensive was, many patrician families fled Naples, thereby clearing the way for a distinctly plebeian political experience inside the city.[136] It can thus be said that "from this new disorder was born a new body politic under the control of the people of Naples, who had stood up to the Spanish occupation and constituted themselves in what for them was a novel experience of political autonomy."[137]

A major incident soon complicated Naples' new situation. Masaniello was the target of an assassination attempt carried out by two brothers close to patricians hoping to step in, pacify the insurgents, and restore the old order. The unsuccessful attempt caused a twofold reaction. On one hand, the Neapolitan plebs violently vented its anger against the hapless assassins, killing them both and dragging their bodies through the streets before decapitating them. Their heads were mounted on poles and paraded through the streets. Through these acts of "popular justice" the plebs were able to take part in the punishment of the wrongdoers and to express their displeasure at the patriciate's misdeeds. On the other hand, the attempt on Masaniello's life enhanced his prestige. He was thereafter regarded as a divine emissary and treated like a king. Even the viceroy, no doubt wishing to avoid a direct confrontation, treated him like royalty.[138]

Masaniello, however, was profoundly disturbed by the attempted assassination. He grew obsessed by betrayal and began to feel surrounded by conspirators aiming to bring down his rule. He therefore renounced his democratic and benevolent policies and adopted "arbitrary, harsh, quasi-terroristic policies."[139] This was the beginning of the end of the plebeian experience in Naples. The head of the popular movement drifted into paranoia and abandoned the free and democratic course he had originally set for the revolt.

To reestablish the old order, the Neapolitan patriciate tried to exert pressure on Masaniello with the aid of the archbishop, who, after considerable effort, managed to convince the fisherman to meet the duke of Arcos. But Masaniello was unwilling to dress like a nobleman for the occasion, claiming that by keeping his fisherman's clothing he would avoid the ostentatious displays of power of the magnates. Nevertheless, the archbishop did eventually overcome Masaniello's objections to noble attire.

A new Masaniello was born: "The suffering body of the poor fisherman was suddenly supplanted by the glorious, almost lordly, body of the new leader of Naples."[140] The effect of this metamorphosis on Masaniello was tangible. He began to defer to the viceroy and even appeared ready to obey him. His erstwhile relationship of equality with the representative of the Spanish crown became one of subordination. Masaniello's compliance with the grandee's dress code seemed to signal his submission to the patrician political model and his repudiation of the qualitative and symbolic difference between him and the magnates. The intractable became tractable, and the downfall of the free and independent city of Naples became inevitable.

Following his meeting with the duke of Arcos, Masaniello appeared to sink deeper into madness. His language became irrational, proposing that a palace be constructed on the market place for his personal use and attacking his own supporters.[141] What's more, "the matter of clothing continued to torment him until the very end."[142] Twice when he was making a speech, Masaniello rent his lordly garments to show that his political action was not for his personal gain but for the greater good of the many. Standing naked before the plebs, he displayed a twice-ravaged body: first by the suffering caused by poverty and, second, by the weight of the political responsibilities that he had shouldered since the beginning of the revolt.

But Masaniello would not have to endure his mental anguish for very long. A patrician plot ordered by the viceroy finally succeeded. The plebeian fisherman was assassinated, and the cohesion of the revolt of 1647 was destroyed. Upon learning of the death of the man who had turned tyrant, the initial response of a portion of the plebs was one of relief, even joy. Masaniello was decapitated, and his body was dragged through the streets to cries of "Death to the tyrant!" before being thrown into a ditch. As a "traitor" to the plebeian cause, he was subjected to the worst possible treatment.

However, in light of the duke of Arcos's subsequent conduct, the people changed their minds about Masaniello. The viceroy's government was imprudent enough to introduce a measure that was a direct strike against the people's welfare. The measure reminded the Neapolitans that, contrary to Masaniello, the Spanish crown remained completely subordinated to patrician interests. The result was a revision of the people's collective memory such that the plebeian fisherman was thereafter considered with respect and even reverence. His body was retrieved from the ditch, and, in a mystical, almost religious gesture, attempts were made to reattach his head. Masaniello was given a grand funeral, with every military honor, attended by more than six thousand people.[143] Henceforward, Masaniello would be remembered as a plebeian hero whose action, however ephemeral, represented a political experience of liberty.

This political experience of the plebs remains significant. By organizing the pillage of the rich for the benefit not of the insurgents but of the poor, and by assembling a people's militia able to drive back the Spanish occupation troops, Masaniello proved that the plebs could take charge of public affairs just as well as the patriciate. In fact, certain contemporary foreign commentators of the events were struck by this illustration of the political capacities of the many. The English translator of a history of the Neapolitan revolution published soon after it occurred observed "a contradiction between what had occurred in Naples and the tradition of political thought which attributed the capacity for political direction and military organization to the upper classes, and indeed exclusively to the nobility."[144] It was this very demonstration of the people's political capacity that would make the revolt of Masaniello an exemplar for plebeian revolts to come. Witness the reproduction of the account of the events of 1647 in a publication meant for English Jacobins at the time of the "making of the English working class" at the end of the eighteenth and the beginning of the nineteenth century.[145]

Masaniello's revolt aptly illustrates the question of the "intractable," which is based on the premise that resistance to attempts to domesticate popular political forces was possible so long as the plebs maintained its separation from the dominant political order. Let us briefly examine this notion, which is drawn from the work of Jean-François Lyotard and developed further by Miguel Abensour.[146]

EXCURSUS 2: ON THE "INTRACTABLE"

There are five features characterizing the notion of the intractable. To start with, the intractable is "that which resists any practice of transformation, or processing [*traitement*]." It defines any phenomenon that manages to avoid the neutralization of its alterity. The intractable is also what refuses to be "processed": it cannot be integrated into a system. It follows that the intractable exposes the lie of totality. The next feature of the intractable is that it reveals itself especially in the political field, and it does so in two ways. First, it designates the "forgetting" that underpins political communities wishing to expel from the political sphere "a force or situation that may potentially weaken collective existence [*l'être-en-commun*]." Second, the intractable in the political field points to what cannot be subjected to sharing in common. The political processing implies the creation of a "commons," which by definition can be shared by all. But it is in its separation from the political order that the intractable takes shape; hence, it delineates the political field and shows "the thing to which collective existence tries to respond." The intractable cannot be located: it is a motif more than a representation. Thus, it is a "secret from which, according to Jean-François Lyotard, all resistance draws its energy."[147] Finally, the intractable is not found where it has historically manifested itself, that is, in social and political struggles, but rather on the margins of contemporary collective existence. However, one must avoid bending those margins so as to make them coincide with the new possible figures of the "historical subject" (women, the insane, illegal immigrants, etc.).

To illustrate the nature of the intractable, M. Abensour examines Lyotard's analysis of the case of paganism (*cas païen*) with reference to the dechristianization campaign during the French Revolution, and his analysis of the case of contemporary forms of resistance in society, which is related to his reflections on postmodernity.[148] We will restrict our discussion here to the first case, because it is more closely linked with the plebeian experience and also because it is a historical rather than a contemporary manifestation of the intractable. After all, Lyotard himself states in this connection that today the intractable must not be sought in social and political struggles as in the days before the end of the "grand narratives," that is, before the advent of the postmodern condition.

In "Futility in Revolution," Lyotard endeavors to understand how the dechristianization campaign of 1793 bore witness to the intractable. He identifies two ways in which that campaign brought to light the untamable nature of the intractable. The first, contained within the unfolding of the French Revolution, relates to the Jacobins' political system, which was unable to "neutralize" the dechristianization movement. The second has to do with a certain contemporary system of historiographic interpretation that is incapable of comprehending dechristianization. Here, Lyotard is targeting the work of the historian Daniel Guérin.[149]

At the time of the dechristianization campaigns, Jacobinism was established as a veritable system of government. The creation of the Comité de salut public and the setting up of revolutionary committees were only two components of the Jacobin political system. But dechristianization was a political initiative emanating from popular organizations, more exactly the Hébertistes. It enjoyed, if not the agreement, then at least "the support of the revolutionary bourgeoisie," specifically that of the Jacobins. However, the Jacobin politicians soon grew distrustful of the tumultuous and disorderly character of the dechristianization campaign, that "irresistible torrent."[150] Robespierre was particularly hostile to what he saw as "ultra-revolutionary"—hence, falsely revolutionary—behavior,[151] especially since the revolutionary bourgeoisie seemed to associate dechristianization with disruption, the uncontrollable, and even madness. For Lyotard, such a view reveals the utterly *intractable* nature of this event, which the Jacobin political system could not integrate.

Daniel Guérin's work also lays bare the inability of a preestablished system to integrate dechristianization. The rigidity of his interpretive system (modeled on Leon Trotsky's theses) prevents Guérin from accounting for the events of 1793 other than by reducing them to maneuvers aimed at diverting the class struggle. On this basis, Guérin attempts to press dechristianization into the mold of the "permanent revolution" (as theorized by Trotsky), thereby subjecting "this movement to an external unity"[152] that fails to seize the movement's true nature. For Lyotard, Guérin's interpretive move is comparable to Robespierre's attitude to dechristianization: "However much one may admire Guérin's book, it partakes of the same performative terrorism . . . , the same procedure that governs Robespierre's thinking."[153] Only through a libidinal and pagan history, Lyotard contends, can one account for the intractable in the dechristianization campaigns, because a history of this kind is attentive to the irreducible alterity of events and to the strength of the impulses driving such moments. The advantage of a "libidinal-pagan" history remains its openness to the plurality of the phenomena enabling humans to escape from power and to criticize in situ the dominant political practice.

Furthermore, according to Lyotard, the intractable is an indication of the dividedness of political communities. Revolutions are therefore understood to be attempts to move closer to what has been excluded from the community because of its intractability. Hence Abensour's intuition, expressed as a question: "Is it not to the intractable that we owe the strangeness whereby, underneath the 'beautiful revolution' that receives the almost unanimous approval of observers, another revolution suddenly awakens, unknown, anomic, 'hideous' in the eyes of the new masters of the political process who yield to the rage of the One?"[154] So the revolution is twofold: There is the "official" revolution that everyone is familiar with, and the underground, unrecognized revolution. Here, we must return to the political history of the plebs, more specifically, to the revolt of Masaniello in Naples.

As we have seen, Masaniello remained faithful to the political principles of the many until the moment he yielded to the Church hierarchs who were pressing him to meet the duke of Arcos and to dress like a nobleman for the occasion. This symbolic concession to the established order signaled the beginning of the end of democratic rule. In acting this way, he allowed himself to be *processed* by the patrician order: for Masaniello to abandon his position of refusing to be co-opted by the magnates amounted to his domestication by the patricians. The passage from the "intractable" to the tractable in this plebeian political experience is problematical because it signified a turn away from the initial democratic principles of the revolt. The question of the intractable in connection with the revolt of 1647 also points to the recurrent and thorny issue of the plebs' leadership.

For Masaniello seems to have partaken in both the grandeur and misery of the revolt. It must be recognized, on one hand, that he was an exceptional individual endowed with great political qualities. In bringing cohesion and open democratic guidance to the people's discontent, he was able to provide fair government. Through his modest, intelligent actions, Masaniello, for as long as the revolt lasted, embodied what was best in plebeian collective existence. On the other hand, however, he shared in the misery of 1647. His descent into madness and paranoia entailed the obliteration of the new possibilities that had arisen with the establishment of a free political regime in Naples. The fall of Masaniello coincided with that of the Neapolitan plebs. By accepting to be processed, the fisherman abandoned the secession from the patrician order and sounded the death knell of the hopes born of this plebeian experience.

The preceding sketch of the historical emergence of the plebeian principle—from the first plebeian secession in Rome, to the revolt of the Ciompi in Florence in 1378 and the carnival of Romans in 1580, through to the 1647 revolt of Masaniello in Naples—has brought to light the historical existence of an important though little-known political subject: the plebs. Far from being confined to the immediacy of the order of biology, the plebs revealed their engagement in the human political condition. The analysis of these political experiences also exposes the features of the plebeian principle and its related issues. We have observed, for instance, with respect to the four events in question, the assertion of the political capacity of the many as well as the presence of an originary division of the social. We have furthermore seen that the "intractable" nature of the plebs can sometimes be equivocal, as it is subject to processing by the dominant political order and even by the political order *in statu nascendi*.

There is one essential constant running through the historical constitution of a plebeian principle: the plebs' desire for liberty. One can discern at each moment of our "brief history of the plebs" the impulse to give the dominated access to involvement in public life. Melded with the feeling of revolt, the desire for freedom acts as a kind of invariant, to the point where it seems to be *constitutive* of plebeian political struggles. During the first Roman secession, the plebs forced the patriciate, through the creation of the tribunes, to open up the *res publica* to the participation of the plebs. In the case of the Ciompi revolt, the plebs fought for the advent of a truly democratic balia, in which political power would no longer be shared among a few prominent patrician families. For the plebs of Romans the limited but real power exercised in the city's poorer neighborhoods gave birth to a political space open to all. Finally, Masaniello's Neapolitan revolt took shape in an experience of political autonomy and freedom in a city under foreign control. All of this clearly indicates that the plebs were the agents of a people's politics and of political freedom.

Another characteristic of plebeian politics arises when the same desire for
freedom encounters the problem of the plebs' leader. For a better understanding of why this is a problem, it is useful to examine this question as it relates
to each of the plebeian experiences. Livy recounts that in the course of the first
secession in Rome the plebs set up on the Aventine Hill a camp "without any
officer to direct them." This apparently innocuous observation takes us to the
very heart of the issue. During that "inaugural" plebeian experience as a political subject expressing a desire for freedom and for the suppression of patrician
domination, the plebs refused to reproduce a division within their ranks by
designating a leader capable of pronouncing the Law.

The matter becomes particularly complicated with the 1378 revolt of the
Ciompi. The role of the leader named by the Florentine plebs, Michele di
Lando, in quashing the popular movement lays bare the difficulties involved
in conceptualizing the question of the plebs' leadership. For Quinet and Weil,
di Lando's behavior typifies (according to Quinet) a leader panicking in the
face of his "success" or—according to Weil—one ready to betray his erstwhile
comrades-in-arms in order to consolidate his own power. For Machiavelli,
however, di Lando can be viewed as having attempted to "found" plebeian
power and therefore still "deserves to be numbered among the few who have
benefited their fatherland."[155] Thus, the presence of the leader was problematic
for the revolt of the Ciompi. At best, in keeping with Machiavelli's interpretation, di Lando's actions signified that the plebs (or at least their *representatives*) were leaving behind the revolt and entering the political institutions of
Florence. At worst, in keeping with the interpretations of Quinet and Weil, di
Lando signaled the appearance of social division within the plebeian movement itself. A new group of "grandees" arose, ultimately with the effect of introducing a logic of domination.

The carnival in Romans adds certain nuances to this depiction of the issue of plebeian leadership. The part played by Paumier was closer to that of a
"spokesman" than of a political leader. Unlike di Lando, Paumier seems not to
have wanted to supplant the plebeian movement. Instead he endeavored to *articulate* the desires and demands of the plebs, as evidenced by his affronts to the
dominant political power (such as his refusal to kneel before the queen mother,
Catherine de Médicis). If Paumier was different from other leaders, it was perhaps thanks to the circumstances of his political ascension. More specifically,
he was designated as "leader" in the course of the carnival of 1579, and, according to Mikhail Bakhtin, the carnival allows transgression and the challenging
of the hierarchical order of patrician domination. Therefore, a "leader" designated during a carnival cannot be a "normal" leader. The carnival's charac-

teristics—antihierarchical, egalitarian, playful—necessarily affected Paumier's political actions. On the other hand, his being named "leader" made him an easy target for the wielders of patrician power in Romans. Indeed, Paumier's assassination marked the beginning of the end of that plebeian experience. This raises the question whether or not it would have been easier for Judge Guérin to neutralize the plebs had its movement been leaderless.

The figure of Masaniello in the Neapolitan revolt somewhat resembles that of Paumier. Periodization is needed to understand the problem of the plebeian leader in 1647. For, as "leader" of the plebs, Masaniello initially rejected conspicuous emblems of leadership: he continued to wear his fisherman's garb and refused to dress like a nobleman for his meeting with the duke of Arcos. Hence, in the early stages of the revolt in Naples, Masaniello presented himself more as a "spokesman" than a political leader. But the attempt on his life played havoc with the free and antiauthoritarian nature of his government. Consequently, the second phase of the revolt was marked by Masaniello's transformation into a veritable despot rather than a spokesman of the plebs, as previously explained: "The suffering body of the poor fisherman was suddenly supplanted by the glorious, almost lordly, body of the new *leader* of Naples."[156] Masaniello's metamorphosis into a tyrannical political leader put an end to the plebeian experience in Naples. The episode illustrates the paradoxical and deleterious effects of the presence of a leader in a political movement whose goal is to abolish domination.

The question of plebeian leadership may be one of the blind spots of the plebs' political experience. The designation of a plebeian leader is problematic because it involves the establishment of a power *over* others, that is, a coercive power, whereas the plebs' transformation into a political subject represents precisely the effort to construct a power *with* others, in other words, a noncoercive power. The problem's complexity stems from the need to distinguish between leaders who are primarily "spokespeople" of the plebeian movement (Paumier and the "first" Masaniello) and those who arrogate to themselves plebeian power in order to reshape it into a tool for their personal political ascendancy (di Lando, the "second" Masaniello).

A thorough investigation of the leadership problem also requires a shift of perspective whereby the role of the plebs in designating the leader is explored. We have seen that the plebs sometimes actively promoted the rise of a plebeian leader (di Lando, Paumier, Masaniello). As Étienne de La Boétie has shown, the desire for freedom, a constant of the plebeian experience, can change radically and turn into its opposite, the desire for servitude. It should first be pointed out that according to La Boétie, voluntary servitude is not based on habit or custom.[157] The oppressed do not seek to reproduce domination because they are accustomed to being dominated. Voluntary servitude comes about when human beings yield to the enchantment of "the name of one man alone."[158] Voluntary servitude thus arises through the search to recognize oneself in a leader and to recover a lost unity in the name of one man. For Claude Lefort, an attentive reader of La Boétie, voluntary servitude must be viewed in connection with the originary division of the social. When human beings are overwhelmed by vertigo in the face of the abyss resulting from social division and the concomitant threat of social implosion, they can yield to the desire for servitude: "The people want to be named, but the name in which the difference between one and another is abolished, the enigma of the social division . . . is the name of a tyrant."[159] What remains to be illuminated, then, is the particular appearance of voluntary servitude in each plebeian experience.

In the case of the first plebeian secession, the acephalous nature of the insurrection is undeniable. By forming a camp without any "officers," the Roman plebs resisted the attraction of the "name of one man." With the Ciompi, however, voluntary servitude seems indeed to have manifested itself. Michele di Lando enjoyed massive support as leader of the plebs, but the support was short-lived, as di Lando's decision to grant himself an allowance provoked the outrage of the Florentine plebs. Yet rather than taking back control of the city's administration, the plebeians designated new representatives, a new balia called the "Eight Saints of the People of God." This title seems to indicate a desire for the One, for does not the religious character of the new balia point to a call for unity or even for *communion*, which could eventually open the door to a desire for servitude? On the other hand, given the carnivalesque nature of the plebeian experience in Romans, Paumier's presence there cannot be associated with voluntary servitude. The distinctive features of the carnival affected the plebs' leader, such that Paumier's actions were more egalitarian than hierarchical, more democratic than authoritarian. In sum, the plebs of Romans did not seek self-confirmation in Paumier's name. As for the Neapolitan insurrection, the revolt of Masaniello does seem to have succumbed to voluntary servitude. From the outset, the plebs of Naples seem to have yielded to the desire for the One: Masaniello's designation as leader took place in the context of a religious ceremony, and the political experience of the plebs was born precisely the moment Masaniello became leader. Moreover, the plebs' violent overthrow of its leader, followed almost immediately by its change of heart, attests to a political disposition at odds with self-emancipation but consistent with the wish to choose a leader able to lead the revolt.

The case of Masaniello is reminiscent of the enigmatic episode in chapter 6 of *The Prince* where Machiavelli describes how Hiero of Syracuse "from private individual . . . became prince."[160] Plebeian acephalia seems to resist this kind of transformation, and the plebeian spokesman (such as the first Masaniello) holds fast to his "private station" in order to stave off the passage to that of prince or ruler. In this connection, does not the first Masaniello's insistence on wearing his fisherman's clothing bespeak a desire to show that he was a man of the people? Whereas, by dressing like a nobleman, the second Masaniello enacted the mysterious passage from the condition of ordinary man to that of prince. In the case of the Ciompi, di Lando quickly became a prince, while in Romans the spokesman Paumier stood resolutely with those who remained "private individuals." In sum, the plebeian experience includes situations where it is possible to go from being an ordinary man to being a prince.

Finally, the difficult question of the plebeian leader may perhaps testify to the *tragic* nature of the plebeian experience. The four experiences examined thus far demonstrate that plebeian temporality is in the order of a gap, hence unable to endure, although this gap does leave traces. The plebeian experience ends, at best, with the neutralization of the plebs' power (Rome, Florence), and at worst with an antiplebeian massacre (Romans, Naples). In the words of Georges Bataille,

> CAESARIAN UNITY, ESTABLISHED BY A LEADER—A HEAD—IS OPPOSED BY THE HEADLESS COMMUNITY, BOUND TOGETHER BY THE OBSESSIVE IMAGE OF A TRAGEDY. Life demands that men gather together, and men are only gathered together by a leader or by a tragedy. To look for a HEADLESS human community is to look for tragedy: putting the leader to death is itself a tragedy, it remains a requirement of tragedy.[161]

Despite its tragic nature, the plebeian experience leaves its mark and resonates for others who will be subjected to the same political domination in the future. Its relative brevity does not prevent it from inaugurating a *discontinuous* history of political freedom.

This historical birth of the plebeian principle is supplemented by an equally little-known intellectual tradition. While it displays specific features throughout political history, it is important to examine the place occupied by the term "plebs" in the political thought of certain key authors of our tradition and other more marginal ones. To discern the philosophical origins of the plebeian principle in the history of political thought—that is the objective of the next chapter.

2
PHILOSOPHICAL GENESIS OF
THE PLEBEIAN PRINCIPLE

But we do not know, or no longer know, what the people is.
As a political concept, it has dissolved.
—G. Duprat, *L'ignorance du peuple*

The notion of the people has certainly never been a central category of
political philosophy. . . . Forever tempted to either demonize or heroize it, at bottom,
political philosophy does not quite know what to do with the people.
—J.-F. Kervégan, *Dictionnaire de philosophie politique*

THROUGH THE GREAT POLITICAL AND DEMOCRATIC STRUGGLES
they have waged, the plebs have refuted the widespread prejudice that they are
subjugated to their vital needs and consequently incapable of political action.
To make plebeian political action intelligible, we have thus far relied on concepts drawn from contemporary political thought. This has enabled us to assess
the significance of the plebeian principle for our understanding of politics and
democracy. But since political thought has helped us better comprehend the
plebs, would it not be appropriate to map out the place that the plebs occupy
within that tradition? This would involve locating the references to the plebs
as a political subject so as to grasp more firmly the philosophical genesis of the
plebeian principle. We shall therefore endeavor to identify the contribution of
the signifier "plebs" to the political conceptualization undertaken by both modern and contemporary thinkers. For we believe that within political thought a
hidden tradition can be brought to light, a veritable "plebeian thought" that
makes it possible to rethink the major issues of political modernity.

Seven authors take part in this "plebeian thought": Three are "canonical"—
Machiavelli, Montesquieu, and Vico; two are marginal—Ballanche and De
Leon; and two are contemporary—Foucault and Rancière. A selection of this
sort is of course restrictive. It leaves aside thinkers such as Spinoza or, closer to
us, Georges Sorel, who also discuss the plebs.[1] Yet it allows us nevertheless to

make an initial contact with the signifier "plebs" in Western political thought. As for the absence here of Karl Marx, a pivotal theorist of emancipation, this requires some explanation. Although the plebs as an analytical category does appear—secondarily—in his work,[2] Marx does not contribute in our view to the philosophical genesis of the plebeian principle that we wish to bring to light. His emphasis on the proletariat, that is, on the laboring dimension of the people, as well as the distinctions he makes among the figures of domination (*lumpen*, etc.) of the nineteenth century, tend to neglect the particularities of the plebs. By isolating the different components of the people and, especially, by insisting on the economic dimension of patrician domination, Marx disregards the specifically political substance of the plebeian experience. To echo the criticism that Gilles Deleuze formulated in his seminar, it could be said that Marx "proletarianized" the people by reducing it to its working-class element. Moreover, Marx explicitly sets the plebs in opposition to the proletariat. "Hence their anger—not proletarian but plebeian—at the *habits noirs* [black coats]," he writes in 1880 with respect to the people's fury at the intellectuals and other "*conspirateurs de profession* [professional conspirators]."[3] Though a key thinker of emancipation, Karl Marx's work does not treat the plebs as a political subject engaged in the communalist and agoraphilic traditions.

Machiavelli, on the other hand, will help us understand the role of the plebs in the political upheavals testifying to the conflict and division at work within the community. Guided by Claude Lefort's reading,[4] we propose to examine the relationship between conflict and freedom in Machiavelli's thought. We will pursue the study of Roman history by focusing on Montesquieu's *Considerations on the Causes of the Greatness of the Romans and Their Decline*.[5] We will observe how his reading of Rome can be seen as a veritable "extolment" of plebeian disturbances. For his part, Giambattista Vico specifies the role of the plebs in what he calls the "ideal eternal history."[6] Like Machiavelli and Montesquieu, Vico extracts from Roman history the invariables of the plebs' political experience, which, in his view, made possible the transition from aristocratic republics to popular republics. For him, however, the plebs prove to be incapable of preserving their political freedom because they inevitably seek to rid themselves of their desire for liberty through the establishment of a monarchy. In the case of the philosopher Pierre-Simon Ballanche, well versed in Vico's writings but today virtually forgotten, we will seek to determine what he means by a "plebeian principle" that ensures the existence of progress in history. As for the work of Daniel De Leon, by virtue of his role as a political actor and thinker of the far left in the United States, it will help us understand what can be learned from the history of the Roman plebs, even with regard to the political and trade union struggles of American workers on the eve of the twentieth century. Finally, we will turn to two contemporary thinkers, Michel Foucault and Jacques Rancière, who have revived the plebeian question within current debates. In particular, we will observe in Rancière's work that the references to the plebs are recurrent and perhaps even central for our understanding of his political thought.

Since it is with the Roman Republic that we began our investigation of the historical birth of the plebeian principle, let us start our exploration of its philosophical genesis with that singular and enigmatic reader of Roman history Niccolò Machiavelli.

MACHIAVELLI: THE PLEBS, CONFLICT, AND FREEDOM

The work that will be the primary focus of this section, *Discourses on Livy*,[7] presents an extensive analysis of the history of Rome developed through a free-flowing commentary on Livy's *History of Rome*. Having established the precepts of the government of one in *The Prince*,[8] Machiavelli concentrates in the *Discourses* on elucidating the principles of the republican regime. Through the example of the Roman Republic, Machiavelli specifies what, in his view, constitutes the greatness of this type of political regime. Contrary to the widespread image of him as the theorist of despotism and tyranny, we discover in the *Discourses* a Machiavelli concerned about freedom and even democracy in political institutions.

The point of departure for the Machiavellian interrogation in the *Discourses* is the *hic et nunc*, the here and now. Machiavelli proposes to analyze Rome on the basis of political considerations applicable to his times. For him, the political situation in Florence required the construction of a countermodel able to provide it with more liberty and power than it possessed at the beginning of the cinquecento. The procedure he follows in the *Discourses* involves two steps. First, Machiavelli presents the Roman Republic as a political example to be emulated. He furthermore asserts that his project of developing a political understanding of Rome is an original one, one that does not coincide with the Florentine view of Rome at that time. Second, this explains why his rediscovery of Rome depends on a completely new reading of the phenomena responsible for its greatness and might. A certain "deconstruction"[9] of the prevailing image of Rome was needed in order for Florence to experience glory and honors. But why was Rome so important for the political representation of the Florentines?

The reference to Rome was central to the political imagination of the inhabitants of the city on the Arno. Regarding itself as Rome's heir, Florence must govern itself according to Rome's teachings. This representation of Rome stemmed from the humanist tradition whereby the inhabitants of the Eternal City were unquestionably the Florentines' direct ancestors, the humanists' objective being to consolidate and strengthen the patrician institutions of Florence. Thus, "for them, what accounted for Rome's early greatness was civic harmony, the majesty of the Law in the eyes of all, moral purity, the citizens' devotion to the public good, their eagerness to sacrifice themselves for the well-being of the country; it was *the wisdom of the Senate and, generally speaking, of the patricians [and] the discipline of the people.*"[10] It was therefore necessary to condemn whatever, in their opinion, had brought about the ruin of Rome: the divisions between the plebs and the patriciate, moral degeneracy, etc.

According to Lefort, this idealization of Rome bore the stamp of ideology, that is, of a discourse projecting the interests of a particular social class onto the whole of society. The vision of Rome put forward by the Florentine humanists was not intended to make known the true significance of the Roman Republic but rather to consolidate the power base of the governing patricians of Florence. In Lefort's view, the most eloquent proof of this ideological appropriation consisted in the fact that "the development of this discourse . . . coincides not with an extension of democracy but with an oligarchic reaction."[11] In other words, just when this conservative conception of Rome was visibly on the rise, democracy was losing ground in the face of the takeover of Florence's political institutions by powerful patrician families. The knowledge conveyed by the humanists of the bygone freedoms of the Roman Republic could not guarantee a rebirth of those freedoms in the city on the Arno and was in no way meant to do so.

The originality of Machiavelli's approach in the *Discourses* resides precisely in the demolition of the comforting image of a Rome whose greatness and strength were founded on concord and harmony. The Florentine Secretary contends that the Roman Republic was the theater of perpetual division and conflict between two rival "humors." And it is exactly because these humors and the conflict between them existed that Rome's freedom and power were ensured. To grasp fully the Machiavellian conception of Rome, we must first look at the notion of "humor," whose elucidation should make it possible to understand the importance of the plebs for Machiavelli.

The Italian word *umori* is recurrent in Machiavelli's work. This term, borrowed from Renaissance medical science, appears in the *Prince*, the *Discourses*, as well as the *Florentine History.*[12] Machiavelli thereby draws a parallel between the human body and the body politic. The use of such medical metaphors to designate a constitutive feature of the political sphere was commonplace during his time.[13] The political thinker was likened to a doctor inasmuch as he could diagnose the ills of the city and propose remedies.

In Machiavelli's work, "humor" conveys several distinct meanings.[14] Political humors refer to the desires inherent in a specific social group. These desires are natural, and it is imperative that they be satisfied. Humors are universal and have always existed in all human societies: "Whoever considers present and ancient things easily knows that in all cities and in all peoples there are the same desires and the same humors, and there always have been."[15] The substance of those universal dispositions, which cannot be transcended, is relatively simple: there is the disposition of the grandees (who are few), which consists of the wish to dominate, and the disposition of the people (who are many), which consists of not wishing to be dominated or, more positively, of wanting freedom. Or, as Machiavelli puts it, "in every city these two diverse humors are found, which arises from this: that the people desire neither to be commanded nor oppressed by the great, and the great desire to command and oppress the people."[16] In addition to designating the desires of a particular component of the political community, "humor" can sometimes designate the component itself. In the case of the Roman Republic, for example, the patricians and the plebs are referred to as humors. The humors can also be the result of conflict between the two basic elements of the community. Thus, in Machiavelli's writing, the struggle of the humors between the grandees and the people gives rise to humors. Machiavelli observes that the different types of political regimes are set up according to the way in which the struggle between the humors is dealt with. Under the Machiavellian typology, there are three such regimes: the principality, the republic, and license (*licenzia*): "From these two diverse appetites one of three effects occurs in cities: principality or liberty or license."[17] In sum, as previously mentioned, we are presented here with a new political intelligibility that consists of defining a political regime according to the manner in which it treats the expression of the constitutive humors of any city.[18]

The preceding statement can be verified for the three regimes identified in the Machiavellian typology. In a principality, it is the prince himself who must satisfy the humors. To strengthen his hold on power, he must ally himself either with the nobles or the people. In a republic (government of liberty), the active presence of the conflict between the humors is what ensures that freedom exists in the city. As for *licenzia*, there is neither a prince able to ensure order by allying with one of the two components of the city nor a conflictual dynamic providing a basis for liberty. In a regime of license, there are only antagonisms engendering the instability and imbalance of the humors.[19]

This excursus on the topic of the humors highlights the true import of the Machiavellian critique of the Florentine vision of the Roman Republic. By postulating the existence of two antagonistic humors that cannot be transcended and whose confrontation is necessary in order for freedom to bloom, Machiavelli radically challenges the conservative representation of Rome that prevailed in Florence. He furthermore lends legitimacy to the people's claims to dissension since they are a guarantee of liberty. This is why Machiavelli's reading of Rome in the *Discourses* is "daring and arresting."[20] He proposes two hypotheses: (1) that conflict was the primary cause of the freedom and greatness of Rome and (2) that the plebs were the custodians of that freedom. The first troubles the irenic vision of Rome and impugns the ideology of the Florentine humanists, and the second grants the people, that is the plebs, a space for political action. The question of the humors, crucial for the Machiavellian understanding of politics, therefore implies a valorization of plebeian disturbances, owing to the freedoms that they brought to life in the political space of Rome.

It is especially in chapter 4 of the first book of the *Discourses*, titled "That the Disunion of the Plebs and the Roman Senate Made That Republic Free and Powerful," that Machiavelli forcefully sets out his conception of what made Rome great. He writes, "I say that to me it appears that those who damn the tumults between the nobles and the plebs blame those things that were the first cause of keeping Rome free, and that they consider the noises and the cries that would arise in such tumults much more than the good effects that they engendered."[21] Rather than going along with Florentine common sense and reproving the tumultuous and conflictual nature of the Roman Republic, Machiavelli postulates that from the disorder born of the struggle between the Senate and the plebs, order can emerge.[22] In other words, one should not be dismayed by the superficial effects (the "cries and noise") but instead analyze the political consequences of this struggle, which, for Machiavelli, represents an expansion of liberty within the Republic. This statement frames the two basic principles guiding Machiavellian political analysis: (1) that the value of an event can be determined in light of its results and (2) that every community is divided between two different humors.[23]

Machiavelli continues this chapter with a defense of his unorthodox conception of politics, which points to a universal makeup of human communities:

> In every republic are two diverse humors, that of the people and that of the great, and that all the laws that are made in favor of freedom arise from their disunion. . . . Nor can one in any mode, with reason, call a republic

disordered where there are so many examples of virtue; for good examples
arise from good education, good education from good laws, and good laws
from those tumults that many inconsiderately damn. For whoever examines their end well will find that they have engendered not any exile or
violence unfavourable to the common good but laws and orders in benefit
of public freedom.[24]

At the root of laws and, moreover, "good laws," Machiavelli finds the opposition
between the two humors of the community. As we have seen, for Claude Lefort,
Machiavelli has perhaps discovered here one of the rare constants structuring
human communities, that is, an "originary social division."[25]

Machiavelli has a favorable view of plebeian opposition because he maintains that a "free" political regime must allow the plebs to express its "humors."
He writes, "I say that every city ought to have its modes with which the people
can vent its ambition, and especially those cities that wish to avail themselves of
the people in important things." As demonstrated by the pressure that the plebs
applied on the patriciate during the secession on the Aventine Hill in 494 BCE,
the strength of the *res publica* resides exclusively with the people. Machiavelli,
in referring to that first secession, underscores its political outcome, that is,
the creation of the tribunes. According to him, "The desires of free people are
rarely pernicious to freedom," and the Tribunes of the plebs "deserve highest
praise," for they made a twofold contribution to the development of the Republic, enabling the plebs to take part in public office and also "constitut[ing]
a guard of Roman freedom."[26]

Like Claude Lefort, we see in Machiavelli's interpretation of the struggles
between the patriciate and the plebs during the Roman Republic a bias in favor of the plebs. By repudiating the Spartan model of the sage establishing the
law that ensures the greatness of the community, Machiavelli carries out a sort
of democratic revolution with regard to the philosophical perspective, which
shifts from the "nobles" to the "people."[27] He was, actually, the first philosopher
to ascribe to the people the credit for law, freedom, and greatness. Indeed, this
is one of the reasons why Machiavelli is regarded as the founder of modern
political philosophy.[28]

In chapter 5 of the first book of the *Discourses*, Machiavelli seeks to determine "Where the Guard of Freedom May Be Settled More Securely, in the
People or in the Great."[29] It may seem that the people were preoccupied with
acquisition (of more freedom), whereas the nobles wished only to preserve
the established order and civic concord. But the idea that the nobles sought
only to maintain order was based on a patrician deception that is debunked

by Machiavelli. The grandees were also motivated by an unquenchable craving for acquisition "bound up with the unlimited enjoyment of possession, power, and prestige."[30] The grandees' thirst for acquisition can endanger freedom since it rests upon the domination of the plebs. To put it another way, the image of a conservative, peace-loving patriciate is no more than an illusion designed to consolidate the political instruments of its ascendancy over the people. Therefore, the responsibility for the "guard of freedom" must be confided to the plebs. As in the Roman example, "when those who are popular [i.e., the people —Trans.] are posted as the guard of freedom, it is reasonable that they have more care for it, and since they are not able to seize it, they do not permit others to seize it."[31]

However, the idea that Machiavelli is partial to the plebs does raise issues bearing on his work as a whole. We have seen in the previous chapter, for instance, how Machiavelli the historian is opposed to the actions of the plebs in the revolt of the Ciompi. In the *Florentine History*, he even describes Michele di Lando, the renegade leader of the plebs, as "*virtuosamente*," one who "deserves to be numbered among the few who have benefited their fatherland." Yet, as we know, di Lando was responsible for the crushing of the plebeian movement, a movement that had allowed him to accede to the highest level of public office in Florence. Machiavelli's position is all the more enigmatic because he writes that di Lando's merit was to have spared the better class of artisans from having "to bear the stench of the plebs."[32] Such pejorative statements regarding the Florentine plebs of 1378 are furthermore consistent with statements found in *The Prince*, where, for instance, Machiavelli advises the prince to follow the example of the Roman emperor Septimus Severus, who had acted in such a way that the people were "awestruck and stupefied."[33]

But do such comments disprove the idea that Machiavelli is a supporter of plebeian opposition as an expression of the desire for liberty? The answer is no, as can be demonstrated by a separate examination of the case of the Ciompi and that of *The Prince*. With regard to the events of 1378, Machiavelli's position certainly calls into question the action of the many. But the Florentine Secretary criticizes the plebs mainly for having turned against di Lando, who, it should be remembered, had come to power thanks to popular pressure. It was the plebs who had installed him at the seigniory of Florence. He thus symbolized the success of the plebeian revolt and, especially, the *founding* moment of the new Florentine power. Machiavelli, preoccupied by the question of the foundation,[34] seems to believe that the plebs should have been indulgent, even grateful, toward the plebeian leader. Although he does not assert this explicitly, it can be supposed that he considers support for di Lando all the more

important because the latter might have had the same institutional effect as
the tribunes of the plebs during the Roman Republic. Since for Machiavelli, as
we have seen, the tribunes were "constituted as a guard of Roman freedom,"[35]
his defense of Michele di Lando, a "conservative"[36] stance, does not call into
question his attachment to the plebs, expressed in particular in the *Discourses*.

Machiavelli's comments in *The Prince* concerning the people relate to a different problem. Aside from chapter 9, "Of Civil Principalities," where he explains the division of the "humors" between the "nobles" and the "people," it
can be said that Machiavelli does not show much esteem for the people, who
can readily be "awestruck and stupefied" by the prince's actions. However, this
work enjoys special status in the Machiavellian corpus. *The Prince* provides
Machiavelli with the opportunity to discuss in greater depth the question of the
foundation of a political community.[37] The foundation, the supreme political
act, requires not the participation of the "people" or the plebs but rather of a
single man, a particularly gifted prince, since he must be able to set his *virtù*
against the vagaries of *fortuna*. The reason Machiavelli discredits the plebs in
The Prince is that they do not take a direct part in the founding act.[38] In fact,
plebeian politics arrives only once the city has been founded, when the prince
has managed to establish a political realm. Thus, "to conceptualize political
freedom in Machiavelli's work,"[39] it is essential to grasp both *The Prince* and the
Discourses together, as the former explores the question of foundations while
the latter investigates the process whereby the community allows for political
freedom.

This is why we can assert that a duly founded community is free inasmuch
as the division between the plebs and the patriciate is brought into the light
of day. The ultimate effect of the division between the great and the people is
liberty, and it is plebeian action that drives it forward. In the writings of the
Florentine Secretary, the plebs play a central role in the maintenance and development of the free political regime. Machiavelli's contribution to "plebeian
thought" can therefore be summed up as follows: *the plebs is the political actor
who brings to life the desire for liberty within the community by ensuring the
presence of conflict, thanks to its implacable opposition to the great.*

MONTESQUIEU: IN PRAISE OF DIVISION

"One can never leave the Romans; thus it is that even today in their capital one
leaves the new palaces to go in search of the ruins; thus it is that the eye that
has rested on flower-strewn meadows likes to look at rocks and mountains."[40]
Although this avowal by Montesquieu is found in *The Spirit of Laws*, we will

turn to a lesser-known work, *Considerations on the Causes of the Greatness of the Romans and Their Decline*[41] (1734) to understand the role of the plebs for his thought. In this work, Montesquieu, following Machiavelli and using a discourse close to his, undertakes a new reading of Roman history aimed at identifying the areas of strength and weakness of that epoch-making civilization of antiquity.

Montesquieu's *Considerations* is not a historical study of Rome; the true import of this work is philosophical. It should be read, more specifically, as a work of "political philosophy."[42] Indeed, Montesquieu performs a philosophical reading of Roman history based on three methodological premises representing the rejection of a certain approach to history.[43] First, the intelligibility of history cannot be reduced to either a final cause of a teleological nature or to chance or fortune. Second, the philosophical approach to history disregards superfluous facts and details, that is, those not directly relevant to a philosophical understanding of the world. Finally, this approach also dismisses any recourse to "great men" as a factor explaining major historical events.

Two chapters of the *Considerations* deal directly with the question of the Roman plebs: chapter 8, "The Dissensions That Always Existed in the City," and chapter 9, "Two Causes of Rome's Ruin." In chapter 8, Montesquieu discusses the division between the patricians and the people in the Eternal City. In his view, it was because of the encouragements of the patricians, wishing to avoid a return to the monarchy in Rome, that the plebs developed "an immoderate desire for liberty." This rampart against the kings quickly transformed into a stronger demand for political participation. The plebs sought to obtain magistrates, with the result that Rome was changed into "a popular state" where power was returned "to the greatest number." For Montesquieu, the people's hatred for the dominators has existed "at all times." The first plebeian secession also allowed the people to obtain tribunes. It demonstrates that the instruments for the defense of the people's interests inevitably metamorphose into weapons used to attack the prerogatives of the powerful. The creation of plebeian magistracies provided the plebs with the tools and the will to fully assert themselves politically at the patricians' expense. In short, it can be said that Montesquieu describes Rome here as a city perpetually in the grip of agitation, a city not only vulnerable to political divisions but that actually fosters them. He consequently states, "The government of Rome was admirable. From its birth, abuses of power could always be corrected by its constitution, whether by means of the spirit of the people, the strength of the senate, or the authority of certain magistrates." Montesquieu concludes chapter 8 with the assertion that "a *free government*—that is, a government *constantly subject to agitation*—

cannot last if it is not capable of being corrected by its own laws."[44] Hence, there exists a correlation between the degree of liberty in a regime and the presence of political turmoil within it.

Toward the end of chapter 9, which discusses two causes of the decline of Rome, Montesquieu returns to the question of the division within the city. For some, Rome's ruin was brought about by its divisions, especially between patricians and plebeians. Montesquieu, however, argues that such dissensions "were necessary to it . . . they had always been there and always had to be." His rationale is as follows: A warrior republic requires that its citizens may become soldiers. A bellicose spirit abroad must perforce express itself in domestic agitation. The plebs being obliged to transform themselves into an army meant that Roman public affairs were necessarily turbulent. So it was Rome's expansionist objectives that turned "popular tumults into civil wars." For Montesquieu, there is as well the "general rule [that] whenever we see everyone tranquil in a state that calls itself a republic, we can be sure that liberty does not exist there."[45] Tranquility, calm, and peace are therefore synonymous with political servitude and hence with a dearth of freedom.

What is more, Montesquieu refutes the idea of a political union resulting from the absence of conflict or agitation. For him, political union is "equivocal" and is akin to musical harmony, where "dissonances . . . cooperate in producing overall concord." Thus, "In a state where we seem to see nothing but commotion there can be union." That is why, in a tyrannical political regime, such as "Asiatic despotism," where disorder is suppressed, "it is not citizens who are united but dead bodies buried one next to the other."[46] In a word, the absence of agitation implies the absence of freedom and the construction of a sham union based on the enslavement and the death of human beings.

For a proper understanding of Montesquieu's outlook, the references to Machiavelli must not be seen as accidental. In his *Considerations*, Montesquieu in many ways discloses his debt toward the Florentine Secretary. The emphasis on the analysis of Roman greatness and power already indicates a rejection of the approach typical of classical political philosophy, whose goal is to circumscribe the question of the Good and the Just.[47] Rather, Montesquieu emerges here as an heir to Machiavellian realism, with its stress on power and its effective use. Indeed, there are those who see in the *Considerations* an iteration of the Machiavellian gesture par excellence, which involves a veiled critique of Christianity and its political consequences.

Through an examination of the preceding hypothesis, articulated by David Lowenthal, a disciple of Leo Strauss and a Montesquieu scholar, we hope to arrive initially at an understanding of the "design"[48] of the *Considerations*, particularly with regard to the issues of division and the plebs. The point here is to determine the exact nature of Montesquieu's Machiavellian heritage. Does he, as Lowenthal believes, repeat Machiavelli's attack against Christianity? Before addressing the question directly, it may be useful to review briefly Leo Strauss's reading of Machiavelli, with the aim of demonstrating that Lowenthal does in fact take up the Straussian critique of Machiavelli, applying it to the *Considerations*, and that this gesture is significant for his resulting interpretation of Montesquieu.

For Leo Strauss, Machiavelli's writings signal the beginning of the triumph of reason over religion. Machiavelli's works dispense with any reference to a transcendent entity able to judge, from an exterior position, the value of human undertakings. Furthermore, the Florentine Secretary wishes to construct a world on "low but solid"[49] foundations by anchoring the ultimate judgment of things in the final effect of human action.[50] This refusal of the transcendent, which represents a denial of religion, radically challenges Christianity's ascendancy over the Western world. In *Thoughts on Machiavelli*, Strauss strives to show that Machiavelli's work is directed toward a political critique of Christianity, which he considered responsible for the deplorable state of Italian politics during his times. This is why Machiavelli turns to ancient Rome, a pagan political power, in order to develop a counterexample that could help reshape prevailing political practices. The reference to Rome enables him to criticize Christianity indirectly by praising its first political adversary, pagan Rome.

For Lowenthal, Montesquieu formulates in the *Considerations* the same critique of Christianity previously articulated by Machiavelli as read by Strauss. Owing to the particular context in France in 1734, the year the work was published, Montesquieu "could easily anticipate trouble over a work that praised pagan Rome, as distinguished from Christianity, and favored republican Rome rather than its early or later monarchical forms." This would explain the esoteric character of his critique. His particular view of Rome seems all the more anomalous because it was clearly at odds with the tradition of that time, which tended to praise Rome as the Eternal City of Christianity. Pagan Rome, in Montesquieu's analysis, turns out to be a warlike city whose preservation and development were necessarily bound up with and dependent on conquest. Although Montesquieu does not state this explicitly, Roman grandeur was essentially determined by its military strength and its ability to dominate the world. Lowenthal, however, detects in the author of the *Considerations* a wish to minimize what was pitiless, even "inhumane," in the Roman martial spirit.[51] Thus, Montesquieu offers a refined vision of what ancient Rome truly was.

A series of clues point to a sibylline critique of Christianity in the *Considerations*. On one hand, there is a total absence of dates in this work. At no time does Montesquieu mention a specific year. According to Lowenthal, this strange omission is not fortuitous. Montesquieu chooses not to follow the Christian calendar, which plays a role in the erasure of the greatness of Rome. On the other hand, that first omission is followed by a second, involving the absence of references to the life and death of Jesus of Nazareth and to the first years of Christianity. In Lowenthal's view, Montesquieu seeks here to turn his readers away from all things Christian. Finally, with the combined effects of a refined, even "benevolent" reading of pagan Rome and the erasure of Christian references, Montesquieu's goal is to undertake, as Lowenthal puts it, "an attack on the Bible, its leaders and its peoples. To win approval for Rome, Montesquieu must engender oblivion of and opposition to 'sacred' history."[52]

It would appear that this is Montesquieu's "design" throughout the *Considerations*. It is essential to criticize Christianity, which is at the heart of the political problems of modernity. It engenders "civil strife on religious grounds" while promoting servitude and obedience to the Church and the monarch. Christianity also condemns certain measures that are needed for liberty to assert itself, such as tyrannicide. Moreover, one of the most serious political consequences of the advent of Christianity was the weakening of the virtues required for a political regime of freedom to flourish: courage and a public spirit. "In short," writes Lowenthal, Christianity "seems to have made the revival of something like Roman republicanism impossible."[53]

Given this state of the political, what actions must be taken to restore politics to what it was in Roman times? Lowenthal believes that the *Considerations* can be read as an incitement to rebel against the ascendancy of Christianity, especially its political embodiment, that is, the monarch endowed with divine right. Montesquieu describes the "revolts, seditions, and perfidies" specific to the Roman Empire as "great enterprises." He observes that such "great enterprises . . . are more difficult to conduct with us than they were with the ancients."[54] His discourse is thus favorable to uprisings; identifying such moments as "great enterprises" would obviously not leave the reader indifferent. Montesquieu's objective, according to Lowenthal, is to remind people of the existence of conspiracies "against tyrants that . . . at times resulted in the establishment of republics."[55] Therefore, the ultimate goal of the *Considerations* is apparently to foster a transformation of the mentality of European nations by liberating it from the pernicious political sway of Christianity.

These, then, are the reasons why Montesquieu, in Lowenthal's reading of his work, emerges as Machiavelli's worthy heir. Like him, Montesquieu sees himself as a warrior of ideas challenging the spiritual and political power of Christian Rome. The *Considerations* participate in the desired decline of Christianity by preparing the way to another political future where reason and liberty will prevail over faith and servitude. Just like Strauss's Machiavelli, Lowenthal's Montesquieu contributes to the destruction of transcendence and to the advent of a political order built "low yet solid" and that fully partakes in the modern project.

It therefore seems reasonable to assert that Lowenthal takes up the Straussian critique of Machiavelli and applies it to Montesquieu. But, while his analysis is often convincing, it is nevertheless as neglectful as Strauss's with respect to one crucial point, underscored by Claude Lefort, which is the question of division. The author of *Le travail de l'oeuvre Machiavel* notes that Strauss's emphasis on the Machiavellian struggle against Christianity blinds him to the existence of social division.[56] Because of this, Strauss has nothing to say about the role of the plebs in a free political regime. We feel that a similar operation is at work for Lowenthal. In stressing Montesquieu's combat against religion, Lowenthal tends to minimize his approval of the "dissensions that always existed in the city."[57] A brief analysis of Lowenthal's positions on this matter should suffice to demonstrate how he reproduces this limitation of Straussian thought.

In an article published for the first time in *Interpretation*, the journal of American Straussians, Lowenthal affirms that the idea of a necessary "civic harmony," so dear to classical political philosophy, is refuted by Montesquieu in chapter 8 of *Considerations*. Conflicts were considered legitimate in Rome, and it is important to appreciate this if one wishes to understand the internal organization of the Republic. Division, Lowenthal concedes, is not a "political vice"[58] for Montesquieu, since it is the result of Rome's military power and therefore shares in its greatness. Lowenthal moreover agrees that in chapter 9 Montesquieu puts forward a conception of political union necessarily involving active conflict and division. It must therefore be granted that, while Lowenthal does not regard it as central to this interpretation, he does acknowledge this aspect of Montesquieu's thought.

That said, in Lowenthal's introduction to his translation of the *Considerations*, completed under the supervision of Allan Bloom, it is clear that he does indeed minimize the importance of the question of division and conflict in Montesquieu's work. For, although he does not hesitate to discuss this issue in a journal intended exclusively for scholars of political philosophy, he refrains from doing so in a publication aimed at a general readership.[59] Lowenthal quickly sets the tone in his introduction, enumerating the reasons for Rome's greatness according to Montesquieu, but rather than highlighting how division contributed to it, he states that the greatness could be attributed in part to the limited influence of the people in public affairs.[60] In discussing the lack of unity in Roman politics, Lowenthal stresses that the author of the *Considerations* apparently neither supports democracy nor even sympathizes, as Machiavelli does, with the plebeian cause.[61] Montesquieu, in presenting the plebs' recriminations, is at such pains to distance himself from them that Lowenthal considers him less critical of the wealthy than Aristotle. By way of reinforcing this attack against what might be understood as an unequivocal stance in praise of division articulated in the *Considerations*, Lowenthal contends that Montesquieu, though aware of the virtues of the Roman people, recognizes the inherent superiority of that distinctly patrician institution, the senate. Furthermore, if one follows Lowenthal's reading, Montesquieu also avers that the immoderate nature of the plebs' freedom and power in ancient Rome represented "a great evil." Finally, writes Lowenthal, Montesquieu "seems to favour a republic where the people have enough power to protect themselves against grave injustices but insufficient power to direct the state."[62] Lowenthal attempts in this way to neutralize the democratic claims of this work, making the author of the *Considerations* into an advocate not of an egalitarian regime but of the patrician political order. He thus minimizes the question of division in Montesquieu's thought, the effect being to diminish the role of the plebs in Montesquieu's work.

In opposition to such a reading, one that reproduces a blind spot in Straussian thinking, we believe that a different interpretation of the *Considerations* is possible. The democratic, even subversive, character of Montesquieu's philosophical history of Rome stands out clearly when it is compared to similar works published during the same period. The Abbé Vertot's *An History of the Revolutions That Happened in the Government of the Roman Republic*[63] offers an exceptionally striking counterexample for anyone wishing to properly grasp the implications of Montesquieu's assertions on division and conflict. Vertot's views, representative of the prevailing political opinions in early eighteenth-century France, throw the true meaning of the *Considerations* into relief.[64] It should be pointed out that, as evidenced by the catalogue of his library, Montesquieu had access to and was familiar with Vertot's works, including the one on the Romans.[65] For Henri Drei, this work is the one that seems "best integrated in Montesquieu's cultural horizon"[66] and hence deserves particular attention.

Vertot's *Histoire* revolves around three key themes: liberty, revolution, and the people. The Roman Republic was, for him, only a brief parenthesis between two monarchic ages, and its history was marked by decline and even decadence. The love of freedom, which was at the heart of the Roman Republic, brought about the ruin of freedom in that it engendered disturbances and conflicts that ultimately resulted in the destruction of the various forms of freedom. Thus, because it was characterized by great instability, the Republic was comparable to a "nonregime." The conflicts between patricians and plebeians were conducive to major changes that Vertot describes as "revolutions." Yet "the very solutions meant to remedy the divisions among the citizens did nothing but engender new divisions."[67] Hence, far from being a regime of concord and stability, the Roman Republic was chaotic, agitated, and beset with numerous revolutions.

Throughout his *History*, Abbé Vertot makes abundant use of the term "revolution." Vast changes and more or less noteworthy political events are all deemed revolutionary. The Roman Republic, constantly in the grip of revolutions, must necessarily be described as unstable or, worse, dangerous. This broad application of the term "revolution" is hardly innocuous. To depict the slightest event as a revolution tends "to blur, or erase, the difference between a revolution, strictly speaking, and a political development or even a stage in the evolution of the State." Hence, to accuse the Roman Republic of spawning endless revolutions represents a highly effective means of denigrating this type of regime, especially in the context of the ancien régime. In fact, from Vertot's point of view, only the monarch is capable of ending conflicts, which are always harmful for the body politic. That is why the Roman Republic is perceived as a nonregime suffering from a "monarchic deficiency."[68]

In Vertot's opinion, this unreasonable and chaotic state of affairs is the fault of the plebs. The plebeian and patrician protagonists invariably played the same roles, and different revolutions were merely repetitions of the same conflicts. What's more, the plebs proved to be hungry for "novelty for the sake of novelty, blind to its true interests, [and] easy to deceive."[69] As for the tribunes, they were incorrigible subversives. The plebs could thus play no political role, since their participation in the Roman Republic only hastened its ineluctable degeneration.

This explains why the Abbé categorically condemns the plebeian love of liberty, which he considers the cause of numberless revolutions resulting in instability and disturbances in the Roman Republic. Vertot can scarcely hide his contempt for the plebs and his belief in the political inequality of human beings. Abbé Vertot's conservative analysis of the Roman Republic clearly displays the color of his political sympathies. A confirmed monarchist, he interprets the events of the Republic from the perspective of a fierce supporter of the ancien régime and its political practices. He is convinced that the movement of history must defer to the smooth continuity that the monarchic system en-sures. Consequently, theological-political stability is always preferable to the uncertainties and disturbances caused by political events.

Against this backdrop, the meaning of the *Considerations* gains new depth and breadth. In contrast to Abbé Vertot's unqualified and often virulent dis-course, Montesquieu stands as a worthy heir to Machiavelli, the theorist of so-cial division. Through a meticulous and nondogmatic analysis of pagan Rome, he not only acknowledges the importance of the love of freedom and the con-flict that it engendered in the Republic but even applauds the contribution of division to the greatness of Rome. Montesquieu also argues that a political regime must not endeavor to suppress discord in the name of civic harmony or unity. Otherwise, it will experience unity in the form of "dead bodies buried one next to the other."[70]

Montesquieu's statements are all the more consequential because they were published during the same period as Vertot's and sought in a way to respond to this type of "monarchist" analysis of Rome.[71] Although, like Machiavelli, he does not position himself explicitly on the side of the plebs, Montesquieu articulates a reading of the political events of the Roman Republic that is sup-portive of plebeian opposition. He thus adds to "plebeian thought" inasmuch as, according to him, the plebs takes part in conflicts born of division. Mon-tesquieu's contribution to "plebeian thought" therefore involves conceiving of the plebs as *the political actor that rejects tranquility and peace in favor of the disturbances needed to achieve liberty and to express the dissension that guaran-tees the conflictual unity of a free political community.*

VICO: THE PLEBS AND THE "HISTORY OF ALL THE CITIES OF THE WORLD"

Vico conceives all political communities as patterned by recurrent historical moments.[72] The cyclical form that Vico ascribes to history is also found in Machiavelli,[73] with whom he shares, together with Montesquieu, the idea that the example of ancient Rome helps to sharpen one's political vision. Indeed, for the author of *The New Science* (*La scienza nuova*), Roman history provides exactly the model or "paradigm" for this cyclical conception of history, which conceives of the annals of nations in terms of the life process: ineluctable birth, growth, and degeneration. The plebs constitutes one of the active poles of these recurrent historical movements.

Before elaborating on the status of the plebs in Vico's work, it would be help-ful to present the general sense of his political thought and, in particular, what he calls the three "ages" of humanity, the three cyclically recurring movements that mark human history: "The world," Vico writes, has "passed through three ages: that of the gods, that of the heroes, and that of men,"[74] each coinciding with a stage in the development of humanity. According to Vico, during the first "age," that of the gods, a sort of theocracy governed collective existence in the sense that, through the figure of the father, the gods exercised their power over human beings.[75] The father, having access to divine wisdom by means of "auspices and divination,"[76] acted as priest. For Vico, the dissemination of families and the "prepolitical" character of the reign of fathers endow it with the status of "state of nature."[77] Closer to Hobbes than to Rousseau in this respect, Vico does not regard the age of the gods as a "paradise lost" but rather as an epoch marked by violence and cruelty. Not until the advent of the second age, that of the heroes, could humanity leave behind the state of nature and organize itself into truly political communities. A struggle within the families produced the conditions for the birth of the city, the inaugural political form of human history. It was here that the many plebeian struggles for liberty arose. These cities, initially "aristocratic," in the sense that they resulted from the meeting of fathers wishing to maintain their control over the plebs, were transformed through plebeian political action into "popular commonwealths."[78] It was the advent of such democracies that ensured the transition to the last age, that of men. But the age of men does not involve the exclusive rein of "democracies," since monarchies also existed.

It can be observed that humanity's trajectory, from the age of the gods to the age of men, was linear and progressive. However, when they arrived at the final age and corruption took hold, political communities returned to "barbarism,"[79] that is, they regressed to an early period and came back to the age of gods, the state of nature. This regression is characteristic of Vico's cyclical vision of history.

To understand the role of the plebs in Vico's thought, one must return to its origins in the age of the gods and the state of nature. He argues that families, the constitutive units of the state of nature, are composed not only of parents and children but also of *famuli*, that is, the domestics and servants who, in exchange for their labor power, gained the protection of the fathers. The famuli had no rights in the state of nature: they could neither marry nor acquire property,[80] and they had no religious status. The famuli lived in the servitude resulting from the absolute domination of the fathers.

But such domination could not last indefinitely. Vico writes, "The *famuli* . . . must naturally have chafed under [that servile state], by the axiom that 'subject man naturally aspires to free himself from servitude.'" The revolt of the famuli against the fathers made possible the transition from the state of nature to the age of heroes. The author of *The New Science* contends that the first cities or commonwealths emerged in reaction against the emancipatory aspirations of the famuli, the forebears of the plebeians. The fathers, powerless so long as they remained isolated in their respective families, united to guarantee the political hegemony of the order of the "paters" (fathers), who dubbed themselves "patricians." The age of heroes was thus born through the offensive of the strong, the father-patricians, against the weak, the famuli-plebeians. The patricians "swore to be eternal enemies of the plebs," and the ultimate purpose of the political institutions of the aristocratic commonwealths was "to preserve the power of the nobles."[81] That is why the patricians fought so fiercely to uphold the exclusivity of marriage and of the public magistracies. Especially since, from the patrician perspective, the plebeians were subhuman, even "bestial." They therefore could not partake in the domains that ensure one's admittance to humanity: religion and politics. In sum, for Vico, the patricians wanted to preserve the established order whereas the plebeians wanted to transform that order.[82]

As was the case with the domination of the fathers over the famuli, patrician control of politics and religion in the aristocratic commonwealths could not be sustained over time. The plebs demanded to be integrated into the city on a more egalitarian basis. It was precisely when the plebeians became fully aware of their equal share in humanity that they articulated political and religious demands. The plebeians, in Vico's words, should "realize that they were *of like human nature with the nobles* and should therefore be made equal with them in *civil rights*."[83] The plebeian struggle for the extension of liberty within the first cities was such that it transformed the very nature of those cities,[84] which changed from aristocratic to democratic. But the transition to democracy, from the age of heroes to the age of men, took place gradually. Concession by concession, the plebeians succeeded in gaining the recognition of their full participation in the political and religious condition of humanity.

To illustrate this progressive exodus from patrician domination, Vico turns to the Roman political experience, which "reveals the histories of all the other cities of the world," thereby exemplifying "the ideal eternal history." For it is in Rome that the recurrent political configuration common to all political communities can be discerned. The Roman plebs made three major political gains: access to property, access to marriage, and, finally, access to political rights. With the first agrarian law, Servius Tullius granted the plebs "bonitary ownership of the fields" in exchange for their observance of the census and their active service in time of war. Bonitary ownership allowed the plebeians to work the land and enjoy its fruits. But because the patricians did not respect this first agrarian law, the plebs created two plebeian tribunes, whose mandate was to defend "the natural liberty" of the people, as expressed in the bonitary owner-ship of the fields. As soon as this right was consolidated, the plebeians pressed forward with the demand for "quiritary ownership of the fields,"[85] that is, full and entire ownership of the land. This was accomplished through the Law of the Twelve Tables, the second agrarian law of antiquity, which granted quiri-tary rights of ownership over the fields, thus setting in motion the plebeians' exodus from servitude.

The effects of this access to property, however, were diminished because of the impossibility for the plebeians to marry and, therefore, to bequeath either land or estate. For the plebs, being prohibited from marrying implied that they had "no direct heirs, agnates, or gentiles (to which relations legitimate succes-sion was then confined)."[86] Accordingly, the plebs sought to secure the right to marry. The demand for equal access to marriage was not a trivial matter in Rome. It represented a direct assault against patrician privilege, more specifi-cally the exclusive enjoyment of religious rights.[87] Indeed, "the plebeians . . . were in effect asking for Roman citizenship, whose natural principle was sol-emn nuptials."[88] Hence, it was the plebs' acquirement of the right to marry that truly marked the passage from aristocracy to democracy.

Yet the political action of the plebeian tribunes cannot be reduced to the obtaining of the right to property and marriage. Vico stresses that they also succeeded in winning "civil liberty" for the plebs. A change in the census, for example, enabled the plebs to pay a tax to the public treasury rather than to the patricians, thereby strengthening its autonomy. The tribunes also acquired the right to legislate, a wholly political right. Since the patricians systemati-cally opposed the demands of the plebs, these plebeian victories gave rise to conflicts and turmoil in Rome. The political disturbances were such that the Romans resorted to a dictator able to settle numerous disputes between plebe-ians and patricians. Paradoxically, it was thanks to the dictator Publius Philon that Rome was transformed into an authentic popular commonwealth. In par-ticular, Philon decreed that it was forbidden to make a law contrary to the plebiscite, thus effectively granting the plebs a veto. The dictator went so far as to grant the people the power to make laws overriding the will of the Senate, a patrician political institution. Vico can therefore assert, "the plebs had already been made in all respects equal to the nobles by laws to which the latter had agreed. By his most recent move, to which the nobles could offer no opposition without bringing the commonwealth to ruin, the plebs had become superior to the nobles."[89]

The emancipation of the plebs, coinciding with the passage from an aris-tocratic republic to a popular republic, was thus fully realized. By acceding

in stages to property, marriage, and political rights, the plebs asserted its unqualified admittance to Rome. It thereupon took part on an equal footing in
the religious and political condition of human beings. "The plebeian desire for
democracy stems from an overall remodeling of the regime of beliefs."[90] And,
in fact, the plebs was no longer regarded as being of a different nature (subhuman or bestial) from that of the patricians. Using a vocabulary that would have
been unfamiliar to Vico, one might say that the plebeian struggle for freedom
involves the plebs manifesting itself as a "political subject" putting forward
democratic demands.

   That said, it should not be forgotten that, since history is cyclical for Vico,
events are subject to regression and an always possible return to "barbarism."[91]
The problem for popular commonwealths or democracies is that freedom soon
becomes intolerable for the plebs, who remain incapable of bearing for very
long the liberty they had nevertheless fought so hard to win. Vico explains that
when the people hold power, they split into factions that struggle for exclusive
control, and in order to put an end this kind of oligarchic rivalry for power
the plebs turn to monarchy, the political rule of One. After experiencing the
political freedom embodied in a democracy, the people open the door to the
voluntary servitude implicit in the adhesion to monarchy. Vico writes, "monarchy cannot arise save as a result of the unchecked liberty of the peoples, to
which the optimates[92] subject their power in the course of civil wars. When
power is thus divided into minimal parts among the peoples, the whole of it is
easily taken over by those who, coming forward as partisans of popular liberty,
emerge finally as monarchs."[93]

   Yet monarchy does not actually signify a regression for Vico. Indeed, it falls
within the category of "human governments" and consequently belongs to the
age of men. Monarchy in fact represents a political solution to the problem of
the difficult freedom of the plebs. Exhausted by the oligarchs' endless struggle
for power in the popular commonwealths, the plebeians seek the "repose" that
a monarchic regime can provide. Such a regime upholds the equality of its citizens and is moreover characterized by "the equitable rule of law, the mildness
of the relationships among individuals, and all the benefits of civilization."[94]
Vico writes:

   As the citizens have become aliens in their own nations, it becomes necessary for the monarchs to sustain and represent the latter in their own persons. Now in free commonwealths if a powerful man is to become monarch the people must take his side, and for that reason monarchies are by
   nature popularly governed: first through the laws by which the monarchs

seek to make their subjects all equal; then by that property of monarchies whereby sovereigns humble the powerful and thus keep the masses safe and free from their oppressions; further by that other property of keeping the multitude satisfied and content as regards the necessaries of life and the enjoyment of natural liberty; and finally by the privileges conceded by monarchs to entire classes . . . or to particular persons by awarding extraordinary civil honors to men of exceptional merit. [95]

Thus, monarchy is not a return either to the barbarism of the state of nature or to the age of the gods.

How is one to understand Vico's idea of the "plebs" in this context? Three constitutive features stand out: First, the plebs are collectively the actor ensuring change and transformation within human communities. Whenever the established order was altered, there are signs of plebeian action, as evidenced by the passage out of the age of the gods thanks to the impetus of the famuli's opposition to the order of the fathers. The insurrection against patriarchal domination enabled the transition to the age of heroes, but the role of the plebs as catalyst of change and transformation did not end there. It was once again under the impetus of the plebeians that the human race moved from aristocratic republics to human republics. Vico states, "the plebs of the peoples, always and in all nations, have changed the constitutions from aristocratic to popular and from popular to monarchic."[96]

Furthermore, the plebs are the agent of the conflicts that bring about an expansion of human liberty. Through political mobilization, the plebeians demonstrate their rejection of the prevailing order of the community, asserting themselves through protest. In its conflictual relationship with the ruling power (of the fathers, the heroes, etc.), the plebs rises up to acquire greater freedom. The struggle against the heroes, for example, was aimed at obtaining economic, religious, and political rights. Even when it was no longer able to bear the burden of freedom and sought "repose" in a monarchy, the plebs endorsed the regime of the One solely on the condition that equality between patricians and plebeians be explicitly recognized by the new political order. Hence, writes Vico, "the multitude of plebeians, while it had been dangerous to the aristocratic commonwealths, which are and profess to be the property of the few, added to the greatness of the popular commonwealths and much more to that of the monarchies."[97] The greatness referred to here is that of freedom, whose motive force was the conflict that arose through plebeian political agency.

Finally, the plebs as conceived by Vico proved incapable of assuming political freedom for any length of time. The popular commonwealths fell prey to degeneration, losing the thing that set them apart politically, that is, liberty. The only political remedy for the anarchy caused by the oligarch's fight for power in democracies was monarchy. While recognizing the equality of human beings, a monarchy restores order and authority within the political community: "From the brooding suspicions of aristocracies, through the turbulence of popular commonwealths, nations come at last to rest under monarchies," Vico writes. The cyclical character of history postulated by Vico implies that the plebeian experience of freedom in some way represents a gap in "the histories of all the other cities of the world."[98] But although that gap may be sealed for a time, it will always reappear, since the cycle of human history must inescapably follow its course.

To recapitulate, Vico's contribution to "plebeian thought" is to conceive of the plebs as an *agent of the change and transformation of the established order, an agent that, in its conflictual relationship to domination, ensures the growth of liberty within the political community. Unable, however, to assume the greatest possible expansion of that liberty once democracy is established, the plebs invariably seeks to be rid of it under a monarchy.*

BALLANCHE: THE PLEBEIAN PRINCIPLE

In contrast to the works of Machiavelli, Montesquieu, and Vico, Pierre-Simon Ballanche's work has today been generally forgotten. Yet it represents a significant contribution to the "plebeian thought" that we are endeavoring to extract from the history of political thought.

Born in 1776 in Lyon, Ballanche belongs to the generation of thinkers who grew up amid the revolutionary events in France and whose thinking was profoundly shaped by the political climate of the Bourbon Restoration (1814–1830). Ballanche's political thought, much like that of Chateaubriand or Pierre Leroux, has a strong connection with religion. Indeed, according to Oscar Haac, "Ballanche devoted his life to reconciling two major sources of inspiration, the church and the revolution, and to describing the gradual synthesis of aristocratic and democratic principles, of spiritual and social forces."[99] The reemergence of religion after the revolutionary offensive of 1789, a crucial feature of the first half of nineteenth century in France, can also be seen in Ballanche's work.

French politics during the Bourbon Restoration was divided between, on one hand, the ultras, who deplored the revolutionary events and hoped for a return to the monarchy and the theological-political matrix, and, on the other hand, the liberals, who condemned the revolutionary excesses while at the

same time welcoming the break with the ancien régime and the Church. Ballanche adopts a position at variance with those of both the ultras and the liberals.[100] In opposition to the ultras, Ballanche maintains that religion cannot exclude the idea of progress. By fighting for a return to absolutism, the ultras are
defending an idea that is not just obsolete but also dangerous for France, since
it proposes to disregard the improvements to the human condition resulting
from the Great Revolution. In opposition to the liberals, Ballanche asserts that
religion is necessary for human progress. For religion does not represent simply the preservation of the hierarchical order specific to the monarchal world;
it guarantees progress. Thus, Ballanche's political thought is a blend of progressive and conservative ideas. His contribution to the philosophical genesis of
the plebeian principle can be better grasped through an examination of his
"Formule générale."[101]

The "Formule générale" is part of a broader study conceived as a series of
"essays on social palingenesis," a term denoting for Ballanche the rebirth of societies. This rebirth is for him at the origin of the evolution of humankind and
ensures the improvement of human beings. Using analogy, Ballanche proposes
to reconstitute the great deeds of a "universal epic" so as to show the movement of regeneration of societies.[102] His largely unfinished "social palingenesis"
includes various "prolegomena" and three fragmentary parts. The first part,
Orphée, gives an account of human evolution through the myths that are at
the origin of Western civilization.[103] The second part, the "Formule générale,"
situates that evolution in the context of ancient Rome while at the same time
explicitly describing the role of the plebs in Ballanche's thought.[104] The last part,
which includes *La ville des expiations* and *La vision d'Hébal*, outlines a "social
and spiritual reform" yet to come.[105]

Through his essays on social palingenesis, it is Ballanche's intention, in the
early years of the nineteenth century, to substitute the nascent philosophy of
history with a "theodicy of history."[106] He declares, "I wish to articulate the
great thought of my century. I wish to seek out this dominant thought—deeply
sympathetic and religious, which received from God himself the lofty mission
of organizing the new social world—in all spheres of the various human faculties and in every order of sentiment and idea."[107] In the wake of the disruption
ensuing from the revolutionary events, Ballanche's mission is to take part in
the advent of a necessary reorganization of human affairs in accordance with
God's plan. But for this to occur, one must first show what is at work in the
evolution of Western civilization. This is precisely what Ballanche strives to
accomplish throughout his essays. The motor force of human evolution lies in
the struggle between two principles: the stationary or conservative principle

and the principle of motion or progress. As a result of the friction between these two principles, humanity can attain an ever-greater share of liberty. In this struggle between conservation and progress, Ballanche sees the workings of providence.

Because "Ballanche's work appears to be a meditation constantly enriched by its own heritage,"[108] focusing on the "Formule générale" rather than reviewing all the fragmentary components of the "Palingénésie sociale" may provide better access to his thought. By drawing freely on the works of the historians of antiquity Livy and Dionysius of Halicarnassus, as well as on contemporary accounts of Roman history such as those of Montesquieu and Vico,[109] Ballanche reconstructs in his "Formule générale" the history of Rome's three plebeian secessions.[110] The reconstruction is performed in line with the constitutive struggle of the history of humanity, that is, between the stationary and progressive principles. Ballanche takes up his premise of a general pattern of human evolution and tries to understand how it was expressed in Roman history. In the case of the plebeian secessions, the stationary principle is represented by the patriciate and the progressive principle by the plebs.

Among Ballanche's studies of the three plebeian secessions, only one was published during his lifetime, in the *Revue de Paris* in 1829.[111] The second was published in 1959 under the editorship of Oscar Haac,[112] who in addition summarizes the fragments dealing with the last plebeian secession.[113] Generally speaking, the first secession can be said to symbolize for Ballanche the plebs' attainment of the status of human beings; the second represents the integration of the plebs in the civic institutions of Rome; and the third involves the plebs' achievement of full-fledged citizen status. The three plebeian secessions demonstrate how the conflict between the stationary principle and the principle of progress made possible the extension of freedom within Roman civilization.

More specifically, the first plebeian secession in 494 BCE on the Aventine Hill presents the plebs as a "confused troop with neither a civic nor religious fraternity." The plebeians were "mute with civic mutism" because they did not enjoy human status in Rome. Therefore, they could not exercise the defining human faculty of speech. The plebs, in order to survive, were placed in a situation of dependence vis-à-vis the patricians, who were the patrons of the plebeian clients. This radical heteronomy of the plebs "excludes [them] by force of circumstance from the noble Roman city." Excluded and deprived of speech, the Roman plebs "[have] no refuge other than revolt."[114] Which is why, when faced with problems of indebtedness, the plebs chose to secede by withdrawing to the Aventine Hill.

Initially, there was "a confused crowd without rules, laws, thoughts, or words to express its thoughts" on the Aventine. Nevertheless, Ballanche contends, by overcoming "the instinct of need" and extricating itself from the imperatives of the order of biology, the plebs succeeded in acquiring thought and, above all, speech. For, with the encouragement of Servilius, a patrician sympathetic to the plebeian cause, the plebs endowed itself with a divine protector and, hence, with a past. Moreover, those who were "mute with civic mutism" possessed themselves of speech and of a leader able to deal with the patricians in Rome. This man, Paterculus, took the name of Brutus and played a part in "the great transformation" engendered by "a palingenesic movement."[115]

When the patricians delegated Menenius Agrippa to the Aventine, a first breach was made in the plebs' infrahuman status. Indeed, negotiating with the plebs amounted to acknowledging that they had at least a partial share in humanity. However, Agrippa confined himself to telling the fable of the body parts and the belly and was surprised by the plebeian demand to conclude an agreement. Because for him the plebs did not constitute a "society with established rules, legitimate assemblies, magistrates appointed according to ancient rites," under such circumstances, to arrive at a settlement remained "impossible." Yet the patricians authorized him to conclude an accord with the plebs; upon returning to the Aventine he was astonished by the prevailing order and tranquility. Agrippa proceeded to create the plebeian tribunes, thereby establishing the autonomous existence of the plebs. For Ballanche, as an interpreter of Roman history, "the progressive principle [thus] emerges . . . to carry on a ceaseless struggle against the stationary principle."[116]

While the first plebeian secession brought to the plebs an awareness of their own existence in relation to the patricians, the second allowed them to integrate the civic institutions of Rome. This next secession took place on Crustumerium in 449 BCE, subsequent to the martyrdom of a plebeian girl "killed by her father to protect her [sic] honor."[117] Underlying this infanticide was the opposition of one of the decemviri, Appius Claudius, to the education of plebeians outside the home of the patrician patron. Appius Claudius asked, "What law authorizes the plebeians to have their children educated outside the domestic precinct ruled by the patron?" He was outraged that a nameless plebeian could be admitted to a school, itself objectionable, having been "created to instruct the children of a race forever excluded from all knowledge and doctrine, denoting a pernicious tendency toward emancipation." According to Claudius, the plebs must absolutely be kept "in a state of benightedness so as not to be tempted to reject passivity, which civic harmony requires."[118] Since the

plebs did not have the right to a legally or religiously sanctioned marriage, it
could not participate in the civic institutions of Rome. It therefore had no right
to be educated anywhere outside the patron's home.

Rather than let his daughter die at the hands of the patricians, her biological
father chose to martyr her to the plebeian cause. To rouse the plebs to revolt
against the nonrecognition of plebeian marriage, he sacrificed his daughter,
thereafter known as Virginia, "the plebeian virgin." This led to a new secession. The patricians sent a mission to deal with the plebs and put an end to
"the anarchy reigning in the city." But it was a group of senators belonging to
the "council of the profound mystery"[119] who resolved this new conflict between the stationary principle (the patriciate) and the progressive principle
(the plebs):

> As of today the plebeians have acquired a sense of modesty. A father has
> sacrificed his daughter to this sentiment, which is that of human dignity;
> and [his] act . . . was sorrowfully applauded by all. . . . Impunity is abol-
> ished within the sacred walls of Rome; the reign of isonomy has begun.
> Anathema on whoever would attempt to reestablish impunity! Threefold
> anathema on whoever might wish to hasten the slow, majestic march of
> isonomy. [120]

The plebs thereby gained access to certain civic institutions such as marriage
and achieved a civic status greater than ever before in the Roman body politic.
Thus, in principle at least, isonomy came to the Roman Republic.

The third and last plebeian secession occurred on the Janiculum Hill in
286 BCE in a context where acquired plebeian rights were being eroded. Specifically, the Roman Senate wished "to abrogate previously granted rights,
especially the right to legitimate marriage." This attack on the status of the
plebs convinced the plebeian tribunes to organize a new secession. Their goal
was to create a "true homeland" for the plebs, that is, a city where the plebs
might fully assume their role of political subject. The triumph of this secession
was ensured through the enactment of Lex Hortensia, which "concretizes the
plebeians' 'initiation' into the city and completes their accession to power."[121]
From that point on, the plebeians were full-fledged citizens, and the principle
of isonomy, acquired during the second secession, was put into practice. The
progressive or plebeian principle installed itself by overcoming the powers of
the stationary or patrician principle. Plebeian freedom and equality reigned in
the Eternal City.

As indicated by its title, the "Formule générale de l'histoire de tous les peu-ples, appliquée à l'histoire du peuple Romain" (General formula of the history of all peoples, applied to the history of the Roman people) seeks to identify the constants in the evolution of humankind. The first constant for Ballanche, as we have seen, is the conflict between the stationary principle and the progres-sive principle. Beyond the particular case of Rome, focusing on the struggle between the plebs and the patriciate, Ballanche throughout his work designates the stationary principle with the term "patrician" and the progressive principle with the term "plebeian principle" or even "plebeianism." For the author of the "Formule générale," the sociopolitical categories specific to Roman civi-lization can be appropriately used to denote the nature of human conflicts. It is telling that Ballanche planned to title his work on the constitutive struggles of societies "Évolution plébéienne."[122] Hence, in his work, the question of the plebs and the patriciate clearly transcends the Roman example. The antago-nism between patricians and plebeians, Ballanche writes, "is a law of fallen and resurrected humankind, [and] . . . the hidden mainspring of Roman history and all history."[123]

The history of humankind is therefore the history of the struggle between the patrician principle and the plebeian principle. According to Ballanche, of these two "faculties, always parallel throughout every historical period," the patrician principle represents the stationary and passive principle. It evokes the Orient, to that which, in his view, resists the transformation of the world, because the Orient is a civilization where the law of conflict no longer prevails. "Wherever struggle ceases there is stagnation, petrified or stereotyped civiliza-tion, as in the Orient. Society remains unchanged, as in China." What's more, Ballanche maintains that the patrician principle excludes humanity: "The truth is that general human sympathy cannot emerge in the patrician class, but only in the plebeian class."[124]

There thus exists a close connection between plebeianism and humankind in general. In fact, Ballanche holds that "the plebeian is the quintessential hu-man being." In their struggle against the patriciate, the plebeians guarantee humankind's progress "towards its emancipation."[125] The plebs designates all evolution of the human species in the direction of progress. For, as Georges Navet asserts, "to become aware and take possession of oneself is to grow in dignity and, hence, to acquire rights. . . . The plebeian is [thus] the person who performs this movement."[126] Plebeianism is linked to humanity to such an ex-tent that Ballanche goes so far as to assert, "literature and the arts, the honor and glory of humanity, are plebeian productions."[127] As the embodiment of the progressive principle, the plebs is comparable to the Occident, the birthplace of human innovation and transformation, according to Ballanche. And it is precisely because the Occident allows itself to be affected by the antagonism between the two principles that it represents the plebeian principle in the world.

The analysis of Ballanche's "Formule générale" brings to light his theoretical conception of the patrician and plebeian principles. But, on the empirical level, what was Ballanche's attitude toward the plebeians of his times, that is, the oppressed and excluded groups of France in the first half of the nineteenth century? What ties was he able to establish with those who, according to his "theosophy of history," incarnate the progressive principle? Some indications can be found in a letter drawn from his correspondence with Juliette Récamier and dated September 1, 1832. In it, Ballanche gives an account of his participation in a weekly meeting of workers, both men and women, wishing to discuss the theoretical and practical problems confronting them. He recounts that, after hearing his theory on the struggle between the stationary and progressive principles, the workers not only understood his presentation but also were able to apply it to French history. "I was surprised at the intelligence of all those present," he writes. Moreover, Ballanche asserts, "I was better understood there than I would have been in the Académie française." The workers said that they found themselves "in fifth-century Rome," that is, at the moment of the first plebeian secession. Thus, in their opinion, their sociopolitical situation resembled that of the plebeians, who in the fifth century were "mute with civic mutism." They could therefore identify themselves with plebeianism and the ineluctable fight against the patrician principle. Seeing that the workers had absorbed the terms of his vision of human evolution, Ballanche insists in his letter to Madame Récamier that he had been "perfectly understood."[128] To all appearances, the core elements of his thought—"history as emancipation; the emphasis on the conquest of individuality through the combined knowledge of oneself and the world; the plebeian hero as the emblem of humanity making itself"[129]—had struck a chord with the Parisian workers.

There emerges from Ballanche's letter a sense of his respect and even of a certain admiration for the workers whom he met. This esteem was no doubt prompted by the sight of individuals subjected to extremely harsh living and working conditions who nevertheless took the time to reflect on and debate their sociopolitical situation. His admiration seems to be confirmed by the reproaches that Ballanche expresses in a letter about Saint-Marc-Girardin, who had compared "the admission [of] proletarians into civil society to a barbarian invasion." For Ballanche, the use of the term "barbarian" to describe the workers—not unusual at the time—"deeply offended the people in whose company

I found myself, something, I am sure, of which Mr. Saint-Marc is oblivious."[130] In Ballanche's mind, the contemptuous use of the word "barbarian" stemmed from thinking that was "retrograde" and even dangerous, because it betrayed an ignorance of the necessary conflict between the stationary and progressive principles.[131] As an expression of the utter smugness of the most conservative elements among the French patricians, Saint-Marc-Girardin's words attested to the fundamentally antagonistic nature of the patrician principle.

Ballanche thus offers us a theory of conflict. He recognizes the necessity of struggle between the two constitutive principles of human society: the stationary principle and the progressive principle. As previously noted, Ballanche's thought is at once conservative (affirming the importance of the Church, for example) and progressive. The progressive character of his work resides in his plebeianism, which guarantees the evolution and the advancing conquest of liberty. Consequently, Ballanche's contribution to plebeian thought can be summed up as follows: *Embodying humanity, the plebeians are the collective political actor who, in affirming a "plebeian principle," enables the progress and emancipation of the human species to be realized in the political sphere through the struggle waged against the stationary patrician forces.*

DE LEON: THE LEADERS OF THE PLEBS

Ballanche's work has today fallen into oblivion, and that of Daniel De Leon is relatively unknown outside the circle of scholars of the history of the American labor movement. Yet his contribution to political theory has remained significant, with V. I. Lenin, A. Gramsci, and R. Michels figuring among those influenced by his writings.[132]

Daniel De Leon (1852–1914) was born in the Caribbean and educated in Germany. A polyglot, he studied law at Columbia University in New York, where he went on to teach for six years at Columbia's School of Political Science. Trained as a lawyer, he abandoned his academic career in order to devote himself entirely to political activism.[133] In 1890, he joined the Socialist Labor Party of America (SLP) and immediately became the intellectual (though not political) leader of the movement.[134] As editor-in-chief of the SLP's daily newspaper, *The People*, De Leon defined the party's major positions for over twenty years. This explains why the ideology advocated by the SLP is indistinguishable from De Leon's political and social thought.

The SLP is a direct heir to the International Workingmen's Association (IWA), also known as the First International, founded by Karl Marx in 1864. Consequent to the incessant quarrels between the supporters of Marx and those of Bakunin, it was decided in 1872 that the headquarters of the First International would be moved from London to New York. After the dissolution of the IWA in 1876, its members, German speaking for the most part, founded the Socialistic Labor Party. The original SLP became the American branch of the Second International, which put forward a blend of reformist and revolutionary propositions.[135] In 1877, the Socialistic Labor Party disavowed the recourse to reformism and opted for revolution. To signal this change in direction, it became the Socialist Labor Party.

In 1890, when De Leon joined the party, it was only a small German-speaking group with no influence on the American working class.[136] By promulgating socialist ideas, the SLP under De Leon's intellectual leadership became a major, albeit ephemeral, force in the U.S. labor movement. Initially the SLP prescribed the infiltration of American trade (reformist) unions as a way to advance the revolutionary cause.[137] Its relationship with the American Federation of Labor (AFL) was particularly strained because the AFL's president, Samuel Gompers, defended the doctrine of "pure and simple"[138] trade unionism, that is, a reformist and staunchly apolitical approach to union struggles. Gompers's anti-Marxism made him a frequent target of De Leon's writing. In any case, the infiltration attempts by SLP militants were unsuccessful. The AFL, as well as the other major American union, the Knights of Labor, easily countered the SLP's maneuvers.

Hence, in 1895, under the decisive influence of De Leon, the SLP abandoned the notion of infiltrating reformist unions and created its own union, one with revolutionary policies. The Socialist Trades and Labor Alliance (STLA) thus became the economic and trade union wing of the SLP. However, the issue of relationships with the reformist unions gave rise to a split within the party. A large faction of the SLP, favoring infiltration and fearing marginalization vis-à-vis the major trade union organizations, left the SLP and established the Socialist Party of America (SPA). For the SLP this rift was all the more difficult because the STLA was "stillborn."[139] De Leon and the SLP then attempted to form an alliance with a new revolutionary-oriented union, the Industrial Workers of the World (IWW), but a political disagreement put an end to the alliance after just three years. Thus, the central concern of the SLP's and De Leon's political actions bore on the kind of ties that should be maintained with trade unionism. But beyond his revolutionary involvement and the political struggles that he conducted, what are the distinguishing features of De Leon's thought?

Daniel De Leon was a Marxist-inspired thinker and activist of "revolutionary industrial unionism."[140] Dismissing the notion that companies must be state owned, De Leon promoted the democratic control of industry through workers' councils, hence the expression "revolutionary industrial unionism." The aim was to eliminate, through the abolishment of the state and the manifold domination of some human beings over others, the coercive exercise of power. To this end, he wanted the SLP to take power democratically. Favoring the electoral approach implied respect for the democratic process outlined in the U.S. Constitution. According to De Leon, by adopting the electoral method the labor movement could avoid the traps of conspiracy, which would only arouse distrust and provoke state violence.[141] De Leon feared that workers would be massacred by those holding the "legitimate monopoly of violence" in the United States. However, the goal of the SLP in taking part in elections was not to exercise political power. Upon coming to power, the party's first task would be to hand over the control of industry to the workers. Workers' councils would replace the decision-making structures of the private sector. Furthermore, the management of sectors of public interest, such as education, health, and agriculture, would be ensured by worker-elected delegates. Once the new system was established, the SLP would wind up its activities, having carried out the passage from the government of men to the "administration of things."

Both De Leon's political battles and his political and social ideas are presented in *Two Pages from Roman History*, a contribution to plebeian thought.[142] The text represents a part of the debate on the kind of relationship that should exist between the working class and the leaders of reformist trade unions. What's more, this discourse articulates some of the main points of DeLeonist thought. As the title indicates, De Leon proposes to highlight two lessons drawn from ancient Rome. The "first page," concerning the "Plebs Leaders and Labor Leaders," deals directly with the plebeian experience, whereas the "second page," on the political reforms enacted by the Gracchi, does not deal with the question of the plebs. We will therefore focus only on the "first page" in *Two Pages from Roman History*.

De Leon affirms from the outset that the goal of his political battle inside the SLP is the establishment of a socialist republic, which is synonymous in his view with "the emancipation of the working class." This is a "promised land" representing the end of the class domination that has always prevailed in human societies. However, in order for the socialist republic to arrive, more time must be devoted to observation and reflection on the means of action needed for emancipation to be achieved. Strategic knowledge of the labor movement and its adversaries is essential for the advancement of the socialist cause. Yet, as De Leon points out, strategic knowledge does not signify deceit and trickery. Strategic thinking does not mean devising stratagems in order to fool people. Rather, it involves mapping the "topography of the field of action, and of the means at command."[143] The first page, concerning "plebs leaders and labor leaders," is in fact part of the effort to gain a better understanding of the "strategically strong place" held by the adversaries of the socialist movement, the union leaders.

For De Leon, the trade union leader is a type specific to the English-speaking world. It exists in England, the United States, Canada, and Australia but apparently nowhere else in the Western world in the same form. That one man may be at once the representative and the leader of a union and thus fully enjoy the union's power cannot fail to raise questions and point to certain problems. Thus, in the first part of *Two Pages*, De Leon elucidates some major questions concerning the union leader, particularly those pertaining to his strategic position with regard to social issues. He also seeks to determine whether or not the union leader serves to further the labor movement's interests over those of the supporters of the capitalist system. In keeping with the recommendation formulated by Marx in *The Eighteenth Brumaire of Louis Bonaparte*,[144] De Leon turns his analytical attention to the past in order to better decipher and understand the present. Because, he writes, "Other nations, now among the dead, also had to deal with their Social Questions."[145]

De Leon looks back to Rome to understand how the Republic managed to deal with its social question. For him, the Republican period is essential for an understanding of the evolution of Rome, because it marks the beginning of the end of Roman civilization. In his treatment of the social question, De Leon sets out the factors leading to the decline of the Roman Republic. To understand this decisive historical episode one must be aware of the sort of social division that prevailed in Rome, that is, the conflict between the orders. On one hand, there were the patricians, who had religious status, political and economic power, and exclusive access to public speech. On the other hand, opposite those possessing the prestige of the great families, were the plebeians. But they are more difficult to define than the patricians. One must first discard the usual image of the plebeian that has circulated since Shakespeare's *Coriolanus*, where the plebeians are reduced solely to their economic dimension. In *Coriolanus*, the plebeian is poor. Casting aside this misrepresentation of the plebs, De Leon stresses that some plebeians were wealthy and that the true sense of this label is the "multitude."[146] In other words, "the plebs" does not indicate economic status but rather the "many" as opposed to the patrician "few." In fact, the fundamental difference between patricians and plebeians rests on the fact that the latter could enjoy only economic power. Contrary to the patricians, if a rich plebeian lost his possessions, he could not rely on his political power and religious prestige to ensure his survival.

To explain the class divisions affecting the plebs, De Leon resorts to modern terminology: there were plebeians belonging to the "bourgeoisie," a plebeian "middle class," and "proletarian" plebeians.[147] The proletarian plebeians no doubt made up the majority in the Eternal City. The bourgeois plebeians, on the other hand, were the big landowners. Finally, the middle class included the owners of small plots of land. This situation engendered an interplay of alliances in the Roman Republic: patricians and rich plebeians could collaborate to increase their wealth at the expense of the proletarian plebeians. The middle class, as indicated by the name, was caught between the two other groups. But its vulnerability to the appetites of the large patrician and plebeian landowners made it a frequent ally of the proletarian plebeian cause.

The basis for the economic exploitation of the proletarian plebeians was to be found in the Roman military conquests. The Republic was often at war and generally victorious, and the conquered lands were usually annexed. Theoretically, the new lands should have been distributed equally among the Romans. In reality, however, the major landowners grabbed most of them. The middle class might obtain a token concession, whereas the proletarian plebeians were excluded from a share in the booty. An alliance between the patricians and the bourgeois plebeians quickly took shape. The objective was to reduce the middle class to proletarian status so as to gain sole access to the spoils of war. In addition, the massive influx of new slaves resulting from the victories over Rome's enemies gave rise to an economic slump that reduced the proletarian plebeians to unemployment. The combined disgruntlement of the middle class and the proletarian plebeians, who saw their labor power replaced by slave labor, made for an explosive social mixture. The economic struggle of the disinherited classes occasioned a politically unstable situation. This is how the conflict of the Roman orders began.

A new alliance between the plebeian middle class and the proletarian plebs resulted in even closer ties between the patricians and the bourgeois plebeians, who coveted a share in public power in order to consolidate their position in the Republic. Consequently, the patricians accepted the idea of a "plebs leader" invariably chosen from among the bourgeois plebeians. Thus, according to De Leon, this new position was the fruit of a joint policy of the patricians and the bourgeois plebeians. The aim of that policy was to address the plebeians' discontent symbolically while reinforcing the position of the major landowners. The plebs leader, chosen by the patrician consuls, held a seat in the Roman senate but was not entitled to speak. He could express his approval or disagreement only by stamping his feet. For De Leon, this gagging of the plebeian leader is reproduced by that of the union leader, who can accept the honors of the capitalist system only on condition that he keep quiet.

The installation of a leader of the plebeians marked the first "victory" of the plebs, or at least a victory of its bourgeois element. For, as De Leon asserts, the presence of a plebeian in the Roman Senate "relieved not one of the economic burdens"[148] of the plebs. The self-interested motivations of the leader of the plebs were eloquently demonstrated by the first plebeian secession, which occurred after the position was created. Despite the presence of a plebeian in the Senate, numerous economic grievances drove the plebs to leave Rome. The secession also illustrated the dynamic at work after the patricians granted a degree of power to the bourgeois plebeians. The withdrawal of the plebs to the Aventine Hill forced the patriciate to institute a new, exclusively plebeian public office, the tribunes of the plebs. Because these tribunes received no salary, it was virtually impossible for a middle-class or proletarian plebeian to hold this position. Only the bourgeois plebeians, those already eligible to be plebs leaders, could become tribunes. That is why the creation of these new offices could not lead to the emancipation of the plebs. The bourgeois plebeians thus exploited the feeling of revolt of the other plebeians to consolidate their own political power.

The naming of a leader of the plebs inaugurated a series of political and economic victories for the plebeian bourgeoisie. At each stage of this process, patricians and wealthy plebeians secured the economic subjection of the multitude. Hence, the patricians' "concessions" did not succeed in ending internal strife in Rome. In fact, the bourgeois plebeians obscured the economic demands of the many by systematically shifting the demands away from the economic plane. For example, at the moment when the distress of the middle-class and proletarian plebs was at its peak, the plebs leaders fought for the right to have their daughters marry patricians. "The plebs mass demanded bread," De Leon writes, and "the Plebs Leaders qualified for father-in-laws of patrician youths."[149] Consequently, the only accord possible in Rome under the Republic was that achieved between the patricians and the bourgeois plebeians.

It follows from this that the conflict of the orders in Rome was not a struggle between the patricians and the plebeians but, indeed, between the large landowners and the multitude. The leaders of the plebs did not endeavor to put an end to the plebeian condition. Instead, they were "practical" political actors espousing no ideal apart from the protection of their own interests. In striving to strengthen their social and economic position in Rome, the bourgeois plebeians wielded a weapon that was particularly effective for the advancement of their cause: the title of "plebeian." The fact that the bourgeois plebeians shared this designation with the other plebeians created the illusion that they had a stake in a "common cause."[150]

Throughout his analysis of the plebeian bourgeoisie's triumphs, De Leon draws a parallel between the self-interested behavior of the leaders of the plebs and that of the union leaders. One can sense De Leon's contempt for those, like the AFL's Samuel Gompers, who take advantage of the title of "worker" to advocate reformism and reject the transformation of the capitalist order. For De Leon, such leaders are "fakirs," that is to say, magicians and snake charmers who bewitch the labor movement. The careers of reformist union leaders offer ample evidence that all they do is provide the liberal economy with a working-class endorsement. Just like the leaders of the plebs, the trade union leaders regard the economic system in which they take part as something that cannot be transcended. Moreover, both types of leader are "practical" inasmuch as they aim only to minimize the system's deficiencies. Finally, both plebeian and trade union leaders deny that the working class has any capacity for self-emancipation.[151]

The deleterious effects on the working class of the union fakirs' endorsement of capitalism make it imperative to neutralize these strategic capitalist bulwarks. The only way to do this necessarily involves the autonomous revolutionary political action of the workers. And, in fact, the strong resistance of the union leaders to such action attests to their role as defenders of the capitalist order. This is how De Leon answers his opening question on the nature of the trade union leader: just like the plebs leader, the trade union leader serves only his own interests, which are identical to those of industrial capitalism.

As evidenced by the history of the United States in the twentieth century, the efforts that Daniel De Leon and the SLP devoted to organizing the socialist revolution in the United States were altogether unsuccessful. Worse still for the DeLeonists, they were not able to establish a revolutionary labor union section with a substantial membership. Nevertheless, De Leon and his plebeian thought did leave a legacy. Indeed, *Two Pages* attracted considerable attention in Great Britain in the early years of the twentieth century. In 1903, the "impossibilists," a group of left-wing activists, were inspired by De Leon's work and founded the British Socialist Labour Party (BSLP).[152] This party formulated two fundamental propositions: first, the necessity of taking industrial rather than political power, and second, the need to set up popular education institutions for workers. The second proposition stemmed directly from De Leon's premise that the domination of the capitalist system affects the workers' minds as well as their bodies. Popular education would be a way to provide tools allowing the working class to think independently. For the BSLP, popular education was thus emancipatory education.

In 1908, members of the BSLP established a national organization for the promotion of popular education. Drawing once again on *Two Pages*, they named it the Plebs League. The educational philosophy of the Plebs League was decidedly political and aimed to initiate workers to the ideology and culture of revolutionary socialism. The Central Labour College was subsequently founded, and more than six hundred activists were mobilized to organize and dispense popular education courses to British workers.[153] At its height, the college, which stayed open until 1964, welcomed over thirty thousand students. Furthermore, to shore up the idea of an education oriented toward the emancipation of the working class, the Plebs League founded a journal, *The Plebs*, which was published until 1969. *The Plebs* fostered debate and exchange on major theoretical and philosophical issues of the labor movement. Indeed, the journal maintained that the development of a truly proletarian philosophy was indispensable for the advent of a society free from the constraints of liberal political economy.[154] The legacy of De Leon's thought, at least in Great Britain, was to be found in such organizations, whose activities bespoke respect for the members of the working class. In struggling for the emancipation of the plebeians, the Plebs League, the Central Labour College, and *The Plebs* also represented particularly effective means of countering the ascendancy—disastrous in De Leon's view—of the labor union leaders.

Daniel De Leon contributes to plebeian thought through the construction of a political analogy that points up a blind spot in plebeian political practice: the question of the leader. As seen in the first chapter, the political history of the plebs is marked by the difficulties arising from the paradoxical presence of a political leader. Michele di Lando, one of the leaders of the 1378 Ciompi revolt in Florence, is emblematic of the conflict of interests that a leader of the plebs can engender. De Leon's work hence argues for a posture of mistrust toward leaders and, above all, for the idea that the labor movement must rely on its own initiative in order to ensure the advent of socialism. By championing self-emancipation and by urging activists to forge, together with workers, the intellectual tools needed for self-emancipation, De Leon makes a significant contribution to plebeian thought. For him, *the history of the Roman plebs demonstrates the necessity of the self-emancipation of the many, who, being endowed with political capacity, must not let themselves be blinded by those claiming to be their leaders.*

FOUCAULT: THE PLEBS BASENESS OR RESISTANCE?

For Daniel De Leon, the figure of the plebs in its Roman incarnation made it possible to grasp the stakes and challenges of American revolutionary labor unionism at the beginning of the twentieth century. Essentially, the question of the plebs was for him of topical interest. Today, in current political debates, there are two thinkers whose works also make the question of the plebs one of contemporary interest: Michel Foucault and Jacques Rancière. We will consider Foucault's work first and then go on to examine Rancière's treatment of the question of the plebs.

Our purpose here will be to understand the role of the plebs in the general economy of Foucault's thought. Rather than reviewing his entire corpus, however, we will analyze three texts where the signifier "plebs" is used: "Nietzsche, Genealogy, History," "Table ronde" (Round table), and "Pouvoir et stratégies" (Power and strategies).[155] We will then consider a hypothesis that may shed light on Foucault's restricted and equivocal use of the term. For it does indeed seem that the Foucauldian use of the notion of the plebs oscillates between two antinomic meanings: the first refers to the plebs' "base curiosity," hence, a lack of greatness and elevation; the second views the plebs as a core of resistance against the apparatuses of domination constituted by the modern disciplinary archipelago.

In "Nietzsche, Genealogy, and History" (1971), Foucault endeavors to define the concept of "genealogy." To this end, he opposes the genealogical method that characterizes Nietzsche's approach to so-called traditional history, that is, the academic discipline born in nineteenth-century Europe. The first aim of genealogy is to "record the singularity of events outside of any monotonous finality; it must seek them in the most unpromising places, in what we tend to feel is without history."[156] This is accomplished through the patient and meticulous analysis of a great variety of material and requires erudition on the part of the researcher. Above all, genealogy impugns any idea of "origin."

The quest for origin is a search for the essence of human objects and events. But this essence proves to be illusory. At best, what can be found behind things is "the secret that they have no essence." At the origin is "disparity" and not an "original identity." For Nietzschean perspectivism, the central problem of the question of the origin or essence is that it is a presupposition rooted in metaphysics. As such, it remains closely tied to the idea of truth. For Nietzsche, there can be no origin, essence, or truth because there are only perspectives capable of making certain facets of human experience intelligible while obscuring others. Producing a genealogy therefore involves denying the idea of origin; instead "it will cultivate the details and accidents that accompany every beginning; it will be scrupulously attentive to their petty malice; it will await their emergence, once unmasked." While genealogy may be opposed to history, it nevertheless needs history to put an end to the notion of a fixed and singular history. Genealogy is interested as well in the body and its health, because the heterogeneity of events is imprinted on the body. To rediscover the emergence of the multiplicity of beginnings, the genealogist must question both history and the body. To produce the history of emergences and beginnings thus involves producing the history of systems of subjugation and domination, as there is at least one constant determining human experience: the domination of human beings by other human beings.[157]

According to Foucault, Nietzsche relates genealogy to the notion of "effective history." To understand this notion, it must be compared to traditional history. While traditional history identifies continuities, or even a basso continuo, through time, effective history establishes the discontinuities or ruptures in history. Rather than dissolving the singularity of events in continuity, historical sense restores the uniqueness of events. Thus, effective history is explicitly perspectivist. Genealogists do not efface themselves before human objects: effective history "gives equal weight to its own sight and to its objects."[158]

For Nietzsche, it is impossible to dissociate "historical sense" from "the historian's history." In other words, traditional history is closely related to the emergence of the figure of the historian. To understand the former, one must produce the genealogy of the latter. But the historian is clearly of "humble birth." His desire to know everything, to refuse to make choices by determining a hierarchy of human events and experiences betrays "a total lack of taste, . . . a satisfaction in meeting up with what is base." Nothing is lofty for the historian; everything is reduced to the most common denominator. In sum, "Nothing is allowed to stand above him."[159]

It is precisely at this juncture in the text that Foucault brings in the figure of the plebs. His answer to the questions, "What is the source of history?" and "To whom is it addressed?" is straightforward: "To the plebs." The discourse of the historian-plebeian is likened to that of the demagogue who affirms the equality of plebeians and patricians as well as the fundamental "evil" of those who deny this equality. In the case of the historian-plebeian, the present is placed on an equal footing with the past inasmuch as even the great moments in history are not without pettiness and baseness. Under cover of the universal, this demagogy conceals the particular grudge of the historian-plebeian. "The historian's ancestry," Foucault writes, "goes back to Socrates."[160] And, as we know, for Foucault just as for Nietzsche, the decline of the greatness of Greece and the start of the era of Western metaphysics—disastrous for the affirmation of life—began with Socrates.

The historian-plebeian emerges at a specific point in human history: nineteenth-century Europe. For both Nietzsche and Foucault, this is a century of "barbarians," and Europe is the "the land of interminglings and bastardy, the period of the 'man-of-mixture.' "[161] The decadence of Europe is such that only ruins remain, examples of the past to live by. Because of this deplorable state of affairs, Europe is prey to nihilism, to the negation of life, and to the impossibility of distinguishing among events and, hence, of making choices. Foucault writes:

> We can begin to understand the spontaneous historical bent of the nineteenth century: the anemia of its forces and those mixtures that effaced all its individual traits produced the same results as the mortifications of asceticism; its inability to create, its absence of artistic works, and its need to rely on past achievements forced it to adopt the *base curiosity of plebs*.[162]

Thus, the concomitant emergence of the discipline of history and the historian occurs at a time of cultural weakening, even exhaustion, in Europe. In the absence of great works able to stimulate creation and life, people fell back on the past, giving free rein to their "base curiosity." In the final analysis, the nineteenth century as seen by Nietzsche and Foucault was a *plebeian* century.

At first glance, Foucault's use of the notion of the "plebs" in "Nietzsche, Genealogy, History" appears highly pejorative. The plebs is what appears when civilization starts to decline. The "base" gaze of the historians is plebeian. And the historian himself is a plebeian addressing other plebeians. There is neither grandeur nor elevation but only demagogy and baseness in the work of the historian-plebeians, which must be replaced by the work of genealogists, because they alone are capable of uncovering the hazy beginnings and the "the hazardous play of dominations."[163] What Foucault opposes to the history produced by the base curiosity of the plebeian is the gaze of genealogy, which is able to make choices (and thereby show "taste"), locate the discontinuities in history, and adopt a perspective that can invigorate the existence of human beings.

Foucault's assertions about the plebeian's "base curiosity" must, however, be set against his statements at a "round table" discussion organized by the journal *Esprit* in 1972. During the part of the discussion devoted to "laboring classes and dangerous classes," Foucault again refers to the figure of the plebs. In response to the question put by the editor-in-chief of *Esprit*, J.-M.

Domenach—*"How can those currently regarded as maladjusted be situated in social theory? Problems or subjects? A reserve army of capitalism or revolutionary reserves?"*—Foucault begins by challenging the distinction between the proletariat and marginalized individuals. Rather, he affirms the existence of a "global plebeian mass" within which there is a split between the "the proletariat" and "the non-proletarianized plebs."[164] This division among the plebeian masses is necessary for the smooth operation of the capitalist system. That is why modern disciplinary institutions constantly maintain the gap between the proletariat and the nonproletarianized plebs.

The fear harbored by the bourgeoisie "since 1789, since 1848, since 1870" is the fear of revolts or riots. The bourgeois order seeks to divide the "global mass" in order to avert all seditious or revolutionary eventualities. The split between the proletariat and the plebs prevents the "dangerous ferment of riots" resulting from their alliance. To achieve this division, the institutions of capitalist society instill in the plebs values and norms stemming from a "system of power controlled by the bourgeoisie." The plebeians are thereby transformed into proletarians. Through the inculcation of values, the bourgeoisie tries to make the laboring classes understand the impossibility of "direct and violent action." This is how the plebs are neutralized and deprived of their conflictual specificity in relation to the ruling bourgeoisie. Once the split has been realized, the differentiation between the plebs and the proletariat is constantly sharpened. According to Foucault, the proletariat does not share the "ideology of the plebs," and the plebs do not have "the social practices of the proletariat."[165] Therefore, the primary political problem is to show the proletariat the ideological character of the values imposed by the bourgeoisie. Were the proletariat to comprehend the power relationship underpinning such values, it could break with the capitalist order and create a lasting alliance with the nonproletarianized plebs. For Foucault, the plebeians here are what "remains" of the revolutionary forces after the establishment of the modern disciplinary archipelago.

The last of Foucault's texts that are of interest here seems to pursue the conceptualization of the plebs begun in *Esprit*. In "Pouvoirs et stratégies" (1977), he returns to a consideration of the signifier "plebs" in a discussion on the possible relationship between the Soviet gulag and the kinds of internment (psychiatric, penal, or medical) typical of democratic societies. Rejecting reductive correspondences, Foucault doubts that Western-style internment can be equated to the gulag model. He also disputes the idea that "we all have our gulags"[166] and does not believe that the manifold apparatuses [*dispositifs*] of domination can be subsumed under a single category. Instead, Foucault distinguishes between two different problems: the institution of the gulag and the question of the gulag. Leaving aside the first, Foucault endeavors to address the second on various levels of analysis. To raise the question of the gulag means making a political choice that implies a twofold refusal: on one hand, the refusal to restrict the analysis of the phenomenon to the texts of Marx and Lenin, and, on the other hand, the refusal to search exclusively for the causes of the gulag. For Foucault, the issue must be defined in more positive terms. What, for example, makes it possible for the prisoners to resist in the world of the gulags? "What gives them their energy? What is at work in their resistance? What makes them rise up?" The gulag thus remains a phenomenon specific to a particular political regime—the Soviet Union. But there are, Foucault writes, two more problems that must be examined: (1) how to understand the connection between the struggle against the classical apparatuses of internment and the struggle against the gulag, and (2) how to understand the "plebs, that constantly silent target of the apparatuses of power." Because it is impossible to provide a "categorical and individual"[167] answer to the first problem, Foucault strives to explore the question of the plebs in terms poles apart from those used in "Nietzsche, Genealogy, History" and closer to the views expressed at the round table discussion.

"What, then, is the plebeian?" Foucault asks. True to his usual analytical procedures, he begins by specifying what it is not. Not "the permanent base of history" or "the ultimate objective of all subjugations," neither is the plebeian "the never altogether extinguished source of all revolts." In fact, for Foucault the plebeian does not represent a sociological entity. They do not exist concretely as a political or social subject. Yet "there is indeed something, in the social body, in classes, in groups, in individuals themselves, that in a certain way evades power relationships; something that is not the more or less docile or rebellious raw material but is rather the centrifugal movement, the inverse energy, the breakaway." That something is the "plebeian," a sort of energy of resistance that exists in people and makes it possible to elude the apparatuses of power. That is why Foucault asserts that the plebeian as such does not exist. He specifies, however, "there is 'something of' the plebeian." He finds traces of this resistance everywhere in the human and social body: the members of the bourgeoisie and the proletariat have "something of" the plebeian, which can also be found in souls and individuals. Of course, the plebeian energy located in these various entities experiences varying degrees of intensity depending on the situation. Neither is the plebeian exterior to power. It is positioned, rather, at the limits of power relationships because it "responds to any advance of power with a movement so as to be free of it; hence, it is what motivates any new development of power networks."[168] Thus, Foucault affirms that the plebeian is at once what resists power and what allows power relationships to be extended.[169]

According to Foucault, the intensity of this "plebeian aspect" (*part de plèbe*) resistant to power may be reduced in three ways. First, the apparatuses of power can try to subjugate it directly by attacking its points of resistance. By targeting that which challenges the apparatuses of domination, those apparatuses succeed in circumventing the plebeian energy. Second, power can treat this energy as the plebs in the ordinary sense of the term, that is, as an element that is tumultuous, seditious, and threatening for public order. By reducing the "plebeian aspect" to a manifestation of insubordination, power is able to directly attack what resists. Finally, this "plebeian aspect" can do itself harm by setting itself "in accordance with a strategy of resistance."[170] It seems that plebeian energy becomes a menace for itself when it congeals in a specifically defined maneuver.

Having conceptualized the plebs in this way, Foucault can assert the "indispensability" of "the plebs' perspective, which is that of the reverse side and the limit in relation to power . . . for an analysis of its apparatuses." Based on this perspective, the ways in which power operates can be understood. Nevertheless, this approach can in no way "be confused . . . with a neo-populism that would substantify the plebeian or a neo-liberalism that would celebrate its primitive rights."[171] In other words, the plebeian outlook provides unique access to the phenomena of power because it is that which resists (and generates) power relationships. To produce the genealogy of power, it is necessary to adopt the plebeian perspective.

The baseness and demagogy that in Foucault's 1971 text were presented as typical of the plebs are not to be found in "Pouvoirs et stratégies." Rather than dealing with the plebs in a condescending and disdainful way, Foucault seems here to find a certain nobility in the plebs. They are the site of resistance to power, and their point of view is worth adopting for an understanding of power relationships. Foucault thus pursues the reflections on the plebs undertaken in *Esprit* in 1972. Hence the problem of the role of the plebs in Foucault's thought comes into focus. How can his contradictory use of the figure of the plebs be accounted for?

An initial answer can be found in the conclusion of "Pouvoirs et stratégies." Foucault explains in a note the indeterminate nature of his statements: "What I say here is not 'what I think' but, often, that about which I ask myself whether this could be thought."[172] Beyond this caveat expressing the experimental quality of his propositions, there seems to be a modulation in his thinking on the plebs. Effectively, the signifier "plebs" moves from a negative status to the more favorable one of a core of resistance to domination or even a center of freedom.

To understand the modulation in Foucault's thinking on the plebs, it is first necessary to summarize his conception of power and how this conception is related to freedom. This is because Foucault's work, at least its last phase, is largely concerned with the question of power and with its analysis in the Western world.[173] For Foucault, studying power amounts to understanding power relationships.[174] The formation of power relationships involves three operations: (1) the constitution of a domain of knowledge, (2) the establishment of rules that determine what does or does not participate in this domain of knowledge, and, based on this domain and set of rules, (3) the establishment of a field of activity within which human beings position themselves as a specific type of subject (student, wife, patient, etc.).[175] In Foucault's work, power, through this threefold movement, is a normalizing enterprise that subjugates people by limiting the scope of their action. Caught in the web of power relationships, human beings are "governed," in the broad sense of that term, that is, the "the way in which the conduct of individuals or of groups might be directed."[176]

A recurring critique of Foucault's political thought is that his conception of power as subjugation does not open onto an exteriority. This is what the philosopher Charles Taylor contends when he states that the Foucauldian notion of power excludes of the idea of human liberty.[177] Since humans cannot escape from power relationships, they are deprived of the experience of liberty. "A society without power relations can only be an abstraction," Foucault writes.[178] As a result, his thinking seems to be caught in a sort of "catastrophism" whose ultimate effect is the formation of a hellish world in which domination holds absolute sway.[179] From a political standpoint, the problem with such catastrophism is that it suppresses the possibilities of liberating oneself from the techniques of subjugation deployed by modern disciplinary society. It thus abolishes any future prospects other than the continuing domination of some human beings over others.

However, Foucault stresses that the operation of power relationships in the West requires the existence of freedom: "Power is exercised only over free subjects, and only insofar as they are 'free.' By this we mean individual or collective subjects who are faced with a field of possibilities in which several kinds of conduct, several ways of reacting and modes of behavior are available." The relationship between power and freedom should not be conceived as a "a face-to-face confrontation," Foucault claims, "of power and freedom as mutually exclusive facts." This "complicated interplay" implies "agonism" more than antagonism, because it involves a "mutual incitement" as well as "a permanent provocation."[180]

It is precisely on this level that the extent of the modulation in Foucault's thinking on the plebs can be understood. We have noted that in "Nietzsche, Genealogy, History" he clearly articulates a negative conception of "the plebs," which he regards as responsible for the baseness of the historian's gaze and emblematic of a "barbarian" (nineteenth) century, associated with loss, pettiness, and decline. Yet if one compares his conception of the "complicated interplay" between power and freedom as "mutual incitement" and "permanent provocation" to his statements about the plebs in "Pouvoirs et stratégies," there appears to be a certain correspondence between freedom and the plebs.[181] Like freedom, plebeian energy has a relationship with subjugation. And that relationship is "agonic," being at once a resistance *and* an extension of power relationships. In addition, the "plebeian aspect" is consubstantial with the existence of power relationships, just as freedom is. In sum, Foucault can be said to conceive of the plebs, or rather of the "plebeian aspect," as a source of liberty because it is what allows human beings to resist the apparatuses of power. Thus, the plebs—neither base nor petty—achieves recognition.

This moves us closer to the hypotheses of Alain Brossat, the author of an article on Foucault as a theorist of the plebs. His discussion clears illuminating pathways for an understanding of Foucault's relationship to the plebs, while qualifying the vision of the plebeian as bearer of liberty and center of resistance. It must first be noted that for Brossat Foucauldian thought does not propose a global solution to political problems. Instead, it can be viewed as a "toolbox" containing concepts that may renew political theory and practice. One of these "concept-tools" is the "plebs." Taking a "resolutely anti-sociological"[182] approach, Foucault proceeds to define the plebs as an element revealing the hardcore resistance of human beings to the networks of power. Brossat writes,

> Seen in this way, the plebeian bereft of all substance of its own, whether historical or social, appears as the "reverse side" or "the limit" in relation to power. It cannot, therefore, be assigned the position of historical subject whose continuous action would leave its imprint on the course of events. [183]

The plebeian has no materiality of its own and is not a "subject of history" whose "political history" could be delineated.

Brossat discerns a "circle of the plebeian" in Foucault's thought. This circle arises, first, out of the fact that the plebeian is engendered by the modern capitalist system and justifies the introduction of disciplinary apparatuses. To put it another way, the plebeian is spawned by the bourgeois order, and it legitimizes the development of the disciplinary archipelago. The circle of the plebeian subsequently closes because it is what allows the forces of order to "to reactivate continuously a split within the people or the proletariat, to divide the people against itself," so as to reduce the contentiousness of the many. That division makes it possible to defuse the potential threat of the plebeian by opposing "healthy" people on one hand to plebeian violence on the other. The bourgeois is haunted by the fear of "plebeian unpredictability"[184] and its continuing ability to burst into the public arena.

According to Brossat's reading of Foucault, what characterizes plebeian action is its "capacity to lacerate the present, to disfigure it." Among the examples that he offers of this mutilation is "Bin Laden who cuts into the (imperial) world order." The reason Brossat can call the scion of a wealthy Arab family "plebeian" is that for him this term applies to "'anybody' displaying a sustained capacity to rise up" like the "mullahs preaching insubordination in mosque after mosque during the Iranian revolution."[185] The plebeian, in other words, does not defend particular demands, whether democratic or libertarian. Plebeian demands could just as well be fascist or Islamist. This absence of a content specific to plebeian politics can be ascribed to its special relationship to action. For Brossat, the plebs are mute. They do not deliberate; they take action. That is why the plebeian has neither substance nor history in Foucault's thought.

Brossat's contribution, perhaps unbeknownst to him, allows us to understand better the portrait of the plebs in Michel Foucault's work. As a center of resistance against the apparatuses of domination, "the plebeian" covers a set of very diverse political experiences, which could be said to range from Masaniello to the mullahs! It is the name of those who resist, regardless of their ideological or religious choices. The plebs, having no voice, spontaneously engage in action while excluding the recourse to public deliberation. With neither a specific content nor a history, the plebs can take part in any battle. Moreover, the plebs as a "circle" is produced by those who dominate, while at the same time serving to justify the established order. They also participate in their own weakening, as they allows those who dominate to impose a split among the many, between the plebs and the people. The modulation in Foucauldian thinking on the plebs consists in the rejection of the disdainful statements made in the 1971 text and in the articulation of a particular conception premised on the plebeian as something without either substance or history, fully participating in the modern apparatuses of domination.

Can Foucault be regarded as a thinker of the plebs? The ambiguity of his statements and his refusal to consider the plebs as a political subject bearing a people's politics and a desire for liberty prevent him from proposing analytical tools able to account for the plebeian principle. Although he did modulate his thinking, it falls short of what is needed to conceptualize the plebs adequately. For example, it seems difficult to reconcile Foucault's two contradictory discourses on the plebs. In keeping with his antisociological approach, Foucault asserts that the plebeian is not a "historical subject," that is, an actor who bursts onto the stage of human history and "whose continuous action would leave its imprint on the course of events."[186] Yet, at the round table discussion, Foucault stated that the bourgeoisie wishes to divide the plebeian masses because it fears sedition and revolt, and that fear goes back to 1789, 1848, and 1870.[187] These dates refer to historical and revolutionary experiences in which the plebs acted to make the French political sphere more egalitarian and free. Hence, how is one to understand that the plebeian is not a political subject yet arouses a fear that is unequivocally part of the revolutionary history of France? Furthermore, emptying the plebs of all substance is problematical. For Foucault, "the plebeian no doubt does not exist, but there is 'something of' the plebeian. There is something of the plebeian in bodies and in souls, there is something of it in individuals, in the proletariat, there is something of it in the bourgeoisie, but with an extension, of diverse forms, energies, irreducibilities."[188] This indeterminacy of the sites where the "something of the plebeian" manifests itself leaves open the possibility of discerning it where it is not to be found. Brossat's article provides more than one example of the dubious associations authorized by Foucault's refusal to attribute a specific content to the plebs. The assertion that Bin Laden or the mullahs of the Iranian Revolution are plebeian figures is the product of a gross misunderstanding or even a process of mystification with regard to the political history of the plebs. Indeed, how can one bracket the events of September 11, 2001, with those related to the Ciompi revolt and the Romans carnival? Granted, the examples of Bin Laden and the mullahs are provided not by Foucault but by Brossat. The fact remains, however, that Brossat's discussion aptly illustrates the limits of Michel Foucault's thinking on the plebs. In short, there does indeed seem to be a modulation in Foucault's thought, but it remains insufficient to conceptualize adequately the plebs' manifold experiences that we are striving to make intelligible. Because of his inability to consider politics and especially power in terms other than those of domination, his contribution to "plebeian thought" may be suggestive at times but is ultimately disappointing. In the final analysis, it is mainly the "Foucauldian gesture," which consists in reactivating the question of the plebs within contemporary debates, that makes his work truly relevant for "plebeian thought."

RANCIÈRE: THE PLEBEIAN DISAGREEMENT

Michel Foucault takes up the question of the plebs once again in 1977, in *Les révoltes logiques*, a journal whose leading lights were Jacques Rancière and Jean Borreil. Although Rancière acknowledges the influence that Foucault's work[189] has had on him, it does not inform his discussion of the plebs. The question of the plebs arose for Rancière as a result of his work in the *Révoltes logiques* collective and the many years that he devoted to studying the "archives of the workers' dream."[190] Rancière's interest in the plebeian question was aroused as well when he discovered the writings of Pierre-Simon Ballanche thanks to the works of the philosopher-carpenter Gabriel Gauny, that "Socrates of the plebs."[191]

The *Révoltes logiques* collective seems to have played a key role in Rancière's discovery of the plebeian question. According to its statement of purpose, the team of researchers behind the journal *Les révoltes logiques: Cahiers du centre de recherche des idéologies de la révolte*, published from 1975 to 1981 (fifteen issues), proposes to "reconstruct grassroots thought" by thoroughly investigating "the gap between the official history of subversion . . . and the actual forms of its elaboration."[192] In other words, in opposition to an "official history," no doubt subservient to the incorrigible Stalinism of the French Communist Party, the journal puts forward the reality of the myriad intellectual and political struggles of the social movement as a whole. The various issues of the journal include articles on women, workers, children, craftspeople, trade unionists, as well as theorists. The collective also wanted to make sure that the "radical critique of Marxism" and the "elimination of a certain conception of the revolution do not dispense [us] from understanding the issues, the complexities and contradictions of two centuries of militant history."[193]

In addition, *Les révoltes logiques* sought to break with "proletarian metaphysics."[194] Rather than conceiving of the proletariat as a "chosen" class bearing the obligation to emancipate humanity and holding the key to the truth of the human race, the journal takes an interest in the multiple figures of domination (without of course neglecting the working-class dimension). The members of the collective thus refuse to reduce domination to its economic and proletarian component, so as to be open to its manifold dimensions. To analyze the proletarian figure alone excessively constrains the scope of the struggles against the modern mechanisms of subjugation: "There is no voice of the people. There are fragmented, polemical voices, which on every occasion split the identity that they present."[195]

Rancière's prolonged examination of the archives of the "workers' dream" engendered three books:[196] *The Nights of Labor* (a revised version of his doctoral thesis), as well as two volumes anthologizing texts written by French workers in the nineteenth century: *La parole ouvrière*[197] and *Gabriel Gauny—le philosophe plébéien*. These works testify to the twofold concern articulated in the statement of purpose of the *Révoltes logiques*: (1) to move away from the "official history" of subversion and (2) to be rid of "proletarian metaphysics." In *The Nights of Labor*, Rancière attempts to "rediscover the original identity of the thought specific to the working class that Marxist discourse appears to have occulted," so as to effect "a return to a working-class voice that Marxism rejects because of its spontaneous and utopian archaism."[198] This for Rancière is an essential enterprise.[199] One needs to analyze the workers' act of speaking out[200] in order to grasp the nature of the struggles undertaken by those subjected to the domination of the few. Beyond the "sorrowful groan or wild howl of misery . . . workers do not speak mainly to moan or threaten, they speak to be understood."[201] The act of speaking up with the aim of being intelligible is crucial for an understanding of the role of the plebs in Rancière's thought.

Rancière's first encounter with the plebeian question seems to occur in his critique of *La cuisinière et le mangeur d'hommes* by André Glucksmann, in the first issue of *Révoltes logiques*.[202] For Rancière, the conceptualization of the plebs proposed by Glucksmann serves to evacuate, through the problem of the Soviet gulag, the idea of a "revolutionary people." Because, according to Glucksmann, the plebeian is a figure of resistance against the apparatuses of total domination introduced by Soviet power. The plebs "instantly reconstructed the old alliance between the immediate positivity of the popular body . . . and the pure negativity of the resistance to power." All that this reconstruction engendered by the plebs does is to benefit its "spokespeople," the dissidents. The plebeian as seen by Glucksmann is a figure deprived of political capacity and through which politics is reduced to ethics. It tends to support only "the authority of its intellectual spokespeople."[203] Rancière is extremely critical of this peculiar way of understanding the plebs.

It would take the publication in 1983 of the writings of Gabriel Gauny for Rancière to arrive at a reformulation of the plebeian question. Even though he had used the term "plebs" before that time, this was the moment when he encountered the ideas of P.-S. Ballanche, who had conceptualized the "plebeian principle" and profoundly influenced the writings of the philosopher-carpenter Gauny. Rancière's discovery of Gauny's work seems to constitute a pivotal event in his intellectual development. Gauny, whose writings were unknown during his lifetime, epitomizes the exceptional figure of the worker-philosopher and the "workers' act of speaking out" that breaks with the Platonic proscription against craftsmen doing "anything but their work." Gauny's life, however, was in no way exceptional. As was generally the case for workers at the time, he lived in conditions of great hardship and deprivation. But unlike most of his peers, Gauny "encountered philosophy, the one that a child of the people could encounter around 1830: the philosophy of the excluded, the rational mysticism [*mystique rationnelle*] or magical rationalism [*rationalisme ensorcelé*] that is like the popular double of Enlightenment philosophy." For Gauny, the decisive philosophical meeting was with the works of Ballanche. Gauny's "fundamental belief"[204] is in the struggle of the plebeian, progressive principle against the patrician, stationary principle, as theorized by Ballanche. This clearly points to the importance of Ballanche not only for Gauny, the plebeian Socrates, but also for Rancière, who proposes an interpretation of Gauny. Rancière articulates how the plebeian question remains relevant for an understanding of the numerous modern struggles for emancipation. Thus, the discovery of Ballanche by way of Gauny's writings made it possible for Rancière to formulate explicitly his relationship to the plebs.

The chapter titled "Wrong: Politics and Police" of his book *Disagreement: Politics and Philosophy* sets out Rancière's reading of Ballanche's interpretation of the first plebeian secession in Rome in 494 BCE. According to Rancière, Ballanche reproaches Livy for being incapable of viewing the secession "as anything other than a revolt, an uprising caused by poverty and anger and sparking a power play devoid of all meaning." The Latin historian's problem is that he is unable to grasp the true sense of the tale of the belly and the parts told by Menenius Agrippa. To recapitulate, the secession takes shape as a result of popular discontent at the imprisonment of some plebeians for indebtedness. The plebs, angered by what they consider unjust treatment at the hands of the patricians, leave Rome and establish a camp on the Aventine Hill, effectively paralyzing the Eternal City. To pacify the plebs and restore order, Menenius Agrippa, a parliamentary ambassador of plebeian origins, explains to them the need for collaboration between the parts (the plebs) and the belly (the patriciate) in order for the organism (the Roman Republic) to live. Rancière asserts that the originality and interest of Ballanche consists in his "restaging of the conflict in which the entire issue at stake involves finding out whether there exists a common stage where plebeians and patricians can debate anything."[205] Whereas Livy fails to grasp the deeper meaning of Agrippa's gesture, Ballanche regards it as heavily charged with symbolism.

For the Roman patriciate, there is no space for speaking in common with the plebs, since they have no voice. This lack of speech is because within the Roman Republic the plebeians are deprived of a surname and, hence, of filiation. Consequently, they are "deprived . . . of symbolic enrollment in the city." Having no name and unable to state their filiation, the plebs are relegated to a subhuman status, that of a being unable to utter anything but noise, the instinctive voicing of pleasure and pain (*phone*). Reduced to the order of the living, the plebs, from the patrician standpoint, can neither speak nor transmit anything except life, in the strictly biological sense of that word. But Agrippa commits an error that is fatal for the patriciate. By recounting the fable of the belly and the parts, he assumes that the plebs are capable of understanding and speaking, thereby opening a gap in the domination of the few over the many. Agrippa thus contravenes the order of patrician domination, which "recognizes no logos capable of being articulated by beings deprived of logos, no *speech* capable of being proffered by nameless beings."[206]

Gathered on the Aventine Hill, the plebs constitutes a different order, a plebeian order. Rather than accepting subhuman status, the plebeians behave as though they have surnames, thereby appropriating their symbolic enrollment in the city. Pursuing his reading of Ballanche, Rancière writes, "They thereby execute a series of speech acts that mimic those of the patricians: they pronounce imprecations and apotheoses; they delegate one of their number to go and consult *their* oracles; they give themselves representatives by rebaptizing them."[207] By transgressing the patrician order in this way, the plebs grant themselves a right to speak that goes beyond mere grunting. In this way, the plebeians, after hearing Menenius Agrippa's tale, were able to demand that a treaty be negotiated, an eventuality beyond the ken of the patriciate. Agrippa was thus the one responsible for having created a space for egalitarian exchange, because he believed the plebs capable of understanding the meaning of his story and of transcending the imperatives of the biological order.

In his investigation of intellectual emancipation, *The Ignorant Schoolmaster*, Rancière affirms that the essence of the first plebeian secession resides in the staging of equality among speaking and intellectually competent beings. The victory of the plebs does not consist in the establishment of the plebeian tribunes but rather in the recognition of the plebeians' access to human intelligence, as attested to by Agrippa's telling of the fable of the belly and the parts. Moreover, in opposition to those who believe that Roman history is outmoded, Rancière proffers Ballanche's "strange prophecy,"[208] which is that "Roman history, as it has appeared to us up till now, after having in part ordered our destiny, after having entered, in one form, into the composition of our social life, our customs, our opinions, our laws, comes now, in a different form, to order our new thoughts, those that must enter into the composition of our future social life."[209]

Clearly, therefore, the plebs form an important, perhaps central, component of Rancière's political thought. Indeed, Ballanche's narrative of the first plebeian secession illustrates what for Rancière is a constitutive element of political communities: "Politics is primarily conflict over the existence of a common stage and over the existence and status of those present on it."[210] To understand better the significance of the "inaugural scene"[211] that the plebeian secession represents, one must first look at the broad outlines of Rancière's conceptualization of the political.

For Rancière, the political is the meeting of two opposite processes. The first aims to bring together citizens so that the community can take shape through "the distribution of shares and the hierarchy of places and functions"[212] in accordance with the titles to be governed. Rancière calls "police" the process that is akin to government and implies a conception of the political as a site of domination. Based in part on the Foucauldian interpretation of power, "policing"[213] is what ensures the marginalization of the plebs and others without title in the community. The second process constitutive of the political but opposite to the first is related to the question of equality. More specifically, it rests on the idea that human beings are equal and that it is important to verify this equality through practices that challenge the "police" distribution of places and functions. This process is called "emancipation" and constitutes the distinctive feature of *politics*.[214] The meeting between these two antagonistic processes, that is, between police and emancipation, reveals the "wrong" that the order of the community (police) inflicts on equality (emancipation). Rancière's uses "wrong" to designate the fundamental—hence constitutive—conflict of politics, which bears on "the relationship between the speaking being . . . and political capacity."[215] Every political community is affected by a wrong because politics involves a distribution of places and functions that necessarily entails a "miscount" (*mécompte*) of certain social elements, which find themselves excluded from the exercise of collective power. There is a "distribution of the sensible"[216] making it impossible to allocate functions in a perfectly equitable way because a distribution always results in a rejection of part of the community and, hence, a wrong. But the encounter between police and emancipation engenders a political stage where the verification of the equality between everyone and everyone can be realized. This is one of the great lessons of the plebeian secession on the Aventine Hill: the plebs were excluded from civic life, yet their withdrawal from Rome forced the patrician order of "police" to deal with it. The effect of these negotiations was to create a political stage founded on equality. The political exists, therefore, at the junction between police and emancipation and is configured through "the handling of a wrong."[217]

But Rancière stops well short of stating that politics as the verification of equality can be considered a kind of enactment of a principle, an *arche*, of even the principle of equality. Quite the contrary, the political remains *an-archic*, in the sense that "the singularity of the act of the *demos* . . . is dependent on an originary disorder or miscount." Simply by virtue of its existence, the *demos*, that is, the historical vehicle of emancipatory practices, reminds the order of the police that it was originally forgotten. Here, the term "demos" is synonymous with "plebs" because it designates the social component excluded by the policing order. Rancière acknowledges that the enactment of emancipation occurs on behalf of a category disowned by the police, but he writes, "the enactment of equality is not, for all that, the enactment of the self, of the attributes or properties of the community in question. The name of an injured community that invokes its rights is always the name of the anonym, the name of anyone."[218]

Consequently, citizenship or civic belonging is defined through a rejection of the established order and the challenging of the police-based distribution of functions and places. Rancière proposes a vision that locates conflict at the heart of political life, since "dissensus" must prevail over consensus. Citizenship "lives on the difference and conflict"[219] initiated by emancipatory practices that contest the hierarchical order of the community. Thus, the plebs entrenched on the Aventine Hill established a space that was antagonistic and conflictual vis-à-vis the patrician distribution (or, more exactly, *confiscation*) of public offices. And that contestation remained an-archic. Here, one can discern the kinship of Rancière's ideas with the notion of "savage" or "untamed democracy" found in the work of Claude Lefort.[220]

The substance of these emancipatory practices nevertheless remains implicit. What does the plebs do when it challenges the patrician order of the community? For Rancière, when the verification of the equality of everyone with everyone is carried out, a "process of subjectivization" is initiated whose objective is "the formation of a one that is not a self but is a relation of a self to an other."[221] More exactly, "any subjectification is a disidentification, removal from the naturalness of a place, the opening up of a subject space where anyone can be counted since it is the space where those of no account are counted, where a connection is made between having a part and having no part."[222] By way of example, Rancière refers to the trial of the revolutionary Auguste Blanqui in 1832. Blanqui's answer to the state prosecutor's question regarding his trade was "proletarian." In response to the prosecutor's objection that this cannot be considered a profession, Blanqui declared, "It is the profession of the majority of our people who are deprived of political rights."[223] This *dis-*

agreement between the prosecutor and the revolutionary illustrates how the encounter between the police order and the victims of the miscount gives rise to a political subject existing with others to the degree that it is *"in-between,"* that is, "between several names, statuses, and identities; between humanity and inhumanity, citizenship and denial; between the status of a man of tools and the status of a thinking and speaking being."[224] The status of "proletarian" precisely denotes this "in-between" stemming from the initial wrong. The process of subjectivization thus involves an impossible identification, that is, an identification that cannot be fully assumed. Because the victims of the wrong exist exactly in an "in-between" of identity, which implies that they are neither altogether proletarians nor altogether *zoon politikon*, as in the case of Blanqui.

Political subjectivization proves to be a "a heterology, a logic of the other,"[225] and according to Rancière there are three reasons for this. First, the process of emancipation is an affirmation of identity that rejects an identity imposed by another, specifically the police order. Inasmuch as it aims to attribute names, places, and functions to human beings so as to assign to each individual a place in the community, it can be said that the distinctive feature of the logic of subjectivization is to propose *inappropriate* names, places, and functions deriving from a miscount in the established order. Second, since this verification of equality comes in the form of the manifestation or the demonstration of a wrong, it implies the presence of another, even if that other is hostile to the logic that is proper to (or rather *improper for*) emancipation. The confrontation between two antagonistic processes makes it possible to establish a common political space in which the wrong can be received and equality can be verified. Finally, as we have seen, political subjectivization invariably implies an impossible identification, because the victim of a wrong remains caught in an "in-between" of identity. But the "in-between" is heterological, as it stems from the fact that the victim does not stand alone in the face of the police order but with others who share the condition of victim. Ultimately, Rancière writes, "The place of a political subject is an interval or a gap: being *together* to the extent that we are *in-between*—between names, identities, cultures, and so on."[226] Here is how Rancière summarizes his conception of the political, centered on the notion of the "wrong," a key concept that

is simply the mode of subjectification in which the assertion of equality takes its political shape. Politics occurs by reason of a single universal that takes the specific shape of wrong. Wrong institutes a singular universal, a polemical universal, by tying the presentation of equality, as the part of those who have no part, to the conflict between parts of society.[227]

It becomes possible at this point to gauge the effect of Ballanche's interpretation of the plebeian secession in Rome on Rancière's thought. The Roman plebs performed the verification of its equality with the patricians, allowing a wrong to be handled. This "mode of subjectivization" took shape thanks to the creation of a space of mutual intelligibility between plebeians and patricians. The handling was carried out in the name of equality, because the plebeians acquired a filiation, consulted oracles, named representatives, and so forth. In sum, they performed "speech acts" that revealed their shared participation in the political capacity of human beings. Hence, the object of the clash arising from this new space of contention was the rejection of the hierarchical distribution of places and functions by the police order.

All this attests to the importance of the plebs for Rancière's thought. The term "plebeian" is emblematic of the antagonistic processes peculiar to the political and "designates a symbolic relationship"[228] that is essential for an understanding of the workings of politics in both its ancient and modern incarnations. Owing to the "inaugural" nature of the first plebeian secession for Rancière, his contribution to "plebeian thought" can be summed up as follows: *The plebs illustrates the founding conflict of the political, which bears on the existence of a common political stage and rejects the order of domination erected through the police-based distribution of titles and functions. By revealing the wrong of that distribution, the plebs institutes a common stage where the verification of the equality of all can take place. This subjectivization allows the plebs to extricate themselves from the "naturalness" of their place, that is, to perform the passage from the status of* animal laborans *to that of* zoon politikon. *Henceforward, the plebs are full-fledged political subjects endowed with equality and opposed to the domination of the few.*

ANSWER TO THE QUESTION, "WHAT IS 'THE PLEBS'?"

In the first chapter, our intention was to present and analyze some key experiences in the historical establishment of the plebeian principle. With respect to the first plebeian secession, we observed how the plebs displayed political capacities through the creation of a distinct political order on the Aventine Hill. The Ciompi revolt brings to light a blind spot in the plebeian experience: the question of the leader as personified by Michele di Lando, whose political action tarnished the democratic character of the experience. As for the Romans carnival, it can be viewed as a "staging" and an "exposition" of the "originary division of the social" (C. Lefort). Last, the Neapolitan revolt of Masaniello highlights the importance of the "intractable" (J.-F. Lyotard), since the fall of Masaniello coincides exactly with his treatment at the hands of the patrician order. Overall, one can observe that a politics of the people and a desire for political liberty is at work throughout these plebeian experiences.

We subsequently endeavored to understand the philosophical genesis of the plebeian principle, a veritable hidden tradition and a summation of "plebeian thought." Machiavelli has left us with a body of thought where the plebs are regarded as a political subject that animates the body politic with a desire for liberty by ensuring the presence of conflict through its "implacable" opposition to the grandees. Following a line of thought close to that of the Florentine Secretary but formulated in his own terms, Montesquieu, in his *Considérations*, extols the virtues of division, stating that the plebs are defined by their rejection of tranquility in favor of the disturbances required by the dissonance of liberty. Thus, according to Montesquieu, the plebs ensure the conflictual unity of free political communities. Vico, agreeing with Machiavelli and Montesquieu that the plebs are the vehicle of conflict and freedom, nevertheless argues that they prove incapable of assuming that very freedom over the long term. For Pierre-Simon Ballanche, the plebs, due to their struggle against the stationary, patrician forces, are endowed with humanity, being a political subject that makes humankind's achievement of progress and emancipation possible. In another vein, Daniel De Leon believes that the history of the Roman plebs should remind the many, invested with political capacity, of the need for self-emancipation. On the other hand, what makes the work of Michel Foucault interesting is his revival of the plebeian question within contemporary debates, rather than his equivocal theorization of it. Finally, in Jacques Rancière's work "plebeian thought" achieves a certain theoretical culmination, since it proves to be central to his thinking. Based on his exploration of Ballanche's findings with respect to the first plebeian secession, Rancière argues that the secession illustrates the founding conflict of the political, which bears on the existence of a common political stage. By exposing the wrong attributable to the "police-based" distribution of titles and functions, the plebs institute a common space where equality can be verified. They thereby set up a process of subjectivization that extricates them from the "naturalness" of their place and enables the passage from the status of *animal laborans* to that of *zoon politikon*.

Before concluding, it may be useful to come back to an issue touched upon in the first chapter and underscored by De Leon in *Two Pages from Roman History*: the plebeian leader. As political actors, the plebs wish to put an end to the structure of political domination arising from the split between dominators

and dominated. When they designate a leader, the plebs run the risk of neutralizing their desire for freedom and of seeing it transform into a desire for
servitude.

For the plebs, the issue of the leader is thus related to the "desire for servitude" that threatens the desire for freedom. The designation of the leader of the
plebs should hence be understood as a shift in the plebeian experience from
the attempt to achieve self-emancipation to the enchantment "by the name
of one man alone."[229] The problem is this: this enchantment aims to avert the
ordeal of the plebs' "difficult freedom." By transferring the responsibility for
emancipation to a leader, the plebs unburden themselves of the demanding
task of liberating themselves from domination. Perhaps this is how best to understand the weariness of the plebs under popular republics, when, according
to Vico, they seek "rest" in the reign of the One, the monarch. But the leader of
the plebs tends to domesticate the plebs' political force: "The tribune manages,
channels, and institutionalizes the revolts of the plebs; he contains them within
tolerable limits so that the system may continue to operate."[230] The mere presence of a leader in the political experience of the plebs is opposed to the desire
for freedom and, especially, to the self-emancipatory imperative.

In *À bas les chefs!* Joseph Déjacque tries to resolve or go beyond this an-
tinomy specific to the plebeian experience. Déjacque distinguishes between
"governmental authority" on one hand and moral authority—to which he gives
the (peculiar) name of "intellectual or moral dictatorship"[231]—on the other.
Governmental authority excludes liberty; it is the authority of Bonaparte or
even of Blanqui. This is because revolutionaries whose aim is to establish a
revolutionary political dictatorship ultimately strive for the continuing domination of human beings over other human beings.

> The Dictatorship, no matter if it is a hundred-headed or hundred-tailed
> hydra, democratic or demagogic, can assuredly do nothing for liberty: it
> can only perpetuate slavery, both moral and physical. It is not by regiment-
> ing a people of slaves under an iron yoke—for there is indeed iron—or
> imprisoning it in proconsular wishes that one can produce intelligent and
> free individuals. All that is not freedom is against freedom. Freedom is not
> something that can be granted. [232]

Déjacque contends as well that revolutionary movements advocating the establishment of this kind of authority are guided by leaders who are concerned
more with their own position and prestige than with the question of emancipa-

tion. For Déjacque, those who pursue titles and functions must absolutely be mistrusted.[233] Only a "traitor" or a "trickster" would consider political dictatorship a way out of servitude. A position in support of governmental authority calls into question the very idea of revolution. Déjacque asserts:

> Any dictatorial government, whether that is understood as singular or plural, any demagogic power can only delay the advent of the social revolution by *substituting* its initiative, whatever that may be, its omnipotent reason, its civic, imposed will, for anarchic initiative, reasoned will, and the autonomy of each individual.[234]

Through an analysis of the question of authority posed by the events of 1848, Déjacque identifies another approach that would have made it possible to assure human freedom. Such authority belonged to neither Bonaparte nor Cavaignac, that is, to the French government, but instead to Proudhon. Indeed, Proudhon was able to incarnate the movement behind the events of 1848. And his authority stemmed solely from the magnitude of his genius and of his intellectual work. Endowed with genuine "natural" and "moral" authority, Proudhon "has no use for the praetorians. . . . His mission is neither to garrote nor to shorten men but to make them taller by a whole head, to develop them by the whole force of expansion of their mental nature."[235] Contrary to political authority, that of Proudhon does not aim to distribute titles and functions to his followers in order to maintain his domination. Rather, its goal is to free human beings from the bonds of slavery by making them autonomous and capable of acting on their own behalf.

By striving to "vitalize"[236] the minds of human beings, the "dictatorship" of intelligence naturally leads to a form of self-emancipation. The important thing is to bring about the affirmation of freedom. According to Déjacque, Proudhon strives to emancipate by relying on the "political capacity"[237] of the many. He does not wish to impose anything but simply to allow human beings to be aware of their own inner desire for freedom. What matters, therefore, is to

> place each and every individual before the possibility, that is, the necessity of acting, so that the movement, being communicated from person to person, may give and receive the impulse to progress and thus increase its strength a hundredfold. *What is needed, finally, is as many dictators as there are thinking beings, men and women, in society, so as to shake it, to make it rebel, to pull it out of its inertia.*[238]

Proudhon's authority arises through the free association of all. The objective of this association is to emancipate human beings by making them capable of controlling their own destinies. Such authority does not seek to construct a coercive power. Its ambition, rather, is to foster the concerted action of individuals freed from the constraints that ensure the domination of certain human beings over others. Once rid of servitude, humanity can enter "a new era," that of human liberty.

Déjacque's proposition could also be labeled the authority of education. What he calls for is essentially the introduction of "education for emancipation," that is, education aimed at increasing self-reliance and critical thinking. We can thus discern a connection with the ideas of Daniel De Leon, who also denounced the leaders of the plebs and pleaded for self-emancipation. De Leon's thought, actually, was the source of the popular education initiatives taken by the British Socialist Labour Party at the beginning of the twentieth century.[239] A possible solution to the problem of the plebeian leader, therefore, may be found in *education for emancipation*. Consequently, to understand better the situation of the plebs with regard to the issue of the leader, one must be attentive to the educational role played by the political structures of the plebs. It could then be determined whether or not the plebs have managed to avoid the traps resulting from the burdensome presence of a plebeian leader.

The fact remains, however, that Déjacque's invocation of Proudhon is also problematical, because what at first is presented as a "solution" to the difficulties caused by the plebeian leader could ultimately lead to a new experience involving the allure of the name of One. The question of the leader of the plebs therefore remains aporetic: the quest for a definitive solution rests on the illusion of a possible resolution of the enigmas of collective existence.

In the next section we will explore the turbulent world of plebeian political practices during the French Revolution, the making of the English working class, and the Paris Commune of 1871. More precisely, we will analyze those historical experiences through the lens of the "forms of political organization" of the plebs. The elucidation of those forms should allow us to assess the extent to which the plebs ensures the conjunction of communalist and agoraphile traditions. If a "plebeian principle" emerges from this condensed political history of the plebs, we will see that an analysis of the resurgence of the plebeian principle clears the way to a new political intelligibility of the historical events under examination.

PART II

THE QUESTION OF THE FORMS OF

POLITICAL ORGANIZATION

PROLOGUE
ON THE DOMINANT POLITICAL CONFIGURATION
OF MODERNITY

The people are missing.
—Gilles Deleuze, *The Time-Image*

TO UNDERSTAND THE "FORMS OF POLITICAL ORGANIZATION" OF the plebeian experience, the more general question of the "forms" of political organization of democratic modernity must be examined briefly. At the end of the eighteenth century and throughout the nineteenth century, while the political practices of the plebs were developing, a "political configuration" was established, one that would dominate modernity. This "dominant political configuration" involved three phenomena: (1) the introduction of representative government, (2) the creation of the system of political parties, and (3) the emergence of large bureaucracies. The latter, of course, were not consolidated but existed embryonically during the eighteenth and nineteenth centuries and had to compete with other political approaches.[1] Nevertheless, even a summary analysis of this hegemonic political configuration shows that it rested on a "patrician" conception of political affairs, a conception that dismissed any effective participation of citizens in political life. By setting up mechanisms that could channel popular political forces, patrician politics neutralized the political expression of the many. This type of politics can therefore be described as "agoraphobic,"[2] in that it feared the idea of political freedom being exercised by all.

At its inception, representative government was opposed to democracy. The adversaries of political representation, such as Rousseau, as well as its advocates, like Madison and Sieyès, emphasized the difference between the two forms of political organization. For Rousseau, sovereignty cannot be represented (just as it cannot be alienated). The representative system limits the freedom of individuals:

> The English people believes itself to be free; it is gravely mistaken; it is free only during the election of Members of Parliament; as soon as the Members are elected, the people is enslaved; it is nothing. In the brief moments of its freedom, the English people makes such a use of that freedom that it deserves to lose it.[3]

In the view of its advocates, representative government differs from and indeed is superior to democracy. Madison asserts that representation makes it possible

> to refine and enlarge the public views by passing them through the medium of a chosen body of citizens, whose wisdom may best discern the true interest of their country. . . . Under such a regulation it may well happen that the public voice, pronounced by the representatives of the people, will be more consonant to the public good than if pronounced by the people themselves, convened for the purpose.[4]

In the case of the abbot Sieyès, a theorist of the Third Estate, representation is superior because it is the form of political organization most appropriate to modern trading societies where individuals are busy producing and accumulating wealth.[5]

Raymond Carré de Malberg stresses that two doctrines of "representation" exist. The first, inspired by Rousseau, assumes that those elected are "commissaries," that is, "pure proxies, dependent on their constituency." Representation is necessary only because of the large territorial extent of modern political communities. Those elected are not entitled to make decisions on behalf of the people. Their role consists in conveying the wishes of the people to the popular political authorities. The second doctrine, inspired by Montesquieu, considers representation necessary because "the mass of citizens does not adequately possess the capacity and prudence needed . . . to discern the measures that the national interest may demand." The people must therefore choose from among the most enlightened individuals representatives apt to govern on its behalf. Once appointed, they represent the collective body, that is, the nation rather than a specific part of it. Thus, representation aims for the selection of individuals with superior qualities. Based on the writings of the founders of the representative regimes in America and elsewhere, it appears that the second doctrine prevailed over the first. Representative government can therefore be thought of as an "aristocratic"[6] political form, one distinct from democracy. Moreover, it is considered preferable to democracy, as it leaves the government of the community in the hands of a few supremely wise individuals while excluding the citizens from public affairs.

The designation of officeholders through elections concretizes the will to create an aristocratic political form. Elections have the merit of applying a "principle of distinction" between those elected and the citizens while at the same time legitimizing political decision making. The expression "principle of distinction" is used here because this method tends to result in the choice of individuals whose qualities are above average, contrary to an alternative way of choosing officeholders, the lottery system, which enshrines the "strict equality" of citizens. Although elections ensure the aristocratic (or patrician) character of the representative system, they nevertheless lend a democratic "veneer" to political action. By placing the people at the source of the appointment of officeholders, representative government acquires popular sanction. Yet theoreticians of this regime were fully aware of the aristocratic effects of elections. Their desire to have the representatives chosen from among those belonging to a higher social milieu was framed in explicit terms: "Another inegalitarian characteristic of representative government, however, was deliberately introduced after extensive discussion, namely that the representatives be socially superior to those who elect them. Elected representatives, it was firmly believed, should rank higher than most of their constituents in wealth, talent, and virtue."[7]

The emergence of political parties coincided with the gradual extension of suffrage and, consequently, with the arrival of the many on the political scene. Political parties addressed the need for "a methodical organization of the electoral masses by extra-constitutional means and in the form of disciplined and permanent parties."[8] These were conceived so as to channel and control the new political forces. With the advent of political parties, particularly those of the working class, the hope arose that the people could finally achieve political power. For it was supposed that parties would do away with the aristocratic consequences of representation.[9] But as Robert Michels demonstrates in his famous analysis of the "oligarchic tendencies" of political parties, they only heightened the exclusive character of representation.[10] The party soon became the site of social advancement for an "aristocracy" with specific faculties, such as militant enthusiasm and organizational skills. To understand the political significance of this novel form of organization, it is important to grasp its two fundamental features: permanence and totalization.

The establishment of parties implies the creation of permanent structures of political action. Moisey Ostrogorski stresses, for example, the preponderant role of the "caucus" in the ascendancy of political parties in Great Britain at the end of the nineteenth century.[11] The caucus, the basic unit of national political parties, ensured the party's presence and local supervision of militant activities. The many "election committees" that shaped the country's political landscape ably promoted the democratic spirit and induced the many to take part in public affairs, but these objectives were ephemeral. The caucus soon became the place where dubious negotiations went on among "professional" politicians and where militants were manipulated so as to consolidate the power of party leaders. Even when it took an interest in the citizens' political education, the caucus did so in a partisan spirit that put party unity ahead of fostering the ability to reflect freely on political issues. Rather than engendering a democratic dynamic and injecting the party with popular and creative energy, the caucus was responsible for "party life being reduced to calculated performances. All gestures were wholly lacking in flexibility and elasticity, every move was rigid, and procedures were cut and dried so as to exclude any spontaneity."[12] The political party was thus transformed into a kind of "electoral machine"[13] enabling militants who had become professional politicians to gain access to political power.

Parties are also "totalizing" organizations. For Ostrogorski, "totalizing" refers to the fact that parties provide answers to all the issues arising in the political sphere, from agricultural matters to social questions and foreign affairs. The "omnibus"[14] nature of parties signifies that membership in a party implies adherence to all the positions adopted by it. Consequently, the militants' latitude is tightly circumscribed. In addition, totalization has the effect of excluding from public discussion issues that do not fit into the political categories defined by the parties. Political debate is weakened, and the "real societal debates"[15] often take place outside the deliberative framework of the political parties. The imposition of an artificial political divide results in a certain depoliticization by removing from the public sphere various issues deemed nonpolitical.

Bureaucracy, the third component of the dominant political configuration of modernity, also meets the needs of representative government and political parties. The advent of representative government spurred the growth of bureaucracy, which provided this form of government with the "shape and practical stability" it needed in order to affect the social sphere in and over the long term. Indeed, as the expression of the wishes and consent of the collectivity, representative government must "secure an instrument" allowing it to accomplish its core social project.[16] Moreover, relative to successive political parties, the bureaucracy makes it possible to follow through concretely on the omnibus political program when a new party takes power. It is imperative for the state to have the administrative tools needed to practically achieve the programs of the parties. Given the twofold impetus of representative government and political parties, large bureaucracies were thus able to take on vast proportions as of the nineteenth century.

In "What Is Bureaucracy?" Claude Lefort defines it as "a group which tends to make a certain mode of organization prevail, which develops in determinate conditions and flourishes by virtue of a certain state of the economy and of technical development, but which is what it is, in essence, only by virtue of a particular kind of social activity." At the core of bureaucratic operations lies a *"specific type of behaviour"* such that "bureaucracy exists only through bureaucrats and through their collective intention to constitute a world set apart from dominated groups, to participate in a socialized power and to define themselves in relation to one another in terms of a hierarchy which guarantees a material status or prestige for each of them."[17] "Social behaviors" are what determine the substance of the bureaucratic phenomenon. But these cannot be reduced to the sum of the civil servants' individual behaviors. Bureaucracy must be understood in its entirety and not with reference to this or that particular civil servant.

This definition involves the idea that an internal dynamic of bureaucracy compels it to constantly seek to enlarge its ambit. The "destiny" of bureaucracy is imposed not just by the structures within which it acts; it develops according to its own logic, which involves the proliferation of its responsibilities and the reinforcement of relations of dependence. In this connection, Lefort states:

> As the agent of a distinctive form of structuration, it multiplies jobs and departments, separates off different sectors of activity, sets up artificial forms of supervision and co-ordination and reduces an ever-growing mass of workers to the function of carrying out orders, thus subjecting these workers at every level to a form of authority seeking to attain its maximum force by creating a system of relations of dependence which is as differentiated as possible.[18]

Bureaucracy, as Karl Marx well knew, is a self-justifying activity whose ultimate objective remains the ever-greater extension of its operations.

Yet Lefort observes a certain indetermination in bureaucracy. By proposing indetermination as one of its constitutive features, Lefort believes he has identified one of the conceptual difficulties concerning the notion of bureaucracy.

The reason for indeterminacy is that bureaucracy remains "dependent on a properly political activity of unification." In other words, bureaucracy participates in a particular system of domination and could not exist independently of a previously instituted "social form of power."[19] The lack of objective existence makes it difficult to designate bureaucracy a "social class" or even a "specific social milieu." This casts doubt on the possibility of categorizing it as a "parasitic class" (as Trotsky puts it).[20] For Lefort, bureaucracy is characterized, in sum, by a specific type of behavior stemming from a political unification project and whose internal dynamic leads to an ever-greater expansion of its activities.

Just like representative government and political parties, large bureaucracies comprise a kind of aristocracy and operate in accordance with a "principle of distinction" inasmuch as they constitute "a world set apart from dominated groups."[21] But the sort of distinction between dominators and dominated engendered by bureaucracy is not necessarily the same as that engendered by the first two components. Whereas representative government seeks to limit the exertion of power to the "wise and virtuous" alone (hence to the notables), and political parties to their top militants and those adhering most closely to party dogma, bureaucracy favors public administration experts. A new type of aristocrat or patrician emerges from the establishment of large modern bureaucracies: the technocrat. It follows that the hegemonic configuration of democratic modernity inaugurates a public space in which the struggle for power is premised on competition among various categories of patricians: (1) the "virtuous" and "wise" notable (representative government), (2) the gifted and efficient militant (political parties), and (3) the competent and ingenious technocrat (bureaucracy).

Finally, Lefort observes an indetermination in bureaucracy, which arises and takes shape because of a "properly political activity of unification."[22] Bureaucracy itself, whose development depends on a desire for unification, partakes in the realization of the unification project. A political project of unification necessarily strives for a consensus aiming to domesticate the dissension (see J. Rancière) characteristic of the turbulence of democratic life. By participating in the neutralization of modern politics, bureaucracy sounds the death knell for the effective engagement of the many in politics and vitiates the plurality of the political space. Ultimately, competition among different categories of patricians (notables, militants, and technocrats) for the control of political power cannot constitute a truly democratic political space.

From our perspective—our goal being to locate and understand the political experience of the plebs, through whom political freedom stays alive—should not our task be to seek in the margins of political history the material needed to break through below (or perhaps above) the dominant political configuration of modernity and its three components? Is it possible to identify a democratic experience that goes beyond the framework of these institutions to the point of finding expression in a movement opposed to that configuration?

3
SECTIONAL SOCIETIES AND THE SANS-CULOTTES OF PARIS

The experiences of the French Revolution lit a torch that distantly illuminates both ancient histories and, on a nearer horizon, modern histories.
—Pierre-Simon Ballanche, *Oeuvres complètes*

ORIGINALLY PEJORATIVE, THE TERM *SANS-CULOTTE* WAS COINED by antirevolutionary publicists to denigrate the poor of Paris. The emphasis on the lack of breeches was intended to point up the indigence, ignorance, vulgarity, and animality of ordinary people as perceived by the breeches-wearing supporters of the aristocratic order. When the Revolution entered a more radical stage, the term became a "title of glory"[1] (along with *canaille*, i.e., the "rabble") designating the people or the revolutionary throng at the heart of the revolutionary movement up until Thermidor.

Beyond their dress code, the sans-culottes can be defined from three different perspectives: historical, sociological, and political. For some historians, including Patrice Higonnet, "The sans-culotte's existence was therefore very brief, from 1792–1795."[2] While for others, such as Daniel Guérin, the history of the sans-culottes ended with the failure of Gracchus Babeuf (1797).[3] Yet, despite the brevity of their history, the sans-culottes were a product,[4] indeed an essential *actor*, of the French Revolution, whose importance came to light at crucial moments of the history of 1789. As the main initiators of the revolutionary days and, hence, of the key events of the Revolution, the sans-culottes were its driving force.[5] For, in the twofold struggle against the ancien régime and the coalition of foreign countries at war with revolutionary France, the bourgeoisie lacked a force capable of prevailing on both the domestic and external fronts. It was the participation of the sans-culottes that allowed the revolutionary bourgeoisie to consolidate its control of France to the detriment of the ancien régime and the foreign monarchies.[6] In historical terms, the sans-culottes proved to be an indispensable protagonist of the Revolution.

But while their historical role may be relatively easy to delineate, the social composition of the sans-culottes remains enigmatic. Most of the documents that would have enabled us to reconstitute accurately their social makeup were destroyed in a fire at the Hôtel de Ville (City Hall) of Paris in 1871. We nevertheless know that the sans-culottes, who came from ranks of the ordinary people, were the product of an "essentially pre-industrial social structure where the antagonism between employers and wage-earners [was] less strong than that between the 'many' and the 'few.'"[7] From a sociological point of view, the sans-culottes constituted a heterogeneous social stratum bringing together those situated on the side of the "many," that is, plebeians, the economically impoverished and politically excluded.[8] But there was also a portion of the sans-culotterie that came from among the impoverished and excluded petit bourgeoisie. In a word, the sans-culottes were a cross-section of the Parisian population:[9] artisans, shopkeepers, rentiers, wage earners, domestics, journeymen, laborers, small employers, etc. Thus, it was not their inclusion in the same social category that united them but, instead, the fact of being subjected to the same political and social domination, primarily at the hands of the aristocracy but also of the rising bourgeoisie.

The basis of the sans-culotterie's cohesion was, therefore, political. What characterized its members were a political sensibility and a political practice that could lend the movement cohesion in spite of its heterogeneous social composition. Although, as Daniel Guérin writes, "the people [may not be] metaphysicians" and "the new forms of political power that [they] discovered were not creations of the intellect, not the work of doctrinarians,"[10] one can identify three major political principles shared by the sans-culottes and that were the movement's source of strength: equality, action, and openness.

Even though the sans-culottes were especially alive to the question of equality, this did not necessarily imply a wish to share out economic assets equally.[11] Rather, they rejected the aristocratic belief in the natural inequality of human beings. The ways of the ancien regime were repugnant to the sans-culottes, who refused to be treated as subordinates.[12] Yet, while the bourgeoisie allowed that individuals were equal before the law, thereby opening a breach in the notion of natural inequality, the sans-culottes, for their part, pursued this dynamic to its logical political conclusion, to wit, the equal participation of everyone in public affairs. They defended equality of political rights, "an essential dimension of *sans-culotte* egalitarianism."[13]

The enactment of political rights created the possibility of action for the sans-culottes, that is, of putting into practice the desire to exercise direct popular sovereignty.[14] The sans-culottes "could not easily bear the representative system or anything that might impede the direct and immediate expression of the general will."[15] The will to take political action was realized through forms of political organization capable of expressing popular sovereignty—sectional societies, popular societies, etc.—and all such structures of political action testified to the desire to establish direct democracy.[16] That is why "the aspiration for direct democracy [is] the keystone for understanding the *sans-culotte* mentality."[17]

Plebeian politics, however, tends to go beyond the institutional framework and integrates insurrection as a method of political action. In its desire for freedom, the sans-culotterie rose up against the dominant powers and the established order, whether it was the ancien régime or the regime that sought to replace it.

Whatever the specific nature of the sans-culottes' political actions (insurrectional, deliberative, etc.), they had to be carried out in full public view. The desire for openness stemmed from "the *sans-culotte*'s fraternal conception of social relationships."[18] The principle of openness had significant consequences for the political practice and representation of the sans-culottes: the deliberations of popular bodies took place in public, votes were not secret, and denunciation became a civic duty. Openness represented both the guiding principle and an especially effective revolutionary method during political crises.[19]

ORIGIN AND ACTION OF THE SECTIONAL SOCIETIES

The principles of equality, action, and openness were concretized through the sectional societies. This form of political organization particular to the plebs arrived on the scene of the French Revolution[20] at a crucial moment: the insurrection against the Girondins. On June 2, 1793, in the aftermath of the political crisis opposing the Girondins and the Montagnards, the Montagne took power by imposing itself at the Convention thanks to the support of the sans-culottes.[21] It was mainly within the forty-eight Parisian sections, each having a general assembly permanently in session as well as certain important powers and committees on the local level, that the sans-culottes asserted themselves politically. The sectional societies were thus born in the wake of a political insurrection carried out against the Girondin Convention. Their insurrectional origins would leave a lasting mark on the political action of the sans-culottes.

When the Montagne took power, the sans-culottes did not control all the sections. Hence, many sections were ambivalent regarding the crisis that ousted the Girondins from power.[22] More specifically, the moderates controlled the sections from the western part of the city and influenced those from the center. They were therefore quite favorable to the Girondins. On the other hand, the sans-culottes generally prevailed in the sections from the east and center (despite the influence of the moderates), which therefore supported the Montagnards. The result was a fragile and shaky balance in Paris between the moderates and the sans-culottes, who sought to take control of the sectional organizations to ensure the continuation of the revolutionary movement. The struggle for the domination of the sections lasted until the late summer of 1793 and in a way amounted to a "masked civil war."[23]

Both the moderates and the sans-culottes took advantage of the double-edged sword that the permanence of the section assemblies represented. The decisions of the general assemblies changed according to whether the sans-culottes or moderates held the majority at any given time. "Permanence allowed a determined party to show up in numbers, generally at a late hour, after ten p.m., to quash the decisions taken previously and to renew the sectional authorities."[24] For the more perceptive sans-culottes, the development of a basic political organization constituted the very foundation of political action.[25] This explains why in the summer of 1793 the sans-culottes focused all their efforts on taking over the general assemblies and committees that were in the hands of the moderates.

The sans-culottes, holding fast to the notion of permanence as the expression of their driving ideal of autonomy, devised a particularly effective tactic against the moderates: fraternization. To regenerate the popular elements of a section, the sans-culottes sent deputations to fraternize with the members of the assembly, where they proposed—or even violently imposed—their positions. Fraternization, then, was a "sort of mutual assistance pact among sections" whose aim was "to hold at bay the aristocrats and moderates of the whole capital."[26] The tactic was not, of course, in the democratic tradition,[27] for through such fraternization the sans-culottes endeavored to muzzle the potentially majority voices of moderates and other political adversaries. But this "corrective measure" was "inevitable for the sake of the dream of exercising sovereignty directly."[28] The effects of the attraction of the One, which transforms the desire for freedom into the desire for servitude, can be discerned here. Concerning the practice of fraternization, the sometimes brutal methods were based—perhaps paradoxically—on a genuine wish to broaden the political sphere to include the dominated.

After three months of struggle, the sans-culottes prevailed over the moderates and put an end to their influence in most sections. But the political situation of the government committees was too vulnerable to allow the presence of moderates, even if it was restricted to a few sections. The revolutionary government wanted to control the sectional organizations as well. It therefore decided to take the necessary steps to eradicate the moderates' influence and ensure its own ascendancy over the sections by doing away with the permanence of their assemblies. Thus, the consolidation of the revolutionary government was achieved at the expense of the "autonomy of the popular organizations."[29]

The decree of September 9, 1793, suppressed the permanence of the sections and introduced a forty-sous indemnity for participants in the general assemblies. More than a mere tactic designed to consolidate the power base of the revolutionary government and its committees in relation to the moderates and the sans-culottes, the suppression of permanence points to two distinct political conceptions, those of the sans-culottes on the one hand and the revolutionary bourgeoisie on the other. The conception of popular sovereignty, held by the sans-culottes,[30] went beyond theory and was embodied in political forms where citizens could exercise that sovereignty through direct political action. This political ideal inspired their action and represented the practical application of the principles proclaimed by the Revolution. The revolutionary bourgeoisie's political vision, however, assumed that popular sovereignty was justified in theory but not in practice because the people delegated their powers to individuals mandated to exercise sovereignty. This is the guiding political conception of representative regimes, and it is central to liberal political doctrine. The suppression of permanence brought to light an initial difference between the conceptions and political practices of the sans-culottes and the revolutionary bourgeoisie. For "it involved a twofold injury to the sovereignty and dignity of the citizens and was a means for the government to limit popular action."[31]

To circumvent the problem posed by the suppression of permanence and to conserve their capacity for political action, the sans-culottes established a new type of popular organization, the sectional societies.[32] Convened on days when the general assemblies were forbidden, these societies appeared in 1793 and spread throughout the various sections of Paris.[33] For each of the forty-eight sections, there was a sectional society acting as executive committee of the general assembly and guiding the sans-culottes' actions. By reestablishing permanence in this way while at the same time providing itself with a body able to channel the sans-culottes' efforts in each section, the sectional societies illustrated the political vitality of the popular movement as well as its desire to continue exercising popular sovereignty directly.

> The sans-culottes were the more insistent in their claim for retaining permanence as they were convinced that the section was not only an organ for supervising general policies, the source of national representation and the means of control over it, but was also an autonomous body performing its own administrative functions; the section is a sovereign power, its affairs are the concern of its general assembly alone.[34]

Essentially the sectional societies played a double role: education and surveillance. The societies were active in promoting the education of their militants through public readings of their literature, decrees, and political speeches. At the same time, they monitored officials through the deliverance of certificates of public-spiritedness and audited the quality of "military . . . supplies."[35] By assuming these two functions the sectional societies quickly became the center of daily life in the sections.

The proliferation of sectional societies engendered a complex network of political organizations that ensured the control of the general assemblies. The problem that then arose involved determining how much coordination there should be among the various sectional societies. Should they act alone, federate, or accept the tutelage of the revolutionary government? The attempt to federate the sectional societies, undertaken by the Club central du département de Paris (Central Club of the Department of Paris), the so-called Comité de l'Évêché (Committee of the Diocese), was a failure.[36] The notion that the revolutionary government might have tutelage over the sectional societies clashed with the sans-culottes' fervent desire for autonomy. Through practices such as purges the sectional societies became formidable organs of political action striving to influence the revolutionary government; they remained essentially autonomous political strongholds.

The practice of purges, that is, the exclusion of elements deemed undesirable from the sectional societies and section administrations, addressed one of the sans-culottes' fundamental political objectives: to put a stop to the influence of the nobles and other political adversaries.[37] Because of the sectional societies' autonomy, purges were carried out in accordance with the criteria particular to each of the sections, hence, without coordination. Paradoxically, the very logic of the purge was at once a strength and a weakness of the sectional societies. Since only the most loyal militants remained, the societies were dynamic and efficient. But the price for this dynamism was a decline in the number of members and therefore in the impact of their actions. In other words, the purges made it possible to concentrate the revolutionary energy inside the sectional societies but somewhat isolated them from the many. Yet it must be understood as well that the purges were carried out against the general backdrop of the political radicalization of the French Revolution. When the Montagnards took power, the Terror was included in the new government's agenda. On September 5, 1793 (a few days before permanence was abolished in order to thwart the moderates), the revolutionary government decided to accede to popular demands in favor of stepping up repression against the interior enemies of the Revolution.[38] Thus, the purges were part of the climate of suspicion inaugurated by the Jacobin Terror.

The Comité de salut public (Public Safety Committee), the supervisor of both the revolutionary government and the Terror, maintained an ambiguous relationship with the sans-culottes. The strengthening of the Committee's powers was accomplished with their support, and it applied various political and economic measures in response to pressure from the popular movement, including the Terror and the overall maximum.[39] But once it had extended its jurisdiction to include the executive authority as well as local administrations, the Committee sought to distance itself from the sans-culottes so as to position itself as a mediating body for all the constituent parts of the nation. This approach seems to have been dictated by the twofold war effort, domestic and external. While preferring to maintain the support of the sans-culottes, "the Comité de salut public did not want to be at their mercy."[40] It was as though, in return for the sans-culottes' support, the Committee wanted to keep a tight rein on them in order to cement its power over the nation. Here, the Committee's political posture can be described as a desire to ensure the sans-culottes' support while refusing to pursue their political objectives.

The tendency of the "public safety" government was to control every facet of French political life, including the popular movement. The decree of December 4, 1793 (14th Frimaire, Year II), laid the foundations of its authority and established the revolutionary government. The wish to set limits on the action of the sans-culottes and to force them to observe those limits was expressed in particular by the elimination of the sans-culottes who dared criticize the executive power.[41] This was the beginning of the "Jacobin offensive against the sectional societies,"[42] which was declared in September 1793 and came to an end only the following spring.[43]

The multiplication of sectional societies and their integration in all the Parisian sections reflected their importance for the revolutionary action of the sans-culottes. The sectional societies, created by the sans-culottes, managed to avoid the control of both government authorities and municipal bodies. The society of Jacobins, in particular, would have liked to play the role of "head society" in relation to the sectional societies, which could have had the effect of curbing the power of the sans-culottes and transforming the sectional societies into resonators for the Comité de salut public.[44] But the real discord between the Jacobins and the sectional societies was on the level of the new societies' makeup. The Jacobins wanted membership in the societies to be open to all patriotic citizens and not just to sans-culotte militants residing in a given section. This proposition could have transformed the societies into "organs of academic discussion,"[45] thereby hampering their capacity for revolutionary action.

Another source of friction between the revolutionary government and the sectional societies was the conflict with the revolutionary committees. Each of the forty-eight sections in Paris had a revolutionary committee originally rooted in the sans-culotterie and wielding certain powers. These committees, however, "were quickly integrated in the bureaucratic apparatus by the decree of December 4 (14th Frimaire),"[46] which placed them under the tutelage of one of the government committees, the Comité de sûreté générale (General Safety Committee). The revolutionary committees obtained major powers, including the power to establish lists of suspects, which turned them into a kind of "state police."[47] Consequently, the revolutionary committees followed the policies dictated by the revolutionary government and strove to direct the general assemblies' actions along those lines. The conflicts that erupted between the sectional societies and the revolutionary committees reduced the effectiveness of the Jacobin government, thereby nourishing the government's desire to bring the sectional societies to heel.

By contrast, the relationship between the central council of the Commune of Paris and the sectional societies was decidedly less antagonistic. The Commune had to intervene to solve the conflicts that arose in a number of sections where the new sectional societies coexisted with older popular societies. It was important for the Commune that there should be only one "popular assembly" in every section. By using the term "popular assembly" the Commune acknowledged the legitimacy of the sectional nature of the societies, and by calling for a single assembly per section it showed its concern with the effectiveness of the popular movement. This is how the Commune distinguished its policies from those of the government committees and of the Jacobin club.[48] The fact remains, nevertheless, that the sectional societies continued to be coveted by the Commune, which "hoped to turn the activity of these organs of popular power to the advantage of their ambitions."[49]

The sectional societies found themselves caught between the municipal and governmental authorities who sought to benefit from their revolutionary might. Albert Soboul emphasizes that the more clear-sighted sans-culotte militants became aware of these ambitions and tried unsuccessfully to organize a central committee of the sectional societies that could protect their autonomy by reinforcing their capacity for political action.[50] Meanwhile, the Frimaire attempt by Chaumette, the Commune's public prosecutor, to get control of the revolutionary committees to the detriment of the Comité de sûreté général was perceived by the sans-culottes as targeting the sectional societies, especially because Chaumette wanted the Commune's general council to become the "common center" of the sectional societies. But the sans-culottes' violent reactions to these initiatives testified to their ardent wish to preserve the autonomy of their organizations and to their rejection of any attempt to co-opt the popular movement for purposes other than those determined by the sans-culottes themselves.[51] The wish to remain autonomous with respect to the Commune and the revolutionary government amply demonstrates the properly plebeian character of the sectional societies.

The societies soon became immensely powerful. As the rallying point for the various parts of the popular revolutionary movement, they took over the leadership and control of the movement by supplanting the general assemblies, which subsequently turned into mere rubber stamps for the decisions taken by the sectional societies. In many cases, the general assemblies of the sections handed over certain powers to the sectional societies, such as the issuing of certificates of public-spiritedness, thereby enhancing the sections' dynamism. In addition, the sectional societies eventually secured the power to draft reports and issue orders, make appointments, and make decisions, instead of the general assemblies.[52]

The sectional societies' new power exacerbated the government bodies' already acute mistrust. Although the popular movement remained too strong and the simultaneous domestic and external threats too grave for the government to be able to confront the sectional societies head-on, the government committees endeavored to control covertly the popular movement. By means, in particular, of the revolutionary committees, the Jacobin government tried to infiltrate the sectional societies and to manipulate decision making in the general assemblies.[53] The antagonisms caused by these maneuvers effectively disrupted the existence of the sectional societies. As a result, the societies were somewhat discredited, and they tried to restore their public reputation by carrying out purges. However, the sans-culottes' methods (purges as well as surveillance and denunciation) along with their zeal in applying them discredited the plebeian bodies even further. Indeed, the revolutionary government continued to be concerned with the social balance among the various components of the nation, a balance upset by the purges. Hence, Albert Soboul writes, "the sectional societies were never closer to their ruin than at the apogee of their power."[54]

The government's hostility to sectional democracy was manifested in the ever-greater concentration of political powers in the hands of government authorities. The effect of centralization was to deflect popular energies toward the war effort as well as the dechristianization campaign.[55] In fact, "the government, having turned revolutionary under pressure from the masses, endeavored to channel and neutralize both the popular movement and the action of the constituted bodies of Paris in order to direct them toward the objective it had set for itself: the success of the Revolution, but in a bourgeois form."[56]

For Albert Soboul, the Jacobin government's destruction of the sectional societies in the Year II was "the harshest, most consequential blow"[57] among the numerous government assaults against the institutions close to or emanating from the popular movement. By attacking the sans-culottes, the revolutionary government destroyed the founding organs of the popular movement. True, the Jacobins no longer needed to fear a revolutionary rising. But the price paid for this peace of mind was the loss of a formidable "means of applying pressure" that had previously served to wrest power from the Girondins. The domestication of the sans-culottes' autonomous political power thus attested to "the entrenched antagonism between the *sans-culotterie* and the Jacobin bourgeoisie . . . [that] paved the way for Thermidor."[58]

However, the destruction of the sectional societies did not put an end to the political action of the sans-culottes. From Germinal to Thermidor, and even beyond that point,[59] the popular movement continued its quest for political autonomy and greater social justice, despite the sans-culottes' many displays of loyalty toward the revolutionary government. But they pursued their fight without the vehicle that could convey their conception of politics and their desire for autonomy.

Two exemplary political struggles, against centralization and against the "great specialists," bring to light the specificity of the sans-culottes' political action.

FIRST EXEMPLARY POLITICAL STRUGGLE: AGAINST CENTRALIZATION

Alexis de Tocqueville rightly affirms that the political and administrative centralization of France could be attributed neither to Jacobinism nor to Bonapartism but indeed to the ancien régime.[60] In its assault against the political foundations of monarchist absolutism, the revolutionary bourgeoisie was obliged to dismantle the centralism of the French state. This was to a large extent accomplished through the Constitution of 1791, which promulgated democratic principles in tandem with administrative and political decentralization.[61] Henceforth, the electors directly appointed the representatives that would be in charge of local administrative bodies, that is, the communes, departments, and districts. But universal suffrage did not yet exist, so it was only in 1792 that decentralization assumed a truly democratic form.[62] The political significance of decentralization is undeniable, for the role of the autonomous communes in what Michelet considers the "admirable" political apprenticeship of the citizens must not be underestimated.[63]

Decentralization was largely responsible for France's ability to achieve national unity. In 1790–1791, French unity was "accomplished spontaneously and enthusiastically through the voluntary federation of the 44,000 autonomous communes."[64] Hence, decentralization did not pose a threat to national cohesion, which cannot be reduced to or equated with administrative centralization. Therefore, the need to ensure and strengthen the nation's unity could hardly serve as a justification for the increasingly severe centralization of the state.

The revolutionary Jacobin government was in the process of consolidating its power when the effects of decentralization became apparent. On the provincial level, it allowed the Girondins to maintain a continuing presence in the departments and districts where they still enjoyed considerable political support, despite their expulsion from national power. Decentralization also focused a great deal of attention on the political bodies of the sans-culottes. The Commune of Paris, the forty-eight sections, the sectional societies—these structures were open to a political practice different from and, what was worse for the revolutionary government, potentially antagonistic to Jacobinism. The political objective, then, of the French state's reversion to centralization was to crush the opposition on the right (the Girondins) and on the left (the sans-culottes) in order to secure complete control of the revolutionary movement, all under the pretext of the imperative of national unity.

The decree of 14 Frimaire confirmed the usurpation by the Comité de salut public of the power to appoint the members of the revolutionary committees. This represented an important step in the centralization process, because the goal of the Jacobin government, acting through the revolutionary committees (now turned into "docile transmitters of the drive to centralize")[65] was to subjugate the general assemblies of the sections. The revolutionary government also suppressed the sections' right to choose and monitor their representatives at the Commune of Paris.[66] The direct exercise of popular sovereignty was supplanted by centralization in the name of administrative efficiency and revo-lutionary unity. The centralization process was gradually consolidated until 14 Frimaire. For example, the general assemblies lost control of the surveillance committees, which thereby gained additional powers, especially with regard to the police.

The strengthening of the revolutionary committees acting at the behest of the Jacobin government provoked the ire of the sans-culottes. Displaying great insight, the Enragés—the revolutionaries rallied around Jacques Roux and sympathetic to the demands of the sans-culottes—were the first to denounce the centralizing trend of the state institutions.[67] In many sections, the hostility was expressed publically, and the protests of the sans-culottes swelled.[68] The sans-culotte militants may have suspected that the aim of centralization was to put an end to the power of the popular movement by reinforcing the Jacobins' hegemony over French political life.

The sans-culottes' struggle was confronted with a major dilemma: how to combat the institutions acting as guardians of the Terror (and thus capable of containing the counterrevolution) without at the same time endangering the course of the Revolution by opening the door to an offensive on the part of the moderates. To tackle this problem, the sans-culottes could possibly have sought to enforce the policy of the Terror themselves. The result would have been to counter the exercise of a centralizing power particular to the revolutionary bourgeoisie with a direct and local plebeian practice of popular sovereignty.

The idea of a direct practice of the Terror by the sans-culottes raises the broader question regarding a plebeian notion of the politics of the Terror. Or, to put this another way: was there a plebeian conception of the Terror as in-cluded in the political agenda by the Jacobin revolutionary government? To answer this question, the plebs' relationship to violence, to the politics of the Terror, and to Jacobin political practice needs to be examined. On one hand, violence was a feature of popular political action during the Revolution.[69] The sans-culottes' violence was directed against both the aristocracy and the de-fenders of revolutionary moderation. Thus, it was aimed at the plebs' political adversaries and, hence, employed toward a specific political objective. It was in no way gratuitous: the use of violent means was for the sans-culottes "the supreme recourse"[70] rather than the preferred initial form of political action. At the same time, the significance of the sans-culottes' support for the policy of the Terror must be noted. An especially striking illustration of that support was the "glorification" of the guillotine, regarded as an *equalizing* weapon by the sans-culottes. For them, the use of the guillotine as a symbol of the destruction of feudal hierarchies remained "necessary for consolidating the Republic."[71] This indeed proved to be the case, as the guillotine's popularity never waned throughout the Revolution. Finally, in spite of the sans-culottes' support for the policies of the Terror, the tensions and conflicts opposing the sectional societies and the Comité de salut public must be highlighted. The two levels of political action—plebeian and Jacobin—embodied divergent conceptions of democracy. For example, the sans-culottes' practice of "fraternization" can hardly be viewed as a precursor of the Jacobin policy of the Terror. For there is a vast difference between fraternization, which sought to *exclude* the moderates from the Parisian sections, and the Terror, which sought to *eliminate physically* the enemies of a certain idea of the Revolution.

Does a plebeian conception of the Terror exist? One answer to this question could surely be that violence was a major part of the sans-culottes' politics and that they massively supported the policies of the Terror. But certain plebeian practices must not be confused with the Terror. The gap between these two types of politics "expressed a concept of democracy that was fundamentally different."[72] Moreover, although the sans-culottes were largely supportive of the Terror, they did not mobilize to have it directly implemented, which would suggest there was no specifically plebeian conception of the Terror.

Consequently, the hypothesis as to the supposedly "plebeian" origins of the Terror is in doubt. Indeed, François Furet points out that for some historians of the nineteenth century[73] the policy of the Terror can be ascribed to the assumption of power by a social group other than "the cultivated bourgeoisie." The Jacobin takeover of the Convention meant that the common people, also referred to as "the multitude" or "the plebs," were in power. This change of the political guard entailed the transformation of 1789 and put a stain on the "historical dignity" of the Revolution because the terrorist phase signified a radical negation of the first principles of the Great Revolution. Thus, writes Furet, "the plebeian nature of this episode makes it possible to understand how the Terror was also the product of elementary political reflexes, at once egalitarian and punitive." Yet even Furet acknowledges that the idea of the plebs in power is insufficient to explain the Terror. The sans-culottes may have massively supported the policy of the Terror, but the pleas in favor of the Terror were presented by political actors "who had no special relation to sans-culotte activism," for example, Barère, who in the summer of 1793 demanded the "total destruction of the Vendée."[74] The terrorist episode, then, was not solely the result of popular pressure exerted by the ordinary people of Paris. In sum, the policy of the Terror cannot be explained by its allegedly plebeian character.

To return to the plebs' struggle against centralization, the sans-culottes' opposition to bourgeois centralization casts light on its contribution to modern political thought and the communalist tradition. On a philosophical level, the sans-culottes put forward a conception of political action implying the inclusion of more participants in the public realm. By creating local political bodies, such as the sectional societies, they granted themselves the right and made it their duty to take part in the common affairs of the arrondissement (borough). In addition, the sans-culottes' action within the sectional societies points up the tumultuous nature of democracy, which enables the always adversarial plurality of the human race to express itself. The notion that politics supposes the active participation of all in the public space signaled the end of political exclusivism. Politics was no longer seen as the preserve of the few entitled (or not, as in the case of tyranny) to govern. It became, concretely, the affair of the many, whose entitlement to govern lay in the necessarily political condition of humankind. The plebeian political practices of the sans-culottes of Paris marked the effective return of the many to politics, even though, particularly in the case of the sectional societies, the return could not last and was marked by increasingly harsh purges.

Understanding the end of political exclusivism among the sans-culottes is made more complex by the recourse to purges. The revolutionary environment and the pressure exerted by the revolutionary government no doubt go some way to explaining the obsession with spies and potential enemies in the popular political bodies, especially because the revolution evolved within a specific set of historical circumstances, which influenced revolutionary political practices. For instance, in time of revolution it is difficult to ignore questions concerning the distinction between supporters and adversaries. While the specific historical context of the revolution may not justify the practice of purges, it nevertheless helps elucidate the phenomenon and, above all, prevents the events and practices of the Revolution from being judged as if they occurred within a different context. Ultimately, however, the practice of purges vitiated the inclusiveness of the sectional societies.

By granting themselves the right and making it their duty to take part in public affairs, the sans-culottes of Paris clearly asserted their political capacity. The organizational forms they adopted demonstrated that they were spontaneously able to display political skill and creativity. The establishment of sectional societies to circumvent the revolutionary bourgeoisie's suppression of permanence amply attests to the political resourcefulness of the plebs, who thereby erected a stage from which they could verify the equality of everyone with everyone and challenge the government's "distribution of shares and the hierarchy of places and functions."[75] For Jacques Rancière, what was involved was a process of emancipation bearing on the "wrong" inflicted on human equality by what he terms the "police" order. This "wrong" brings to light the fundamental political conflict pertaining to the existence of a common political arena, one that makes it possible to confirm equality because it opens up the public sphere to broader participation. The work of the sans-culottes within the sectional societies was evident as well in this creation of a shared arena. In opposition to the official "leaders" of the Revolution (such as the Girondins and the Jacobins), the sans-culottes presented a political existence and practice attesting to their equal capacities. In so doing, they recalled the "inaugural" moment of the plebs in ancient Rome, the first secession on the Aventine Hill, when, as discussed earlier, the Roman plebs, entrenched in their camp, took steps to inscribe themselves symbolically and politically in the community. Thus, the plebeians "execute a series of speech acts that mimic those of the patricians: they pronounce imprecations and apotheoses; they delegate one of their number to go and consult *their* oracles; they give themselves representatives by rebaptizing them."[76] In the same way (but of course using different means), the sans-culottes' action in the sectional societies enabled their symbolic and political inscription in the French Revolution.

Aside from the end of political exclusivism and the display of the political capacities specific to human beings, the struggle *against* centralization involved adopting a political position offering a fertile ground for liberty. Although the opposition or conflict between the sans-culottes and the revolutionary bourgeoisie was not total, since the sectional societies liked to criticize the government while not hesitating to take part in the war effort and in demonstrations of patriotism,[77] the sectional societies were nonetheless a source of antagonism for the Jacobin government. The political objectives of the sans-culottes were directly at odds with the political imperatives of the Montagnard bourgeoisie. The formulation of a position "against"—against the aristocracy but also the bourgeoisie—signaled the operation of a freedom-producing dynamic. The position "against" necessarily indicates a manifest conflict between two "humors" in the public space, as Machiavelli puts it. As previously explained, for Machiavelli, all communities are inescapably divided between two humors that reflect two essential components of the community: the humor of the Grandees, who wish to dominate, and the humor of the many, who desire liberty. Thanks to the articulation of the conflict between the two antagonistic humors, freedom can arise within the community. In Machiavelli's words: "The desires of free peoples are rarely pernicious to freedom."[78]

In the case of the French Revolution, the sectional societies offered the Parisian sans-culottes the possibility of expressing their desire for liberty and their opposition to the humor of the Grandees (old and new), who wished to dominate. The sans-culottes fought on two fronts: against both the remnants of the ancien régime and the establishment of a new state manifesting the will to dominate the nascent political institutions.[79] The sans-culottes' political battle against centralization was also a battle against the instrument of domination of the "new grandees." This is because, to pursue Machiavelli's line of argument, the two "humors" are coterminous with the very existence of the community. Whenever the people succeed in putting a stop to the domination of a particular component of the political community, they must immediately mobilize to counter the restoration of the desire for domination. For the sans-culottes the incipient desire to dominate resided within the Jacobin government. But it was also expressed by a new type of ruling caste: the "great specialists."

SECOND EXEMPLARY POLITICAL STRUGGLE: AGAINST THE GREAT SPECIALISTS

The struggle against the centralization of the revolutionary institutions supposed a struggle against the administrative personnel in charge of the centralization and whose professional and political position was bolstered by the growing concentration of state power. During the French Revolution, those that Daniel Guérin refers to as the "great specialists" are the ones who by virtue of their expertise in specific areas took advantage of the ongoing administrative centralization to gain considerable political power in relation to the revolutionary bourgeoisie. Among the great specialists at the center of bourgeois power were the financial specialist Cambon; the military strategist Carnot; Barère, specialized in foreign and military affairs; and Jeanbon Saint-André, in charge of the navy.[80] These great specialists constituted a group distinct from the more political members of the revolutionary government, such as Robespierre and Saint-Just. Preferring to focus on strictly technical issues, the great specialists kept their distance from political negotiations and the political practices of the sans-culottes of Paris. However, writes Guérin,

> though they [the great specialists] affected to leave politics and confine themselves to their specialisations, they did not slacken their hold on the essential levers of command, which all the others depended on. With those under their control, they could easily impose so-called technical solutions to this or that problem on their non-specialist, incompetent colleagues,

when their solutions were in fact eminently political, and in line with their class interests.[81]

Considering their technical competencies and their political and administrative situation, the great specialists can arguably be regarded as precursors to the "technocrats" and therefore as having laid the foundations for the modern bureaucratic system.

Of bourgeois background for the most part, the great specialists were also at least partially associated with the ancien régime. For instance, Barère de Vieuzac, as indicated by the preposition in his surname, was a landowner and, as such, collected feudal taxes. On the political level, the great specialists shared certain reactionary sentiments, as illustrated by their opposition to the insurrectional Commune, the Parisian sans-culottes, and the most revolutionary Jacobin faction (i.e., Marat's).[82] Before joining the Montagne and entering the Comité de salut public, they were close to the Gironde. Cambon is a good example of the ties between the great specialists and the Gironde. Born to a prominent family of Montpellier that had supported the Girondin cause, he made only a belated break with the Gironde in July 1793, when his approval of the federalist revolt[83] had unduly compromised his professional position. Notwithstanding their shift from the Girondin to the Jacobin camp, the great specialists maintained numerous ties with the moderate camp throughout their involvement with the Jacobins.[84] The fact that the great specialists could avoid the Thermidor repression speaks volumes in this connection.

As evidenced by the many criticisms addressed to Barère, Cambon, and others,[85] the great specialists were regarded with animosity and suspicion by the Parisian sans-culottes. But the endorsement that the great specialists received from the revolutionary bourgeoisie, especially Robespierre, whom the sans-culottes held in high esteem, lent them a degree of legitimacy and attenuated the mistrust they aroused. This, however, did not prevent the sans-culottes from denouncing those who really held power in the revolutionary government. Even a Jacobin such as Marat, writing in *L'Ami du Peuple*, relentlessly accused the "leaders" of the Comité de salut public, who

quite criminally fulfill their functions in so shameful a manner. There is one among them whom the Montagne has very rashly reappointed, one whom I consider the most dangerous enemy of the nation. His name is Barère. . . . For my part, I am convinced that he is sitting on the fence, waiting to see which party will triumph; he is the one who has paralyzed every vigorous measure and who thereby fetters us in preparation for the slaughter.[86]

The struggle against the great specialists encompassed three notable contributions to communalism and agoraphilia, in addition to the obvious one of negating the principle of exclusion pertaining to the political domain. The fight against the great specialists sought to strengthen the link between politics and daily life. Furthermore, challenging their control over political life amounted to repudiating the homogenization of public space. Finally, the sans-culottes' fight against the great specialists signified in a way the rejection of a certain idea of modern political action (or, rather, "management").

Politics as part of daily existence—that is what the sans-culottes of Paris, assembled in the sectional societies, succeeded in reviving at the heart of modernity. The congenital link between politics and everyday life was a lasting, crucial element of democracy at its inception in Greece.[87] In harking back, perhaps unwittingly, to that originary democratic time, plebeian political practices made an invaluable contribution to political modernity. But the advent of centralization and the attendant predominance of the great specialists in revolutionary political life could only undermine the very foundations of politics as part of daily existence. Indeed, the more power gets concentrated in the hands of a small circle of administrative experts, the more politics becomes a specialized field removed from the daily life of the many. The struggle against the great specialists can therefore be understood as one aimed at preserving the renewed originary link between politics and the everyday, something which the sans-culottes experienced in the sectional societies.

The great specialists' grip on public affairs entailed a form of homogenization of politics. More specifically, homogenization was effected through the rationality underpinning the work of the great specialists. The distinguishing feature of public administration specialists is their application of the principle of efficiency to solutions proposed by the political authorities. The efficiency principle is not neutral but intrinsically implies a value judgment and a worldview requiring an ever-shrinking gap between means and ends. The application of this principle to all political problems therefore supposes a uniform outlook on politics, since everything must be subjected to administrative rationality. The great specialists' work, then, was not situated outside of politics, that is, outside the manifest clash of values and practices within the community but remained an application, indeed an extension, of particular political approaches and techniques, those of the modern state. By subsuming political problems

under the variables of efficiency and rationality, the great specialists participated in the homogenization of modern politics. Thus, in attacking them, the
sans-culottes were defending the heterogeneous nature of community affairs.

But the struggle against the great specialists implied as well the rejection
of a certain idea of politics based on the equation of administrative rationality
with technical rationality. The "managerial" approach to public life stemmed
from a wish to apply the principle of efficiency to every political problem.
Consequently, it was no longer a question of political *action* but of political
management, which tended toward "regulating" and neutralizing conflicts in
the public sphere. Politics as "management" meant seeing it in terms of "work"
(i.e., making) or as a captive of the means-ends couple. The managerial approach toward politics can be contrasted with the notion of action, as Hannah Arendt defines it: the possibility of acting together with others "in order
to begin something new."[88] Unpredictable and irreversible, action remains the
implementation of liberty realized through the spoken or written word and
human plurality.[89] In challenging the work of the great specialists, particularly
in the popular press,[90] the sans-culottes opposed the desire to domesticate politics through a managerial approach with a tumultuous and adversarial practice
of modern politics. Hence, they supported actions against political management and administration, thereby regenerating the political history of liberty
by once again placing action at the heart of the community. The sans-culottes
were staunch agoraphiles because political freedom continued to be a rampart
against an elitist and exclusive conception of politics, whereby public affairs
were the private preserve of specialists of the state apparatus and of its preferred body of knowledge, the law.

A Practice of Insurrection

The sans-culottes took an active part in the sectional societies because, going
beyond the limits of political representation, democracy as they saw it was
direct, immediate, and local. The practice of insurrection also partook of this
conception of democracy as the unmediated exercise of political sovereignty.
Insurrection, that is, insurgence against the established powers, remained "the
ultimate recourse of the sovereign people"[91] against political oppression and
tyranny. As asserted by a Parisian section in 1792, the insurrection would last
"until France shall be purged of its tyrants."[92] "Ultimate recourse" or not, insurrection was not illegal or forbidden by law. As of the spring of 1793, insurrection was a recognized constitutional right appearing in the Declaration of
the Rights of Man decreed on May 29, 1793. The first article of the Declaration

affirms that "resistance to oppression" is one of the "human rights in society" in the same way as "liberty, equality, security, and property." Article 29 is even more explicit in this connection, as it provides that "in any free government, individuals must have the legal means to resist oppression; and when those means are ineffectual, insurrection is the sanest of duties."[93] That duty would be reasserted in the Constitutional Act of June 24, 1793.[94] The Constitution of 1793 introduced an additional dimension to the practice of insurrection, which was henceforward conceived of as both a duty and a right. Article 35 stipulates, "When the government violates the rights of the people, insurrection is for the people and for each portion of the people *the most sacred of rights and the most indispensable of duties.*"[95] It is telling that the Constitution of Year II (1795) did not renew the people's right and duty to rise up.[96] The "omission" was neither haphazard nor innocuous.

Insurrection is a collective experience of resistance to tyranny and the abuse of power. It is the people's insurgence, "their refusal to obey laws which they did not accept, their reassertion of their sovereign rights, their insistence on their elected representatives rendering an account of their activities and fulfilling the decisions of the people."[97] Popular uprisings are not necessarily violent. Strange as it may seem, the sans-culottes' insurrections were often peaceful. For example, in Year I a Parisian section declared itself to be in a state of insurrection, which would imply "a continual state of useful defiance, of activity, of surveillance, of patriotic concern, a state which every good republican should be in until freedom be established on firm ground."[98] This enumeration articulates the nonviolent modes of popular insurrection. Thus, the notion of peaceful resistance to tyranny was pertinent for the sans-culottes' activities. To rise up means to oblige the holders of public office to respect the will of the people. Consequently, there is such as thing as an "*insurrection morale,*"[99] that is, a peaceful insurrection aiming to shape political action through nonviolent acts and statements.

Standing in contrast to "moral insurrection," however, was "brutal insurrection."[100] When peaceful means proved inadequate to put an end to political domination, the sans-culottes did not hesitate to resort to violence or to the threat of violence, a method they often employed. Thus, when peaceful means failed, the sections were apt to raise the specter of a mass uprising against the established powers.[101] Hence, if insurrection was the ultimate political recourse of the Parisians plebs, then armed insurrection could only be "an extreme manifestation of popular sovereignty."[102] In other words, taking arms was not something the sans-culottes did lightly. Brutal insurrection was an exceptional measure taken in response to exceptional circumstances. It was only when the great principles of the Revolution were truly in jeopardy that the ordinary people engaged in violent mobilizations against the established political institutions. The "revolutionary days" testified to the people's recourse to insurrectional violence.

As a sans-culotte militant put it, "when the tocsin sounded, the Convention no longer counted."[103] In other words, the call to insurrection (made by sounding the tocsin or the call to arms) signified that the established powers were dissolved and that the laws were no longer valid. The Convention, the high place of political authority during the Revolution, immediately lost its legitimacy for the sans-culottes. Under such circumstances, the sans-culottes provisionally took over the full exercise of sovereign rights. A violent insurrection implied that "the people are all-powerful: they can make laws, dispense justice, perform every function of the executive. They alone are in command as soon as they are in insurrection."[104] By taking arms the plebs granted themselves legislative, executive, and legal power. Thus, for a specific length of time they bent the course of the Revolution to their will.

Insurrection as a political practice involves a particular historical context: it unfolds within "the time of the *caesura* between two State forms."[105] With respect to the sans-culottes of Paris, insurrection can be considered a breach arising between the newly founded revolutionary power (for example, the Convention or the Thermidorean regime) and the supporters of the old power and order (aristocrats and other reactionaries). Insurrection, then, is the moment that breaks the "normal" rhythm of political life and arrives when the plebs refuse both the "new" and "old" grandees. In this case, the plebs went through the difficult experience of a relentless temporality calling for continuous and, above all, manifold political action. They became at once the legislative, executive, and legal power, which necessitated constant vigilance and exemplary political skill.

THE INSURRECTION AGAINST THE GIRONDINS

The insurrection against the Girondins in a way marked the birth of that plebeian form of political organization, the sectional society. But the circumstances surrounding the removal of the Girondin representatives were complex and the subject of differing historical interpretations.[106] Rather than rehearsing the sequence of events or reviewing all the various interpretations, we prefer to focus on the political objectives of the Enragés during the insurrection. Without subsuming the role of the sans-culottes under that of the Enragés, we believe the latter can be regarded as a "laboratory" of plebeian politics. Jacques Roux and the other "spokesmen of the popular vanguard"[107] managed to articulate the demands of the Parisian sans-culottes because they embodied the political ideal nurtured by the ordinary people during this insurrectional experience. Thus, writes Daniel Guérin,

> A few men, close enough to the people to experience their suffering yet not subject to long hours of work every day, whose bourgeois education had given them the necessary eloquence, had to speak for the *bras nus* in their place. Called "Enragés" by their enemies, Jacques Roux, Theophile Leclerc and Jean Varlet were, in 1793 the direct and true interpreters of the mass movement.[108]

By returning to the outlook of the Enragés, we can throw into sharp relief the conflict between two distinct conceptions of democracy that faced off during the Revolution: that of the revolutionary bourgeoisie and that of the sans-culottes. The primary political goal pursued by the Enragés during the insurrection was to transform the French political system.[109] They wanted to replace representative government, the political system of the revolutionary bourgeoisie, with direct democracy based on the local assemblies, from which delegates would be chosen. These would be only *proxies* for the will of the people, as expressed in the institutions of direct democracy. The delegates would then be given a political mandate from which they must not depart. This was the practical incarnation of the idea of the *"mandat impératif"*[110] dear to the Enragés. The project of a new political system founded on direct democracy effectively expressed the ideal of full participation in public affairs that motivated the sans-culottes of Paris. To better understand this struggle between the two types of democracy, let us limn out the political stakes involved in the ouster of the Gironde.

The popular insurrection leading to the fall of the Girondins grew out of a "divorce" or "split" within the revolutionary bourgeoisie.[111] The Girondins, just like the Jacobins, were in favor of private property, acknowledged the importance of work,[112] and supported representative democracy. However, the two factions were at odds when it came to applying those shared principles. Moreover, whereas the Jacobins wished to maintain the support of the popular movement, the Girondins expressed their mistrust toward the sans-culottes, sometimes to the point of openly voicing their contempt.[113]

According to Guérin, the antagonism within the revolutionary bourgeoisie reached its peak when the Girondins chose to put "their immediate interests before the higher interests of their class" by opposing "any emergency economic measures and any of the other radical solutions which were all that could give at least partial satisfaction to the people" and which, because they ensured the people's support, were the only means of saving the Revolution. Thus, the practical divergence between the Girondins and the Jacobins, combined with the Girondins' agoraphobia, made collaboration between the two factions of revolutionary bourgeoisie untenable. In the face of the twofold threat of interior and exterior enemies and because the plebs were needed in the war effort, the Jacobin faction "after some hesitancy and beating about the bush . . . decided to remove the Girondin leaders from power."[114] To carry out this delicate maneuver the Jacobins had to resort to methods that were effective and relatively safe. Without giving a detailed account of the myriad intrigues leading up to and marking the days of insurrection of May 31 and June 2, 1793, we can confidently assert that the Jacobins called on the Enragés to arouse the sans-culottes' distrust of the Girondins and to foster insurrectional ideas.[115] The Jacobins' strategy, then, consisted of fomenting revolt through "extra-legal organs,"[116] especially the Comité de l'Évêché, a kind of "Central Committee" of the Parisian sections. The Comité in fact established a "Comité insurrection-nel," which included the Enragé Jean Varlet. However, just because Robespierre and the Jacobins wished to use the Comité insurrectionnel as a weapon against the Girondins, it was not necessarily a passive agent of the Montagnards' manipulations. Quite to the contrary, Varlet's presence added a particularly radical dimension to the Comité's activities.

The Jacobins thus played "a political game with uncommon virtuosity,"[117] as they needed to challenge the legitimacy of the Girondin representatives while at the same time maintaining the legitimacy of the parliamentary and representative system. To borrow a contemporary trope, the strike against the Girondins of the Convention had to be "surgical" so as to avoid "collateral damage" that might destroy the Convention's authority and, consequently, the Jacobins' political power. That is why Robespierre strove to restrict popular action to an insurrection against "corrupt" representatives. As Slavin suggests, Robespierre wanted a "moral" rather than a "brutal" insurrection because this would preserve the authority of the Convention, the political institution of the revolutionary bourgeoisie, while neutralizing its political adversaries.[118] Robespierre thereby showed once again his adherence to a representative conception of democracy.

On May 23, the Gironde had Varlet—"for whom the Convention was but a 'law-shop' "[119]—placed under arrest. His brief detention (he was released four days later) did not keep Varlet from playing a crucial role in the preparation of the insurrection against the Gironde. On May 29, Robespierre publically endorsed the idea of an insurrection, but the endorsement "stayed within strictly parliamentary bounds."[120] On the evening of May 31, Varlet declared at the Évêché that the insurgents were sovereign and could destroy the authority of the Convention.[121] Hence, whereas the Montagne and the Enragés shared a common target (the Girondins), the same was not true of their respective aims in the insurrection.

It is precisely in this regard that the action of the Enragés stands as a "laboratory" of plebeian politics. The Jacobins' desire to circumscribe, indeed to domesticate, the insurrection was confronted with the plebs' determination, conveyed through Varlet's words, to go beyond the strict framework of representative democracy. The Enragés' struggle during the insurrection against the Gironde thus heralded the fight of the Parisian sans-culottes to exercise directly political sovereignty in the sectional societies. The conflict between these two conceptions of democracy was manifested in the political action of the Enragés. For example, on May 31, under the leadership of Roux and Varlet, the sans-culottes swarmed into the Convention and presented petitions calling for the arrest of the Girondin representatives as well as "the creation of a sans-culotte army; and . . . a temporary restriction of the right to vote to sans-culottes."[122] The Jacobins' response, on the other hand, attested once again to their hostility toward the direct democracy demanded by the Enragés. To ward off the widening of the insurrection, which might undermine the legitimacy of the representative bodies, the Jacobin-controlled "official bodies" succeeded in weakening the influence of the Enragés by reining in the "extra-legal power"[123] (i.e., the Évêché) at the head of the insurrection against the Girondins. Though the insurrection did in fact take place on June 2, it was confined to the political framework determined by the Montagnard bourgeoisie. By shutting out the Enragés, the Jacobins made sure that the Évêché would not seize power, thereby protecting both their own power base and the interests of the bourgeoisie.[124]

While the arrest of the Gironde representatives signified a radicalization of the Revolution (as evidenced by the sectional societies, the policy of the Terror, etc.), it did not result in a thoroughgoing transformation of the representative system. True, the political project of the Enragés was for a time embodied in the sectional democracy of the sans-culottes. Nevertheless, for liberal historians the insurrection against the Gironde marked a point of no return for the French Revolution. For it was from that point on that the "hideous" revolution emerged and tainted the merits of the "beautiful revolution"[125] of 1789. The putative horror of the French Revolution in the spring of 1793 is for some observers due precisely to the assault on parliamentarianism perpetrated in the insurrection. This bias is very cogently articulated by Denis Richet:

June 2, 1793, marked an important turning point in the history of the Revolution. Until then the whole bourgeois revolution rested, even in democratic dreams, on the dogma of representative government. This was a late-eighteenth-century innovation. By reawakening the old popular passion for direct power, June 2 dealt a mortal blow to parliamentarianism. The assembly found itself a prisoner, and it mattered little whether it was held today by the sections or tomorrow by the army. . . . The day it accepted the violation of the representative principle, the parliament renounced its own legitimacy.[126]

Richet's analysis highlights the crux of the struggle of the Enragés and the sans-culottes against representative democracy and parliamentarianism. It also makes quite clear that the plebeian political practices of the sans-culottes were in opposition to the essential components of the "dominant political configuration" of modernity. Furthermore, rather than presenting themselves as "new grandees" wishing to exert a different form of domination on the plebeian movement, the Enragés acted more as spokespersons than as "leaders" of the plebs.[127] This is what enabled them to avoid the pitfalls of plebeian leadership.

THE INSURRECTION AGAINST THE THERMIDOREANS

Whereas the insurrection against the Gironde marked the beginning of the sans-culottes' sectional democracy and the blossoming of plebeian politics in Year II, the insurrection against the Thermidoreans in Year III indubitably marked the end of the political experiment of the Parisian sans-culottes. For "the period from 9 Thermidor Year II to the advent of the Directory [was] marked by a violent reaction and an attempt at bourgeois stabilization of the Revolution." The "reaction" and "stabilization" necessarily required the prior neutralization of the plebs' political strength, in particular the eradication of "the democratic ideas of 1793 and Year II."[128] The goal of the Thermidorean regime at that point was to do away openly with popular political action and the notion of the sans-culottes directly exercising political sovereignty.

The neutralization of the sectional societies was carried out by the Jacobin revolutionary government. In the aftermath of Robespierre's death, the purpose of the Thermidoreans, the "new grandees," was to pursue the project of state Jacobinism. Following the liquidation of the sans-culottes' form of political organization, the only road open to the Parisian plebs was the practice of insurrection. Hence the importance of the idea of insurrection for the sans-culottes in Year II: "The insurrections of Germinal and Prairial were the ultimate manifestations [of the] autonomous *sans-culotte* movement." We have chosen to limit our examination of the insurrection of Year III to the Prairial insurrection, owing to its "considerable significance."[129] According to the historian Kåre Tønnesson,

> the failed insurrection [of Prairial] allow[ed] the government to strike a blow against the sans-culotterie and paralyze the popular movement. The repression [took] the form of mass arrests and disarmament. The Jacobin and sans-culotte left ceased to pose a threat to the bourgeois Republic. Not before 1830 would a new popular insurrection break out.[130]

Clearly, then, the crushing of the Prairial insurrection had catastrophic consequences for the plebs. In anticipation of the next phase of the plebeian experience, the effects of this suppression on the "social movement" seemed to foreshadow those of the "bloody week" that tragically marked the end of the Paris Commune of 1871. Analyzing the events of Prairial is also useful because of the demands put forward by the insurgent plebs, demands linking the resolution of the social question to the exercise of political rights.

The political apprenticeship of the sans-culottes in the sectional societies played a major part in the unfolding of the Prairial insurrection. The political experience of Year II had also facilitated the dissemination among the common people of specific political ideas, including that of the right to insurrection. For Tønnesson, it was part of a veritable *"insurrectional ideology"*[131] that inspired the sans-culottes of Year III. When the public authorities do not abide by the wishes of the general population, the people have the right to rise up. In doing so, they temporarily suspend the state's political power in order to exercise it directly.

The Prairial insurrection can also be explained by the particular political and economic circumstances of the Thermidorean reaction. On the political level, the Thermidoreans explicitly attacked the political movement of sectional democracy. The attacks took two forms: "persecution of sectional personnel" and *"dé-sans-cullotisation."* On one hand, the Thermidoreans encouraged internal struggles against former sectional "leaders." On the other, they forcibly ejected the sans-culottes from public life and, especially, from the state administration. *Dé-sans-cullotisation* also involved the public vilification of the sans-culottes: "The Thermidorean reaction saw in 'simplicity' not virtue but rather vulgarity and unenlightenment."[132] The ignominy was all the more jarring because before Thermidor the sans-culottes had enjoyed widespread esteem and even a degree of prestige.

On the economic level, Thermidor was a period of pronounced inequalities and severe hardship for the plebs. While the triumphant bourgeoisie was increasingly ostentatious in parading its wealth, the sans-culottes were hard hit by food shortages. The contrast between the wealth of the few and the poverty of the many was so blatant as to arouse nearly unprecedented discontent in the capital. The situation was depicted in stark terms by Georges Duval, a contemporary member of the bourgeoisie: "The balls continued, and so did the famine, so that upon leaving the dance halls between midnight and one in the morning, the first thing one saw was lines already formed at the bakers' door."[133] The people's anger, provoked by "suffering" as well as by the "glaring"[134] inequalities, was expressed in the form of insurrection.

The failure of the first attempt at insurrection in Germinal opened the door to harsher political repression and even more pronounced economic inequalities. Yet the popular movement was not demoralized by this political defeat. The intensification of Thermidorean political repression and the worsening of economic hardship (there was a veritable famine in Floreal) actually emboldened the sans-culottes and incited them to renewed insurrection.[135] The days of Prairial were looming. It was the distribution of a pamphlet on Prairial 1, Year III, that triggered the second insurrection against the Thermidor régime. The pamphlet, titled "Insurrection du Peuple pour obtenir du Pain and reconquérir ses Droits" (People's insurrection for bread and to regain their rights),[136] paved the way for the insurrection by setting out its political objectives. The issue of subsistence was predominant among the plebeians' demands along with that of political rights.

The people, considering that we are being inhumanly starved to death by the government . . . have made the following determination: . . . Today, without delay, the citizens of Paris, both men and women, will proceed en masse to the National Convention to demand: (1) bread; (2) the abolition of the "revolutionary government," of which every faction, each in turn, has taken advantage to ruin, starve, and subjugate the people; (3) . . . the immediate proclamation and establishment of the Democratic Constitution of 1793; (4) the removal of the current government . . . and the arrest [of its] members.[137]

The document clearly articulated not just the political goals of the insurrection but also the means needed to achieve them. The sans-culottes were to converge en masse on the Convention in "fraternal disorder"[138] for the purpose of imposing their demands on the Thermidorean regime. In addition, soldiers were invited to join the insurrection. As a result of this mass uprising, the powers of the Convention were suspended, and the people invested themselves with legislative, executive, and legal powers.

The watchword of the Prairial insurrection—"*Du pain et la Constitution de '93!*" ("Bread and the Constitution of '93!")[139]—concisely and instructively linked social demands with political ones. By demanding food staples (bread) and political rights (the Constitution of 1793), the sans-culottes made "the issue of subsistence dependent on a libertarian revolutionary outcome."[140] Perhaps, then, they were drawing the contours of a public space different from that of the revolutionary bourgeoisie, one amalgamating the resolution of the social question with the unmediated exercise of popular sovereignty. A public space of this sort refuses to distinguish between the fundamental dimensions of human existence, that is, between humans as a species of animals governed by the biological order and humans as *zoon politikon* fulfilling themselves in and through political action.[141]

On the early morning of Prairial 1, the alarm bell rang out in the poor suburbs of Saint-Antoine and Marceau, signaling the start of the insurrection. The mobilization was massive, thanks especially to the strong involvement of women.[142] In Paris, the most intense insurrectional activity took place in the traditionally sans-culotte eastern and central districts. In response, the Thermidorean Convention declared "leaders of demonstrations" to be "outlaws" and called on "all good citizens" to take up arms.[143] The insurgents converged on the Convention and, with the women in the forefront, succeeded in laying siege, taking advantage of the situation to read their political program out loud—without, however, trying to implement it. Nor did they even attempt to occupy the "offices of the government Committees," leaving the Committees free to prepare the Thermidoreans' return to political power. The primary goal of the government Committees was to eject the insurgents from the Convention so as to "give the 'oppressed national representation' its freedom back."[144] In order to safely expel the insurgents, the Thermidoreans waited for the crowd surrounding the Convention to disperse. Toward midnight, the government battalions removed the sans-culottes without much difficulty. This was the beginning of the end of the Prairial insurrection. "Over the next few days the insurrection petered out."[145]

The Prairial defeat brought heavy political consequences for the popular movement. The Thermidoreans decided "to put an end *once and for all* to the 'insurrectional machinery' "[146] that the plebeian movement had become. They disarmed the sans-culottes, made massive arrests (ten thousand sans-culottes were arrested within a few days),[147] purged the sections, and, as the coup de grâce, adopted the Fructidor 5 Constitution of Year III suppressing the right to popular insurrection.[148] By means of this fierce and merciless repression, the Thermidoreans secured the political hegemony of the bourgeoisie and dealt such a heavy blow to the plebeian movement that it would take a number of years before it would once again be able to act on the French political stage. The sans-culottes found themselves in profound disarray, having been deprived by the Jacobins of the sectional societies in Year II and then losing the right to insurrection in Year III. "After Prairial," writes Daniel Guérin, "the mass movement was suppressed for a long time. Desperate, deprived of their guides, the *bras nus* sank into doubt and apathy."[149] The work of the Thermidoreans was taken up and pursued by the Directoire, a veritable "liquidation regime."[150] For the sans-culottes of Paris the Revolution was truly at an end.

Through an analysis of the sectional societies, the form of political organization of the Parisian sans-culottes, and of the practice of insurrection, we can observe the resurgence of the plebeian principle in modern history. Though short-lived (hence occurring within the temporality of the "gap"), that resurgence nevertheless allows us to grasp the sans-culottes' contribution to the communalist and agoraphile tradition. The struggle against centralization and the great specialists stands as a reminder of the originary link between politics and action, that is, between on one hand the exercise of public power and human freedom and, on the other hand, the link between politics and everyday life. The sans-culottes of Paris also bequeathed to the history of modern democracy certain elements essential to its realization as an organizing principle of collective existence in contemporary Western societies: the idea of the natural political equality of human beings, the necessity of conflict, the rejection of a management approach to collective existence, etc. For its part, the practice of insurrection reveals how profoundly attached the plebeians were to the principle of the direct exercise of popular sovereignty. This political practice of the plebs, in both its "moral" and "brutal" incarnations, stemmed from a conception of democracy upheld by the common people. The purpose of insurrection was to put an end to tyranny and to stop the authoritarian drift of the constituted powers through the effective exercise of public power. As a tyrannicidal weapon, insurrection clearly participated in the construction of a people's politics (communalism) as well as in the advent of political freedom (agoraphilia). Ultimately, the sans-culottes' practice of insurrection sought to democratize the political sphere rather than engender a new form of domination of certain individuals over others.

But the action of the Parisian sans-culottes is not a unique phenomenon in modernity. Among the experiences sharing in this tradition is that of the English Jacobins at the time, described by E. P. Thompson, when the English working class was in the making.[151] The English Jacobins are all the more appropriate as a case in point because they belonged to the same historical period as the sans-culottes and shared the same desire for liberty: "*Both* sans-culottes *and* Jacobins . . . compell[ed] the people to be free."[152] An analysis of the English Jacobins' form of political organization—the London Corresponding Society— should therefore facilitate our understanding of the political expression of this desire for liberty.

4
THE LONDON CORRESPONDING SOCIETY AND THE ENGLISH JACOBINS

Hence, every large workshop and manufactory is a sort of political society,
which no act of parliament can silence, and no magistrate disperse. . . . [A] sort of
Socratic spirit will necessarily grow up, wherever large bodies of men assemble.
—John Thelwall, *The Rights of Nature*

E. P. THOMPSON'S MAGNUM OPUS, *THE MAKING OF THE ENGLISH Working Class*, constitutes a genuine work of political thought that illuminates the inventiveness and richness of the English plebs' political practices, especially as regards English Jacobinism in the late eighteenth century. Indeed, he attributes the transformation of social relationships that occurred during the Industrial Revolution as much to the collective action of the plebs as to the structural transformations of the economy, the international situation, or the various religious movements. Thompson maintains that the politically and economically excluded members of society had their own values and political practices. As a reminder of the tumultuous and adversarial world of plebeian political practices, this political reading of the beginnings of the English working class opens onto "a renewed consideration of the specificity of modern democracy."[1]

The implication of Thompson's analysis is that the London Corresponding Society (LCS) was the English Jacobins' major contribution to communalism and agoraphilia. Just like the Parisian sectional societies, the LCS was a decisive political body in that it set the tone for and established the parameters of the English Jacobins' actions both in London and the rest of the country. It represented the core of Jacobinism and, what is more, the hub of the English oppositional forces' deployment. The LCS was thus the site from which the plebeian principle could assert itself on the political scene of eighteenth-century England.[2]

ON THE PLEBS: THINKING WITH THOMPSON AGAINST THOMPSON

In an article that first appeared in the *Journal of Social History* in 1974, Thompson outlines a definition of the plebs.[3] In his view, the opposition between patricians and plebeians originated in the language practices of the English ruling classes in the eighteenth century,[4] who, in order to identify a split within English society, appropriated terminology drawn from Roman antiquity.[5] In Rome, as noted earlier, the plebs were initially conceived of as a subpolitical entity. But in the case of England, the patrician/plebeian "polarization of class relations doesn't thereby deprive the plebs of all political existence." But, as Thompson points out, the plebs must not be confused with the working class. Unlike the latter, the plebs had no definite "class consciousness" or any specific idea of their political objectives. Yet they were indeed a political actor, as evidenced by the numerous upheavals that marked the eighteenth century. While not displaying any "deference" toward the English patricians, plebeian political culture was in no way revolutionary or even protorevolutionary. They did not seek to overturn the social or political order. The upheavals that they brought about were the result of "riots but not rebellions; direct actions but not democratic organizations."[6] Nevertheless, to avoid conceiving of the plebs as a primitive, or even subpolitical, political figure, one must resituate them in their proper political context rather than view them through the lens of the working class's development in the nineteenth century.

Thompson identifies three features of plebeian politics. First, he sees a tradition of anonymously denouncing political power. Eighteenth-century English society was characterized by clientelism as well as *simulated* plebeian deference. The risks involved in openly declaring one's opposition to the regime were in fact great enough to give rise to a tradition of anonymity. By denouncing the injustices of the English system incognito, the plebeians voiced their indignation without at the same time putting themselves and their families in jeopardy. The proliferation of "anonymous letter[s]" intended to sow fear among the patricians is emblematic of this first characteristic of plebeian politics. Second, the political actions of the plebs took the form of a sort of "counter-theatre" responding to the patricians' "contrived style" of theater. The plebs affirmed their political presence by creating a theater of threats and sedition. Here one finds the authentically political dimension of the plebeian "crowd" loudly execrating domination when those entitled to govern made public appearances. England in the eighteenth century in fact witnessed numerous popular demonstrations against political leaders, and even the king was the target of such expressions of plebeian animosity. The last feature of plebeian politics was the capacity to carry out direct and swift actions expressing the plebs' political disgruntlement. This characteristic includes the first two, since such actions were performed by anonymous crowds proceeding in a theatrical fashion. For Thompson, riots provoked by food shortages represent typical cases of the plebs' direct and swift action. However, refuting the notion that the crowd acted "blindly," he affirms that it was "often disciplined, had clear objectives, knew how to negotiate with the political authorities and above all brought its strength swiftly to bear."[7]

Thompson acknowledges that his idea of the plebs remains derivative of a Marxist conception of class conflicts.[8] But he refrains from ascribing a class identity to the plebs because, with regard to the historical development of the popular movement, the period in question precedes the "making of the working class." To better think *with* Thompson, his definition of the plebs obliges us to think *against* him. He discerns a process of transformation of the plebs into a "working class" that in our view corresponds to a plebeian experience, that is, the plebs' attainment of political dignity. In other words, the fact that Thompson's reading of the plebs remains within the Marxist framework occults their political dimension. If one adheres to his conceptualization, it is difficult to recognize the democratic and revolutionary nature of plebeian action. Curiously, E. P. Thompson's work seems to provide elements for an agoraphile and communalist plebeian politics while at the same time remaining ambivalent as to the acting political subject: is it the working class or the plebs? Notwithstanding this ambiguity, our task will be to locate in his work those elements testifying to the political affirmation of the plebs.

ON THE ENGLISH JACOBINS

Thompson contends that the English Jacobins cannot be confused with the French Jacobins. Instead of being composed of an educated elite, as was the case in France, the English Jacobins included working people, some of them illiterate, as well as professionals, all of them motivated by radical political ideals. It is in the sans-culottes that Thompson sees a French equivalent to the English Jacobins: "These English Jacobins . . . resembled the *menu peuple* who made the French Revolution. . . . Indeed, they resemble less the Jacobins than the *sans-culottes* of the Paris 'sections,' whose zealous egalitarianism underpinned Robespierre's revolutionary war dictatorship of 1793–4."[9]

Yet the English Jacobin "strongholds" were not the recently industrialized cities but rather the old urban industrial centers sinking into inactivity because of the new factories and whose social-economic makeup was based on urban, sometimes specialized, craftspeople. Shoemakers comprised the "hard centre" of English Jacobinism, which lends weight to the comparison with the sans-culottes of Year II.[10] In their fight against domination they radicalized the principles framed by one of the most important theoreticians of English Jacobinism, Thomas Paine. Uncompromising opposition to the monarchy, the aristocracy, and the state and its taxes, as well as the goal of establishing an "absolute" democracy—such were the shoemakers' basic tenets.

But shoemakers were only one component of the English Jacobin movement. Just like the Parisian sans-culottes, this movement's social composition was heterogeneous. The Jacobins of England were supported by "small shopkeepers, . . . printers and booksellers, medical men, schoolmasters, engravers, small masters, and Dissenting clergy at one end; and . . . porters, coal-heavers, labourers, soldiers and sailors at the other."[11] In short, the composition of the English Jacobins can be said to reflect accurately what Claude Lefort calls the "originary division of the social," that is, the community's division into two "humors," that of the Grandees, who wish to dominate, and that of the common people, who desire freedom. The English Jacobins tended to rally the common people (part of the many), in other words, those "below," for whom domination remained a constitutive experience of everyday life.

The writings of John Thelwall, another theorist close to the militant base of the English plebeian movement,[12] very effectively illustrate the difference between the English and French Jacobins. His analysis of the French Revolution and the Terror, more specifically, turns out to be neither Jacobin nor Girondin. While deploring the excesses of the Revolution, Thelwall applauds its contribution to emancipation and its recognition of natural equality. His critique of the Terror makes no concession to the counterrevolutionaries and other opponents of the advent of democratic modernity. The Terror is not, in his estimation, the product of the implementation of revolutionary principles but of "the old leaven of revenge, corruption and suspicion which was generated by the systematic cruelties of the old despotism." At Robespierre's death, Thelwall even drew a parallel between Robespierre and Pitt, the head of the English government and prime mover of the counterrevolutionary mobilization in Great Britain. Despite the excesses of the Terror, Thelwall insisted on being indentified as a Jacobin because the principles of Jacobinism coincided with his most profound political convictions. He thus defines Jacobinism as *"a large and comprehensive system of reform, not professing to be built upon the authorities and principles of the Gothic customary."*[13]

In comparison with its French counterpart, English Jacobinism was an "oppositional Jacobinism" that developed *"outside* of power." The difference between it and French Jacobinism resided to a great extent in their differing outlooks and orientations. Oppositional Jacobinism remained firmly anti-tyrannical in thought and action and therefore "exempt from the accusation" of being the womb of future totalitarian regimes.[14] At the heart of the English Jacobins' political vision was the recognition of a split between the governors and the governed.[15] In this way English Jacobinism sought to open the political sphere to the excluded. It also promoted humanist values—including internationalism, freedom of thought, social equality, and political tolerance—while at the same time shunning the thirst for revenge on the dominators, a thirst that only the physical elimination of its enemies could quench.

Eighteenth-Century England and the French Revolution

By way of explaining the political solidity of the London Corresponding Society as a form of organization, Thompson endeavors to demonstrate how its convictions were forged,[16] in particular through contact with two distinct phenomena: the subpolitical beliefs[17] of eighteenth-century England and the French Revolution. By underscoring the Englishness of oppositional Jacobinism, Thompson heads off attempts to reduce it to a minor phenomenon of French origin and hence foreign to English political history and tradition. Quite to the contrary, Thompson argues, English Jacobinism (and its forms of political organization) shares in the history of England and was part of an underground tradition too often forgotten by standard historiography. He also emphasizes that popular beliefs are modified by events and current affairs such that they gain undeniable political effectiveness.

Subpolitical popular beliefs tying the eighteenth to the nineteenth century stemmed from the widespread notion of "the Englishman's 'birthright,'" an idea deriving from the equation of the "Constitution [with] Liberty." According to popular thinking, the Constitution granted everyone the enjoyment of certain freedoms. Among them were freedom from foreign control, freedom from absolute power, equality before the law, freedom from arbitrary arrest, freedom to travel, and freedom to sell one's labor power. According to Thompson, these freedoms "embody and reflect a moral consensus in which authority at times shared, and of which at all times it was bound to take account." Thompson therefore maintains that the subpolitical attitude of England's plebs in the eighteenth century was more "anti-absolutist" than prodemocratic, that is, favorable to greater openness of the political sphere in English society. Englishmen thus saw themselves as having few affirmative rights but as nevertheless shielded from the abuse of state power by a set of laws. This rather liberal individualism could, however, turn into political revolt (albeit short-lived) when "free-born Englishmen" felt their basic rights had been violated. The legitimacy of the right to rebel was rooted in the idea that "the Glorious Revolution afforded a constitutional precedent for the right to riot in resistance to oppression."[18] Moreover, in the minds of the English plebs, the Glorious Revolution of 1688 seemed to take precedence over the one of 1640–1642, the first modern revolution. Although the English Jacobins in fact took up the demands put forward in the previous century by the Levellers, this was not an indication that the first English revolution was of central importance for them.[19]

The recourse to constitutionalism was, according to Thompson, the "central paradox" of the eighteenth century as well as the "'illusion of the epoch.'" That political theory was imbued at the time with constitutionalism is evidenced by the fact that conservative thinkers and their liberal adversaries alike confined their political conceptualization to the limits established in 1688. The paradox, at least inasmuch as the plebs was concerned, was that this theory allowed the simultaneous establishment of both "a bloody penal code" and "a *liberal* and, at times, meticulous administration and interpretation of the laws."[20] In other words, while the penal code was openly biased in favor of property owners, hence of the well-to-do few to the detriment of the many, the latter could nevertheless find effective protection in certain constitutional provisions (e.g., habeas corpus and popular juries) against arbitrary legal measures. Hence, the plebeians' recourse to the Constitution to justify antidespotic rebellion. The same sort of recourse was also to be observed among the French plebs, as demonstrated by the watchword of the sans-culottes' Prairial insurrection in Year III: "Bread and the Constitution of '93!"[21]

Another convention of plebeian constitutionalism was the demand that the "free-born Englishman" be left alone. The desire that the state not interfere in people's daily lives was one of the primary subpolitical attitudes of the eighteenth century. This was clearly expressed in the rejection of a standing army and of recruitment through press-gangs. The same can be said of the creation of a true police force, which the plebs instinctively knew would act in the service of the despotism of the few. The potentially authoritarian nature of a police force was understood to be an extension of a tyrannical system designed to threaten public freedom,[22] especially because the expansion of the central state's powers meant that the local traditions and customs dear to the plebs were being called into question. Thus, beyond its exclusively individualist aspects, the "right to be left alone" also embraced a collective dimension.

Alongside the plebs' wish to be left alone, there was the "belief in the equality of rich and poor before the law." The sensationalist popular press reported cases where aristocrats and bourgeois magnates were condemned, thereby strengthening the impression of equality. Of course, some radicals cast doubt on this formal equality by stressing the role of personal fortune in the legal process. But even the most fervent English Jacobins were convinced "that the rule of law was the distinguishing inheritance of the 'free-born' Englishman." For Thompson, it was thanks to this defensive stance that, by a dialectical reversal, demands for new rights arose on the English political scene. John Wilkes, for example, went from defending ancient rights to adopting an offensive position advocating the extension of political rights to all British subjects.[23] His arguments (like those of the conservatives) were always based on recourse to tradition, in the sense that there existed a constitutional convention in support of granting the free-born Englishman new political rights. This departure from the defensive posture enabled the initiation of a process favoring the growth of freedom in the community beyond the mere defense of acquired rights rooted in political tradition.

The new surge of demands took the form of an "extraparliamentary" pressure group known as the Platform, which set specific political objectives and used various methods for raising public awareness: publications, large rallies and meetings, petitions, etc. This unprecedented form of political organization added, "*in practice*," a new political dimension that went beyond recourse "to the accepted procedures of the Constitution." It thus helped to transcend reference to the Constitution, a reference that ensured the legitimacy of certain institutions responsible for the political subjection of the plebs, such as the monarchy. For the plebs to go from simply holding subpolitical beliefs to being a full-fledged political actor, it was necessary to transcend the constitutional reference. "For a plebeian movement to arise," Thompson writes, "it was essential to escape from these categories altogether and set forward far wider democratic claims."[24] But it would take more than "extraparliamentary" practices to put an end to plebeian constitutionalism. It was on this level that the impact of the French Revolution was most keenly felt in England, through the dissemination of the theoretical writings of Thomas Paine, a leading light of English Jacobinism.

Before discussing Paine's political works, they must be located within their proper historical context, that is, the English response to the French Revolution and, more specifically, the debate sparked by the writings of Edmund Burke.

The year 1789 marked the introduction into history and political practice of a precedent with new implications: a Constitution "drawn up, in the light of reason and from first principles, which threw 'the meagre, stale, forbidding ways/ custom, law, and statute' into the shadows." But the French Revolution inevitably clashed with the conservative sensibilities of the English ruling classes, of which Burke was a representative. In *Reflections on the Revolution in France* (1790), Burke affirms the importance of tradition in politics, as this alone can ensure the connection between the present, past, and future. The French Revolution is not an example to be followed because its aim is to put a definite end to the authority and legitimacy of the ancien régime, thereby breaking the thread of tradition. However, the importance of tradition in Burke's thought transcends the strictly political framework and involves "man's moral nature in general." But, like Paine, Thompson stresses that Burke is more concerned with the "moral nature" of the many, whom he describes as the "swinish multitude," than that of the "corrupt aristocracy."[25] Burke's reading of the French Revolution therefore bears the stamp of class interests and is a plea for the maintenance of the political status quo in England, that is, the preservation of the "patricians'" instruments of domination.[26]

Thomas Paine's *Rights of Man* (1791–1792) was written as a plebeian answer to Burke's *Reflections*, and for Thompson it remains "a foundation-text of the English working-class movement."[27] For Paine, tradition represents the authority of the dead and as such must not restrict the action of the living. Quite the contrary, every new generation has the right to determine the institutions and rules of democratic collective existence. These two principles provide Paine with grounds for challenging English constitutionalism and the conservative recourse to tradition: a country governed according to principles of tradition bases its legitimacy on "conquest and superstition," that is, on purely arbitrary phenomena. Among the principles marked by contingency but lying nonetheless at the heart of the English political system Paine firmly and boldly censures the hereditary principle. Here is how he portrays the establishment of monarchic systems:

> A banditti of ruffians overrun a country, and lay it under contributions. Their power being thus established, the chief of the band contrived to lose the name of Robber in that of Monarch; and hence the origin of Monarch and Kings.[28]

Using vivid, colloquial language, Paine then calls into question the hereditary succession of the monarchy, which tends to treat people as mere chattel that royal families pass on through inheritance. Moreover, kings succeed each other like "animals," that is, without any distinctions as to the talents and abilities required to govern the kingdom. It is enough merely to meet the biological requirement of being human and to find oneself in a position to inherit in order to accede to the highest political functions.

Paine portrays society as divided along class lines between taxpayers on one hand and, on the other, those who live on those taxes. The English Constitution is openly biased in favor of the idle class drawn from among the few, thus placing the state and its actions on the side of the well-to-do, to the detriment of the interests of the many. The opposition between these two classes gives rise to a "war of the propertied and the unpropertied,"[29] because of the rights of the poor being stripped by the wealthy, which in turn engenders the plebeians' desire to dispossess the wealthy of their property. Thompson points out that this political vision is close to an anarchist theory of politics. In his view, what Paine wishes is not the reform of the state but indeed its elimination. Paine writes, "the instant formal Government is abolished, society begins to act."[30] He believes that local structures of political administration can provide society with the tools needed to ensure the good conduct of public affairs.

Beyond this twofold theory (admittedly somewhat cursory) of society and the state, Paine framed a series of social measures that made his book hugely popular with the English plebs. Progressive income tax, welfare payments to families, free public schools, the right to a retirement pension, social housing, maternity benefits, and funeral expense allowances were among the ideas that enthused the many and lent originality to Paine's work. These political propositions supplied the concepts and arguments underpinning what would soon become a key demand of the plebs' political action: radical egalitarianism. Paine's insight also allowed him to "set a course towards the social legislation of the 20th century." Nevertheless, Paine did not seek to expand the state's economic influence and role. He was too averse to the modern state to want to grant it additional responsibilities in the life of the community.[31]

Thomas Paine had a decisive impact on English Jacobinism.[32] Because of his defense of the destitute, his denunciation of the structures of political domination, and his desire to open up the political sphere to everyone, he was in reality an advocate of the notion that the public sphere must be inhabited by a diversity of opinions and currents.[33] This belief in a society where each individual has the right and duty to think and speak freely in fact constituted one of the characteristics of the oppositional Jacobinism that arose in England. As E. P. Thompson puts it, Paine "saw that in the constitutional debates of the eighteenth century 'the nation was always left out of the question.' By bringing the nation *into* the question, he was bound to set in motion forces which he could neither control nor foresee. That is what democracy is about."[34]

This is how popular subpolitical beliefs dating from the eighteenth century were transformed through contact with the French Revolution, whose effect was to mobilize the plebs in support of properly democratic demands. Ultimately, the political turbulence of the many was not merely a repercussion of the French Revolution. "It was an English agitation, of impressive dimensions, for English democracy."[35] And, in political terms, Paine's writings as well as the tradition of the "free-born Englishman" were what allowed the plebs to fully assume their obligations concerning the human political condition. What they needed thereafter was to discover a form of political organization that could serve as a vehicle for the demands of English Jacobinism.

"THAT THE NUMBER OF OUR MEMBERS BE UNLIMITED"

The London Corresponding Society (LCS) gathered for the first time in January 1792. The nine individuals present in the tavern where the inaugural meeting was held came to an agreement on parliamentary reform whose goal would be the franchise for all British subjects. The first "principle" of this new form of political organization aptly illustrates its political orientation: "That the number of our Members be unlimited."[36] The founder of the LCS, the cobbler Thomas Hardy, describes the first meeting in these terms:

> After having had their bread and cheese and porter for supper, as usual, and their pipes afterwards, with some conversation on the hardness of the times and the dearness of all the necessaries of life . . . the business for which they had met was brought forward—*Parliamentary Reform*—an important subject to be deliberated upon and dealt with by such a class of men.[37]

At this initial gathering they also developed the general plan for a political organization able to rally the many and encourage their participation in public life through the promotion of political education.[38]

After two weeks, the LCS grew from nine members to twenty-five and then to over two thousand six months later. The conditions for membership were simple: answer in the affirmative three questions, the main one of which concerned the appropriateness of extending the franchise to all Englishmen. As a political body, the LCS held debates on parliamentary reform. Such debates presented the reasons why it was essential for England and the advent of

English democracy to extend the franchise. As indicated by its name, the London Corresponding Society sought as well to establish ties with radical political organizations throughout the kingdom. The LCS allowed those excluded from the political sphere to meet, discuss political issues, and correspond with other similar English organizations.

The LCS is often regarded as the first properly working-class form of political organization in England. Historically speaking, this is incorrect since it had been preceded by corresponding societies in Sheffield, Manchester, Norwich,[39] and other English cities. Thompson also notes that after the American War of Independence (1775–1783), there existed in London political debating societies attended by workers and artisans. "It may become more accurate to think of the L.C.S. as a 'popular Radical' society than as 'working-class.'"[40] Given its heterogeneous social makeup and its political demands, the LCS was more akin to a popular radical or, one might say, "revolutionary" and "plebeian" society. It was "revolutionary" in relation to English politics at the time and "plebeian" because it was made up of individuals who refused political exclusion in order to transform themselves into *zoon politikon*.

"Radical" London was receptive to the LCS, and its influence spread among the various strata of London society. It could count on the participation of the patrons of the taverns, cafés, and "Dissenting Churches off Piccadilly, Fleet Street and the Strand, where the self-educated journeyman might rub shoulders with the printer, the shop-keeper, the engraver or the young attorney."[41] It also mobilized the older working-class communities located to the east and south of the Thames. Thompson points out that the social fabric of London had always been more variegated and fluid than was the case in the cities of the Midlands and the north, where there were a limited number of staple industries. The diversity of "radical" London partly explains why the dissident movements based there rarely displayed strong ideological cohesion and political solidity. In addition, the English metropolis was more open to new ideas than were the large provincial industrial cities.

It was precisely this openness to new ideas that made the LCS the hub and "junction-point" of the English revolutionary movement. While other corresponding societies may have been older than the LCS, they were not as dynamic nor as well disposed toward the new ideas and proposals that underpinned the plebeian democratic movement. Furthermore, in comparison with other corresponding societies, the LCS appeared to be a new form of organization containing the embryonic features of "working-class organisation[s]" to come. The secretary of the LCS was a worker, weekly membership fees remained modest, and its deliberations, blending political and economic issues, took place according to formal procedures that were strictly adhered to. Moreover, the LCS's meetings combined political action with socialization and interaction among friends. Thompson nevertheless stresses that "there is [in the Society] the determination to propagate opinions and to organise the converted, embodied in the leading rule: 'That the number of our Members be unlimited.' "[42] That rule, which was paramount for the LCS, allowed it to recruit members among both the destitute and the well-to-do open to its radical political ideas.[43]

The LCS's internal structure was based on "divisions" that could include no more than thirty members. When a division exceeded that limit (but not until it was forty-five or sixty strong), it was obliged to split in two. Each section appointed a delegate to the weekly General Committee, as well as a subdelegate acting only in an advisory capacity. The delegates were subject to recall by the divisions, which were entitled "to be consulted on questions of principle."[44] It can be seen from the minutes that the LCS's meetings were altogether democratic.[45] Discussion between the Committee and the divisions was vigorous, and the divisions kept an eye on the powers of the General Committee. After 1794, to deal with government spies, the divisions granted significant powers to an executive, the "committee of correspondence of the General Committee, composed of about five members."[46]

Though it may be difficult to confirm the exact number of LCS members, especially because figures from various sources are inconsistent or lack credibility, Thompson states that the high points came in the fall of 1792, the spring of 1794, and during the second half of 1795. In his estimation, LCS membership for the period between early 1794 and late 1795 can be broken down as follows: two thousand active members, five thousand paying members, and "a paper membership" of over ten thousand. Whatever the precise number of its members, the LCS represented a vigorous political force.[47]

With respect to the financial management of the LCS, Thompson asserts that it was always meticulous, with "severe attention to democratic principle."[48] For instance, the LCS covered travel expenses and even paid certain delegates, in keeping with the principle of payment for services. This also protected the LCS against the influence of affluent individuals who might wish to neutralize its political strength.

One of the LCS's major areas of activity was education. Francis Place, who played a key role in the Society, underscores the instructive nature of the meetings held in the private homes. Readings followed by discussions enabled members to educate themselves and acquire practical and theoretical political knowledge. By drawing the many away from their preferred forms of entertainment, the LCS had significant "moral effects." But the LCS's events were not as peaceful and educational as Place would have us believe. As reported by informants working on behalf of William Pitt's government, "Almost everybody speaks . . . and there is always a very great noise, till the delegate gets up. People grow very outrageous and won't wait, then the delegate gets up and tries to soften them."[49] In addition, meetings were not always held in private homes. The poorest divisions met in taverns, where satirical songs, tobacco, and beer were all part of the program. In sum, among the English Jacobins "austere and puritanical 'saints'" rubbed shoulders with "hedonistic and turbulent fellows."[50]

The LCS fought more for constitutional reform than for the power to exercise popular sovereignty directly.[51] Here, the form of political organization of the English Jacobins did not reproduce the revolutionary political demands of their Parisian comrades, the sans-culottes. The LCS, in framing its demands in its first address,[52] emphasized the repressive nature of taxation, unjust laws, and limitations on freedom. It also censured the English authorities for squandering public funds. For the LCS, only the fair, equal, and impartial representation of the people in parliament could do away with these ills. It therefore refused to resort to violence and sought to achieve reform exclusively by means of public persuasion. Despite its apparently rather moderate demands, the LCS was subjected to repeated and sustained persecution at the hands of the English authorities. For, although the political content of the LCS's demands were not quite "revolutionary," its existence, basic principles, and methods were.[53]

There was, nevertheless, a significant gap between the democratic operation of the plebeian organization and its political demands aimed at achieving better parliamentary representation. Together with Günther Lottes, we can question the absence of demands for direct or radical democracy. To elucidate this paradox, Lottes explains that political representation remains an almost natural component of the English political imagination. The Jacobins could therefore have only a stunted awareness of the need for the direct exercise of political sovereignty.[54] In addition, the LCS's persecution by the state must be taken into account. The speed with which the state attacked this organ of plebeian power dissuaded it from putting forward overly radical demands for fear of arousing the mistrust of the political authorities.

This particularity (functioning on the basis of direct democracy while presenting reformist demands) is already perceptible in the work of John Thelwall, one of the theorists and "leaders" of the Jacobin movement. His ambivalent use of revolutionary and reformist ideas can even be seen as emblematic of that movement. In spite of an apparently antirevolutionary discourse denouncing political violence, Thelwall pleaded for the extension of the franchise in England and strived for the creation of political bodies open to all. Considering the English political environment, these two demands can only be viewed as revolutionary.[55] Furthermore, in his political speeches, Thelwall used rhetoric that, while cloaked in figurative language, implied a real threat of revolution.[56]

"The Liberty Tree"

The year 1792, when the LCS was founded, marked the beginning of major revolutionary turbulence in England. Because of the LCS as well as the impetus provided by the writings of Thomas Paine, the government of Prime Minister William Pitt became aware of the magnitude and extent of plebeian unrest and lost its assurance as to the political stability of the kingdom. This uncertainty was furthermore linked to external events, specifically the radicalization of the French Revolution and the upsetting of the diplomatic balance in Europe owing to the expansionism of the new French Republic. At the same time, however, "the depth and intensity of the democratic agitation in England" must not be underestimated; that agitation altered the political orientation of the English government, which subsequently became "the diplomatic architect of the European counter-revolution."[57] Moreover, it was not just the English government that was transformed in the wake of plebeian agitation and the events in France; the entire ruling class was galvanized by the fear of plebeian power, that is, by the specter of democracy.

The plebs' political mobilization was quite real and not a figment of the ruling classes' paranoia. The second part of Thomas Paine's *Rights of Man*, for example, enjoyed "phenomenal" success.[58] Thompson puts the number of copies sold in 1793 alone at two hundred thousand (the United Kingdom's population at the time was only ten million). The book's distribution throughout the country drew a line of political demarcation dividing "the gentlemen reformers and patrician Whigs, from a minority of radical manufacturers and professional men who sought an alliance with the labourers and artisans, welcomed Paine's social and economic proposals, and looked in the direction of a Republic." The triumph of Paine's writings led to a government offensive against him. He fled to France to avoid public slander and, especially, state persecution. Prime Minister Pitt's decision to prosecute Paine marked the "opening of the era of repression"[59] against those advocating radical reform in England.

The counteroffensive of the ruling classes took a variety of forms. The court gentry campaigned against Paine with publications intended for the many. Societies of magistrates and gentry were strengthened, in particular through the decisive role played by the decidedly anti-Jacobin Association for Preserving Liberty and Property Against Republicans and Levellers founded by John

Reeves.[60] Such societies aimed to renew the old tradition of popular violence in the name of church and king (and were hence known as the "Church and King Mob").[61] Sections of Reeves' association were established in small villages, and anti-Paine rallies were held throughout the country. Given this especially harsh environment for English Jacobinism, Thompson stresses,

> If the distribution of Rights of Man was nation wide, so also was the pro-motion of anti-Jacobin societies. Hence in England the revolutionary im-pulse had scarcely begun to gather force before it was exposed to a counter-revolutionary assault backed by the resources of established authority.[62]

In time, however, the spurious, artificial nature of the loyalist demonstrations was exposed. For some, it was the rabble (a reference to the most miserable and bigoted elements among the people) and not the people who took part in the anti-Jacobin rallies.

Despite the counterrevolutionary offensive, there was an observable trans-formation of popular mentalities. Not that most Englishmen became Jacobins, but they grew more tolerant of the agitators and radicals within English society, notwithstanding the foreign and domestic events that might have made the Jacobin cause less palatable: the execution of Louis XVI, the start of the war with France, and the Pitt government's persecution of the Jacobins. On the other hand, it should not be assumed that the conflicts with the young French Republic were of no consequence for the English Jacobins. "These experiences," Thompson writes, "provoked the first phase of that profound disenchantment, in an intellectual generation which had identified its beliefs in too ardent and utopian a way with the cause of France. The unity between intellectual and plebeian reformers of 1793 was never to be regained."[63]

The popular societies nevertheless survived the persecutions of early 1793, thus demonstrating the force of the plebeian movement. This was true, in par-ticular, of the popular societies founded in 1792 and firmly rooted in their local environments, as was the case in Sheffield, London, and Norwich. There was, of course, a drop in membership (the middle classes, especially, experienced a certain disaffection), but the societies still managed to improve their organiza-tions, a sure sign of vitality. The situation of the LCS is more difficult to ascer-tain. It seems to have faced grave difficulties in early 1793, as illustrated by its launching a nationwide petition that garnered only six thousand signatures. By contrast, the summer of 1793 appears to have been a more fruitful period. Cor-respondence between the LCS and regional societies resumed with renewed vigor, indicating that the societies were active and attracting new members.

The minutes of LCS proceedings indicate that the meetings were well attended and well organized. New members were joining, and new divisions were being created.

Although the societies resisted the government offensive, they were none-theless transformed by it in terms of both their orientation and the style of their actions. The influence of Paine's writings declined, and the republican tone, Thompson notes, shifted to a "renewed emphasis upon restoring the 'pu-rity' of the Constitution. (In June 1793, the L.C.S. went so far as to define this in terms of the 1688 settlement)." There is nothing particularly surprising about this return to constitutionalism. The Pitt government was intent on prosecut-ing anyone who went beyond what it regarded as the pale of political criti-cism, that is, the terms defined in 1688. On the other hand, the counterrevo-lutionary offensive radicalized certain societies, particularly those of Scotland, Norwich, and Sheffield. That is why Thompson observes that the hub of Jaco-binism shifted from London to the radicalized societies. Whereas the leaders of the popular societies were professionals and artisans, the membership was increasingly composed of wage earners, small tradesmen, and small masters. This change brought with it two new sets of demands: the first concerned "eco-nomic grievances and social remedies," and the second expressed the desire to imitate the "French example, forms of organisation and of address."[64]

Among the major figures of English Jacobinism, four men, all close to the LCS, stood out: Thomas Hardy, Maurice Margarot, Joseph Gerrald, and John Thelwall. Hardy was an effective, scrupulous organizer. His work in the LCS served as a longstanding example for his successors. According to John Binns, an active member of the LCS, Hardy was an unpretentious, plainspoken, and personable man who played an important role in the development of Jaco-binism. Maurice Margarot, the president of the LCS, was the son of a wine merchant and consequently spent much of his childhood abroad. Because he had studied at the University of Geneva, he was dubbed "the Frenchman." He was, in Thompson's words, "energetic and audacious, but badly bitten by the characteristic vice of the English Jacobins—self-dramatization."[65] Yet neither Hardy nor Margarot had the stuff of a national leader. For Thompson, only Joseph Gerrald and John Thelwall came close to displaying the qualities of a national leader and theorist.[66] For example, Gerrald was persuaded that the success of English Jacobinism depended on "the calling of a National Conven-tion of British reformers."[67] This strategy, discussed for the first time in Paine's writings, represented the worst scenario for the Pitt government. An alliance of all the radical and reformist forces of the United Kingdom (including Scotland and Ireland) could have seriously jeopardized Pitt's control over the country.

This prospect prompted the government to step up the persecution of English Jacobins and tighten its grip on the plebeians.

With respect to the law, government persecution was faced with the "paradox" of English constitutionalism. Although the law was biased toward the owners, certain provisions protected individual freedoms. It was therefore difficult in England to obtain long prison terms for Jacobin activists. Scotland, however, offered a highly favorable terrain for securing penalties against the Jacobins, especially because of the particularities of its judicial and legal systems (jurists more attached to the state than to the law, a dysfunctional method of jury selection, etc.). With the trials in Scotland the Pitt government took aim at not just the Scottish societies but the English ones as well. Two trials, those of Thomas Muir and T. F. Palmer, raised the red flag for the English Jacobins. These two thinkers were handed heavy sentences for having participated in the Scottish Jacobin movement. "The example was made upon two gifted professional men, who had been unreserved in their willingness to co-operate with plebeian reformers."[68]

But the Jacobin societies of Scotland were not easily intimidated. They were apparently emboldened by the two trials, going so far as to provoke the English authorities by calling for a national convention.[69] They hoped thereby to strengthen their ties with the English societies and better protect themselves against Pitt. The LCS responded favorably to this call, delegating Margarot and Gerrald to represent the society. Aside from Sheffield, the other Jacobin societies did not attend the convention because they were unable to finance the trip to Edinburgh. The English delegates from London and Sheffield were consciously defying the Scottish courts to deal with them in the same way they had dealt with Muir and Palmer.

The so-called Edinburgh Convention assembled three times before being outlawed by the Pitt government, which then sought to arrest the participants. The tenor of the debates, however, was moderate. Yet the very idea of a convention was considered thoroughly revolutionary by the government. The presence of Irish observers and the use of French forms of procedure and address further highlighted the revolutionary character of the event. Moreover, the minutes of the proceedings were dated "First Year of the British Convention," and a resolution was adopted "authorising the calling of an immediate emergency Convention at a secret place in the event of the suspension of Habeas Corpus, or the introduction of legislation against the reformers."[70] All of this stoked the animosity of the Pitt government.[71]

Margarot and Gerrald, together with others, were arrested, and their trials unfolded along the same lines as the trials of Muir and Palmer. Through them the government wanted to indict the Edinburgh Convention as such.[72] They were eventually sentenced to fourteen years of exile. Meanwhile, Gerrald, though he easily could have absconded, pleaded on his own behalf (as did most of the reformers), taking the opportunity to expose the deceitfulness of the ruling classes' constitutional discourse. According to Gerrald, the deceit (for instance, referring to the Constitution while violating its principles) was intended to anaesthetize the people in order to consolidate the power of the ruling classes. Gerrald's condemnation and subsequent death (already seriously ill, he died after a year in exile) gave rise to a wave of sympathy for the reformist cause. That wave resulted in the acquittal of other Jacobin conventioneers, such as Thomas Walker and Daniel Eaton. Thus, writes Thompson, Joseph Gerrald's death was in a way a sacrifice that "helped to save England from a White Terror."[73]

The English societies were in no way demoralized by the trials of Margarot and Gerrald. On the contrary, they remained combative, and their political activities resumed with renewed vigor. Of course, the difficult economic juncture fostered this political revival, but the trials were a major factor as well. Dormant societies were roused, and attendance at the LCS was such that during a general meeting the floor gave way under the weight of the crowd. The national Society for Constitutional Information (established in 1780, this Mecca of reformist thinking for the English middle classes had been in sharp decline since the start of the war against France) once again took up its political activities and passed a motion affirming, in terms borrowed from the French Revolution, that the LCS had "deserved well of their country."[74] Forty thousand copies of the motion were printed and distributed throughout the kingdom, breathing new life into popular societies outside London. The idea of a new convention began to spread in reformist and Jacobin circles. The LCS and the Society for Constitutional Information resolved to form a joint committee to organize it. Jacobin agitation also began to reach the most impoverished districts of the country, such as the East End. Plebeian rallies held all across England were massively attended. For instance, in Sheffield, six or seven thousand individuals took part in a Jacobin demonstration.

To attack the Jacobin movement and put a stop to the political affirmation of the many, the Pitt government suspended habeas corpus, arrested SCL and Constitutional Society leaders, and seized archives, creating a secret parliamentary commission to examine them.[75] This was followed by further arrests of Jacobin leaders in the provinces. To win over public opinion, the government fabricated anti-English conspiracies and plots purported to have been hatched in popular societies—more particularly, in collaboration with

France. Flyers accusing the Jacobins of treason were distributed throughout the country. *The Times* even published a satirical piece concerning a forthcoming English revolution during which Pitt's current political prisoners would enjoy "sanguinary power."[76]

English public opinion was highly susceptible to these accusations. The Jacobins, especially in the provinces, were subjected to the violence of loyalist committees; the local authorities did nothing to stop such criminal—indeed, *sanguinary*—acts. In Nottingham, for example, Major Cartwright reported that the homes of Jacobins were "broken open and persons dragged out, halters were put around their necks, and they were plunged into the muddy brook by the side of the town."[77]

Once again, the effects of the repression were the opposite of what the Pitt government had envisioned. Rather than dissolving, the LCS grew even more radical, appointing a secret executive committee and openly declaring its wish to overthrow the English government. Despite the arrests of Thelwall, Hardy, and others, LCS recruitment efforts gained momentum, and it succeeded in attracting new members and forming new divisions. As a consequence of government repression, only the most radical elements remained in the LCS. But the executive committee encountered serious problems, especially with regard to the security of its correspondence with the societies in the provinces. The nub of the problem lay in the presence within the executive committee of an informer working for Pitt. This was "Citizen Groves," a figure emblematic of the English tradition of spies, a "long line which runs through Oliver to the Chartist years and beyond."[78] His detailed reports on the committee's deliberations allowed Pitt to thwart the LCS's initiatives.

The trials of the reformist leaders projected an image of English Jacobinism that was not the one conveyed by the state and the press. Instead of power-hungry, bloodthirsty revolutionaries, the people of England saw in Thomas Hardy, for example, "one of those images of independence in which the 'free-born Englishman' delighted: a firm and dignified commoner, defying the power of the State."[79] The verdict was eagerly awaited not only in Jacobin circles but also among ordinary citizens, and his acquittal undoubtedly prevented rioting in the streets of London. The two other major anti-Jacobin trials, those of John Horne Tooke and John Thelwall, also resulted in defeats for the Pitt government. Thompson remarks that these setbacks for the English state kept Pitt from unleashing a White Terror. Indeed, the government had made ready to arrest some eight hundred reformers.

In spite of these legal victories, the trials dealt a heavy blow to the reform movement in general and the English Jacobins in particular.[80] The Society for Constitutional Information began to decline following the trial of Horne Tooke, who thereupon withdrew from political life. Hardy left the LCS, which was in the grip of severe internal strife as well as grave financial difficulties,[81] especially because of the costs entailed by the trials. For weeks, LCS members debated the advisability of instituting new internal rules, "one section arguing that *all* constitutions were an impediment to direct democracy, the other section arguing that persecution should be met by a stricter internal discipline."[82] Two divisions decided to break away and form new societies: the London Reforming Society (with John Bone as secretary) and the Society of the Friends of Liberty (initiated by John Baxter). But the LCS was even more divided over the tactics to be applied than the demands to be put forward. Socioeconomic problems had worsened, so that the resolution of the social question could garner widespread support and be the central demand of the LCS. But as a result of the splits, only seventeen LCS divisions were left in March 1795. Furthermore, it no longer corresponded with the regional societies. Even Thelwall withdrew from the movement on the pretext that he would be more useful on the outside.

Following these abandonments, the LCS presented a more united aspect.[83] A large demonstration was held to demand the franchise for men as well as the yearly convening of Parliament, and this revived the organization.[84] Membership increased throughout the year, and the society was able to attract more and more wage earners.[85] In addition, new clubs "with a new stridency of republican rhetoric"[86] appeared around the LCS and its offspring. These new groups were more militant than the LCS and advocated the entrenchment of considerable local powers while at the same time extolling the French Revolution, especially its Jacobin and terrorist tendencies.

In the fall of 1795, the LCS decided to hold another large rally at Copenhagen House. Thompson maintains that between one hundred and one hundred and fifty thousand people attended. The speakers addressed their remarks directly at the king, calling on him to explain why so many people in England were starving (1795 was an especially harsh year for the many), even while the wealth of the few was more and more on display. A vote was passed censuring the king and decrying the indigence of the people.[87] In the words of an anonymous observer, "harmony, regularity, and good order prevailed . . . *it was a day sacred to liberty.*"[88]

Barely three days later, London witnessed a most unusual scene: two hundred thousand people greeted the king with hoots and his prime minister with insults. The window of the royal carriage was smashed (apparently by a stone), and the king believed he was the target of an attempt on his life. The LCS denied all responsibility, but the response of the English government, in a panic

162   THE QUESTION OF THE FORMS OF POLITICAL ORGANIZATION

over this potentially revolutionary incident, was swift and severe. A proclamation against seditious meetings and a bill concerning *Two Acts* were submitted to Parliament. The freedom-destroying bill prohibited, on pain of death, incitement to express contempt or hate for the king. It also made it mandatory to obtain a judge's permission to hold a rally of over fifty people. Last, the bill contained measures tailor-made to suppress once and for all the English Jacobin movement, such as the right to shut down reformist lecture halls, on the pretext that they were "disorderly houses." The British historian G. A. Williams writes of the *Two Acts*, "this was the most serious invasion of traditional liberties since the Stuarts."[89]

The few weeks between the submission of the bill on the *Two Acts* (November 10, 1795) and its approval by the king (December 18, 1795) were at once the final and most intense period of plebeian political action in England.[90] Even the parliamentary opposition (headed by Charles James Fox) openly joined the popular societies in denouncing the bill. The LCS organized another rally at Copenhagen House that brought together two hundred thousand demonstrators. Given the participation of women and children, there could be no doubt as to the peaceful nature of the gathering. A final mass meeting was held in December at Marylebone Fields, where the speakers did not mince words with regard to the British government. One of them, John Gale Jones, even spoke in favor of the public execution of Prime Minister Pitt.[91] However, an account of the day reports that this was not an incitement to violence. On the contrary, Jones's words were received calmly, and those who did not support brutal methods were respected: "No tumult took place: nor was any offence given to such as did not hold up hands, or join in the plaudit."[92] Demonstrations were held throughout the kingdom, and the Jacobins' opposition to the bill even elicited support from members of the military, represented in particular by Colonel Thornton, who stated that there were soldiers ready to join a popular uprising against the *Two Acts*. Pitt himself acknowledged that, were he to resign, "my head would be off in six months."[93]

But the law was a victory for the English state and brought to a close the period of Jacobin political unrest in the United Kingdom. Although the provisions of the *Two Acts* were not often enforced, the fear they aroused among English Jacobins was sufficient to put a stop to their political agitation. From that point forward, "public political life had become impossible."[94] At first, however, the LCS wanted to defy the law. Representatives received the mandate to rebuild a national organization by establishing ties with societies around the country. Initial contacts were fruitful and gave rise to government persecution of LCS delegates and to the violent intervention of the state. The LCS subsequently tried to regroup so as to circumvent the legislation by creating new subdivisions with no more than forty-five members, five fewer, that is, than the number requiring judicial authorization according to the law.[95] But with the imprisonment of the main leaders of the LCS, correspondence with the provinces grew increasingly sparse. The repercussions of the law obviously weighed heavily on the morale of radical plebeians. Thus, "the London society . . . turned in upon itself and entered into a phase of internal dissension and disintegration."[96]

Its last gasp would come at the end of 1796. Following the implementation of the *Two Acts*, members of the LCS sensed that government spies were ubiquitous, and some of them felt it was futile, even dangerous, to hold meetings. Yet the LCS persisted, and in Westminster an informal alliance was forged between Whigs and radicals in preparation for the general elections. However, toward the end of 1796 the lack of participation, financial difficulties, as well as the arrest of LCS leaders got the best of the organization, at least its public component.[97]

According to E. P. Thompson, historical sources indicate that after the fall of the LCS at least two sections continued the political struggle of the English Jacobins, the first openly and quasi-legally, the other preferring to operate secretly and outside the law. In the second case, the reformers were active throughout the great political upheavals of 1796 through 1799. This "clandestine" section was involved in the Scottish weavers' uprising in 1797 as well as the United Irish rebellion that led to the war against England in 1798. However, its presence made itself felt above all in the naval mutinies of 1797.

In April and May of that year, English sailors, subjected to extremely harsh conditions, rose up against the English government. The participation of some former members of the LCS, such as Richard Parker, in the mutiny added a revolutionary dimension to the sailors' demands. Indeed, their discourse was sometimes reminiscent of Paine's *Rights of Man*. Yet the behavior of the English Jacobins with respect to the mutineers was problematical, as some mutineers were reproved by the Jacobins, displeased perhaps by the development of the mutinies. Still, their role in these events seems to have been significant. For Thompson, "these great mutinies, and the Irish rebellion of the following year, were indeed events of world-wide significance, and they show how precarious was the hold of the English *ancien régime*."[98] The significance was worldwide because a successful mutiny would have upset the diplomatic balance in Europe to the detriment of Great Britain and its global strategic interests. And the hold was "precarious" because it would not have taken much to destabilize the Pitt government and undermine the established political regime. Thus, the work of the Jacobins continued despite being forced underground.

The Irish rebellion of 1798 aroused the sympathy of the English Jacobins, and the LCS (which, in the meantime, had adopted a new internal constitution better suited to clandestinity) published a declaration addressed to the Irish insurgents denouncing English despotism and saluting the courage and generosity of the Irish nation. In addition to expressing support for the Irish cause, the declaration also appealed to the English soldiers in Ireland to refuse to be complicit in the repression. The statement demonstrates that, beyond the essentially religious opposition between Catholics and Protestants, the conflict between Ireland and England involved the more political cleavage between the many and the few. This throws into relief the universal nature of the Irish struggle against domination and for emancipation, that is, for the emergence of the Irish from their minority status.

The persecution of the Jacobins was such that in 1799 the former leaders of the LCS were either imprisoned or exiled. The treatment of political prisoners as well as their families was especially harsh. The extent of the repression completely extinguished revolutionary hopes, in particular among Jacobin intellectuals but also, though perhaps to a lesser extent, among the plebs. Popular societies, including the LCS, were banned by Parliament on July 12, 1799.[99] Nevertheless, writes Thompson, "It is wrong to see this as the end, for it was also a beginning. In the 1790s something like an 'English Revolution' took place, of profound importance in shaping the consciousness of the post-war working class."[100]

Certainly, the revolutionary impulse in England was "nipped in the bud," making it difficult if not impossible to carry out the plebeian political project. Still, it must not be forgotten that the struggle for emancipation through the English Jacobins' political organizations (the LCS and other popular societies) concretely opened up spaces of freedom in which the many could fully assert themselves. Thus, the popular societies enabled them to demonstrate their participation in the human political condition. The liberty tree had been planted, and "even in the darkest war years the democratic impulse can still be felt at work beneath the surface."[101] This is the work of political equality expressing itself in the possibility, available to all, of enjoying political freedom or, to use a more revolutionary phrase, public happiness.

A Heritage Without a Testament?

It can be seen through this account that the London Corresponding Society and the English Jacobins made five major contributions to communalism and agoraphilia: the principle of plurality, political capacity, the acceptance of otherness, the creation of new political spaces, and active citizenship. These shaped the democratic impulse in Great Britain in the late eighteenth century and throughout the nineteenth century, and, taken together, they comprise the political heritage of English Jacobinism.

PLURALITY

The first principle of the LCS was that there should be no limit on the number of its members. To fully grasp the magnitude and radical nature of this principle, one must understand what it stood in opposition to, that is, the exclusiveness of the political practice of England's aristocracy and bourgeoisie. Indeed, English politics rested on various criteria and titles of nobility but, above all, on titles to property, the aim being to restrict the political sphere to property holders. For Jacques Rancière, what was involved here was a "police" distribution of places and functions based on titles to govern.[102] The English political order was then the product of a "police" order and therefore of a conception of politics as an instrument of the domination of the many by the few. To circumscribe access to public space in this way amounted to denying the principle of human plurality, which remains the sine qua non of a truly democratic practice. But this restriction of politics by means of symbolic or material requirements (respectively, titles of nobility or titles to property) was not exceptional in Europe at the time of English Jacobinism. On the contrary, political exclusiveness constituted the norm in the vast majority of European countries during that period. Hence Thompson's assertion that the principle of unlimited membership so central to the LCS's work was "one of the hinges upon which history turns "and which it would be wrong to "pass over . . . as a commonplace."[103]

However, though it may have been a historical hinge, this principle was not a radical innovation in the political annals of England.[104] The principle of unlimited membership harks back to the struggles of the English levelers, who sought to dissociate political rights from property requirements. But the Jacobins added new intensity to the dynamics of openness and thus represented an "essential contribution of the plebeian public sphere to modern politics."[105] The contribution was characterized by a twofold rejection: of political exclusiveness and of the exploitation of the many in the name of a political project. Just like the sectional societies of Paris's sans-culottes, the LCS sought to put an end to political exclusiveness, that is, the widespread notion whereby politics could never really be the concern of all. By openly encouraging participation in the life of the community, the English Jacobins showed deep respect for the many, who were assigned the eminently political tasks of constructing collective existence, of establishing the rules governing the life of the community, and of building a society embracing the values of the many. That participation rested on the simple fact of being human rather than on titles to govern.[106] The plebeian experience could take shape thanks to the English Jacobins' political organizations, because it was there that individuals could move from the status of *animal laborans*—that is, a subpolitical existence—to that of *zoon politikon*. The plebs thereby acquired the full human dignity that comes with active involvement in the life of the community. Moreover, by creating bodies of political participation, the English plebs constructed a stage where the equality of everyone could be verified.[107] What the plebeian "dissensus"[108] revealed was the wrong inflicted by the police order, and structures were then established that opened the way to self-emancipation.

The principle of plurality implies as well rejecting attempts to exploit the people for political ends. Throughout English political history, the many, often referred to as the "mob," have been used on a number of occasions by radical groups to pressure the government. The assumption underlying this fundamentally contemptuous tactic is that the many are incapable of organizing themselves "in pursuance of [their] own ends."[109] For the English Jacobins, the plebs' emancipation movement must be one of self-emancipation. Neither the "gentlemen reformers" nor the "radical property owners" could appropriate it. "That the number of our Members be unlimited" hence represented a critique of the dominant practice of political exclusiveness and the plebs' affirmation of autonomy and their readiness to take on the most crucial political tasks. Thus, in addition to being a political critique, it also signified a displacement of politics from the realm of domination to that of liberty. It is in this sense that the English plebs instituted a veritable people's politics and fully participated in the revolutionary communalist tradition.

However, the question of women's position within the LCS somewhat complicates the picture. In *The Struggle for the Breeches*, the feminist historian Anna Clark observes the lack of female participation in the political activities of the English Jacobins. Yet the primary intellectual source of Jacobinism, Paine's *Rights of Man,* expresses a nonsexist attitude. Indeed, the notion of citizenship put forward by Paine points to a dynamic that makes possible the recognition of women's political rights.[110] For Clark, the absence of women in the LCS was the result of the English Jacobins' indifference to the women's question as well as to the fact that women themselves were more concerned about social issues than political rights. At the same time, Clark stresses that, to the LCS's credit, it had in fact planned to establish a patriotic society made up exclusively of women.[111] Moreover, historical documents attest to the presence of women at major gatherings, such as those at Copenhagen House and Marylebone Fields.

POLITICAL CAPACITY

The principle "that the number of members be unlimited" led to another contribution of English Jacobinism to communalism and agoraphilia: the idea that all people have equal political capacities. What is meant by "political capacity" is the notion that, in part thanks to a prior initiation to political matters, every person is able to understand and make the fundamental choices required by political communities. The reason the LCS wished to open wide the doors of its organization was, in particular, that it believed everyone was endowed with the same political capacity. So, while the aptitudes needed to assume the responsibilities of political leadership are not equally distributed among individuals, the ability to take political decisions and participate in the deliberative process counts as one of the most fundamental human potentials. The Jacobin form of political organization, writes Thompson, was "based on the deliberate belief that every man was capable of reason and of a growth in his abilities, and that deference and distinctions of status were an offence to human dignity."[112] For instance, the LCS address to the nation dated July 8, 1793, was intended to "awaken the sleeping reason"[113] of English citizens, thus confirming the belief in the equal possibility of taking part in the res publica.

More than a mere beneficial byproduct of the principle of plurality, the active belief in individuals' equal capacities was essential for the advent of modern democracy. The moment liberal societies accepted the principle of universal suffrage, they became, theoretically, democratic.[114] But the example of the English Jacobins goes further than liberal democracies, in that they not only adhered to a liberal conception of political capacities but also established structures of public participation and deliberation. In other words, the SCL and English popular societies took this belief to its logical conclusion: the creation of radical democratic bodies. Such forms of organization were all the more important because they were of plebeian origin; they allowed the plebeians to feel both valorized and responsible thanks to bodies, procedures, and rules that were specifically their own.[115] They represented islands of political freedom in a regime still subjected to the imperatives of the domination of the few entitled to govern. Once again, the plebeians on the British side of the Channel took part in the communalist revolutionary tradition because they recognized the political capacity of the many.

OTHERNESS

The Jacobin's open attitude to "otherness" stemmed from the principle of plurality. The notion of "otherness" refers to two distinct yet related phenomena. The first is the fact of being willing to welcome others and their difference relative to oneself. Here, otherness is situated on the plane of interpersonal relationships, where an open attitude to otherness focuses on the other as an individual. Second, openness to Otherness is the disposition to welcome Others and their difference in relation to what we know and experience as subjects integrated into a social, political, and cultural fabric that precedes and transcends us. Here, Otherness is embodied not in an individual but in a social, political, and cultural entity such as a foreign country or an unfamiliar culture. In is on these two levels of openness to otherness that the Jacobins' major contribution to communalism can be identified.

The LCS and its members displayed their openness both toward individuals embodying otherness and to societies embodying Otherness. On one hand, the LCS was receptive to dissension and conflict, as attested to by the fact that it did not foist any doctrine or ideology on its members. Beyond support of basic demands for parliamentary reform, the LCS did not require its members to pledge allegiance to any credo. Actually, from a strictly strategic perspective, it may have been an organizational weakness not to ensure greater internal cohesion. The many struggles inside the LCS certainly played into the hands of England's counterrevolutionary forces. But what may have been a shortcoming with respect to political objectives nevertheless provided an example of tolerance and openness, a tolerance not necessarily underpinned by theory but experienced on the ground through the Jacobins' political practice. Francis Place writes in his autobiography, "The discussions in the divisions . . . opened to them views which they had never before taken. They were compelled by these discussions to find reasons for their opinions, and to tolerate others. . . . It is more than probable that a circumstance like this never before occurred."[116] In this respect, the English Jacobins contributed to communalism by revealing a democratic practice, "conceived, intended as the reign of the multiple, as the search for diversity, indeed, for assortment . . . instituted through the rejection of a homogenizing unification."[117]

In connection with Otherness—the openness to other societies and cultures—the LCS, through its stand alongside the Scots and Irish and even in its relations with the young French Republic, showed the very same openness. The joint struggle with the Scots and Irish may be somewhat surprising, given the historical animosity between the various components of the United Kingdom. It is all the more surprising because the military superiority and political domination of the English over the other nations could have fostered if not mutual mistrust then at least (especially among the English) a wish to subordinate and to erect hierarchies. Often, the geographically and culturally closest Other is the most difficult to accept. Yet, in spite of such considerations, the English Jacobins proved to be open, indeed solidary, toward the struggle in Scotland against the domination of the few and toward Ireland's fight for national emancipation.

The case of the English plebs is equally unique with respect to their relations with France. The Franco-British wars, colonial rivalry, cultural differences, and political oppositions might have played a decisive role in making France a political model to be rejected. Yet the English Jacobins, no doubt deeply impressed by the audacity of the French revolutionaries, were able to rise above the prejudices and rivalries of that period and to welcome French Otherness. Thus, through its relationships with Scotland, Ireland, and France, English Jacobinism bequeathed what is a common feature of the many faces of communalism, "the tradition of internationalism."[118]

NEW POLITICAL SPACES

English Jacobinism also passed on a heritage of "new political spaces," which here refers to the places that the Jacobins occupied politically. While Parliament, City Hall, and the streets remained the usual sites where political life occurred, it must be acknowledged that the English Jacobins transformed apolitical spaces of daily life into centers of political action. As Thompson observes,

> The countryside was ruled by the gentry, the towns by corrupt corporations, the nation by the corruptest corporation of all: but the chapel, the tavern and the home were their own. In the "unsteepled" places of worship there was room for a free intellectual life and for democratic experiments with "members unlimited."[119]

The political reappropriation of spaces was consequential for the politics carried out in these sites of everyday existence.

The meetings of certain LCS divisions took place in taverns, coffee houses, and sometimes even workshops and factories. Unable to gain political legitimacy in the eyes of the ruling classes, who monopolized the traditional sites of power, the English Jacobins were obliged to innovate. They went to the people's "natural" environments: their places of work and social interaction. By melding work and politics as well as socializing and politics in this way, the plebeian forms of organization promoted the forging of a political bond. For a bond to exist, there must be a site likely to foster its emergence. But no site is neutral; it necessarily affects the politics that take place within it. The Jacobins gathered in spaces, especially taverns and cafés, where social and economic distinctions tended to fade and where equality was experienced in a direct, almost radical manner. In such places, a cobbler could mix with a lawyer, or an intellectual could make the acquaintance of a weaver without social distinctions necessarily standing in the way. This "dissolving of the markers of [social] certitude" promoted a more egalitarian exchange, which could in turn have an effect on political deliberations.[120] In other words, a climate favorable to the recognition of natural equality enabled the emergence of a politics that developed without ever losing sight of that egalitarian acknowledgment.

John Thelwall, moreover, affirms, "every large workshop and manufactory is a sort of political society."[121] There occurred a veritable transformation of the workplace into a political society where human relationships were defined in terms of equality. This transformation represented a critique, through action, of the capitalist system's structures of domination concretized through the physical and psychological constraints of the workshop and factory. The wish to create, at the very heart of English capitalism, egalitarian political spaces where all could express themselves freely and openly was indeed a critique of, indeed a challenge to, the authoritarian and hierarchical tendencies specific to the liberal economic system. In opposition to the distribution of places and functions characteristic of nascent industrial capitalism, the English Jacobins advanced an egalitarian political practice.

ACTIVE CITIZENSHIP

The English Jacobins presented an active conception of citizenship, as opposed to liberal practice, which supposes that political activity is restricted to citizens' participation in the election to public office of professional politicians invariably belonging to the few. By contrast, an active conception of citizenship implies the possibility for everyone to take a direct part in public life on a daily basis. Thompson underscores the importance of this tenet for the Jacobins: "The Radical and free-thinking artisan was at his most earnest in his belief in the *active* duties of citizenship."[122] By founding the LCS, the English Jacobins endowed themselves with political rights. The plebs' subsequent participation in popular societies amply expressed the desire to involve themselves in public affairs.

The political participation advocated by the Jacobins can be better understood through an examination of LCS operations. As E. P. Thompson puts it, "*Every* citizen on a committee was expected to perform some part, the chairmanship of committees was often taken in rotation, the pretensions of leaders were watched."[123] Three elements are worth noting here. First, the emphasis is clearly on the participation of all in common affairs. This seems to be a constant for English Jacobinism, which refused to exclude anyone from political functions. Second, the rotation of the chair is a reminder of a method of designation forgotten by modern democracy—lottery (or sortition). As a method of selection, the lottery represents a deeply democratic procedure that consecrates the equality of all with all. It can therefore be contrasted with elections whose outcome is aristocratic. Bernard Manin demonstrates this by setting Florentine democracy (which resorted to the lottery) in opposition to Venetian aristocracy (which preferred elections) during the Renaissance.[124] By choosing to appoint committee chairmen on a rotating basis, the Jacobins asserted their belief in the genuine equality of citizens and in values that could underpin a democracy.

Wariness with regard to the ambitions of leaders also seems to point to a wish to put an end to the age-old structure of domination that reproduces the division between the few and the many. It was an attempt to forestall the differentiation and empowerment of a new leadership caste able to establish another form of domination, which would engender a "dialectic of emancipation."[125] This dialectic, whose core mechanism transforms emancipatory movements into their opposite—domination—eventually proves fatal for freedom and for equality. Hence the importance of defusing any attempts to recreate the gap between dominators and dominated. Similarly, the distrust of the ambitions of potential leaders may also have stemmed from the desire to prevent the professionalization of politics, in the sense of the formation of an oligarchy composed of careerists assuming the right to speak and decide on behalf and instead of the many. For an authentically democratic space to exist, access to public expression and power must be open to all and not just to professional politicians. It should be added that by proceeding this way the English Jacobins circumvented the difficult problem of the "plebeian leader." Within the LCS, none of the leaders acted as a true head. In keeping with its educational mission, the LCS counted on the authority of "Intelligence" or of education (as advocated in the nineteenth century, for example, by J. Déjacque),[126] because its aim was to allow its members to arrive at their own political judgments. What this "education for emancipation" indicates is that the English Jacobins were more concerned with having people treated as adults than with the privileges that might be derived from being named leader of the plebs.

English Jacobinism's contribution to a people's politics and to political freedom resides in the valorization of active citizenship within genuinely democratic political bodies. By illuminating the political will and capacity of the many, the English Jacobins revealed the possibility for citizens to play an active role in the modern political space. Beyond the distinction—closely associated with liberal thought as articulated, in particular, by Benjamin Constant[127]—between the political freedom of the ancients and the private freedom of the moderns, the English plebs displayed not just a desire but an aptitude for public life and political affairs within modernity. That desire and aptitude blur the distinction between the freedom of the ancients and that of the moderns. The history of English Jacobinism constitutes a major contribution to the modern democratic revolution and reminds us that "freedom . . . is actually the reason that men live together in political organization at all. Without it, political life as such would be meaningless. The *raison d'être* of politics is freedom, and its field of experience is action."[128]

Through an exploration of English Jacobinism, particularly as seen by E. P. Thompson, we can better grasp the political possibilities of modern democracy. Despite its lack of success in the short run, the Jacobins' action remains an integral part of *our* political heritage. We thought it important to summarize this political history, with particular reference to the London Corresponding Society, and at the same time indentify the principal contributions of that political experience to communalism and agoraphilia. Moreover, this approach has allowed us to offset a certain neglect of significant political events, which can no doubt be ascribed to the short time span covered by the events, for the experience of the English plebs also falls within the temporality of the gap.

There is an obvious kinship between the English Jacobins and the sans-culottes of Paris: a comparable social makeup, the same desire to take an active part in public affairs, a common determination to create forms of political organization in their image, a similar rejection of domination, and an analogous demand for self-emancipation. In sum, the same resurgence of the plebeian principle. But what of the Paris Commune of 1871? How was it akin to the actions of the sans-culottes and the English Jacobins? It remains for us to reconstitute the political form of organization that arose in 1871 and subsequently to identify its contribution to both communalism and agoraphilia.

5
THE PARIS COMMUNE OF 1871
AND THE COMMUNARDS

There was agreement only on this watchword: create a plebeian government,
render powerless the classes deemed responsible for so much public
suffering and hardship. This was the general nature of the Commune of 1871,
of which it can be said that for the last time in our history the word [Commune]
recovered a little of its primitive meaning, of its power to call for the
unity of fellow citizens against the oppressors.
—C. Petit-Dutaillis, *Les communes françaises*

IN CONTRAST TO THE PREVIOUS CHAPTERS, OUR ANALYSIS OF THE
political experience in Paris in 1871 focuses not on a particular form of organization but on a series of political forms that contributed to the advent or the
historical deployment of the Commune. Through a host of political bodies, the
Paris Commune of 1871 marked the establishment of a political form intended
to put an end to state power, that is, power based on coercion, in order to institute a power constructed through the concerted action of the citizens. The
Paris Commune stands as a refutation in practice of a certain line of thought
whereby the state is considered desirable, or even indispensable, for the collective existence of modern individuals. However, the Communards' political
action was not exempt from myth, particularly that of the Great Revolution
of 1789, as evidenced by the creation of an ersatz Committee for Public Safety,
which presaged the Commune's demise. The Paris Commune was a fragile undertaking; an experiment in freedom vulnerable to the desire for the One and,
hence, in constant danger of turning into its opposite.

What Is a Communard?

Just like the expressions "sans-culotte" and "English Jacobins," the term "communard" was initially pejorative. Although it has gained currency today, it was

"very rarely used"[1] during the events of 1871. Actually, "communard" replaced the equally pejorative epithet "*communeux*," which was widely used at the time of the Commune, especially by its adversaries. Beyond its "ignoble" origins, "communard" came to designate all sympathizers and members of the Commune and not just its elected officials or functionaries.

The social makeup of the Communards continues to be the subject of significant historical debate. Depending on the perspective adopted (e.g., the Commune as "the last revolution of the nineteenth century" versus the Commune as "the revolution of the future"), the Communards are presented as either artisans or proletarians. Rather than choosing between the two, we concur with the American historian Martin P. Johnson that an analysis of the social fabric of the Commune reveals its essentially composite nature: artisans, laborers, petit bourgeois, professionals, wage earners, merchants, etc. The Commune attracted women and men from a variety of social backgrounds and a wide range of trades and professions. In response to the proponents of either interpretation of the Commune, it can be objected that, in typically plebeian fashion, it was characterized by plurality. The political bodies of the Commune were not the preserve of one socioeconomic class but rather a rallying point and a forum for the expression of the same revolutionary desire to assert oneself as a political subject.[2] This is what prompts the leading French historian of the Commune, Jacques Rougerie, to state that the Communard "is in no way the modern proletarian."[3]

The nature of the Communards' cohesion was more political than socioeconomic. The use of the term "citizen" to address both male and female Communards testifies to their view of themselves as bound together in the same struggle for a more democratic political sphere. Hence, a Communard was "firstly an activist of the Revolution."[4] The designations "worker" and "proletarian" rarely occurred in communalist discourse.[5] Yet this does not imply that social issues were considered secondary. On the contrary, such issues were inseparable from the creation of democratic communal bodies. Without doubt, the political cohesion of the Communards constitutes a distinctive feature of the plebeian experience.

TOWARD THE PARIS COMMUNE: A POLITICAL APPRENTICESHIP

The period preceding the establishment of the Paris Commune was a time of exceptional political and revolutionary ferment.[6] In retrospect, it can be regarded as a stage of political apprenticeship for the communalist movement. This training was to be decisive because the communalist forces learned to act in a concerted way and to seize the opportunities arising out of the political conjuncture in order to advance their political project.

During the siege of Paris (September 19, 1870–January 28, 1871) there were two coalitions seeking to establish an autonomous Commune and to neutralize the defeatist policy of the Government of National Defense.[7] The first coalition, characterized by its moderation and a certain lack of coordination and organization, tried unsuccessfully to set up a Paris Commune in October 1870. Out of this failure came a second, more radical coalition whose aim was to establish a revolutionary Commune by going beyond the electoral process through the designation of its members from among the political clubs and societies of Paris. This more revolutionary coalition initiated two fruitless attempts to create a Commune in January 1871.

Both coalitions included militants active in popular political bodies. Thanks to Napoleon III's legislation concerning public meetings, the many opponents of the French bourgeoisie's regime could gather and make themselves more widely known to a public not restricted to political activists.[8] The supporters of Auguste Blanqui, for example, gained notoriety for their oratory skills and their ability to arouse the sympathy of Parisian students and workers. The International Workingmen's Association (IWA), founded in 1864 and later known as the First International, also took part in preparing the Commune of 1871, with many of its members acting as elected officials and functionaries of the Commune. The First International refused to get politically involved, on the pretext that politics "means suppression, conquest and force,"[9] but some of its key actors did not hesitate to do so. All this attests to the ideological diversity within the Commune.

The creation in 1870 of the Comité central républicain (Republican Central Committee), known simply as the Comité central, of the twenty arrondissements (districts) of Paris was to be crucial for the future Commune.[10] The Central Committee, established at the instigation of activists from the International, was composed of members from a number of dissident political committees and groups in Paris. A vigilance committee was formed for each district. The Central Committee acted as the federative body, ensuring the coordination of efforts throughout the city. The vigilance committees had the "twofold objective" of defending both Paris and the Republic.[11] Here is how Gustave Lefrançais describes the responsibilities of these new plebeian political bodies:

> The twenty vigilance committees were . . . revolutionary municipal structures, collecting whatever information was available on the operations of the official administrations in order to make known their true nature to a

central committee comprising delegates sent by the vigilance committees. The central committee was in turn responsible for coordinating any action designed to oppose the reactionary machinations of the Hôtel de Ville [City Hall] or to denounce them to the population of Paris.[12]

The reason the Central Committee played an essential role in the political action leading up to the Commune was in part because the International was divided as to its participation in the events surrounding the creation of the Paris Commune. Those like Gustave Lefrançais, Eugène Varlin, and Benoît Malon, who encouraged the International to get politically involved, were important actors within the Central Committee.[13] But the latter cannot be reduced to a mere branch of the International,[14] as that would be an offense against the heterogeneity of the Central Committee's members and the plurality of their backgrounds.[15]

It was precisely because of this diversity that the Central Committee was from the outset split as to its political objectives and actions. The internal divisions became apparent during the demonstrations that began on October 5, 1870, when three separate demonstrations were held in the name of the Central Committee. Given the lack of organization and coordination, all three rallies were failures, and the rifts among Central Committee members deepened. Nevertheless, as the hardships caused by the siege grew more severe, the clubs in Paris experienced a degree of activity such that they were able to fill the political vacuum resulting from the discord within the Central Committee.[16]

The twists and turns of France's faltering military strategy in face of Bismarck's armies as well as the negotiation of an armistice to allow Paris to replenish its supply of basic goods further inflamed the anger of Parisians, already kindled by various revolutionary actions. On October 31, 1870, they rose up against the National Defense government. The insurrection was triggered by the Parisians' spontaneous initiatives, and the popular bodies, more specifically the Central Committee, provided the guiding framework. The Committee organized a march on the Hôtel de Ville and demanded that elections be held to establish the Paris Commune.[17] Despite some confusion concerning the leadership of the revolt (at least three members of the Central Committee somehow fulfilled this role: G. Lefrançais, G. Flourens, and A. Blanqui), the mayor of Paris agreed to hold elections. While the Central Committee was negotiating, the vigilance committees launched assaults on a dozen *mairies d'arrondissement* (town halls). This, according to M. P. Johnson, was no mere coincidence but proof that there was a degree of coordination among popular organizations during the siege. However, the insurrection of October 31 was not initiated by the Central Committee but was the product of the spontaneous actions of Parisians combined with the coordination effected by the popular organizations.[18]

The Government of National Defense had no intention of allowing the insurgents to set up a Commune in Paris. In the early morning of November 1, 1870, it took control of the Hôtel de Ville, which had been almost entirely abandoned by the revolutionaries, who were convinced of having won the day. To mollify those remaining (including Blanqui), the government promised to hold municipal elections. The maneuver enabled General Trochu, president of the National Defense government, to regain control of the political situation in Paris. He did indeed order the holding of elections but only on the level of the mairies d'arrondissement. He also pledged to step up the fight against the Germans, thereby strengthening his political base in Paris. Ultimately, the government reneged on its promise to amnesty the revolutionaries and arrested those who had taken part in the October 31 insurrection.[19]

In addition to the arrest of some of the key actors in the communalist movement (including Blanqui, Lefrançais, Pyat, and Vallès),[20] the Parisian revolutionaries suffered a serious blow when the National Defense government held a plebiscite with the aim of consolidating its political base. More than 322,000 Parisians voted to support the government while only 54,000 voted against it. Trochu took advantage of the favorable political circumstances to tighten his authoritarian grip on Paris.[21] The leaders of the revolutionary opposition were thus obliged to rethink the movement's overall strategy. What emerged out of the first, generally moderate coalition was one decidedly more radical and revolutionary in terms of both its goals and methods,[22] one that drew a lesson from the October 31 failure and the subterfuges of the Trochu government. The radicalization of the Parisian opposition gave rise to new organizations, while the Central Committee temporarily stood back.

Three new plebeian organizations stepped in: the Légion garibaldienne (Garibaldi Legion), the Club central (Central Club), and the Ligue républicaine de défense à outrance (the Republican All-out Defense League). The Légion, founded by militants close to the International, was established as a semiclandestine revolutionary federation striving for the advent of a democratic, social republic in France.[23] The purpose of the Club central was to gather and disseminate the propositions formulated at public meetings. It should be noted, however, that the Club seems to have suspended its activities between October 31 and the beginning of December. Finally, the Ligue républicaine brought together radical and moderate revolutionaries, which is why it would play a crucial role in the future Commune. The Ligue, which was quite secretive at the outset, was responsible for the publication of two revolutionary newspapers and for the creation of the Club de la solidarité (Solidarity Club), which sought to associate itself with the popular organizations of Paris. Notwithstanding the moderates in its ranks, the Ligue républicaine carried out its activities under the leadership of its most radical members (the Blanquistes in particular).[24]

The new plebeian organizations marked a turning point in the communalist movement's strategy. To outwit the police, closed and secret meetings were held, and more emphasis was placed on clandestine activities than on public gatherings. After October 31, the vision of the Commune to be created was altered. Henceforward, the revolutionaries fought for a revolutionary Commune, one based not on popular suffrage but on the clubs and committees of Paris. The Blanquistes played a decisive role in this shift, because they were able to persuade the various elements in the communalist movement of the validity of the new approach.[25] Furthermore, for supporters of the Commune the results of the plebiscite had discredited the ballot box solution.

On January 1, 1871, the Comité Central républicain des vingt arrondissements became the Délégation des vingt arrondissements (Delegation of the Twenty Districts), thereby signaling a renewed wish to constitute a Commune in Paris as well as elsewhere in France. Indeed, the Delegation sent representatives to the provinces to encourage and prepare the establishment of a communal power. However, the change of name implied more than a mere renewal of the Central Committee's political will. The general assembly of local vigilance committees (in the districts) that voted the name change also proclaimed the dissolution of the Central Committee. The innovative and revolutionary nature of this change must be underscored. The Delegation represented a new coalition of the Left, which, following the events of late October and early November, chose to establish the Commune in Paris through revolutionary means.[26]

In fact, the Delegation of the Twenty Districts saw itself as the Commune to be constituted. The creation of a comité d'exécution (executive committee), also known as the comité d'initiative (initiative committee), made up of a limited number of members chosen from among those most dedicated to the communalist cause, suggests that the Delegation was seriously preparing for its arrival at the Hôtel de Ville.[27] The task incumbent upon the Committee was to organize the insurrection against the National Defense government. To this end, the Committee sat on a permanent basis and put forward the idea of a "red poster" with which the city would be placarded to announce the insurrection and publish the demands of the communalist movement. The demands reiterated the minimal program of the revolutionary clubs and committees of Paris: the distribution of foodstuffs to the needy, a fairer social sharing of the hardships caused by the siege, etc. As William Serman notes, the red poster signified a certain erasure of the "ideological differences"[28] among the components of the communalist movement. It also incited Parisians to mobilize en masse against the blockade and encouraged them to overthrow the Government of National Defense. It furthermore provides an indication of the level of coordination and organization of the plebeian revolutionary bodies.[29] The many meetings of the supporters of the Commune preceding the circulation of the poster throughout Paris (January 6, 1871) confirmed its seditious and revolutionary character, with the speakers setting out exactly what needed to be done to ensure the Communards' takeover of power.

The effects of the siege were especially harsh for Parisians. Each week over a thousand of them died of the disease and famine ensuing from the Prussian blockade. Hence, supporters of the Commune hoped that the red poster's call would be taken up by large numbers of people. But they underestimated the strength of many Parisians' continuing faith in their government. The poster failed to arouse the enthusiasm of the masses or even of large crowds. Only a few hundred people responded. Worse still for the communalist movement, the number of posters immediately torn down was so great that one communalist club voted for a new printing.[30]

However, the effects of the siege of Paris were so devastating that by mid-January the potential existed for a new insurrection. Especially since the National Defense government appeared to be preparing to sign an armistice, with the implication that the Parisians' sacrifice and suffering would have been in vain. This is what led communalist militants, more specifically the Delegation of the Twenty Districts, to organize an attempt to seize power on January 22. The clubs and committees in the districts made ready, and a secret "execution" committee coordinated the operations of the communalist movement's different components.[31]

However, as had been the case with the red posters, only a small number of insurgents showed up on the appointed date. The government brutally crushed the insurrection. Contrary to the claims of certain historians and participants who witnessed this episode firsthand, Martin P. Johnson argues that the failure of January 22 cannot be ascribed to a lack of organization within the communalist political bodies.[32] Instead, the events of January 22 demonstrated their high degree of organization as well as the absence of the minimal level of popular support that all revolutionary movements require. To intimidate the Trochu government, Parisians would have to mobilize on a massive scale. For this to occur in the strongly patriotic climate of 1870–1871, a conjunction of the national and communalist causes was required.[33]

Reacting to this failed uprising even more severely than it had after the revolt of October 31, 1870, the Trochu government cracked down on the revolutionaries. It not only closed the clubs and banned public meetings of the communalist forces, but it also censored two major opposition newspapers: Félix Pyat's *Le Combat* and Charles Delescluze's *Le Réveil*. For Johnson, the closing of the clubs, the arrests of many key militants, and the signing of the armistice (January 26, 1871) had the combined effect of closing a chapter in the communalist movement's development. Although this period was marked by failures, the political lessons drawn from it were considerable: "the months of agitation and the experience of coordinating initiatives and combining efforts had forged a viable revolutionary coalition and a radical political culture."[34]

The Delegation of the Twenty Districts, which brought together the most revolutionary elements—including members of the International, supporters of Auguste Blanqui, and Jacobins—was at the core of revolutionary activities. Other clubs, such as the Republican League, were more broadly based, drawing moderate elements favorable to republicanism into the communalist movement. The revolts of October 31 and January 22 enabled these organizations to learn to work in concert in order to advance a shared political project: the establishment of a communalist democracy in Paris.

The period immediately preceding the inauguration of the Paris Commune (from the armistice of January 27 until March 18, 1871) witnessed the creation of a coalition whose objective was to institute a specific political project: a revolutionary, socialist Commune. In comparison with the previous clubs and associations, this coalition displayed greater ideological cohesion and strived for a stronger focusing of revolutionary efforts. Ideologically, its goal was the political empowerment of workers, the destruction of the dominant political oligarchy, the end of industrial feudalism, and the achievement of political freedom through social equality.[35] At the center of the new movement were the Delegation of the Twenty Districts, the International Association of Workingmen, and the Chambre fédérale de sociétiés ouvrières (Federative Chamber of Workers' Associations). The coalition was thus made up of the most dedicated communalist bodies and the most determined activists.

In parallel to the establishment of the coalition, the Comité central de la garde nationale (Central Committee of the National Guard) was created. The formation of a coordination center of the people's army, the Garde nationale, would prove decisive in the communalist forces' takeover of power. The Central Committee's goal was to federate the numerous sections of the National Guard. As some members of the Central Committee belonged to the communalist movement, a strategy aimed at "merging" the revolutionary socialist movement and the National Guard could be carried out. What occurred on March 18, 1871, was the fruit of that merger.[36]

The political context in the early part of 1871 remained a difficult one for the communalist movement. The Government of National Defense banned the communalist clubs and associations, and the Delegation of the Twenty Districts disappeared after January 22. Many of its members were either imprisoned by Trochu or on the run. But the elections planned for February 8 induced the Delegation to reemerge. In preparation for that date, the key components of the "revolutionary socialist" movement—the Delegation, the IWA, and the Federal Chamber—produced a common slate of candidates. This was one of the first gestures of the new coalition.[37] Among the list of revolutionary socialist candidates were familiar names such as Garibaldi, Blanqui, and Pyat as well as those of lesser-known militants belonging to the IWA and the movement of communalist clubs and associations.

The election results transformed France's urban centers into republican islands "in an ocean of monarchist peasants."[38] In Paris, the majority of those elected were moderate republicans, but a few "revolutionary socialist" candidates were also victorious (B. Malon, H. Tolain, and F. Gambon), along with other left-wing candidates. M. P. Johnson puts the proportion of votes in favor of "revolutionary socialists" in Paris at approximately 15 percent; thus, the communalist option represented a significant minority in the capital.

The monarchists' overwhelming victory nourished the apprehensions of the republicans and revived the fear, especially in Paris, of a monarchist restoration. The new National Assembly, convened in Bordeaux, refused to proclaim the republic and constituted a government composed of a monarchist majority under the leadership of Adolphe Thiers. Pointing to the state of public finances, the Assembly refused to pay members of the National Guard in Paris who were unable to prove that they were destitute. The exodus of a part of the Parisian bourgeoisie to the provinces and the scarcity of soldiers of the French armed forces enabled the revolutionaries to strengthen their base in the capital. What's more, there were in Paris 240,000 armed National Guard soldiers disappointed by their treatment at the hands of the Bordeaux monarchists. In addition, the economic effects of the siege and the war continued to weigh heavily on Parisians, especially the poor and the petite bourgeoisie. Finally, for many Parisians the loss of Paris's status as capital provided more evidence of the Thiers government's intention to restore the monarchy.[39]

Taken together, these factors created favorable conditions for a new attempt to establish a Commune. The "revolutionary socialist" movement was particularly active throughout this period. As a body engaged in direct political action, the coalition was rooted in the popular organizations and promoted the active participation of militants in the coming revolution. For example, the IWA encouraged its members to seek election in the National Guard's central committee in order to rally it to the communalist cause. This is precisely what took place in the first weeks of March, when the majority of seats in the central committee were taken by revolutionary socialist militants.[40]

On March 18, 1871, the supporters of the Commune finally succeeded in taking power. Thanks to the fraternization of the people of Paris with the troops deployed by Thiers early that morning to take control of the capital (as well as the National Guard's artillery), the Communards took Paris's Hôtel de Ville by storm, together with a number of town halls in the districts. By the afternoon, the police was in retreat, thereby confirming the triumph of the Commune and leaving the power in the hands of the National Guard, now an essential component of the communalist movement. While the events of March 18 were not the results of prior planning on the part of the Delegation or the IWA, the Communards took power thanks to the political experience they had acquired in the committees and associations.[41] The people's involvement in the overthrow of the French state proved—to say the least—decisive.

POLITICAL CLUBS UNDER THE COMMUNE: A RADICAL DEMOCRACY

Analyzing the "political clubs" active during the Paris Commune offers fertile grounds for understanding the foundations of the Communards' political action. It was in the local political organizations that the plebeian experience took shape through the institution of a communalist "people's politics" and the revival of the agoraphilic democratic tradition. The expression "political club" refers to associations whose raison d'être was political debate and action. Such clubs first appeared during the French Revolution and were hallmarks of nineteenth-century politics.[42] The clubs multiplied during the Paris Commune of 1871, with education, discussion, and, ultimately, political action as their objectives. Members could keep abreast of news in the district, take part in discussions, and organize upcoming political actions. As conduits between the official organs of the Commune and the Parisian plebs, the clubs made it possible to minimize the distance between the governed and the governing. Within the three major sites of communal power (the Hôtel de Ville, the district town halls, and the streets), the political role played by the clubs was primordial.[43] Indeed, two-thirds of the elected members of the Commune came from the clubs, and eighteen out of twenty districts were represented by a majority of Communards belonging to the club movement. The importance of the clubs for the Commune was such that a top official of the French Interior Ministry would forcefully underscore the major responsibility of the clubs and associations in the revolution of March 18.[44] Thus, not only did plebeian political practice during the siege lead to the advent of the Commune, but it was also a determinant in the growth of radical democratic bodies. This genuine apprenticeship in political action and democracy engendered a climate where political freedom and self-emancipation could occupy center stage on the political scene. The main actors of the Commune wanted to consolidate and develop this new political spirit, as reflected in the forms of political organization of 1871.

There were three levels of communalist political power. First, the civil and military administration, for which the Hôtel de Ville of Paris was the decision-making headquarters. Second, the district town halls, where the communalist vigilance committees and clubs played a crucial role. Finally, the streets, squares, and neighborhood meeting places, where public opinion was formed and expressed and where the presence of communalist militants made itself most strongly felt. In fact, supporters of the Commune played a part at every level of power.[45] Moreover, the communal power structure ensured the involvement of the capital's inhabitants in the various decision-making bodies.

Following negotiations with the district town halls, the Central Committee of the National Guard, installed at the Hôtel de Ville since March 18, decided to hold elections based on universal suffrage in order to lend the communalist revolution electoral legitimacy. A number of important actors in the Delegation of the Twenty Districts wanted the Commune to adopt a more revolutionary approach. Nevertheless, the Delegation endorsed the idea of elections and mapped out a strategy to ensure the presence of its militants at Paris's city hall and the district town halls.[46] In so doing, it opened up the communalist project to both moderate and radical republicans. For the Delegation, the outcome of the March elections was a major victory, which indeed "revenged" the disastrous results of February.[47] The political experience gained in the previous contest no doubt served to enhance the Delegation's electoral vigor in March. But the victory was attributable primarily to the work of the vigilance committees in every district.[48] Among the various groups competing in the elections, only the communalist movement could count on a critical mass of experienced and committed activists. The result of this numerical and organizational advantage was the election of a majority of Commune supporters in March,[49] which contributed to the success of communalist ideas and representatives in Paris. The elected Commune was thus consistent with the pre–March 18 communalist movement, thanks to the political apprenticeship acquired in the local clubs and associations.

The exact number of clubs and associations that existed in Paris during the Commune is nearly impossible to ascertain. This is because certain clubs were quite short-lived, and others changed their names and locations. M. P. Johnson nevertheless maintains that this movement, born prior to March 18, began to expand as of that date. At its peak (early May 1871), there were between thirty and thirty-five large clubs as well as an even greater number of committees and associations specialized in areas such as education and social issues.[50] The frequency of meetings is also difficult to determine. Some notices in the daily newspapers of that period refer to daily meetings, whereas the assemblies of other clubs were convened only three times a week. Although certain districts were more active than others (clubs in the popular districts were more dy-namic than those in the bourgeois districts), the clubs' activities affected the districts of Paris as a whole.

In several districts, the participation of the local vigilance committees, the rank-and-file organizations of the Delegation of the Twenty Districts, was vital for the movement of clubs and associations. In the fifth and sixth districts, for instance, they promoted activities and meetings. Furthermore, the vigilance committees acted as liaisons among the various clubs in the districts, thereby consolidating the base of the communalist movement while at the same time enabling the many to take part in public affairs. One of the vigilance com-mittee's goals was, in fact, to foster the multiplication of clubs and associa-tions throughout the city. The vigilance committee in the nineteenth district, for example, wanted to divide it into subdistricts, each of which would have a communalist club.[51] This project expressed a desire to disseminate the spirit of the clubs and associations as widely as possible and to ensure that strong ties existed among them.

The attendance at clubs and committees varied according to their missions. In general, the large clubs concerned with the affairs of a single district brought together the inhabitants of that area. However, the associations and committees specializing, for instance, in education or issues related to the place of women in the communalist revolution attracted citizens from various districts.[52] But the number of participants in the specialized associations was small, no doubt because they were scattered throughout Paris. Nevertheless, as Serman points out, it was in the clubs that "the anonymous masses voiced their opinion."[53]

Meetings of clubs and associations typically included women and even chil-dren. The communalist public space was thus open to individuals regarded until then as "apolitical."[54] This broader—and, what's more, sustained—participation is surprising, especially in the context of a civil war, which might have dissuaded many citizens from getting involved. Yet attendance at the large clubs in the districts remained strong throughout the Commune's brief career.

Small groups of militants were responsible for ensuring the orderly running of club and association meetings and of the drafting of communalist manifestos and newspaper articles. Most clubs appear to have had such cores of dedicated activists whose function was to act as public speakers. The same was true of the mairies d'arrondissement and the Paris Hôtel de Ville, where civil and military administration tasks were performed by committed rank-and-file militants.

Given the close ties between the clubs and the vigilance committees and between the vigilance committees and the communal administration in Paris, the Commune can be said to have maintained an ongoing connection with the popular movement: "In these circumstances the distance between the leadership and the rank and file was virtually nonexistent."[55] By virtue of the operation of the clubs and associations, the Commune managed to create local democratic bodies while administering the city at the same time. The free and open character of the local political bodies points to the genuinely democratic nature of the Paris Commune and its founding organizations.

An examination of the political culture engendered by the communalist clubs and associations brings to light the Communards' ideological cohesion centered on the notion that the Commune was engaged in a struggle between two worlds: on one hand, the old world of hierarchy, competition, and domination, and on the other, the new world (yet to be built) based on equality, association, and liberty.[56] This can also be framed in terms of a Commune setting a new, scientific era of politics against the old world of the government and the clergy. The "Declaration to the French People" adopted by the Commune affirms:

The communal Revolution, initiated by the people on March 18, inaugurates a new era of experimental, positive, and scientific politics. It puts an end to the old world of governments and clerics, of militarism, bureaucracy, exploitation, speculation, monopolies, and privileges, to which the proletariat owes its servitude, and the country its misfortunes and disasters.[57]

First among the ideals impugned and the enemies identified by the Communalists was perhaps the clergy.[58] As provider of public instruction and medical care, the Catholic Church exercised a great deal of influence and played a decisive role in maintaining the rule of the few over the many throughout the nineteenth century. The communalist fight for secularization was conducted largely by rank-and-file activists, who on occasion would take certain members of the clergy hostage but were generally content to expel them from the schools and hospitals. In this struggle the Communards sometimes resorted to violence, both verbal and physical. It was the militant base of the Commune that applied the anticlerical policies.[59] In particular, the hatred of the clergy paved the way for the appropriation of churches for the purpose of holding club and association meetings. In fact, former churches were among the most important sites of action and discussion in "Paris Libre 1871."

This struggle points to a significant difference between 1848 and 1871. Whereas the revolutionaries of June 1848 believed that religion was compatible with the revolution, this was evidently no longer the case in 1871. In this connection, one must keep in mind the major impact of positivism on the evolution of the communalist revolution,[60] as evidenced by the Commune's homage to the socialist philosopher Pierre Leroux. Indeed, while it underscored Leroux's contribution to socialism, the Commune refrained from "any solidarity with the religious tendencies that always served to support [his] system of social transformation."[61] For most Communards, science was closely associated with social progress, whereas religion was an agent of obscurantism and subjugation.

The Communards were motivated by a certain idea of "revolutionary justice," one based on a distinction between "legality" and "rights." Legality referred to what was allowed by current laws, which were deemed nothing more than instruments for preserving the established order, hence biased in favor of the dominators at the expense of the dominated. Rights, on the other hand, set in motion a dynamic favorable to the emergence of justice, notwithstanding the dominant groups' demands for social or political conservation. Revolutionary justice, closer to rights than to legality, therefore implies obedience to a Law transcending the codes voted by politicians.[62] It is on these grounds that the Communards, when they were tried by Versailles after the fall of the Commune, would refute the illegality of certain actions.

Even though physical violence was rare, verbal and symbolic violence as well as the potential for physical violence produced a climate of fear in Paris for the opponents of the Commune (known as réfractaires, i.e., recalcitrants), a climate for which the club and association membership was largely responsible. However, the Communards did not resort to gratuitous violence. For them, acts of violence came under the head of revolutionary justice, and they believed such acts to be compatible with the building of the "new world" of the Commune. It must be stressed, however, that the Communards did accept differences of opinion concerning the operation or direction of the Commune. In other words, a space for discussion and action was open to those who accepted the principle of the Commune. People were free to challenge its key actors as well as the actions of the Central Committee. But political tolerance did not extend to the recalcitrants. Thus, certain adversaries of the Commune were arrested and imprisoned by militants of clubs and associations in the districts. In addition to priests, former police officers and property owners were targeted by the Communards.[63] More than mere discussion groups, the rank-and-file political organizations of the Commune were sites of direct political action.

The communalist conception of revolutionary justice involved a specific vision of equality among citizens. For the Communards, equality could no longer be abstract; hence, it was less a subject for debate in the clubs and associations than a principle for action whose application in everyday life was imperative. Hardships as well as responsibilities and duties had to be shared among the various groups making up Parisian society. For example, communalist activists wanted the Commune to pursue the policy, introduced by the National Defense government, of requisitioning foodstuffs. The requisition policy ensured that the poor had the same access to basic goods as the wealthy. Beyond equal access for the dominated and the dominators, there was also a desire for genuine equality among Communards. Therefore, the salaries of the officials and representatives of the Commune were capped so as not to exceed four times the average salary of a worker.[64]

It was through the struggle for true equality among citizens that the Communards succeeded in reversing certain traditional social relationships. The reversal involved the transformation of an established power relationship into its contrary, a transposition that was widespread under the Commune. Among the more significant reversals was the arrest of former police officers by liberated political prisoners, as revolutionary justice sometimes requires the detention of agents of the fallen regime. Other instances include atheist meetings held in churches, anticlerical speeches delivered from the pulpit, as well as "dressing up idols to look like canteen women or national guards."[65] Conversely, the street—formerly a Mecca for militant communalist demonstrations—gradually turned into a meeting place for the moderate and conservative forces of Paris.[66] Ultimately, the equality advocated by the Communards entailed a threefold destitution of the dominant classes: political, economic, and social. This was without doubt the most consequential reversal effected by the Paris Commune and may in part explain the bourgeoisie's outpouring of hate and vindictiveness during the Bloody Week.

The creation of a Committee for Public Safety manifested the desire to situate the Commune within the French revolutionary tradition. Its establishment furthermore represented a decisive step in the history of 1871, because it broke the revolutionary alliance between the majority wishing to adopt radical and authoritarian methods to defend the Commune and the minority supporting a more democratic approach. This measure was connected with the communalist movement that had developed in the clubs and associations of the districts.[67] The initial impetus in support of a Committee for Public Safety had originated in the vigilance committees of the nineteenth district.[68] Not one club or association spoke out against the idea of such a committee, and many voiced their endorsement.

In May, the Communal council came out in favor of creating a five-member committee empowered to take strong measures to protect the Commune and ensure military victory over the Versailles forces. The split between the "authoritarian" majority and the "democratic" minority was accentuated by the makeup of the Committee for Public Safety, whose members all belonged to the majority. In addition, the democratic minority was excluded from the Communal commissions, in particular the military commission. On May 15, 1871, the minority temporarily withdrew from the Communal Council and published a manifesto stating the reasons for their opposition to the Committee for Public Safety.

For the minority, "concerned with social and anti-authoritarian measures,"[69] the creation of a Committee for Public Safety represented the centralization of power and the marginalization of the democratic ideal that the Commune must embody. It appeared to be a backward step, whereas the Commune was supposed to be forward looking. Thus, the Committee for Public Safety seemed to the minority a "parody of the past" and a "revolutionary pasticcio," whose power would lack authority.[70] The painter Gustave Courbet, a minority member of the Communal council, aptly describes the minority's sense of the impossibility of returning to the past:

I would like for all the titles and words belonging to the Revolution of '89 and '93 to be applied to that period alone. Today, they no longer mean the same thing, nor can they be used with the same appropriateness or the same acceptations. The titles Public Safety, Montagnards, Girondins, Jacobins, and so forth cannot be used in the republican socialist movement. We represent the years between '93 and '71 with the mentality that must characterize our own temperament and emanate from it. To me, this seems all the more evident because we resemble plagiarists, and we are reproducing to our detriment a terror that does not belong to our times. Let us use terms that our revolution suggests to us.[71]

The minority not only decried an initiative that it regarded as anachronistic, but it also rejected the idea of a dictatorship imposing a specific policy on the Commune and its local bodies.[72] That is why it withdrew from the Communal Council and returned to the district town halls to work more closely with communalist activists. The minority also included anti-Robespierrists, such as Jules Vallès,[73] who no doubt did not wish to see a repetition of the Jacobin offensive against the sans-culottes in Year II. The concern about the fate of the Communards belonging to the local associations and clubs stemmed also from the memory of the sans-culottes in the sectional societies.[74] It attests to the democratic ideal found in Paris in 1871. Despite breaking with the majority, the minority recognized in its manifesto their common adherence to the same broad objectives, specifically, "political freedom [and] the emancipation of the workers."[75]

For the majority, whose members included Jacobins and Blanquists as well as "Independent Revolutionaries,"[76] the creation of the Committee for Public Safety was necessary for the sake of efficiency in the fight against Versailles. Indeed, the properly democratic proceedings of the deliberative organs of the Commune appear to have slowed up decision making, which was a problem insomuch as the imperatives of war required a swifter administrative process.[77] In response to the accusation of wanting to establish a dictatorship, it could be argued that the Committee for Public Safety was accountable to the council of the Commune, which remained free to determine its own composition. Finally, the Committee for Public Safety in fact did not organize a new "Terror."[78] With respect to military organization, the Committee proved so inefficient that its composition had to be modified soon after it was established.[79]

Beyond the divisions between the majority and the minority in the Communal Council, the words and symbols of the French Revolution affected the revolutionaries' political analysis and activism in France throughout the nineteenth century.[80] The Great Revolution in a way served as an analytical framework for the purpose of making political events and issues intelligible. During the Commune, communalist speakers and journalists did not hesitate to situate the revolution of March 18 in a continuum with 1793, and they held up its major protagonists—Robespierre, Marat, and other celebrated names of the

Revolution—as role models. The Committee for Public Safety can therefore be viewed as a product of the French Revolution's undeniable power of attraction.

The language and institutions of the French Revolution remained at the heart of the struggle for the Commune. By creating an ersatz Committee for Public Safety, the majority in the Communal Council and the communalist militants who supported this initiative yielded to the "myth of 1793," the idea that history could repeat itself but with results different from those of 1793. But what if this yielding to the myth of 1793 were viewed as indicative of the transformation of liberty into its opposite, servitude? From that perspective, the Commune, an example of a people's politics opening the way to political freedom, can be thought of as having succumbed to the One, to the desire for unity as represented by the Committee for Public Safety. Accordingly, the reliance on the Committee would signify the beginning of the Commune's decline as a political regime of liberty. The establishment of such a committee implies the introduction of "leaders of the plebs" and, hence, of the possibility of a "Dictatorship." The Commune no longer evolved in keeping with the desire to achieve self-emancipation based on the "natural . . . authority" or "intelligen[ce]"[81] that would enable the many to acquire true political autonomy. With the creation of the Public Safety Committee, the legacy of the French Revolution proved harmful for freedom and emancipation. That is perhaps why Gustave Lefrançais, a member of the minority, wrote:

> "Happy are the peoples who have no history!" says the philosopher, whose name has been forgotten. And we readily add: How happy the Commune would be if it had no revolutionary traditions! For indeed, the sole concern of the vast majority of its members, preoccupied with historical memories, was to take up—as the accepted phrase would have it—"the great tradition of '93" interrupted by the fall of the Hébertistes, say the Blanquistes; by Thermidor, say the Jacobins.[82]

Karl Marx as well, no doubt concerned about the direction taken by something as precious as a communalist revolution, affirms that the task of the Communards would be "not to recapitulate the past, but to build up the future."[83] Thus, the French Revolution's hold on the minds of the Communards prevented them from being creative and imaginative in the face of the threats confronting the Commune. Rather than blazing its own potentially original trail, the council of the Commune engaged in pastiche, thereby sacrificing the democratic nature of the free political regime established through the communal insurrection of March 18, 1871.

THE COMMUNALIST CONTRIBUTION:
CRITIQUE OF POLITICS, PRACTICE OF FREEDOM

It remains for us to specify the Commune's contribution to the communalist and agorophile traditions. The Paris Commune of 1871 was an attempt to build a modern form of political organization outside the framework of the state. Indeed, it belonged to a movement opposed to the modern nineteenth-century state. It established a noncoercive power and thus introduced a different organization of collective existence, one better suited to the idea of a democracy where active citizenship is a crucial element of the community's overall functioning. It is Karl Marx who must be credited with having identified the Paris Commune's antistate contribution. His reading of the communalist revolution offers a fruitful approach to analyzing the Commune's contribution to our understanding of a people's politics and of modern political freedom.[84]

In the third part of *The Civil War in France* (1871), Marx presents an interpretation of the Commune that situates it within the antistate current. For him the Commune could have been content to take over the instruments of the modern state and put them at the service of the dominated, especially since those instruments were ubiquitous in French society at the time. The central power of the state, in particular through the standing army, the bureaucracy, and the police, as well as the clergy and the legal system, had developed greatly since it was born under the ancien régime. Indeed, the centralized power of the state had been consolidated by the Empire. And this state power "assumed more and more the character of the national power of capital over labor, of a public force organized for social enslavement, of an engine of class despotism." According to Marx, the Empire increased the subordination of social groups to the class of property owners, whose economic hegemony it ensured. Thus, the bourgeoisie was able to develop enormously under the Empire: "Its industry and commerce expanded to colossal dimensions; financial swindling celebrated cosmopolitan orgies; the misery of the masses was set off by the shameless display of gorgeous, meretricious and debased luxury."[85] While the bourgeoisie was busy accumulating vast wealth, the power of the imperial state was corrupted. For Marx, it represented the ultimate development of the tool enabling the bourgeoisie to liberate itself from the snares of feudalism. That liberation, however, required the subjugation of all social classes to the imperatives of capital. This was accomplished thanks to state power and implied that the accumulation of capital would be the primary objective of the Empire's economic policy, to the detriment of fair wages for workers.

Consequently, the Paris Commune of 1871 was for Marx the "direct antithesis to the empire." Under the Commune, Paris became the site of an attempt to abolish class domination through the abolition of state power. Since the state as political form was historically the propertied classes' tool for dominating the nonpropertied classes, the Commune did not seek to put the modern state apparatus in the hands of the dominated. To the contrary, in fact, one of the Commune's first acts was to eliminate the standing army and replace it with the National Guard, that is, the "armed people."[86] By thus abolishing one of the most crucial (and most visible) components of state power, the Commune constructed a collective existence different from the one established by the ancien régime and reinforced by the Empire. The Commune thereby attacked the symbol par excellence of the sovereignty of the modern state, that is, the state force responsible for protecting the country's territorial integrity. That is why for Marx the revolution of 1871 proved to be a revolution against the state.

The political form adopted by the Commune was an innovation in the form of the modern state. Not quite an executive power nor altogether a legislative power, it combined both inasmuch as its members deliberated and then applied the ratified decisions. It also dealt with the apparatuses of central power. The police, for example, "was at once stripped of its political attributes, and turned into the responsible and at all times revocable agent of the Commune." The bureaucratic apparatus generally underwent the same treatment as the police: "Public functions ceased to be the private property of the tools of the Central Government."[87] Instead they were put in the service of the Commune and, hence, of the needs of the many.

The Commune took on not only the tangible instruments of state and bourgeois domination but also the spiritual bedrock of that domination: the Church. As we have seen, the struggle against the clergy was fervently waged by the militants of the clubs and associations in the districts. According to Marx, this anticlerical struggle was part of the communal attempt to break the power of the state. Moreover, removing education from the dominance of the priests and the state made it possible to liberate science "from the fetters which class prejudice and governmental forces had imposed upon it."[88] The spiritual control of the French bourgeoisie through the intermediary of the Church was thus undermined by the Communards' offensive against Catholicism.

The establishment of the Commune could have altered the political structure of France as a whole. Indeed, the Communards wished for the Commune's political form to be adopted throughout the land, so as to become "the political form of even the smallest country hamlet." A system of delegation from one administrative level to the next would have made communes the basis of a new form of national unity, with truly democratic foundations, since it would have enabled everyone to take part. Concretely, from the hamlet to the county seat, from the county seat to the department, and from the department to the National Assembly in Paris, elected and revocable delegates would have made decisions and implemented the policies of the communes of France. In opposition to national unity ensured by "State power which claimed to be the embodiment of that unity independent of, and superior to, the nation itself,"[89] the Commune put forward a sort of democratic federation of communes of which the Paris Commune would be the hub.

For Marx, an original political form such as the Paris Commune was commonly apt to be mistaken for older political structures. Hence, March 18, 1871, was believed by many to be a return to the medieval communes that had preceded and later served as the foundations for state power. Furthermore, the fight of the Paris Commune against state power was also "mistaken for an exaggerated form of the ancient struggle against over-centralisation." But, writes Marx, the Commune of 1871 can hardly be reduced to such formations or historical struggles. The novelty of the Commune resided above all in its desire to liberate "all the forces hitherto absorbed by the state parasite feeding upon, and clogging the free movement of, society."[90] In other words, by freeing society from the grip of the modern state's coercive power, the Commune could ultimately have set free the lifeblood of French society. The acknowledgment of this unprecedented task would suffice to set aside any identification of the Paris Commune with older historical political forms and struggles.

It is at this point in his analysis that Marx introduces the enigmatic notion of the "Communal Constitution." Though not developed at length, the idea of a "Communal Constitution" enables us to grasp more firmly the political innovation of which the events of 1871 were the vehicle. The "Communal Constitution" struggles against the state as "a parasitic excrescence," which ineluctably strives to serve its own interests. The Communal Constitution would seek to guarantee the free development of citizens while at the same time recognizing "municipal liberty." Thus, the Communal Constitution could have "initiated the regeneration of France."[91] But the Communal Constitution could have this effect only on one condition: that it be a working-class government. As such, it could have brought about the emancipation of, as Saint-Simon puts it, "the most numerous and poorest class." According to Marx, by emancipating the proletariat, the Communal Constitution would have prepared the way for the emancipation of humankind.

For Marx, the "secret" of the Commune was precisely that "it was essentially a working-class government," that is, the political form capable of "work[ing]

out the economic emancipation of labour."[92] As the end product of the struggle between the dominators and dominated, or between the workers and the
bourgeoisie, the Paris Commune represented the establishment of a political
administration whose objectives coincided with the needs of the dominated.
The Commune was therefore a revolution against the state but not against the
idea of government.

Marx nevertheless recognizes that the policies implemented by the Commune were modest. Still, the elimination of the night shift for bakers indicates
the direction that the Commune's initiatives would have taken. The bias in
favor of ordinary people was perceptible in most of the measures taken by the
Communal Council. Yet, writes Marx, "the great social measure of the Commune was its own working existence."[93] That is why the particular measures of
the Commune cannot in themselves serve to evaluate an emancipatory undertaking such as this.

The identification of the Commune as a revolution against the state is perhaps the most fertile element of Karl Marx's interpretation, especially since
this outlook was shared by certain actors of the Commune. Gustave Lefrançais, for example, asserted that the Communards who endorsed the creation
of a Committee for Public Safety (i.e., the majority) failed to understand that
the Commune as a political form rejected the modern state. Unaware of the
antistate specificity of the Commune, the majority succumbed to the myth of
1793 and, especially, to the "raison d'état,"[94] which explains the recourse to an
instrument as bureaucratic and potentially lethal for liberty as the Committee
for Public Safety.

The writings of Lefrançais also point to the regeneration of politics of which
the Commune was an agent. For, as Marx maintains, while its negative content was the rejection of the modern state as an inevitably self-serving form,
the Commune's positive and innovative contents resided perhaps in the idea
of the possibility for everyone to take part in public life. In other words, the
Paris Commune's contribution to the communalist and agoraphile traditions
has been the creation of a democratic regime based on the blossoming of a
civic life open to the participation of all citizens favorable to the communalist
enterprise. Through the clubs and associations in the districts, the Commune
embodied the resurgence of political freedom in the heart of modernity. By
struggling against state—that is, coercive—power (a power exercised on others), the political experience of the Commune brought in a noncoercive form
of power, one that emerges through the concerted action of the citizens (a
power exercised with others).

Gustave Lefrançais's writings testify to the twofold mission of the Commune: challenging state power and building a free political regime based on power that arises with others. He asserts,

> The revolution of March 18th ... did not bring with it mere modifications of the administrative and political workings of the country. Its goal was not simply to decentralize power. On pain of giving the lie to its initial affirmations, it had the mission of erasing Power itself, of restoring to all members of the social body their effective sovereignty by substituting the right to direct initiative of those concerned—the governed—for the pernicious, corrupting, and henceforth impotent action of the government, which it had to reduce to the role of an ordinary administrative agency.[95]

What does this signify? Perhaps Lefrançais chooses to capitalize the term "power" in order to underscore its majesty and imperial sovereignty. From his decidedly antiauthoritarian perspective, "Power" can only refer to state power, to the state's exercise of coercive force. By suppressing "Power," the Commune therefore had to place "effective sovereignty" in the hands of the citizens in order to bring about a form of self-government. In the words of Jacques Rougerie, "The communard revolutionary wants full and complete popular sovereignty. Full sovereignty through the direct government of the people, by the people, is a demand that one sees constantly affirmed."[96] What Lefrançais suggests here is that in opposition to the coercive and corrupt rule of the dominators, the Commune proposes to the dominated the right to direct political initiative. Hence, a noncoercive "power" arises, a power whose wellspring is the concerted action of citizens.

By referring to the Paris Commune's antistate struggle, one can identify two distinct models of "government," the first being the state as government imposing a direction on collective existence and the second being the Commune as a government founded on the concerted action of the citizens. The first case involves a gubernator[97] state, a state government that, like a ship's captain, controls the rudder of political and social life. In this situation, the vision of collective existence is nurtured primarily by "agoraphobia." Indeed, this conception of the state rests on the distancing of citizens from public affairs. The sovereign state seeks to impose itself on the political community, or, to borrow Marx's terms, it constantly strives for greater independence from social life. This desire for autonomy, which expresses itself through an increasingly stifling authoritarianism, enables the gubernator state to occupy—in the manner of a "parasitic excrescence"—more and more space in the daily lives of individuals while at the same time denying them daily access to its domains.

The Commune, as a different form of government, was constituted through the recognition of the citizens' role in community affairs. The communal government had no wish to direct, as the gubernator state does, but accepted the reciprocity between the various organs of government and the local democratic bodies. The communal experience was based precisely on the idea of sovereignty being not restricted to the government apparatus but exercised in the associations and clubs of the districts. By ridding the Commune of the coercive force proper to the gubernator state, the Communards established a political institution involving a truly democratic rule of Law. Would this be the deeper meaning that Marx intended with the enigmatic phrase "Communal Constitution"? If so, a "subterranean" continuity can be drawn between what the young Marx meant by "true democracy" in his 1843 manuscript *Toward a Critique of Hegel's Philosophy of Right*[98] and the notion of a "Communal Constitution" found in his later text on the Paris Commune, *The Civil War in France* (1871).[99]

In *Souvenirs d'un révolutionnaire*, Gustave Lefrançais reexamines the distinctiveness of the Commune as an attempt to organize modern democratic collective existence in a new way. He advances the hypothesis that the attempt to introduce a plebeian political configuration was precisely what aroused the murderous hatred displayed by the Versaillais during the Bloody Week. Addressing the bourgeois anti-Communards, Lefrançais writes,

> The Commune demonstrated that the proletariat was ready to manage itself and could get along without you, whereas you claim to be the only ones able to "run things." The obvious proof of this was the immediate reorganization of the public services that you had abandoned. . . . The Commune attempted to substitute direct action and the citizens' continuous supervision for your governments, all based on the "raison d'état," which conceals and shields your pillaging and every sort of government villainy.[100]

Hence, what the Paris Commune opposed to the "raison d'état" and the crude "Machiavellianism" of the French state exiled in Versailles were forms of political organization that respected the human political condition, forms that above all were attentive to the many and allowed citizens to participate actively in decision-making bodies. By rejecting the "raison d'état" and its freedom-destroying imperatives, the Commune shows us the possibility of building a truly free political regime in the heart of modernity.

It remains for us to determine what sort of "reason" the Commune wanted to substitute for the "raison d'état." Given the brevity of the communal experience, there can be only a partial answer to that question. We can affirm, nevertheless, that such "reason" was not based on instrumental objectives. Indeed, instrumental rationality is characteristic of the "raison d'état." Nor does the communal rationality seem to have been that of communicative action or rationality as theorized by Jürgen Habermas.[101] Communal democracy was more than deliberative; it involved a significant element of direct action that cannot be reduced to a communicative activity. Rather, what the communal experience points to is an alternative conception of rationality concerned more with justice than with economic performance or efficiency, as confirmed by the previously mentioned example of the elimination of the night shift for bakers.

As a critique of the politics of the modern state and a practice of politics as a site of human freedom, the Paris Commune is exemplary in that it attempted to institute a different organization of modern collective existence, and it did so in the exceedingly difficult context of a civil war followed by a military defeat. The analyses of Marx and Lefrançais enable us to grasp both the negative and creative contributions of the communalist revolution. On a more practical level, what emerges from the above examination of the communalist political enterprise is the shape of the "new politics"[102] (or "new world") that the actors of the Commune hoped for. The Communards strived for a world with more solidarity, more justice, and more equality among the various social groups. These plebeian aspirations could be realized only through the establishment of local democratic bodies, such as the district clubs and associations. For such aspirations to be fulfilled, the modern state, that instrument of political domination, had to be done away with. And the communalist political bodies were the only possible political alternative to state power.

Tumultuous, adversarial, and sometimes even violent, communalist political action was founded upon the possibility for everyone to take part in political life. Thus, the Commune bore witness to the political capacity of the many. To those who consider the plebs to be subpolitical, the experience of the Paris Commune of 1871 shows that the many are capable of instituting a politics of the people and that when they do, political freedom ensues. Here, communalism and agoraphilia once again emerged together through this further modern affirmation of the plebeian principle.

PART III

THE NATURE OF THE HUMAN BOND

PROLOGUE
SOCIAL BOND, POLITICAL BOND,
AND MODERNITY

Queer, the affection you can feel for a stranger!
—George Orwell, *Homage to Catalonia*

THE QUESTION OF THE FORMS OF POLITICAL ORGANIZATION established during plebeian experiences relates to a particular conceptualization of the notion of "power." In the case of the sectional societies, the London Corresponding Society, and the numerous clubs and associations at the root of the communalist movement of 1871, the "power" of the plebs did not rest upon the "monopoly of the legitimate use of violence" (M. Weber). Quite the contrary, in each of those experiences, the plebs' forms of organization fought *against* the wielder of the "monopoly of the legitimate use of violence," the state. Instead, these plebeian organizations suggest a kind of "power" that arises when individuals act together in a concerted fashion. Such power is not exerted *over* others but emerges *with* others. Hence, through action, the plebeian experience refutes a definition that reduces power to domination and violence. The refutation clears a political path scarcely explored in our political tradition. This path, which we will refer to as "communalist," situates power as collective action at the heart of human affairs. It thus participates in a different conception of human beings, especially of their relationship to others.

The issue of power as concerted action is connected with that of the "human bond," defined as the elements and factors that bring together individuals, by definition singular, within the same community. The human bond pertains to what incites dissimilar individuals to agree to live together and form a community. Studying it therefore involves identifying the foundations of collective existence. However, as noted by the sociologist Francis Farrugia, the human bond or, to borrow his terminology, the "social bond," as a research subject is at once an analytical category and a value.[1] As an analytical category, the social bond is an analyzable and describable empirical phenomenon. Yet, when regarded as a value, the social bond can be the object of a critique aimed at assessing its presence and efficacy in human communities or societies. In that context, describing the social bond amounts to evaluating it and, consequently, evaluating the bodies that engender the bond.

The question of the human bond as a "social bond" is central to sociological thought. The founders of the discipline, such as Auguste Comte, Ferdinand Tönnies, and Émile Durkheim, devoted themselves to exploring that bond.[2] In classical sociological thought, this question revolves around the dichotomy between community and society. Following Tönnies, the author of a seminal work of sociology, *Community and Society*,[3] Durkheim maintains that the social bond is to be sought in the community, which constitutes human beings' only natural and organic group, while society creates no more than a simulated or, rather, an artificial social bond. In fact, society is instituted through a contract that considers only a single aspect of human existence—the mercantile dimension.[4] This founding contract of modern society leads directly, according to Durkheim, to anomie, that is, to the destruction of sociability and community values and to the disappearance of collective laws and organization. Consequently, to reestablish the social bond or indeed the *community* bond, one must return to an organic community within which individuals feel naturally bound to one another.

From a firmly political perspective, these few sociological considerations on the social bond seem to omit a constitutive facet of human existence: politics. Yet "sociability and politicalness [*politicité*] must not be confused. Only the latter creates social bonds."[5] A type of bond other than the social may be created through political action. The nature of sociology, which posits the social as the central element of modern life, leads it to neglect the distinctions between the social bond and the political bond.[6]

Therefore, to avoid any ambiguity, let us distinguish among three terms: "human bond," "social bond," and "political bond." The "human bond" is inextricably linked to human existence. Throughout life we bond with others. The "human bond" denotes the most general level of human sociability. The phrase "human bond" signifies that human life cannot be absolutely solitary; we cannot exclude others from our existence.[7] A "human bond" will exist so long as there is a *human* community.[8] The human bond can be expressed in two ways.

First, in the form of a "social bond" that arises in and through *collective existence*, which means that the social bond depends on the very nature of society. It relates to the social as a set of shared institutions, mores, and values within a specific community. On the other hand, the human bond can be expressed as a "political bond." In that case, concerted action rather than society is what produces the bond. The political bond therefore denotes the human relationship established through *common action*. Whereas the social bond depends on society, the political bond depends on the political community. Thus, the "human bond" designates the general form of interhuman relationships, which can assume either a social form ("social bond") or a political form ("political bond").

To understand better the political character of the bond that can exist among individuals, a brief analysis is required of that quintessential enterprise of the destruction of politics, totalitarianism. Such an analysis should make it possible to demonstrate that politics is conterminous with a particular bond, because in order to destroy politics, totalitarianism must attack the bond among human beings.

In opposition to a persistent and problematical "misinterpretation"[9] of totalitarianism as an excessive politicization, Miguel Abensour contends that total domination represents an attempt to destroy the space between individuals. This space, according to Hannah Arendt, is the guarantor of politics because it allows individuals to bond with others while at the same time conserving a place sheltered from political matters.[10] Rather than politicizing every sphere of human life, as a certain contemporary mantra claims, totalitarian domination seeks to put an end to politics by attacking the human bond through a sustained assault on the spaces between individuals.

The field of architecture offers a convincing interpretation of the totalitarian treatment of the human bond. In *De la compacité*, Miguel Abensour shows that the aim of gigantic and extravagant totalitarian architectural projects (like Albert Speer's "Der Grosse Platz" in Berlin, 1937–1940) is to subject the "mass" to a "radical heteronomy" in the face of the state. By creating monumental spaces, totalitarian architecture strives to do away with the phobia of contact and to foster a desire among individuals to merge together "in a compact body."[11] The result is a "density" that addresses the human desire to live in an intensely close and basely egalitarian society. This is what Élias Canetti asserts in *Crowds and Power*: "In that density, where there is barely any space between, and body presses against body, each man is as near the other as he is to himself; and an immense feeling of relief ensues. It is for the sake of this blessed moment, when no-one is greater or better than another, that people become a crowd."[12] By creating density through excessively large spaces capable of bringing the mass together and which make it absurd to gather in small numbers, totalitarian regimes *abolish* the vital distance between individuals.

Imprisoned in density, the individual sees himself deprived of what separates him from others. The totalitarian suppression of the space between individuals makes the formation of a political bond inconceivable. When individuals live in density and meet others only on the basis of an intense closeness, it becomes impossible for them to open up to others and to form relationships. They become a "mass." The totalitarian enterprise succeeds in creating masses within the gigantic spaces that it constructs. But because the masses are presented with instances of substitution, the political appeal addressed to them represents the destruction of all political subjects. Denied any political action, the mass is entitled only to a "depoliticizing mobilization" through rituals, music, and *mises-en-scène* that transform political action into ideological belief: "What is specific to totalitarian regimes is not so much the violence it does to a problematical human essence, nor even the displacement of the boundaries of the human, but rather the assault on the human bond, the destruction of relationships among individuals, of the interhuman order. . . . What is at issue here is the social bond and the political bond among individuals."[13] In sum, in order to destroy politics, totalitarianism strikes at social and political bonds through the vital spaces that such bonds require.[14] Hence, there appears to be a significant, even constitutive, connection between the question of the human bond and politics.

While seeking to distinguish between the "social bond" and the "political bond," how can one understand the issue of the human bond in the French Revolution, the making of the English working class, and the Paris Commune of 1871? The purpose of the following chapters is to answer that question. By identifying the nature of the bond in those three political experiences, we will be able to grasp the nature of the human bond formed in the communalist and agoraphile traditions.

6
THE SANS-CULOTTES
A POLITICAL BOND OF FRATERNITY

The essential characteristic of the political behavior of the sans-culottes . . . is based
on fraternity. This is to be understood not as an abstract virtue but as the feeling,
indeed the sensation of unity among the sans-culottes.
—Albert Soboul, *Les sans-culottes parisiens en l'an II*

YEAR III OF THE FRENCH REVOLUTION MARKED THE END OF THE
plebeian political practices of the sans-culottes. Aside from Babeuf's conspiracy in the year IV,[1] the main political contribution of the sans-culottes came to
an end with the repression of the Prairial insurrection and the political fallout
of that defeat, that is, the attack against the popular movement and the concomitant suppression of the right to insurrection in the Constitution of 1795.
However, it was the revolutionary bourgeoisie's liquidation of the sectional
societies in the year II that signaled the end of the sans-culottes' political experiment: "Seeing their aspirations flouted, their organizations destroyed, the
sans-culottes detached themselves from the revolutionary government, found
refuge in passivity or muted resistance; this was the climate that nurtured the
tragedy of Thermidor."[2]

The development of a particular human bond can be discerned in this plebeian experience, despite its neutralization. The relationships maintained by
the Parisian sans-culottes appear to have been determined by the revolutionary and republican principle of "fraternity."[3] This constituted a "political" bond
because the cohesion of the sans-culottes' movement was achieved in and
through the political action that set it in motion. But the revolutionary political
context in which the plebs' action was deployed rendered the "political bond of
fraternity" complex and fragile.

THE SANS-CULOTTES: A POLITICAL BOND

As observed in chapter 3, *sans-culotte* designates a group composed of individuals belonging to a variety of socioeconomic categories. Workers as well as small property owners and artisans took part in the political bodies of the Parisian plebs. The term *sans-culotte* encompasses all those without economic power or political status. Hence, to be a sans-culotte implied "a feeling of solidarity among the ordinary people [transcending] the boundaries between wage earners, independent artisans, and small business owners."[4] The politics of the sans-culottes were characterized by the intertwinement of their economic and political demands, and the cohesion of their movement rested precisely on this convergence of *both* social *and* democratic demands.

Albert Soboul underscores, for instance, the role of "hunger" in the political actions of the Parisian plebs. It is, for him, an "essential factor in the popular movements [and] the cement binding together categories as diverse as the artisan, the shop owner, and the laborer, who coalesced around a common interest in opposing the big merchant, the entrepreneur, the noble or bourgeois speculator." But Soboul goes on to state that "political factors"[5] resulting from their social situation motivated the sans-culottes to engage in political actions. In fact, the association of social and political issues seems to be a distinguishing feature of plebeian political struggles.

This explains why the resolution of the social question necessarily required direct political action. The sans-culottes sought to end the political and economic domination of the few through the establishment of a genuine political democracy in Paris. The human bond of the sans-culottes was therefore a political one because it involved relationships that were indeed political.

FRATERNITY IN ACTION

As the historian Mona Ozouf has noted, "fraternity" is the revolutionary and republican principle that is the least rooted in the founding intellectual tradition of the French Revolution, that is, the European Enlightenment. For while the ideas of liberty and equality are clearly expressed in that tradition, the idea of fraternity appears only marginally. Moreover, "fraternity" does not enjoy the same status as liberty or equality. As a "moral obligation,"[6] fraternity does not represent a right that might give rise to demands. It is in a way a requirement of republican citizenship. The fact that fraternity appears only incidentally in the major texts of the Revolution attests to its ambiguous status throughout the revolutionary events. Thus, it was not until 1848 that fraternity was finally added, alongside liberty and equality, to the motto of the Republic.[7]

The quasi-absence of the principle of fraternity from the official texts of the First Republic does not mean, however, that it did not play an important role in the Revolution. In fact, its presence and influence were considerable, especially among the sans-culottes: "Hence it scarcely matters that the word does not appear in legislative texts. It was present everywhere else."[8] Ultimately, the absence of fraternity from the official documents bespeaks its plebeian character. The recourse to fraternity made it possible, in particular, to distinguish the popular movement from the Jacobin authorities.[9] Furthermore, fraternity emerged as one of the major "horizon[s]" of the Revolution. Its extension and scope seemed limitless.[10] By placing fraternity at the heart of political action, the sans-culottes created an opening that inaugurated a distinct political experience. But the substance of the principle of fraternity remains implicit. What was fraternity for the sans-culottes? How did it affect the human bond? How did it lead to a new political practice?

Soboul proposes the following definition: "Fraternity can be understood as not only the bonds of affection among citizens but signifies as well that they are fused into a mass where all are equal."[11] Accordingly, fraternity implies reciprocal relationships and feelings of affection but also a collective ("fused into a mass")[12] and egalitarian vision of political action. What enabled the sans-culottes to join together was the impression that each of them had of being part of the same enlarged family, the human family. The bond of fraternity is political because it was formed, as Soboul specifies, "among *citizens*."[13] Its collectiveness involved a very pronounced egalitarian dimension. The bond was therefore premised on a political practice that challenged the idea of a natural inequality among human beings.

The sans-culottes' notion of fraternity covered two meanings: (1) an ideal, abstract meaning and (2) a concrete meaning linked to a set of practices through which it was implemented. Fraternity was, on one hand, closely related to the ideas of "union" and "unity." In the vocabulary of the sans-culottes, who used them interchangeably, the differences between the three terms were blurred. The "triangular quasi-synonymy" designated both the necessary "fraternity-union-unity" of the Parisian sections and that of the French Republic. For example, the appeal to "fraternity-union-unity" issued by the poorer sections in the east end of Paris was intended to persuade the wealthier sections of the city "to make common cause with [them]."[14] Albert Soboul even suggests that the sans-culottes' political action was based on this threefold idea.

The political behavior of the sans-culotte was "grounded in fraternity. This is to be understood not as an abstract virtue, but as the feeling, indeed the sensation of the *unity* of the sans-culotte movement."[15] That is why those who rejected the feeling of fraternity could only be enemies of the Revolution. To participate in the revolutionary enterprise, it was necessary to share the idea of "fraternity-union-unity." Nevertheless, during the revolutionary events the ideal aspect of fraternity remained secondary.

At the same time, the concrete meaning of fraternity refers to a set of political and social practices. On the political level, fraternity among the sans-culottes was linked to "fraternization," a key political practice of the plebs to which we will return. On the social plane, fraternity was tied to the question of dignity. As a dominated group freed from the multiple controls of the ancien régime, the sans-culottes were very sensitive to violations of their equal share in human dignity. Any offense against that dignity was considered an offense against the fraternity at the core of the new world inaugurated by the Revolution. Certain social attitudes were hence deemed incompatible with fraternity:

> The sans-culottes tolerate neither arrogance nor contempt: these are aristocratic sentiments contrary to the spirit of fraternity that must prevail among equal citizens, and they obviously imply a political position hostile to democracy as practiced by the sans-culottes in their general assemblies and popular associations.[16]

The sense of fraternity was sufficiently strong among the sans-culottes to modify certain longstanding and widespread language usages. For example, rather than addressing a stranger as *Monsieur*, the sans-culottes used the title *Citoyen* (Citizen).[17] This title was more political and also more fraternal. In fact, *Citoyen* implied a connection between strangers, whereas *Monsieur* carried no such connotation. Similarly, claiming that the use of the formal second person, *vous*, created a distance between individuals and separated them, the sans-culottes fought to have it replaced by *tu*, the informal second person. The wish to impose the fraternal *tutoiement*—the use of *tu*—among citizens of the First Republic represented to some extent a means to further "de-hierarchize"[18] French society, the *vous* being perceived as a vestigial legacy of feudalism. As free citizens, the sans-culottes hoped that the use of *tu* would become the expression par excellence of fraternity.[19]

Fraternization as Political Practice

As a political practice, "fraternization" was conceived as a response to a specific problem of the French Revolution. In the spring of 1793, a struggle for control of the revolutionary government pitted the Jacobins against the Girondins. In order to win this battle for power, the Jacobins needed the support of the Parisian sans-culottes. Now, the power of the sans-culottes was manifested essentially through the various Parisian sections. The forty-eight sections of Paris were permanently in session; that is, the session was never adjourned. The sans-culottes' control of the sections depended largely on the socioeconomic makeup of each one. The poorer a section was, the more the sans-culottes could express themselves. Conversely, in the wealthier sections, the moderates and other political adversaries of the sans-culottes held the reins of local power. Consequently, a decision made at section headquarters could be reversed in accordance with the political affiliation of the assembly membership. For example, a large contingent of moderates could vote for a "moderate" measure in the afternoon only to see the decision overturned by a large contingent of sans-culottes arriving later that evening.

It was precisely to ensure the sans-culottes' control over the Parisian sections as a whole that fraternization was put forward. It functioned as a sort of call for assistance sent out by sections where the sans-culottes were in the minority to those where they held the majority. Fraternization would then involve "swamping" a moderate section with the massive, noisy presence of sans-culottes from another section. Thus, a section controlled by moderates could swing to the camp of the plebs. In the struggle between Jacobins and Girondins, fraternization strengthened the political base of the Montagne while undermining support for revolutionary moderation as embodied in the Girondins.[20]

The sans-culottes nevertheless pursued their tactic of fraternization after the Jacobins took power on June 2, 1793. Throughout the summer of 1793 the sans-culottes continued to fraternize the moderate sections to ensure that the voice of the plebs found political expression in all the Parisian sections. The strategy's effectiveness was such that after three months of struggle with the moderates the sans-culottes succeeded in gaining the upper hand in most Parisian sections. However, the Jacobins' revolutionary government shut down the sections on the pretext that its power was threatened by the moderates' control of some sections. The practice of fraternization thus came to an end with the Jacobin offensive against "the independence of popular organizations."[21]

Fraternization proved to be an especially powerful political weapon against the moderates.[22] It owed its strength to the whole gamut of procedures, rites, and gestures deployed by the sans-culottes over the course of fraternization. The maneuver combined vigorous tactics with appeals for the unity of the body politic. Of course, aggressive actions (purges, expulsions, etc.) seem contrary to the spirit of fraternization underpinning this political practice. But fraternization also included rites and gestures consistent with the ideal of fraternity: "kisses of peace, accolades, oaths of unity, and enthusiastic speeches in which they congratulated themselves on having subdued the 'hydra of moderatism.'" Moreover, it should be understood that the sans-culottes' fraternity was limited to individuals sharing the same desire to spread the work of the Revolution to the utmost, particularly its democratic and egalitarian dimension. The practice also created the possibility of "effecting the division"[23] between supporters of a radical revolution and those of a moderate or even "frozen" revolution (to borrow Saint-Just's term), which explains the blend of violent and nonviolent elements encompassed by fraternization.

The plebeian practice of fraternization also depended on the immediate political context of the Revolution. At the outset it was performed in a manner that excluded physical attacks against others. But following the radicalization of the Revolution and the enforcement of the Jacobin policy of Terror, the sans-culottes resorted more often to violence. Catherine Chalier writes:

> While in the camp of the sans-culottes the demand for fraternization—in the name of hatred for the tyrant that obliged everyone to choose: brother or enemy—initially maintained a minimum of respect for individuals, during the Terror fraternity and fraternization established ties with death that left no room whatsoever for such respect.[24]

This appraisal, however, needs to be qualified, since the violence of the sans-culottes remained more symbolic than physical, as we shall see.

Fraternization enacted two fundamental principles of the political practices of the Parisian plebs: public action and unity. Public action refers to the sans-culottes' wish to see political actions carried out openly, for all to see. They rejected any move in the direction of secret dealings, feeling that too often this meant the execution of malevolent plans. The desire for transparency "stems from the sans-culottes' fraternal conception of social relationships." Fraternization took place publically and excluded the possibility of hidden or clandestine schemes. Unity, another fundamental principle of sans-culotte politics, was "founded on unanimity of feelings and convictions [and] enabled *concerted actions*, thereby appearing to guarantee victory." This explains why the sans-culottes set such great store on fraternization: through it "unity"[25] was achieved because it enabled the sans-culottes in every Parisian section to express themselves. Since the sans-culotte mentality allowed for a distinction between unity and fraternity, it was in fraternization that the two ideas converged.

The recourse to fraternity also seems to have been a way to ward off nascent individualism, a significant phenomenon of the Revolution. Fraternization appears to have been an attempt to transcend the predominance of private interests, as advocated by the revolutionary bourgeoisie, in order to overcome the splits and divisions affecting French society.[26] In seeking unanimity through fraternization, the Parisian plebs manifested their will to ensure the integrity of the body politic. This certainly affected the quality of the human bond among the sans-culottes.

POLITICS, VIOLENCE, AND FRATERNITY: A TENUOUS POLITICAL BOND

The sans-culottes' actions involved the blend of fraternity, politics, and violence characteristic of fraternization. However, assertions about the place of violence need to be qualified. Although violence was certainly used, sometimes extensively, the sort applied by the sans-culottes against the opponents of the Revolution did not result in the "physical elimination of their adversaries, even those suspected of systematic obstruction."[27] The violence of the sans-culottes was more symbolic than physical and consisted of intimidation tactics designed to muzzle the voices of their numerous political enemies.

The expression "fraternity or death"[28] hence proves to be reductive for an understanding of the sans-culottes' relationship to fraternity and violence. Indeed, the practice of fraternization shows that the sans-culottes' violence was real but limited and did not entail the execution of political adversaries. Quite to the contrary, "an analysis of the fraternization process has shown that, at least within the framework of that process, the strong attachment to a fraternity retaining a minimum of human respect prevailed over the unleashing of a hateful eagerness to spill blood."[29] The slogan "fraternity or death" does not, therefore, explain the political bond among the sans-culottes any more than it does their relationship to violence.

Therefore, we cannot subscribe to Jean-Paul Sartre's theses on the necessarily violent nature of fraternity and the relationship between fraternity and the Terror, at least with regard to the specific case of the Parisian sans-culottes. For the author of *Critique of Dialectical Reason*, the bond of fraternity "is the *right of all* through everyone and over everyone. It is not enough to recall that it is also violence, or that it originated in violence: it is violence itself affirming itself as a bond of immanence."[30] For the sans-culottes, the bond of fraternity was not "violence itself" since a political practice such as insurrection (also rooted in fraternity) could be realized nonviolently.[31] The stress that Sartre lays on the violence of fraternity during the French Revolution may result from a somewhat exaggerated insistence on "lynching" as a political practice. But in light of historical sources, the role of lynching or even of violence in popular actions must be relativized, for it constituted a "last resort"[32] and not the sans-culottes' primary form of action.

Although lynching did exist, it remained a marginal practice of the Parisian sans-culottes, one of several actions, including "hanging effigies," "pillage," and "setting fires."[33] To return to the example of the insurrection, even when it turned "brutal," as in Prairial of Year III, lynching was infrequent. When the sans-culottes took over the Thermidorian Convention during the great Prairial insurrection, only one lynching occurred, that of the representative Féraud. In this connection, Kåre D. Tønnesson even points out that the circumstances surrounding the representative's death were never "elucidated." Nevertheless, the sans-culottes took advantage of Féraud's death to intimidate the Thermidorian forces by parading his head "on a pike,"[34] as if a lynching had indeed taken place. This was arguably a case of violence that was more symbolic than real.

Yet however symbolic this may have been, it was violence nonetheless. The bond of fraternity among the sans-culottes certainly involved an undeniable portion of violence. Political practices stemming from the principle of fraternity—surveillance and purges, for instance—implied a belligerent conception of public space. The objective pursued through such methods was clear: "to eliminate . . . property owners from the general assemblies and . . . quash the influence of the Jacobin middle-level bourgeoisie in the sections."[35] With regard to "surveillance," the physical presence of the sans-culottes, armed with pikes and prepared to "do whatever was necessary"[36] to achieve victory, constituted a real and clearly intimidating threat for the enemies of the plebs. But this measure was so effective that the sans-culottes did not need to "do whatever was necessary" to win the day. The sans-culottes' violence thus remained virtual. This said, the practice of surveillance is a good illustration of the blend of violence and politics subsumed in the political bond of fraternity among the Parisian sans-culottes.

Concerning the "purges," that is, the expulsion of section members deemed undesirable, the use of violence reveals the fragility of fraternity. Here, "fragile" signifies that the bond could easily disintegrate. The fragility resulted from the relationship between violence and politics in the political bond among the sans-culottes and from the problem of fraternity. By purging the sections, the sans-culottes sought to achieve unquestioning adherence to the principles of the plebeian movement. The effect, however, of introducing this kind of symbolic violence into sectional democracy was to negate the principle of "plurality," that is, respect for the uniqueness of every human being. Uniqueness implies that individuals are naturally distinct and express different points of view and orientations. Consequently, violence undermines plurality and, hence, weakens the political bond existing among plebeians.

At the same time, the fragility of the plebeian bond is attributable to its relationship with fraternity, inasmuch as, for the sans-culottes, fraternity is linked to unity, union, and even unanimity. But if one assumes that "politics is based on the fact of human plurality,"[37] striving to ensure unity and, what is more, unanimity proves to be problematical. For how can one hope to find unanimity among individuals who are by nature distinct and unique? Paradoxically, by seeking at all costs to achieve the unity of the movement through the fraternal bond, the sans-culottes created a particularly vulnerable political bond. This gave rise to a vicious cycle: in seeking unity and unanimity, the Parisian plebs obtained only division and discord, thereby hindering the development of the fraternal bond.

With the quelling of internal dissensions and conflicts, that bond became difficult to sustain. Its extension was restricted in order to preserve the purity of convictions. It is possible, then, to conceive of the fraternal bond as a bond of *undividedness*, in that it endeavored to transcend the splits and oppositions marking the Great Revolution. This bond of undividedness may go some way to explaining further the transient career of the sans-culotte movement. It does in fact appear difficult to maintain a movement founded on a political bond entailing purges in the name of that very bond, in this case, of fraternity.

ROUSSEAU'S LEGACY? ON UNDIVIDEDNESS AMONG THE SANS-CULOTTES

How is one to explain the limits of the political bond of fraternity? We believe that they can be attributed in part to the philosophical legacy of Jean-Jacques Rousseau.[38] Indeed, his ideas had a considerable influence on the theory and practice of the French Revolution.[39] Because of its uncompromising critique of inequality among individuals and, subsequently, of the ancien régime's social hierarchies, Rousseau's thought was especially apt to resonate among the political actors of the Revolution. Robespierre, for example, referred to the idea of a "civil religion"[40] when he tried unsuccessfully to establish the "cult of the Supreme Being."[41] The impact of Rousseau's ideas was not limited in 1789 to "great men" alone but echoed as well in the minds of the many: "Rousseau

[was] extolled by the people of the Revolution, who erected monuments in his honor and constantly paid tribute and homage to him at each of its major celebrations."[42]

However, the dissemination of Rousseau's ideas among the popular classes must not be confused with a grasp of the intricacies of his thought or even with a general knowledge of his works. For the sans-culottes, Rousseau's ideas constituted, above all, general ideals that could serve to guide political action. In the words of Daniel Guérin, "The people are not metaphysicians."[43] Boiled down to their bare bones, Rousseau's ideas resonated powerfully among the sans-culottes of Paris. Just as there is a "Machiavellianism" based on a "collective representation"[44] of his thought, during the Revolution there also existed a kind of "Rousseauism" based on a limited but widespread understanding of the writings of the citizen of Geneva. For Albert Soboul, "the fact is obvious": "The popular masses of Paris, in their behavior, their social aspirations, and their political tendencies, seem to have been steeped in a vague Rousseauism."[45] This observation is especially pertinent because the French Revolution, at least in its Jacobin incarnation, was meant to enact Rousseau's principles, and the movement of the sans-culottes fully shared in that project.

Soboul identifies three "channels" through which Rousseau's ideas were able to spread throughout the popular milieux: "chapbooks," "singer-songwriters" (*chansonniers*), and "oral propaganda." In the eighteenth century, chapbooks comprised a literary genre intended for the underprivileged classes, and played a paramount role in the development of the popular mentality in France. During the Revolution, an "Anthology of Rousseau's Most Beautiful Thoughts" (*Almanach des plus belles pensées de Rousseau*) met with great success among the sans-culottes.[46] However, the potential distribution of chapbooks was considerably hampered by the low rate of literacy among the popular classes.

Thus, to better understand the reception of Rousseau, we must turn our attention to oral means of transmission. Singer-songwriters and popular songs actually played a significant role in the dissemination of his ideas. In a collection of patriotic songs that was broadly distributed (and sung) during the Revolution, there is a "Hymn to Liberty and Equality" composed by citizen Desmarets, which includes this verse:

Liberty, then, exists only in the law;
The law, supreme will of all,
Is my work, it is made for me.
Subject to the law, I obey myself.[47]

Clearly, this excerpt contains more than mere traces of Rousseau's political ideas.

Finally, it was mainly through "oral propaganda" that Rousseauist thinking spread throughout the Parisian plebs. The political education provided to the sans-culottes by the section associations referred explicitly to the ideas of Rousseau.[48] Furthermore, the popular press, the speeches made at the Convention, and the Constitutional Act of 1793, all pervaded by Rousseau's ideas, were given public readings in the sections. In other words,

> through oral propaganda or chapbooks, the Enlightenment . . . filtered much earlier into the popular milieux, becoming, as it were, diluted along the way. From the Montagnard or Jacobin bourgeoisie to the illiterate lower classes, the formulation changed and it distorted the original thought; the common substance is the same—it is that of the philosophical thinking of the century influenced by Rousseau.[49]

To explain the decisive impact of Rousseau's thought on the development of the political bond of fraternity among the sans-culottes, we must first point out that the idea of "fraternity" exists only indirectly, even marginally, in Rousseau's philosophy. Works as important as the *Discourse on the Origin of Inequality* and *On the Social Contract* contain no more than allusions to the question of fraternity. Marcel David notes that in the dedication of the *Discourse* the terms "brother" and "fellow-citizen" are used interchangeably, a fact testifying to the marginality of the notion of fraternity for Rousseau. Moreover, scattered throughout his work, David identifies allusions to fraternity expressing Rousseau's nostalgia for the brotherly feelings that he experienced during the "public celebrations of his youth." Thus, fraternity occupies only a "modest place" in his thought. It is for Rousseau "neither a founding principle, nor a teleological—nor even an ethical—outlook on society."[50]

Catherine Chalier nevertheless argues that although Rousseau's idea of fraternity certainly sprung from his memories of "public celebrations," it gave rise to his goal of replacing the pact of domination (the first unjust social contract) by a pact of association founded on the general will.[51] This can be inferred from the great significance that Rousseau attached to the notion of a "civil religion" able to supplant Christianity. It was a matter of preserving the Christian idea of "fraternity" without, however, prolonging the "servitude and submission" engendered by Christianity.[52] According to Chalier's reading of Rousseau, only the social contract and the civil religion will be able to give fraternity the legal and political expression it requires. Therefore, in order to surpass the ephemeral and illusory *feeling* of fraternity experienced in celebrations, the *principle* and the *promise* must be enshrined in the law.[53]

The Rousseauist filiation of fraternity is due essentially to both the Jacobins' cooptation of the notion of fraternity (which they attributed to Rousseau) as well as the actual presence of this idea in Rousseau's writing. Moreover, the Genevan philosopher's influence on the political bond of the sans-culottes depended more on the "osmotic"[54] infiltration of some of his ideas into the mentality and political practices of the sans-culottes than on his definition of "fraternity."

Rousseau's thought expresses a desire to transcend the splits and divisions characteristic of social life. Rousseau observes that the transformation of self-love into *amour propre* results in an insatiable thirst for esteem. As human qualities are not distributed equally, this leads to covetousness and envy. Social life then becomes unpleasant, even intolerable. To overcome the harmful effects of inequality, Rousseau proposes that the unjust social contract governing modern society be replaced by a new social contract that can bring about a political bond other than one based on comparison.

The cornerstone of the political bond produced by this new social contract is the "general will," a concept whereby "obedience to a law one prescribes to oneself is freedom." Observance of the general will leads to the convergence of the individual's particular will and the general will. Thus, the general will creates equality "by right" between individuals. As a political bond, the general will makes it possible to go beyond the constitutive divisions of modern society. What is more, the general will aims to establish the unity and undividedness of the political community.[55] Because the general will commands obedience to the laws that it frames for itself, it tends to suppress the turmoil and other expressions of conflict within the *res publica*. However, to express itself in this way the general will require the political alienation of the individual. Political assemblies, for example, must as nearly as possible achieve unanimity. The general will as a political bond rests on both the quest for unanimity and on the idea of the necessary undividedness of the body politic.

It is precisely on this level that Rousseau's legacy came to bear on the political bond of the Parisian sans-culottes. While they were unfamiliar with the subtleties of Rousseau's thinking, the sans-culottes learned from it the importance of unanimity. Through fraternization and purges, they endeavored to realize it in order to ensure undividedness. To quote Albert Soboul,

Rousseau articulates what others feel more or less violently: the aversion to extreme positions, to opulence as well as indigence—the *passion for unity* so strong among both the Jacobins and the sans-culottes—a certain "*unanism*" that would mark the high points of the Revolution.[56]

In addition, fraternity, serving as the political bond among the sans-culottes, seems intrinsically to have included an appeal to unity and undividedness. The growing insistence on loyalty to the principle of fraternity resulted in the failure to remain faithful to it. The sans-culottes were always at risk of falling short of the ideal of fraternity, which implied the exclusion of an increasing proportion of members. Caught in the vicious circle of fraternity, the movement gained in intensity what it lost in breadth.[57] The end result of this process was no doubt the elimination of almost all the sans-culottes in the name of what was to unite them. The bond of fraternity thus led to a weakening of the political space in the sense that it did not respect the principle of plurality. As Hannah Arendt reminds us, the concept of "fraternity" in the eighteenth century continued to prove incapable of founding a common world because it rested on phenomena incompatible with the public sphere.[58] Catherine Chalier therefore contends that for Arendt, "fraternity presumably pleaded . . . the case for compassion, fusion, and acosmism."[59] Hence, Rousseauism advances an idea that is especially problematical for the goal of ensuring the human bond: unanimity. By taking it up, the sans-culottes forged a bond of fraternity that was fragile at best. At worst, this political bond could create the very conditions of its disappearance. Hence, for the Parisian plebeian experience, Rousseau's legacy represented a double-edged sword. Fraternity, being subject to the desire for undividedness, could not assure a lasting bond.

Beyond the diffuse but significant influence of Rousseau's thought, one can discern in the importance that the sans-culottes attributed to "fraternity-union-unity" a slide from the plebeian desire for freedom to the desire for servitude. Indeed, the wish for the undividedness of the sans-culottes body politic suggests an inclination to create a political space of nearly absolute fusion. Or, to put it another way, the One lurks in the political practice of the sans-culottes. It remains to be seen whether the desire for the One is the result of the revolutionary circumstances in which the plebs' action unfolded or, rather, if it is a constitutive feature of the plebeian experience. The answer to this question will emerge from an analysis of the bond among the English Jacobins and among the Communards of 1871.

7
THE ENGLISH JACOBINS
A POLITICAL BOND OF PLURALITY

In some of the lost causes of the people of the Industrial Revolution we may discover
insights into social evils which we have yet to cure.
—E. P. Thompson, *The Making of the English Working Class*

WHEREAS THE POLITICAL BOND OF THE SANS-CULOTTES WAS
forged through the disappearance of the ancien régime and the attendant advent of democracy at the time of the French Revolution, the human bond of
the English Jacobins was created largely within the context of the Industrial
Revolution, which left a deep imprint on the late eighteenth century and the
nineteenth century in Europe. The "Industrial Revolution" refers to the passage
from small-scale production to the large-scale manufacturing made possible
by the introduction of mechanized factories requiring an abundant, unskilled
labor force. For Karl Polanyi, this "great transformation" represents the establishment of a new type of economy, the "market economy."[1]

To counter the harmful effects of the Industrial Revolution on the traditional human bond, the English Jacobins adopted measures designed to recreate a bond based on the principle of plurality. The term "plurality" should
be understood here in the sense defined by Hannah Arendt, that is, as the
fact of "living as a distinct and unique being among equals."[2] This condition is
achieved through common actions and in words. To grasp the full meaning of
this "bond of plurality," it would be appropriate to start with an outline of the
consequences of the Industrial Revolution in England.

The Industrial Revolution in England

The first factory, a silk mill, appeared in England in 1721. The mill was built on an island in the River Derwent, near Derby. The enterprise employed children for the most part and hoped to supplant the labor of small weavers thanks to its efficient output. But the English Industrial Revolution did not enter its critical expansion period before 1790. Throughout the eighteenth century artisans coexisted with the factories and to some extent managed to resist the attraction of industrialization. However, as of 1790 the artisans started to attack the industrial machines. In 1791, for example, a large plant was set on fire in Albion even before its construction was completed.[3] During this period, numerous struggles and conflicts erupted in England between rich owners seeking to impose the reign of the machine and artisans wanting to defend their independence and preserve their knowhow.

Beyond the story of the clash between two worlds, one must examine the effects of the Industrial Revolution in England in order to comprehend the nature of the plebeian bond. Among those effects, the rural exodus stands out as a decisive phenomenon for the English plebs.[4] The factories and mills that sprung up in the large cities toward the end of the eighteenth century exercised an attraction on country dwellers such that many of them went away to find work in the nascent industries. The rural areas were drained of their populations to the advantage of the industrialized urban centers. The plebs thus found themselves obliged to recreate bonds and traditions in the places where they had migrated in search of work. For, as will be seen below, they could not transpose their rural habits and customs into urban areas.

Out of the migration to the major centers emerged a new population.[5] It was composed mainly of artisans whose labor power proved indispensable for the operation of industries. For many observers, such as Robert Owen, "the general diffusion of manufactures throughout a country generate[d] a new character in its inhabitants."[6] In fact, the new population elicited mistrust among the wealthy, who feared the potential turbulence and agitation of the many gathered together in the cities, especially because the distinctive features of the "new character" included the vitality and energy that the operation of industrial machines required. For the propertied city dwellers, this new workforce represented a somehow "barbaric"[7] or even "dangerous"[8] class, unfamiliar as it was with the manners and customs of the urbanites.

E. P. Thompson nevertheless invites us not to reduce "the making of working-class communities"[9] to the sole variable of the Industrial Revolution. He stresses the continuities between the older political and cultural traditions and the development of a new collective working-class existence. The Industrial Revolution certainly gave rise to a radical mutation of the means of production, but it was not the only cause of political, economic, and cultural change, for "the changing productive relations and working conditions of the Industrial Revolution were imposed, not upon raw material, but upon the free-born Englishman."[10] The combined effect of the older traditions and the Industrial Revolution engendered the figure of the English worker. That is why Thompson's central thesis in the *Making of the English Working Class* is that the workers fully participated in their emergence as a social class.

Nevertheless, an analysis of the Industrial Revolution enables a better understanding of how the English working class took shape. Thompson believes that one must return to the "classic" view of the Industrial Revolution as a catastrophe of major proportions (which is the position of, among others, Marx, Toynbee, and the Hammonds).[11] Thompson decries the empiricist and revisionist historians and economists[12] who claim that the Industrial Revolution constituted a moment of economic growth unprecedented in Western history and that the problems of that period were due more to wars and economic uncertainties than to the effects of that revolution. The premise whereby this time of transformation unfolded under the banner of progress and the general improvement of the living conditions of the many rounds out this soothing interpretation of industrialization.[13] Contrary to the "classic" catastrophic view, the empiricists and revisionists reject the notion that the Industrial Revolution set up a system of economic exploitation hitherto unknown in human history. They argue, rather, that the hardships endured by "people of small means" (P. Sansot's "*gens de peu*")[14] were caused by factors extrinsic to the Industrial Revolution, such as war and a limited knowledge of the economy's operation. Moreover, since the workers enjoyed a higher "standard-of-life" than before, their hardships may even have been imaginary.

To revive the catastrophic vision of the Industrial Revolution, E. P. Thompson sets the idea of "way-of-life" against that of "standard-of-life," so near to the hearts of historical revisionists.[15] The notion of "standard-of-life" is grounded in a quantitative and statistical analysis of production and of the distribution of economic wealth. For the defenders of the revisionist thesis, the economic well-being of the Industrial Revolution generation of workers was superior to that of preceding generations. This, they believe, justifies their views on the putative progress and improvement of workers' lives.[16] The idea of "way-of-life," on the other hand, is an attempt to provide an accurate account, in qualitative terms, of the transformations brought about by industrialization and experienced by individuals. In support of the explicative potential of "way-of-life,"

E. P. Thompson argues simply that "it is quite possible for statistical averages and human experiences to run in opposite directions."[17] In other words, the workers may have been somewhat "richer" than their forebears, but this new "richness" was obtained at the cost of a deteriorated "way-of-life."[18]

E. P. Thompson consequently pleads for a return to the "classic" vision of the Industrial Revolution as a catastrophe. An analysis of the workers' "way-of-life" reveals that the radical transformation of the economy placed exploitation rather than well-being at the core of working-class experience. By way of evidence, Thompson quotes extensively from a cotton worker's account dated 1818 that relates the many ways in which his way-of-life had declined. His observations include (1) the development of a new caste of masters whose power was not circumscribed by any tradition, (2) the loss of independence and status in relation to industrial machines, (3) the weakening of the traditional family, and (4) the end of moments of leisure and recreation in his daily life.[19] This man's depiction of working-class life during the period of industrialization relativizes the statistical analysis performed by English revisionists. Of course, the cotton worker earned more than his father had. But he was thereafter deprived of the pleasures that had run through traditional life. His existence was entirely devoted to factory work and, in private life, to the satisfaction of his bodily imperatives.

To provide a detailed illustration of the catastrophic effects of the Industrial Revolution on the way-of-life, E. P. Thompson examines four key elements of the workers' existence: goods, homes, life, and childhood. For each element, he identifies how industrialization affected workers' daily lives. With regard to goods, Thompson applies a sort of sociology of nutrition whereby he analyzes alterations in diet. For example, the greater importance of the potato represents an impoverishment because the tuber replaced valued staples like bread and oats. This is especially true because the potato was at the heart of the Irish regime and as such emblematic of its poverty. For the "free-born Englishman," the predominance of the potato seemed to be part of a plot aimed at reducing him to Irish levels of indigence.[20] Similarly, the replacement of beer and milk—indispensable beverages of daily life—by tea was met with universal disgruntlement. Concerning housing, urban dwellings were severely deficient, particularly with respect to heating and water supplies. On top of this there was industrial and human pollution as well as the overcrowding of certain neighborhoods, making the quality of life of urban workers unquestionably inferior to that of country dwellers. Industrialization also entailed reduced life expectancy among workers and soaring rates of infant mortality. Finally, the Industrial Revolution had a tragically negative effect on childhood because it relied massively on child labor. Though this had been the case for some time in certain areas of activity such as agriculture, the conditions of children working in factories were especially harsh. They were obliged to work longer and longer days, executing increasingly dangerous tasks, making them the most exploited victims of industrialization. In light of this analysis of goods, homes, life, and childhood, it is difficult to describe the Industrial Revolution as anything but "catastrophic" for English workers,[21] even though from a statistical perspective workers were slightly "better off" than their predecessors.

THE BREAK-UP OF THE TRADITIONAL SOCIAL BOND

The cataclysmic nature of the Industrial Revolution was felt especially in the traditional communities of the English plebs. The ideology particular to the industrialization of England, a blend of Methodism and Utilitarianism, fully participated in the destruction of such communities.[22] Methodism, which had emerged within Anglicanism in 1729, had a major revival during the war with France. Its strong asceticism was expressed in the desire to master human passions through instruction on the need to repress turbulent impulses that could lead individuals to transgress the rules ensuring the smooth operation of society, particularly the mills and factories. For its part, Utilitarianism reduced all evaluation to a calculation of the advantages of any action. In fine, for this school of thought, whatever was useful was good. The alliance between Methodism and Utilitarianism thus guaranteed that workers would absorb the discipline needed to make them docile. Worse still, it justified this domestication by demonstrating its potential benefits for the workers themselves.

The church and the factory were, in sum, the headquarters of disciplinary training. But the effects of this domestication spread to every corner of the workers' daily lives. It was for this reason that traditional communities, historically founded on the rules, customs, and laws specific to the many, were cruelly affected by the Industrial Revolution.[23] A new moral order arose, as evidenced by the founding of the Society for the Suppression of Vice,[24] whose raison d'être was to promote, indeed, to impose that order. The leaders of the society were of the opinion, moreover, that the plebeians' political Jacobinism flowed from their pronounced moral laxness, hence the crucial importance of instilling the so-called inferior classes with discipline and moral order.

Among the traditions targeted by this new moral order were the "fairs" and other popular celebrations. As discussed in the first chapter, there is a link between such celebrations and revolt. For example, the carnival—plebeian celebration par excellence—was a way for the dominated to thumb their noses at the dominators. For the English plebs, feast days and fairs played a fundamental economic and cultural role. In particular, they allowed one to acquire certain goods that were not readily available. In cultural terms, they were sites of popular socialization. People engaged together in merrymaking and, so, established relationships among themselves. Furthermore, these playful activities were rare opportunities for ordinary people to indulge in "spending" that was not useful but necessary for the mental balance of the "free-born Englishman." As E. P. Thompson notes, "the working man's year was made up of cycles of hardship and short commons, punctuated with 'feast' days when drink and meat were more plentiful, luxuries like oranges and ribbons were bought for the children, dancing, courtship, convivial visiting and sports took place."[25]

It must be stressed, however, that the ideology of the Industrial Revolution did not succeed in completely eradicating popular traditions and customs. There was constant resistance to the repeated assaults of Methodism and Utilitarianism. Industrialism even gave rise to renewed interest in ancient traditions. Thompson nevertheless asserts that this was "a conscious resistance to the passing of an old way of life."[26] To put this another way, workers were well aware that the new moral and disciplinary order would eventually sound the death knell of their traditions. Thompson even underscores that the disappearance of certain old English customs did not represent a loss. The suppression of ancient superstitions and dubious practices constituted a form of progress for the many. Yet in spite of this, the assault on the traditional communities was designed to neutralize their potentially disruptive force and to channel their physical and mental energies toward the needs of industrialization. Methodism, especially, played a major role in the eradication of traditions predating the industrial transformation. An account given by an observer in 1834 testifies to the fact that the Industrial Revolution meant loss and decline and brought about a profound metamorphosis of popular communities:

> I have observed it not only in the manufacturing but also in agricultural communities in the country; they seem to have lost their animation, their vivacity, their field games and their village sports; they have become a sordid, discontented, miserable, anxious, struggling people, without health, or gaiety, or happiness.[27]

How did all this affect the human bond? To the extent that the Industrial Revolution undermined ancient customs and ways of life, it can be supposed that it severed the traditional human bond based on solidarity. It should be specified that this bond appears to have been more *social* than *political*, since it concerned collective life rather than collective action. By attacking fairs and feast days, the new moral order underpinning industrialism was directed against forms of popular socialization, the fair and the feast day being moments of collective spending and merrymaking conducive to the forging of bonds. According to Polanyi, the Industrial Revolution represents a "calamity" or even a "catastrophe" because the advent of the market economy erased the social and cultural bearings of the many.[28]

With domestication as its objective, Methodism openly attacked the moments of socialization that set the rhythm of daily life. Hence, it banned the traditional Sunday visits. People "should refuse to entertain even friends and relatives (from among the unconverted) who might call; and if such visitors could not be turned from the door they should be entertained only by Bible-reading, holy discourse and hymn-singing."[29] Developing and maintaining social relations became difficult under such circumstances. Finally, the exodus from the countryside to the urban centers left people rudderless. They inhabited overpopulated neighborhoods where the sites of socialization were different from those in villages and rural communities. As a result, industrialization ultimately brought about the destruction of the traditional social bond. Alone in the factory and the large towns and cities, the "free-born Englishman" felt the full monadological brunt of Manchester liberalism.

The breakup of the traditional social bond represents, however, only one facet of the attempt to destroy the human bond caused by industrialization. As we have already stated more than once, the existence of humans was reduced to factory work and to the satisfaction of physiological needs in the private sphere. In other words, only within the private sphere did they enjoy a measure of freedom. But this submission to the factory and to the private sphere was a radical denial of plurality and therefore of the human political condition. For Hannah Arendt plurality occurs only in common action and in speech.[30] Only with great difficulty could common action and speech take place in the factory,[31] and they surely did not exist in the private sphere. Under the effects of industrialization, the individual was confined to a private existence devoted to the cycle of production and consumption characteristic of work and of that antipolitical figure, *animal laborans*.[32] Hence, industrialization tended, in its early stages, to prevent the development of a political bond.

REBONDING: THE LONDON CORRESPONDING SOCIETY

In the face of the Industrial Revolution's catastrophic effects on the social and political bond, the London Corresponding Society attempted to create a new human bond. Although such a project was not explicitly articulated in the

LCS's objectives, it can be thought of as one of its byproducts. But however derivative it may have been, this project was not secondary, because the creation of a different human bond was part and parcel of the two tasks central to the LCS's actions: (1) resistance to industrialization and to the political counterrevolution, and (2) political practice as a site of freedom.

It was as a gathering place of the plebeian experience that the LCS contributed to the formation of a new bond. It was primarily a place where discussion, debate, and correspondence took place in a spirit of equality and liberty for all. Indeed, members were invited and encouraged to take part in the public deliberations of the LCS's divisions. The deliberations were open and democratic and enabled the creation *in situ* of spaces of freedom where the many displayed their political capacity.

In addition, the instruction provided at LCS meetings was intended to ensure the development of self-reliance. Thus, the English Jacobins gave their militants a form of political education for emancipation, thereby evading the traps stemming from the thorny problem of the plebeian leader. On every level, the LCS's actions allowed its members to form relationships based on respect for differences, freedom, and equality. The LCS also favored the progress of plebeian collective existence. Within this political framework, the plebs could act concertedly in order to achieve common goals. In doing so, the LCS constructed a form of political organization that produced a truly political bond. Despite the breakup of the traditional social bond, the plebs could gather together and forge a bond through plebeian collective action. For it must not be forgotten that the chief objective of the LCS was the extension of democratic political rights to the many.

LCS meetings were not, however, exclusively political and educational. They were also key moments of socialization. While being initiated into public affairs, the Jacobins could get to know each other, develop common affinities, and establish friendly or even emotional ties with others. Learning and political debate were thus melded with the development of friendships. The loss of the traditional social bond could thus be offset through attendance at LCS meetings. The founders of the Society fought the harmful effects of industrialization on the social bond by offering the many the possibility of creating a political bond.

That the activities of the Society's divisions took place in the sites of urban socialization furthermore points to the LCS's role in the development of a political bond. Cafés, taverns, and even factories were politically invested, a phenomenon that illustrates the LCS's contributions to the development of a different human bond. Here is how John Thelwall, a theorist of the Jacobin movement, puts it:

> A sort of Socratic spirit will necessarily grow up, wherever large bodies of men assemble. . . . Whatever presses men together . . . though it may generate some vices, is favourable to the diffusion of knowledge, and ultimately promotive of human liberty. Hence every large workshop and manufactory is a sort of political society, which no act of parliament can silence, and no magistrate disperse.[33]

In spite of the Industrial Revolution's effects, the very sites of economic exploitation were transformed into a "political society" that could be neither silenced nor banned.

Thelwall's statement indicates a possible "plebeian public sphere" by revealing one of its key components. The term "public sphere" must be understood as a sphere of human reality located between the private and state spheres.[34] The public sphere comprises a culture and a set of political practices. It includes, more specifically, a written press through which ideas are disseminated and points of view circulated.[35] By equating workshops and factories with political societies, Thelwall acknowledges the appearance of a new political species, one that combines *animal laborans* and *zoon politikon*, thus blurring the distinctions made by Hannah Arendt. Thelwall, who witnessed the politicization of the workshops during the period of industrialization, draws attention to the plebeian worker who no longer differentiates between factory and political society. From this perspective, a plebeian public sphere seems indeed to have existed in England.[36] This public sphere transcended the separation between work and action. What is more, in transcending the opposition between the order of the living and political life, it demonstrates the possibility of joining together political action and physical labor.[37] It can thus be compared to the practice of the Prairial insurrection in Year III, where, it should be recalled, the watchword was "Bread and the Constitution of '93!" By blending social and political demands, the sans-culottes also blurred the sharp distinctions between the order of life and political condition. The political equality embodied in the plebeian public sphere made it possible to combine, but not confuse, economic demands and political demands.

"UNLIMITED NUMBER": PLURALITY AS POLITICAL BOND

In chapter 4 we analyzed the political consequences of the first principle of the LCS: "That the number of our Members be unlimited." The vision of modern democracy as the reign of plurality had a considerable effect on the political practice of the English Jacobins. According to Thompson, this principle "signifies the end to any notion of exclusiveness, of politics as the preserve of any hereditary élite or property group."[38] This was a radically new approach to the extent that English political practice, just like the political practice of modernity, was built on the idea that citizens need to be politically qualified. Such qualifications could include, for example, titles of nobility or of property. The LCS thus proposed to break with a fundamentally antidemocratic approach by "pluralizing" the English public sphere.

As evidenced by the social makeup of the movement and the internal functioning of the LCS, plurality was not simply a principle to be observed "in theory" but was fully applied within the Society. Its raison d'être can be accurately summarized as the experience of "living as a distinct and unique being among equals"[39] through common actions and in speech.

Craftsmen without doubt made up the core of the LCS. The English Jacobins nevertheless managed to attract members from a broad range of professions and social classes. It was a movement "which drew the support of thousands of small shopkeepers, of printers and booksellers, medical men, schoolmasters, engravers, small masters, and Dissenting clergy at one end; and of porters, coal-heavers, labourers, soldiers and sailors at the other."[40] Far from being confined to the so-called lower ranks, the LCS welcomed all those sympathetic to the democratic cause in Great Britain. In this context, the human bond that the English Jacobins were able to establish was decidedly plural, for, notwithstanding the traditional barriers, individuals from different milieux could form fundamentally egalitarian social and, above all, political relationships.

The internal functioning of the LCS's divisions also reflected a plebeian adherence to the notion of plurality. The LCS was organized in accordance with the principle of an "unlimited number" of members. Thus, section heads were appointed on a rotating basis; they could not permanently occupy a position. Consequently, all members had equal access to political office. The idea implicit in this organizational arrangement was that politics was the domain of the many and not the preserve of a small group of individuals entitled to govern. In order for plurality to be instituted, appointment to public office had to be regulated on the basis of equality; otherwise the LCS would have lost its democratic character. Because plurality was experienced directly and immediately, the political bond put forward was one founded on a radical openness to alterity and on the observance of the principle of equality.

A POLITICAL BOND OF DIVISION?

How is the political bond to be understood? In the case of the sans-culottes, the "bond of fraternity" was particularly fragile because it sought to establish the undividedness of the body politic. Under the diffuse, indirect, but none-theless real influence of Jean-Jacques Rousseau's ideas, the sans-culottes set up an apparatus designed to achieve unanimity and harmony. They therefore tended more toward the desire for the One than toward the desire for liberty. With regard to the English Jacobins, what matters is determining the political consequences of their openness to difference and alterity.

The political bond of plurality among the English Jacobins seems to have been a "bond of division," that is, a bond with others formed through conflict and aimed at preserving individualities while at the same time ensuring the existence of a human bond; there was no wish to attain unanimity. Indeed, the LCS was regularly caught in the grip of division and conflict. For instance, following the English government's legal actions in 1794 against the leaders of the movement (including its founder Thomas Hardy), the LCS was profoundly divided as to which tactical course it should adopt.[41] Rather than trying to conceal this division, the LCS agreed to make it public. They seemed truly to have recognized the power of conflict to create bonds.

On several occasions throughout its career, the LCS proved to be open to dissension and allowed dissident voices to be heard. Granted, motions were passed in some sections with the goal of expelling the defenders of this or that position, but the LCS never enforced motions that would be fatal for liberty, especially since it did not defend a strong and unified doctrine. The "unlimited" number of members were thus not subjected to strict or intensive in-doctrination. On the contrary, the objective of the educational component of the movement was autonomy: the English Jacobins "sought, by education and agitation, to transform 'the mob' (in Paine's words) from 'followers of the *camp*' to followers of 'the *standard* of liberty.'"[42] The many were called upon to ex-press themselves freely on the most pressing political issues. A political bond of plurality always involves the expression of differences, implying openness to conflict and division.

For conflict and dissension to be acceptable to a political movement, that movement must be convinced of the legitimacy of tolerance. The theory and practice of tolerance were in fact at the heart of the LCS's operations. As E. P. Thompson stresses, "The English Jacobins argued for . . . the toleration of Dis-senters, Catholics and free-thinkers, for the discernment of human virtue in 'heathen, Turk or Jew.'"[43] Their relationships with Ireland, based on solidarity and mutual assistance, show that the English Jacobins not only preached toler-ance but practiced it as well. Rather than acting as condescending dominators toward the Irish, the Jacobins respected their difference. A theory and practice of tolerance allowed the English Jacobins to retain differences (or plurality) while maintaining a political bond. The bond of plurality is therefore a bond of division inasmuch as the expression of difference and conflict does not obviate the possibility of forming egalitarian relationships with others. Unlike the bond of fraternity, the bond of plurality attests more to the desire for liberty than to the desire for the One.

The political bond of division grounded in plurality can be associated with the human bond that would later emerge in the utopian practices inspired by Robert Owen and in English Chartism.[44] These two political experiments appear to have involved the type of bond that had been central to the English Jacobins' experience. The Jacobins introduced a political dynamic that, despite its political defeat, would survive in the nineteenth century. Ultimately, then, the English Jacobins bequeathed a lasting legacy.

What about the nature of the human bond during the Paris Commune of 1871? It would appear that the Communards as well proposed an original conception of the human bond. What is the connection between it and the human bond established by the sans-culottes and the English Jacobins?

8

THE COMMUNARDS

A POLITICAL BOND OF ASSOCIATION

There was no doctrinal unity among the delegates [of the Commune], although most of them manifestly wished for an abrupt severance of the existing social bond. Every tendency recognized its point of impact in the idea of the Commune— the symbol of equality and association, the rallying point, the revolutionary forces' place of convergence, and then, as soon as the insurrectional government was installed, the center of divergence.

—C. Rihs, *La commune de Paris 1871. Sa structure et ses doctrines*

UNLIKE THE GENERAL CIRCUMSTANCES SURROUNDING THE English Jacobins, the context of the Commune was marked by a series of political rather than economic events. Those events started, roughly speaking, during the final months of the Second Empire and ended when the Commune was proclaimed. Between those two moments a war and a change of regime took place, followed by a siege and the beginnings of a civil war. A host of incidents led to the establishment of "Paris libre 1871" (J. Rougerie). A review of the sequence of events is necessary precisely because the existing human bond did not emerge unscathed from a political conjuncture so exceedingly taxing for Parisians. Against this background, the political action that founded the Commune created a human bond governed by the principle of "association." The term "association" is used here to refer to a principle of collaboration based on equality and rejecting all forms of hierarchy. The Commune represented the end product of the work accomplished over a long period of time by the social and revolutionary movement, which, according to Pierre Leroux, sought as of 1830 to establish a modern collective existence underpinned by the principle of association.[1] And the specificity of this bond stemmed from the acceptance of division and conflict within the newly established public space.

The Political Situation in France Before the Commune

Any analysis of the Paris Commune requires a review of the circumstances surrounding its constitution as a political form. This involves, first, outlining the key events marking the final moments of the Second Empire, because the Commune, the Empire's "direct antithesis,"[2] was also the end result of "a revolutionary movement born under [that regime]."[3] It is therefore necessary to understand the political form within which it developed and in opposition to which it arose.

On the whole, the distinguishing features of Napoleon III's long reign (1852–1870) can be summed up as military debacles abroad and measures promoting the economic development of French industries at home.[4] Such economic development did not mean, however, that the quality of life of French workers was generally improved.[5] As of 1864, workers formed associations and tried to establish ties with workers outside the country, despite the restrictions imposed by the French state. The French section of the International Working Men's Association, for example, was created in 1865. This period also witnessed the proliferation of texts and debates on the place of workers in the political and economic life of France.[6] Given that the Second Empire stood essentially for "economic development and the erasure of the political" and that the "absent political debate moved into clandestinity or into the exaltation of hatred,"[7] the evolution of the political thought and practice of the many during the final years of the Empire would be decisive for the coming Commune.

Beginning in 1869, the Empire underwent a sort of "exhaustion." Economic growth slowed, and the parliamentary majority backing Napoleon III "was dangerously diminished" after the legislative elections of 1869. Although the results of the imperial plebiscite of 1870 renewed the emperor's legitimacy, "it soon became apparent to certain thinkers of the regime . . . that the prestige of an effectively prosecuted war would be of decisive use"[8] in ensuring the continuation of the Bonapartist "dynasty." Moreover, the rise of Bismarck's Prussia, an imperial rival capable of taking over the Second Empire's role in European international affairs, stirred up the bellicose sentiments of Empire supporters. The consequence of this conjuncture was the Franco-Prussian war, which lasted only from July to September 1870.

Poorly prepared, lacking allies, and underestimating the military capacity of the Prussian adversary, France suffered a crushing, indeed spectacular defeat.[9] In early August, after a string of key victories (Wissembourg, Forbach, Froeschwiller-Woerth), the Prussian army crossed the French border. At Metz, one hundred thousand French soldiers were encircled by Bismarck's troops.

In a desperate attempt to relieve his soldiers, the emperor himself led a "hastily mustered" army. The outcome of this expedition was the rout at Sedan on September 2, 1870: "3,000 dead, 14,000 injured, and capitulation, with 83,000 prisoners, including 39 generals and the emperor."[10] With such a bloody, stupefying defeat, the Second Empire had signed its own death warrant.

The Sedan fiasco triggered a political transformation in France. On September 4, 1870, barely a day after Paris had learned of the defeat, a "government of National Defense" was formed under the leadership of General Trochu. This government was composed of moderate and even conservative Republicans who were "extremely punctilious on the issue of order and property."[11] To ensure the city's defense, the Trochu government decided to revive the National Guard, "a veritable popular army" whose battalions received "pay and weapons through the municipalities, elect[ed] their leaders and [developed] their political awareness."[12] Despite its title of "National Defense," the government was unable to halt Bismarck's advance toward Paris. On September 19, 1870, the Prussians blockaded Paris. This was the beginning of a punishing siege of the city, which brought hardship to its inhabitants while heightening their ardor and determination.

General Trochu immediately asked his minister of foreign affairs, Jules Favre, to explore with Bismarck the conditions of a Franco-Prussian peace. The news of negotiations that would entail the capitulation of Paris aroused the Parisians' mistrust toward the Trochu government. However, a plebiscite held on November 3 strengthened its position, which had been considerably shaken by the attempted insurrection of October 31.[13] With the arrival of winter, the siege began to severely affect Parisians' quality of life. A great many of them survived thanks exclusively to the pay received by the members of the National Guard.[14] On January 28, 1871, Jules Favre signed an armistice with Bismarck. The price of France's capitulation was especially steep; Parisians were devastated by the news.[15]

After legitimizing the armistice, the National Defense government called legislative elections for February 8 with the aim of designating a new National Assembly likely to ratify the accord with Bismarck. The assembly resulting from these elections brought to light the profound crisis splitting the country: in the provinces, a majority of "rural monarchists" were elected, "that is, people who had raised the specter of the working-class threat, of the risk of revolution, [and of] the fear of large urban centers."[16] Paris, meanwhile, elected a majority of republicans. Trochu stepped down as head of government and handed over power to Adolphe Thiers, who, rather than seeking to reconcile the capital with the provinces, adopted measures penalizing the Parisians.[17] He demanded, for example, that only those members of the National Guard able to prove their neediness should be paid by the state. This was particularly humiliating for soldiers who had valiantly defended Paris and survived the privations of the siege.

Worse still for Parisians, the National Assembly, which convened in Bordeaux rather than the capital, voted to transfer the seat of government from Paris to Versailles. By depriving Paris of its status as capital, the "rural monarchists" expressed their hostility toward it and, more specifically, toward the revolutionary and republican ferment that had gripped the city since the end of the Second Empire. A move of this sort was obviously taken as "an affront, a twofold affront, because the Assembly preferred the monarchist city to the republican *Cité*, and . . . gave the impression that the resistance against the Germans and the tribulations of the siege counted for nothing."[18] The last act before the proclamation of the Commune was played out on March 18, 1871. Thiers ordered his troops to disarm Paris by seizing the National Guard's artillery, located in Belleville and Montmartre. Parisians rose up against this act, which they considered intolerable with regard to the city's autonomy. This was the beginning of the Paris Commune and the "civil war in France."[19]

How is one to understand, in the context of such radical change, the state of the human bond in Paris? The events leading up to the establishment of the Commune unfolded over a period of about eight months during which the existing human bond was severely tested. It was no doubt weakened, perhaps even broken, by the various traumas. Certainly, the main actors of *Paris libre 1871* wished for "an abrupt severance of the existing social bond,"[20] but it is quite possible that this had already occurred. A particularly telling example of the state of the human bond during the developments heralding the Commune was the Parisians' response to the news of the capitulation of the National Defense government. P.-O. Lissagaray, who witnessed the events, asserts that "the town remained gloomy" in face of the armistice and that "the days of anguish had stunned Paris."[21] Rather than arousing furor among Parisians, the news of the armistice was received with resignation. Yet patriotic fervor had been at an especially high pitch in the capital, and the hardship of the siege had been tolerated because the people of Paris refused to submit to the Prussians. Nevertheless, when the armistice was announced, Parisians seemed unable to muster the energy needed to create a bond that might breathe life into the resistance. No doubt exhausted by the exceptional circumstances of the preceding months, they fell prey to anomie, that is, to the disappearance of the founding law of collective existence.

A Core Principle of Communal Action: Association

To deal with the situation, the Communards needed to innovate. Rebuilding the human bond meant advancing a principle likely to institute another kind of bond. This posed a serious challenge because the new bond had to be able to rally Parisians, who had been abandoned by the French state and were threatened by both the foreign enemy (the Prussians) and the domestic enemy (the "rural monarchists").

As the "direct antithesis" (Karl Marx) of the Second Empire, the Commune displayed political features diametrically opposed to those of the Empire. Whereas the Empire was characterized by economic, political, and social inequality, the Commune endeavored to promote an egalitarian political practice that would result in economic and social measures fostering greater equality among citizens. The Empire, moreover, was singularly hierarchical. Contrary to the Republican regime, it revived the monarchic principle of dynastic succession, reintroducing a decidedly hierarchical principle in French society. Furthermore, the political practice of the Second Empire, especially in its early years, was authoritarian. The banning of workers' associations and the restriction of freedom of the press were just two examples of the Caesarism typical of Napoleon III's reign. A particularly effective way to fight the inequality, hierarchy, and authoritarianism of the Second Empire was to establish the principle of association. This was exactly what the Paris Commune of 1871 did.

The principle of association was instituted but not invented by the Commune. As noted earlier, it had been central to the demands of the social and revolutionary movement since 1830 and partook of the French revolutionary tradition: "Its roots may be found in the popular assemblies of the Great Revolution, in the socialist manifestos of the 1840s, in mutual aid societies and artisanal *compagnonages*."[22] The idea of association continued to flourish in France throughout the nineteenth century and appears to have been a point of convergence for various discrete revolutionary tendencies. In the Commune, the principle of association was accepted by all, despite the many disagreements as to the Commune's objectives.[23]

The principle of association is also referred to in the works of certain thinkers who had a major impact on the Commune's political action, such as Pierre Leroux and Pierre-Joseph Proudhon.[24] For them, association constitutes an essential way for the many to gain access to emancipation. According to Leroux, association is one of two "systems"—the other being individualism—that can found the political sphere.[25] But unlike individualism, association represents the true goal of politics. Thanks to association among human beings, that is, "an anti-hierarchical form of relationship,"[26] society can accomplish its "march toward equality." The advent of association also requires the establishment "of moral, scientific, and historical beliefs."[27] This is why virtue and science are so essential for Leroux. What is more, the idea of association is intimately linked to that of humanity, which underpins all his work.[28] Without reviewing the general premises of the concept, one can nevertheless assert that humanity guarantees the existence of an "invisible bond" among human beings. Association therefore represents not only a form of egalitarian relationship but also an unlimited openness to the alterity and the plurality of the human race, thereby enabling the advent of "Humanity as a great living thing."[29] In sum, association excludes the possibility of the domination of some individuals by others.

In the work of Pierre-Joseph Proudhon, the idea of association is found especially in the mutualist system theorized in *De la capacité politique de la classe ouvrière*. Drawing inspiration from the working-class initiatives of his times, Proudhon contends that the idea of mutuality encompasses the ideas of reciprocity and justice. Rather than basing collective existence on a hierarchical principle, Proudhon turns to an associative principle grounded in the symmetry of social and economic relationships. Mutualism makes it possible to achieve "the social unity of the human race"[30] without the intermediation of any state centralization. Indeed, Proudhon stands in opposition to the centralizing tendencies of certain social and political theories of his period. To put an end to the destructive effects of centralization, a system must be established that encourages the free association of individuals, industries, and political bodies. Consequently, in conjunction with federalism, the idea of association subsumed under mutualism has the potential to hasten the emergence of a society "where socialism and freedom are not incompatible."[31]

In the polemic between Leroux and Proudhon concerning the state (and religion), Leroux argues that Proudhon does not "understand association,"[32] as evidenced by Proudhon's statement that the recourse to the idea of government rests on a kind of "faith" comparable to religious faith. For Proudhon, then, the necessity of a government is no more obvious than the existence of God.[33] According to Leroux, this blindness particular to Proudhon's anarchism stems from its inability to distinguish among different forms of authority. For example, "Republican authority," Leroux maintains, is based on association, whereas "monarchic authority"[34] is founded on the domination of some individuals by others. In his critique of the governmental function Proudhon ignores such distinctions, which is why he remains incapable of grasping the true meaning of association. However, in Proudhon's defense, his political thinking did evolve to the point of theorizing federalism, a sort of "compromise between anarchism and statism."[35] Notwithstanding Leroux's criticism, mutualism and federalism do indeed open the way to the principle of association.

Thus, the idea of association has a twofold filiation. On one hand, it was present in French revolutionary practice, while on the other hand it was part of the political and social thought nurturing the reflections of the actors of the Commune. Indeed, the thoughts of Pierre Leroux and Pierre-Joseph Proudhon both participated in the ideological proliferation surrounding the Paris Commune. It remains to be seen how the principle of association underpinned a social, political, and economic practice that engendered a "bond based on association."

ASSOCIATION AS POLITICAL BOND

The government's attempt to confiscate the National Guard's artillery on March 18, 1871, was the event that triggered the Commune. The "fraternization" between the soldiers of the French state exiled in Versailles and the ordinary people of Paris transformed this attempted disarmament into a communalist revolution. This "fraternization" must not be confused with the political practice of the sans-culottes in the Year II. The "fraternization" of March 18, 1871, refers to the soldiers' refusal, at the people's behest, to follow the orders to shoot the men, women, and children impeding their work.[36] By disobeying their superiors, the soldiers acknowledged the validity of the popular demands and, hence, of the participation of the many in the human political condition. The soldiers rejected the hierarchical principle, recognizing instead the political equality and dignity of the people of Paris. Rather than accepting the subordination inherent to the military function, the soldiers broke the chains of servitude by choosing to *associate* with the people. This inaugural scene of the Commune set the tone for the plebeian experience of 1871: association, not hierarchy, would thereafter govern the human bond.

Over the seventy-two days of the Commune's existence, the principle of association developed on three fronts: economic, social, and political. True, the Commission of "Work, Industry, and Exchange," which, under the direction of Hungarian-born Léo Frankel, was responsible for the Commune's economic affairs, failed to effect a radical reorientation of economic life.[37] Lacking time and, especially, economic activity, it was hard put to lay the foundations of a new sort of economy. However, through an examination of an initiative involving "cooperative workshops," one can observe the possibilities of the associative economy that the Commune wanted to construct.[38] On May 3, 1871, a women's organization named the Union des femmes pour la défense de Paris et les soins

des blessés (Women's Union to Defend Paris and Care for the Wounded) submitted a petition to the Frankel Commission demanding work for women.
A few days later, Frankel presented a project to organize workshops whose
objective was to have women work at home. Rather than elaborating this project alone, the Commission agreed to leave the Women's Union in charge of
its preparation.[39] In doing so the Frankel Commission displayed its profound
commitment to the practice of association. Through its neighborhood committees, the Women's Union conducted a thorough inquiry on the needs of
unemployed women. Out of this work came cooperative workshops operating on the basis of association. The first workshops "did not assemble women
assigned to jobs according to their trades, but centralized orders and distributed tasks to the female workers, who accomplished them at home. When they
were finished, the women brought the finished products back to the workshop,
which then took care of delivery."[40] By creating the conditions required for
the economic association of these unemployed women and by eliminating the
intermediary between the manufacture and sale of economic goods, the Commune adopted an innovative system of work organization, one that fostered the
workers' dignity while ensuring the production of goods necessary for modern life. In both form (collaboration between the Commune and the Women's
Union) and content (cooperative workshops), the Commune championed an
economic ideal based on association.

On the social plane, the Commune proposed, most notably, major education reforms resulting from the work of "Éducation nouvelle" (New Education). Born under the siege, this association brought together teachers and
parents intent on reforming and modernizing the French education system.
On April 1, 1871, the association presented the Commune with a program of reforms designed to make education free, mandatory, and secular. Instead of an
education based on religious principles, Éducation nouvelle's goal was to pro-
gressively apply experimental or scientific methods to instruction. The members of the Commune expressed their agreement with the program's objectives.
This gave rise to a "fruitful [collaboration] between the Commune and Éducation nouvelle." Once again, the Commune did not hesitate to associate with a
noncommunal organization in advancing the cause of emancipation. One of
the first outcomes of this collaboration was the nomination of a commission
mandated to reorganize the educational system. A number of members of Éducation nouvelle sat on this commission, which was directed by the Blanquist
Édouard Vaillant. Among the commission's various initiatives, it proposed to
give women and men equal access to education with the aim of hastening true
social equality. Similarly, Vaillant decreed that male and female teachers should

earn equal pay for equal work.[41] These reforms were crucial for the question of association because under the Commune the aim of education was not only vocational training but also to make good citizens out of the women and men of Paris. For them to be independent and politically active, they had to be inculcated with the principle of association from their first years in school.

Finally, in the political realm, association as a human bond was established on two levels. On one level was the proliferation of local clubs and committees that formed the base of the communalist movement in Paris. As explained in chapter 5, thanks to the numerous possibilities of political participation under the Commune, Paris became a focal point of radical democracy. The local political bodies considered themselves sovereign and allowed citizens to meet, discuss, and take action in connection with their common affairs.[42] As was true of the English Jacobins grouped together in the sections of the London Corresponding Society, the Communards, thanks to the clubs and associations, could openly share as equals in the human political condition. Within these spaces of common deliberation and action, Parisians could forge egalitarian relationships and realize not a power exerted *over* others but one emerging *with* others. The Paris Commune, whose foundation comprised local organizations functioning on the basis of the principle of association, ensured that a bond of association was applied politically. Here, then, the human bond proved to be a *political* bond.

Second, the relationship between those sitting in the Commune and local political bodies was also governed by the principle of association.[43] It should be pointed out that the elected members of the Commune were not regarded as representatives entitled to impose decisions according to their personal political desires. They were invested with only an "imperative mandate,"[44] meaning that they were emissaries and not representatives of the popular will. They could not override the political interests and wishes of the many. Gustave Lefrançais therefore proposed that the Commune's officials and elected members take part in meetings of the local clubs and associations in order to understand better the political tendencies of the many and to fulfill their political responsibilities as proxies of the people.[45] Speaking in support of this approach, Arthur Arnould, an elected member of the Commune, asserted, "an elected member is not and must not be the living, speaking conscience of his electors. The day his conscience is no longer in agreement with theirs, it is he who is wrong. The only thing he can do is to resign and to fight, elsewhere, on his own behalf."[46] The Commune's rank-and-file organizations can be seen as having acted as "intermediaries" between the Commune and Parisians.[47] The Commune therefore had to associate with the local political bodies to retain its democratic legitimacy. Association thus became the cornerstone of the political bond because it was encouraged at all levels of political action in Paris—among citizens within local organizations and between the elected members of the Commune and members of the local organizations.

DIVIDEDNESS OR UNDIVIDEDNESS AMONG THE COMMUNARDS?

Whereas the sans-culottes' political bond of fraternity sought to ensure the undividedness of the body politic, while the English Jacobins' bond of plurality resulted in the acceptance of division, the bond of association comes even closer to being one of plurality. Association recognizes the uniqueness of human beings while assuming the need to carry out concerted actions that respect that very uniqueness. The acknowledgment of the inevitability of division was manifested specifically in three ways during the Paris Commune: (1) in the doctrinal or ideological fragmentation of the Communards, (2) in the decentralized and antihierarchical political organization of the Commune, and (3) in the majority/minority split within the council of the Commune.

Doctrinal fragmentation was a key characteristic of the Paris Commune. There are two reasons why it would be difficult to identify any ideological unity within it. First, the influence of a variety of thinkers can be seen in the Communards' declarations and actions: Saint-Simon, Proudhon, Leroux, Fourier, Comte, and Blanqui were only a few of those whose writings nurtured the Commune's actions. Second, the actors of the Commune came from a host of different political associations, including the Association internationale des travailleurs (International Workingmen's Association), the Ligue d'union républicaine des droits de Paris (League of Republican Unity for the Rights of Paris), the Comité central de la garde nationale (Central Committee of the National Guard), and the Freemasons. Given this doctrinal and organizational heterogeneity, the division of the Communards according to their various schools of thought and political practices seems to have been unavoidable. Within this fragmented environment, the principle of association underpinning the human bond during the Commune served as a shared variable able to rally the many but without performing the synthesis of the different doctrines and approaches. The bond of association led to neither unity nor undividedness. It guaranteed a form of accord resting on the recognition of differences with regard to ideas and approaches.

In addition, the Commune can be viewed as a decentralized and antihierarchical form of political organization. With local clubs and associations in the arrondissements participating in public affairs, the Commune remains perhaps the most decentralized political regime in recent political history. This is especially true because the elected members of the Commune were accountable to the local bodies and could not impose their own views at the expense of the people's wishes. In this connection, the Commune advocated a political conception based on merit rather than patronage or family ties. We have seen, moreover, that some of the Commune's key initiatives were implemented in conjunction with extracommunal bodies. Rejecting the hierarchical distribution of titles and functions as well as the centralization of decision making, the Commune recognized the divisions and conflicts inherent to political life.

Finally, the split between a majority and a minority within the council of the Commune also related to the acknowledgment of division and conflict. The majority/minority division, which was especially visible during the debate on the appointment of the Comité de salut public (Committee of Public Safety), was coterminous with the very existence of the Commune. Indeed, differences in tendencies and orientations were apparent within the council from the very start of communal deliberations.[48] The bond forged through association did not lessen them, but it nevertheless ensured a certain degree of collaboration among the factions existing in the Commune. Association is thus a principle that makes it possible for different individuals to work together while maintaining their differences. Ultimately, the bond of association does not express a desire for undividedness but attests to a legitimation of division and conflict in politics. That is why the political bond under the Commune was constituted through the ongoing resistance of the desire for freedom against its opposite, the desire for servitude.

CONCLUSION

Men fight and lose the battle, and the thing that they fought for comes about in spite
of their defeat, and when it comes it turns out not to be what they meant, and other
men have to fight for what they meant under another name.
—William Morris, *A Dream of John Ball*

OUR PURPOSE IN THESE PAGES HAS BEEN TO RECONSTITUTE A
little-known, or even occulted, experience of our political history: the plebeian experience. It arises when people excluded from the *res publica* transform
themselves into political subjects able to act in concert. Hence, from the first
secession of the Roman plebs through to the Paris Commune of 1871, the plebeian experience attests to the abiding presence of a communalist politics of
the people, that is, politics based on the direct action of the many. It also attests
to a desire for freedom, as opposed to the desire for domination characteristic
of the patrician politics of the few entitled to govern. The plebeian experience
thus confirms the existence of communalist and agoraphile political traditions
throughout Western political history.

While numerous experiences may have revived the plebeian principle, it
must be acknowledged that none of them could be sustained for any considerable length of time. The Paris Commune of 1871, for example, lasted no more
than seventy-two days. Indeed, the temporality specific to the plebeian experience seems to be that of the gap. In other words, faced with the absolute domination of "oligarchy,"[1] the plebs rebels and challenges the established order but
without being able to found a sustainable new political order. However, as the
historian Boris Porshnev has perceptively observed, plebeian movements leave

"traces."[2] Thus, precisely because the political experience of the plebs is not without "testament," it is important to identify its specificity.

The plebeian experience, then, is characterized by a temporality of the gap that leaves traces. The memory of the Neapolitan revolt of Masaniello in 1647 illustrates the specificity of plebeian temporality. Almost a century and a half later, at the time when the English working class emerged, a publication intended for the English Jacobins related the exploits of the plebeian experience in Naples.[3] The memory of Masaniello therefore served as a reminder and lesson for the English plebeians. Similarly, the struggle of the sans-culottes in the Republican Years II and III was a source of inspiration for the political action of the Communards in 1871. It becomes plausible, then, to speak of a kind of "plebeian memory" that acts as a resource capable of reviving the plebeian principle and of nurturing the action of those for whom domination remains a constitutive dimension of everyday life.

The temporality of the gap that leaves traces makes it possible to establish the existence of a "plebeian memory." This memory opens onto a larger question concerning the persistence of the plebeian experience beyond the historical events analyzed here. Having observed the temporality specific to the plebs, we could, in the future, focus our attention on plebeian experiences that took place throughout the twentieth century. For do not the German Revolution, the Spanish Civil War, and the events of May '68 in France also partake of the communalist and agoraphile traditions? Hence, the work of bringing to light the plebeian principle should be pursued, its new task being to analyze the persistence of the plebeian desire for freedom during the twentieth century and through to today.

But the events of the twentieth century make a true understanding of the plebeian experience especially complicated. To grasp the plebeian "trace" we must first come to grips with two crucial political phenomena: "totalitarian domination" (Claude Lefort) and the consolidation of "the modern disciplinary archipelago" (Michel Foucault). In the first case, one must understand the effects of this unprecedented form of domination on the very capacity of individuals to transform themselves into "political subjects" in a context of total domination. This is because the totalitarian (non)regime may make political subjectification, if not impossible, at least extremely difficult. In the case of the modern disciplinary archipelago, the capacity to develop properly political "experiences" seems jeopardized. The movement toward the intrusion of biopolitics into all dimensions of daily life no doubt makes it harder to engage in political action, a move characteristic of the plebeian experience. Despite this new complication, a reconstitution of the plebs' action during the twentieth century will undoubtedly sharpen our insight into the political phenomena affecting current events here and now.

Finally, the plebeian experience, inasmuch as it reveals a discontinuous history of freedom, remains in many ways a reactivation of the principle of *isonomia*. Isonomia, the founding principle of democracy at its genesis in ancient Greece,[4] designates both the equality of citizens before the law *and* their equal participation in the formulation of the law. Now, to those whose political horizons are limited to the liberal constitutional state, the plebeian desire for full and integral isonomia may appear *utopian*, but this qualifier in no way invalidates the political experience of the plebs. Quite to the contrary, it indicates the utter importance of that experience, because its utopian nature reminds us that modern democracy cannot be reduced solely to the equality of citizens before the law. In face of patrician opposition to the equal participation of all in lawmaking, the plebeian experience testifies to the persistence throughout history of the desire for liberty. In face of the contemporary denigrators of utopia, plebeian politics opposes the utopian actuality of an ever-possible and more-than-ever necessary emancipation. If modern democracy remains an "unfinished project" (Habermas), the contents of that incompletion may reside in the plebeian experience of a *utopian isonomia*.

NOTES

PREFACE

1. Hannah Arendt, "Labour, Work, Action," Speeches and Writings File, Hannah Arendt Papers, Manuscript Division, Library of Congress, Washington, D.C., 1967, 1–17.
2. Georges Bataille, *Inner Experience*, trans. Leslie Anne Boldt (Albany: State University of New York Press, 1988), 7.
3. Niccolò Machiavelli, *Discourses on Livy*, trans. H. C. Mansfield and N. Tarcov (Chicago: University of Chicago Press, 1996), book 1, 83–84.
4. Niccolò Machiavelli, *The Prince*, trans. H. C. Mansfield (Chicago: University of Chicago Press, 1998), 39.
5. Machiavelli, *Discourses*, 16, 17.
6. Claude Lefort, *Machiavelli in the Making*, trans. Michael B. Smith (1972; Evanston, Ill.: Northwestern University Press, 2012), 223.
7. Machiavelli, *Discourses*, 16.
8. Étienne de La Boétie, "The Discourse of Voluntary Servitude," trans. H. Kurz, in É. de La Boétie and P. Bonnefon, *The Politics of Obedience and Étienne de La Boétie* (Montreal: Black Rose, 2007), 112, 114.
9. Ibid., 128, 112.
10. Ibid., 121–122.
11. Jacques Rancière, *Staging the People: The Proletarian and His Double*, trans. David Fernbach (London: Verso, 2011), 38.
12. Jean Borreil, "Le combat des 'muets du mutisme civil,'" in *Les sauvages dans la cité. Auto-émancipation du peuple et instruction des prolétaires au XIXe siècle*, ed. J. Borreil (Seysell: Champs Vallon, 1985), 37. All translations are ours.

13. Livy, *A History of Rome: Selections*, trans. M. Hadas and J. Poe (New York: Random House, 1962), 90.
14. Or the Sacred Mount. However, Livy follows the traditional narrative whereby the plebs withdrew to the Aventine. Ibid., 92.
15. Livy, *The Early Roman History*, trans. A. De Sélincourt (New York: Penguin, 1981), 141. [Because the Hadas edition omits certain passages found in the original, the De Sélincourt edition will also be cited at times. —Trans.]
16. Ibid.
17. Ibid., 142.
18. Ibid., 141.
19. Jacques Rancière, *Disagreement: Politics and Philosophy*, trans. Julie Rose (Minneapolis: University of Minnesota Press, 1999), 23.
20. Ibid., 23.
21. Ibid., 24.
22. Ibid.
23. Michel Humbert states that in 494 BCE the Roman plebeians organized themselves "in an insurrectional commune." M. Humbert, *Institutions politiques et sociales de l'antiquité* (Paris: Dalloz, 2003), 243. All translations are ours.
24. Oskar Anweiler, *The Soviets: The Russian Workers, Peasants, and Soldiers Councils, 1905–1921*, trans. R. Hein (New York: Pantheon, 1975), 3.
25. Ibid., 4.
26. Humbert, *Institutions*, 243.
27. See Roger Dupuy, *La politique du peuple* (Paris: Albin Michel, 2002). Our translation.
28. Anweiler, *The Soviets*, 4.
29. Francis Dupuis-Déri, "L'esprit antidémocratique des fondateurs de la 'démocratie' moderne," *Agone* 22 (1999): 112–113; "The Political Power of Words: The Birth of Pro-Democratic Discourses in the Nineteenth Century in the United States and France," *Political Studies* 52 (March 2004): 118–134. All translations are ours.
30. Dupuis-Déri, "L'esprit antidémocratique," 112.
31. Hannah Arendt, *Between Past and Future* (New York: Viking, 1969), 5.
32. Boris Porchnev, *Les soulèvements populaires en France au XVIIᵉ siècle* (1963; Paris: Flammarion, 1972), 290. All translations are ours.
33. Oscar Negt, *L'espace public oppositionnel* (Paris: Payot, 2007), 34. All translations are ours.

1. Historical Genesis of the Plebeian Principle

1. Pierre-Simon Ballanche, *Oeuvres complètes* (Geneva: Slatkin Reprint, 1967), 344, 319. The "plebeian principle" in Ballanche's thought will be examined in the following chapter. All translations are ours.
2. Jean-Claude Richard, *Les origines de la plèbe romaine: essai sur la formation du dualisme patricio-plébéien* (Paris, Rome: BEFAR, 1978), xi. All translations are ours.
3. Jean Gagé, *Les classes sociales dans l'Empire romain* (Paris: Payot, 1964), 123.
4. Richard, *Les origines*, xix.

5. Max Weber, *The Agrarian Sociology of Ancient Civilizations*, trans. R. I. Frank (London: NLB, 1976), 287. Italics added.

6. Chaïm Wirszubski, *Libertas as a Political Idea in Rome* (Cambridge: Cambridge University Press, 1950), 1.

7. Henrik Mouritsen, *Plebs and Politics in the Late Roman Empire* (Cambridge: Cambridge University Press, 2001), 9.

8. Wirszubski, *Libertas*, 3.

9. Ibid., 4.

10. Ibid.

11. Ibid., 8.

12. Ibid., 14.

13. *Autoritas* and *dignitas* were also important notions for Roman politics. But they are not central to my analysis of the plebs in the Roman Republic.

14. Mouritsen, *Plebs and Politics*, 3.

15. Ibid. See also F. Miller, *The Crowd in Rome in the Late Republic* (Ann Arbor: University of Michigan Press, 1998), 6–7.

16. Numa-Denys Fustel de Coulanges, *The Ancient City: A Study on the Religion, Laws, and Institutions of Greece and Rome*, trans. Willard Small (1874; New York: Doubleday, 1955), 307.

17. Weber, *The Agrarian Sociology*, 267.

18. Mouritsen, *Plebs and Politics*, 4.

19. Richard, *Les origines de la plèbe*, 433.

20. Mouritsen, *Plebs and Politics*, 11.

21. The political genesis of the plebeian principle is discussed in the next chapter.

22. Livy, *A History of Rome: Selections*, trans. M. Hadas and J. Poe (New York: Random House, 1962), 129. For a critical analysis of Livy's presentation of the plebeian secessions, see J. Bayet, "Appendice," in Titus Livius, *Histoire romaine* (Paris: Les Belles lettres, 1969), 3:115–153.

23. Livy, *Selections*, 90.

24. Ibid., 91.

25. Livy, *The Early Roman History*, trans. A. De Sélincourt (New York: Penguin, 1981), 131.

26. Ibid., 133, 134.

27. Ibid., 135–137.

28. Ibid., 140.

29. Ibid., 141, 143–144.

30. Weber, *The Agrarian Sociology*, 283.

31. Livy, *The Early Roman History*, 141.

32. Ibid., 142.

33. Ibid.

34. Humbert, *Institutions politiques et sociales*, 243.

35. Livy, *Selections*, 141.

36. Edgar Quinet, *Les révolutions d'Italie* (Brussels: Imprimerie et lithographie de Ch. Vanderauwera, 1853), 147. All translations are ours.

37. Simone Weil, "A Proletarian Uprising in Florence," in *Selected Essays: 1934–1943*, trans. R. Rees (London: Oxford University Press, 1962), 55.

38. Ibid.

39. Michel Mollat and Philippe Wolff, *The Popular Revolutions of the Late Middle Ages*, trans. A. L. Lytton-Sells (London: Allen & Unwin, 1973), 22.

40. Ibid., 24.

41. Ibid., 24, 80, 25.

42. Weil, "A Proletarian Uprising," 59.

43. Mollat and Wolff, *The Popular Revolutions*, 28–29.

44. Weil, "A Proletarian Uprising," 56.

45. Mollat and Wolff, *The Popular Revolutions*, 79.

46. Ibid., 144–145.

47. Niccolò Machiavelli, *Florentine Histories*, trans. L. F. Banfield and H. C. Mansfield Jr. (Princeton, N.J.: Princeton University Press, 1988), book 3, 116.

48. Weil, "A Proletarian Uprising," 59.

49. Machiavelli, *Florentine Histories*, book 3, 117.

50. Weil, "A Proletarian Uprising," 59.

51. Mollat and Wolff, *The Popular Revolutions*, 149.

52. Ibid., 149–150.

53. Weil, "A Proletarian Uprising," 60.

54. Machiavelli, *Florentine Histories*, book 3, 128.

55. Quinet, *Les révolutions d'Italie*, 160.

56. Machiavelli, *Florentine Histories*, book 3, 128.

57. Quinet, *Le révolutions d'Italie*, 160.

58. Ibid., 161.

59. Mollat and Wolff, *The Popular Revolutions*, 155.

60. Machiavelli, *Florentine Histories*, book 3, 129.

61. Weil, "A Proletarian Uprising," 60.

62. Quinet, *Les révolutions d'Italie*, 162.

63. Mollat and Wolff, *The Popular Revolutions*, 156.

64. Quinet, *Les révolutions d'Italie*, 162.

65. Mollat and Wolff, *The Popular Revolutions*, 156.

66. Quinet, *Les révolutions d'Italie*, 166–167.

67. Mollat and Wolff, *The Popular Revolutions*, 157.

68. Machiavelli, *Florentine Histories*, book 3, 130.

69. Martine Leibovici, "From Fight to Debate: Machiavelli and the Revolt of the Ciompi," *Philosophy and Social Criticism* 28, no. 6: 660n21.

70. Quinet, *Les révolutions d'Italie*, 160.

71. Ibid., 161.

72. Weil, "A Proletarian Uprising," 61.

73. Quinet, *Les révolutions d'Italie*, 166.

74. Mikhail Bakhtin, *Rabelais and His World*, trans. Hélène Iswolsky (Bloomington: Indiana University Press, 1984), 7.

75. Ibid., 8, 7, 9.

76. Ibid, 9.

77. Ibid., 10.

78. Ibid., 11–12.

79. On the "wedding" of festival and revolt throughout history, see Yves-Marie Bercé, *Fêtes et révoltes. Des mentalités populaires du XVIᵉ au XVIIIᵉ siècle* (Paris: Hachette, 1976), 72.

80. Michael D. Bristol, *Carnival and Theater: Plebeian Culture and the Structure of Authority in Renaissance England* (London: Methuen, 1985), 50.

81. Emmanuel Le Roy Ladurie, *Carnival in Romans*, trans. Mary Feeney (New York: Braziller, 1979), 315–316.

82. Ibid., 20.

83. Ibid., 23–24.

84. Ibid., 100–101.

85. The text of this testimony, in both Old and Modern French versions, is included in Philippe Venault et al., *Un soulèvement populaire: Romans—1580* (Paris: Albatros, 1979), 38–117.

86. Le Roy Ladurie, *Carnival*, 126.

87. Le Roy Ladurie, "Présentation," in Ph. Venault et al., *Un soulèvement populaire*, 10. Our translation.

88. Ibid., 11.

89. Ibid.

90. Le Roy Ladurie, *Carnival*, 229, 230.

91. Ibid., 249, 263.

92. Ibid., 283.

93. Ibid., 290–292.

94. Bristol, *Carnival and Theatre*, 51.

95. Ibid., 52.

96. Gilles Labelle, "Maurice Merleau-Ponty et la genèse de la philosophie politique de Claude Lefort," *Politique et Sociétés* 22, no. 3 (2003): 37. All translations are ours.

97. Marcel Gauchet, *La condition historique* (Paris: Stock, 2003), 174. All translations are ours.

98. Claude Lefort and Marcel Gauchet, "Sur la démocratie: le politique et l'institution du social," *Textures* 2–3 (1971): 7–78. All translations are ours.

99. Augustin Simard, "Les formes politiques de la modernité. Signification et portée de la démocratie dans la pensée de Claude Lefort," master's thesis, Laval University, Quebec City (2000), 14–16.

100. Machiavelli, *The Prince*, 39, 40.

101. Machiavelli, *Discourses*, 16.

102. Claude Lefort, *Machiavelli in the Making*, trans. Michael B. Smith (Evanston, Ill.: Northwestern University Press, 2012), 223.

103. Machiavelli, *Discourses*, 16.

104. [The English translation does not include Lefort's interpretations of certain "exemplary readings" of Machiavelli such as Leo Strauss's, from which this reference is taken. See the original French edition: Claude Lefort, *Le travail de l'oeuvre* (1972; Paris: Gallimard, 2005), 304. —Trans.]

105. Labelle, "Maurice Merleau-Ponty," 35.

106. Miguel Abensour, "Appendix: 'Savage Democracy' and the 'Principle of Anarchy,'" in *Democracy Against the State: Marx and the Machiavellian Moment*, trans. Max Blechman and Martin Breaugh (London: Polity, 2011), 104–105.

107. Machiavelli, *Discourses*, 17.

108. See Miguel Abensour, "Réflexions sur les deux interpretations du totalitarisme chez Claude Lefort," in *La démocratie à l'oeuvre. Autour de Claude Lefort*, ed. Claude Habib and Claude Mouchard (Paris: Éditions Esprit, 1993), 79–136.

109. Claude Lefort, *Un homme en trop* (Paris: Seuil, 1976), 68.

110. Claude Lefort, "Le nom d'Un," in Etienne de La Boétie, *Le discours de la servitude volontaire* (Paris: Payot, 1976), 267.

111. Claude Lefort, *L'invention démocratique. Les limites de la domination totalitaire* (1981; Paris: Fayard, 1994), 41–42. Our translation.

112. Claude Lefort, "Préface," in *Éléments d'une critique de la bureaucratie* (Paris: Gallimard, 1979), 23–25.

113. Joseph-Yvon Thériault, "Sur les traces de la démocratie avec Claude Lefort," *Conjonctures* 20–21 (Fall 1994): 139. Our translation.

114. Lefort and Gauchet, "Sur la démocratie," 8, 9. All translations are ours.

115. Ibid., 12, 13.

116. Ibid.

117. Ibid.

118. Maurice Merleau-Ponty, *The Visible and the Invisible*, ed. Claude Lefort, trans. Alphonso Lingis (Evanston, Ill.: Northwestern University Press, 1968).

119. Maurice Merleau-Ponty, *Phenomenology of Perception*, trans. Colin Smith (1962; London: Routledge, 2002).

120. Claude Lefort, "Qu'est-ce que voir?" in *Sur une colonne absente: Écrits autour de Merleau-Ponty* (Paris: Gallimard, 1978), 152. Our translation.

121. Simard, *Les formes politiques*, 14. Our translation.

122. Merleau-Ponty, *The Visible and the Invisible*, 169.

123. Ibid., 124. Italics added.

124. Miguel Abensour, "Réflexions sur les deux interprétations du totalitarisme chez Claude Lefort," in Claude Habib and Claude Mouchard, eds., *La Démocratie*, 102. Our translation.

125. Machiavelli, *Discourses*, 16–17.

126. Ibid., 17.

127. Peter Burke, "The Virgin of Carmine and the Revolt of Masaniello," *Past and Present* 99 (May 1983): 3.

128. Rosario Villari, "Masaniello: Contemporary and Recent Interpretations," *Past and Present* 108 (August 1985): 125–139.

129. Miguel Abensour, "Ça se passe bien! Pour François Châtelet," *La Mazarine*, special issue, "L'épuisement du politique" (March 1988): 11. All translations are ours.

130. Burke, "The Virgin of Carmine," 9.

131. Abensour, "Ça se passe bien!" 12.

132. Villari, "Masaniello," 120.

133. Burke, "The Virgin of Carmine," 12.

134. Abensour, "Ça se passe bien!" 12.

135. Burke, "The Virgin of Carmine," 13.

136. Villari, "Masaniello," 128.

137. Abensour, "Ça se passe bien!" 12–13.

138. Burke, "The Virgin of Carmine," 15, 16.

139. Abensour, "Ça se passe bien!" 13.

140. Ibid., 14.

141. Burke, "The Virgin of Carmine," 16.

142. Abensour, "Ça se passe bien!" 14.

143. Burke, "The Virgin of Carmine," 17.

144. The translator was James Howell, whose translation from the Italian of Alessandro Giraffi's work was titled *An Exact Historie of the late Revolutions in Naples and of their Monstrous Successes not to be Parallel'd by any Ancient or Modern History* (London, 1650). The quoted passage is Villari's paraphrase of Howell's views. See R. Villari, "Masaniello," 128.

145. The story of Masaniello appeared in Thomas Spence's periodical "Pig's Meat; or lessons for the Swinish Multitude." On the presence of Masaniello, see David Worrall, *Radical Culture: Discourse, Resistance, and Surveillance, 1790–1820* (Detroit: Wayne State University Press, 1992), 23.

146. See in particular Jean-François Lyotard, "Chapitre 4: futilité en revolution," in *Rudiments païens* (Paris: UGE, 1977), 157–212; Miguel Abensour, "De l'intraitable," in Gérard Sfez and Dolorès Lyotard, eds., *Jean-François Lyotard. L'exercice du différend* (Paris: PUF, 2001), 241–260. All translations are ours.

147. Abensour, "De l'intraitable," 243–245.

148. Ibid., 246.

149. Daniel Guérin, *Class Struggle in the First French Republic*, trans. I. Patterson (Sydney: Pluto, 1977). [Ian Patterson's translation is an abridged version of Daniel Guérin, *La lutte de classes sous la première république, bourgeois et "bras nus" (1793–1797)*, 2 vols. (Paris: Gallimard, 1968). Whenever the quoted passage is not included in the English translation, the reference is to our own translation of the French original. —Trans.]

150. Guérin, *Class Struggle*, 137, 142.

151. Abensour, "De l'intraitable," 247.

152. Ibid., 248.

153. Lyotard, "Chapitre 4: futilité en revolution," 174–175.

154. Abensour, "De l'intraitable," 250.

155. Machiavelli, *Florentine Histories*, book 3, 130.

156. Abensour, "Ça se passe bien!" 14. Italics added.

157. La Boétie, *The Politics of Obedience*, 128.

158. Ibid., 112. Italics added.

159. Lefort, "Le nom d'Un," 274. Our translation.

160. Machiavelli, *The Prince*, 25.

161. Georges Bataille, "Nietzschean Chronicle," in *Visions of Excess: Selected Writings, 1927–1939*, ed. Allan Stoekl, trans. A. Stoekl et al. (Minneapolis: University of Minnesota Press, 1985), 210.

2. PHILOSOPHICAL GENESIS OF THE PLEBEIAN PRINCIPLE

1. Benedict de Spinoza, *Theological-Political Treatise*, trans. J. Israel and M. Silverthorne (New York: Cambridge University Press, 2007); Georges Sorel, *Matériaux d'une théorie du prolétariat* (Paris: Marcel Rivière, 1921).

2. See Karl Marx and Frederick Engels, *The German Ideology*, ed. C. J. Arthur (New York: International Publishers, 1970).

3. Quoted by Walter Benjamin in "The Paris of the Second Empire in Baudelaire," in his *Selected Writings, 1938–1940*, ed. Howard Eiland and Michael W. Jennings (Cambridge, Mass.: Harvard University Press, 2003), 4. [The reference note originally provided by Benjamin reads, "Marx and Engels, Review of Chenu and of de la Hodde, p. 556." —Trans.]

4. Claude Lefort, *Machiavelli in the Making*, trans. Michael B. Smith (Evanston, Ill.: Northwestern University Press, 2012).

5. Charles Montesquieu, *Considerations on the Causes of the Greatness of the Romans and Their Decline*, trans. David Lowenthal (New York: Free Press, 1965).

6. Giambattista Vico, *The New Science of Giambattista Vico*, trans. T. Goddard Bergin and M. H. Fisch (Ithaca, N.Y.: Cornell University Press, 1984), 57.

7. Niccolò Machiavelli, *Discourses on Livy*, trans. H. C. Mansfield and N. Tarcov (Chicago: University of Chicago Press, 1996).

8. Niccolò Machiavelli, *The Prince*, trans. H. C. Mansfield (Chicago: University of Chicago Press, 1998).

9. Claude Lefort, "Préface," in Niccolò Machiavelli, *Discours sur la première décade de Tite-Live* (Paris: Flammarion, 1985), 14. All translations are ours.

10. Ibid. Italics added.

11. Ibid., 15.

12. See Machiavelli, *The Prince*, 38–42; Machiavelli, *Discourses*, 16–17; Niccolò Machiavelli, *Florentine Histories*, trans. L. F. Banfield and H. C. Mansfield Jr. (Princeton, N.J.: Princeton University Press, 1988), 105–106.

13. Gérald Sfez, "Machiavel: la raison des humeurs," *Rue Descartes* 12–13, "Passion et politique": 22.

14. Anthony J. Parel, *The Machiavellian Cosmos* (New Haven, Conn.: Yale University Press, 1992), 104–107.

15. Machiavelli, *Discourses*, book 1, 83.

16. Machiavelli, *The Prince*, 39.

17. Ibid.

18. Parel, *Machiavellian Cosmos*, 107.

19. Ibid., 108.

20. Ibid., 122.

21. Machiavelli, *Discourses*, book 1, 16.

22. Lefort, *Machiavelli in the Making*, 223.

23. Parel, *Machiavellian Cosmos*, 124.

24. Machiavelli, *Discourses*, book 1, 16.

25. Claude Lefort, *Le travail de l'oeuvre, Machiavel* (1972; Paris: Gallimard, 1986), 304. Our translation.

26. Machiavelli, *Discourses*, book 1, 17.

27. On the question of Machiavelli's partiality and its consequences for modern political philosophy, see Pierre Manent, "Toward the Work and Toward the World: Claude Lefort's Machiavelli," in his *Modern Liberty and Its Discontents*, trans. D. J. Mahoney and P. Seaton (Lanham, Md.: Rowman & Littlefield, 1998), 47–63.

28. See Pierre Manent, *Naissances de la politique moderne. Machiavel, Hobbes, Rousseau* (Paris: Payot, 1977).

29. Machiavelli, *Discourses*, book 1, 17.

30. Lefort, *Machiavelli in the Making*, 230.

31. Machiavelli, *Discourses*, book 1, 18.

32. Machiavelli, *Florentine Histories*, book 3, 130.

33. Machiavelli, *The Prince*, 30.

34. Ibid., 21–25.

35. Machiavelli, *Discourses*, book 1, 17.

36. Martine Leibovici, "From Fight to Debate: Machiavelli and the Revolt of the Ciompi," *Philosophy and Social Criticism* 28, no. 6: 660n21.

37. See Mansfield and Tarcov, "Introduction," in Machiavelli, *Discourses*, xxvii–xxxiii.

38. Christian Nadeau, "Machiavel. Domination et liberté politique," *Philosophiques* 30, no. 2 (Autumn 2003): 302.

39. Ibid. Our translation.

40. Montesquieu, *The Spirit of the Laws*, trans. A. M. Cohler et al. (Cambridge: Cambridge University Press, 1989), 172.

41. Montesquieu, *Considerations on the Causes of the Greatness of the Romans and Their Decline*, trans. David Lowenthal (Ithaca, N.Y.: Cornell University Press, 1965).

42. Lowenthal, "Introduction," in Montesquieu, *Considerations*, 1.

43. Melvin Richter, *The Political Theory of Montesquieu* (Cambridge: Cambridge University Press, 1977), 55–56.

44. Montesquieu, *Considerations*, 83, 84, 87, 88. Italics added.

45. Ibid., 93.

46. Ibid., 93–94.

47. David Lowenthal, "Introduction" in Montesquieu, *Considerations*, 6.

48. David Lowenthal, "The Design of Montesquieu's *Considerations on the Causes of the Greatness of the Romans and Their Decline*," *Interpretation* 1–2 (Winter 1970): 144–168.

49. Leo Strauss, *Thoughts on Machiavelli* (Chicago: University of Chicago Press, 1978), 296.

50. Leo Strauss, *What Is Political Philosophy?* (Westport: Greenwood, 1959), 40–50.

51. Lowenthal, "The Design of Montesquieu's *Considerations*," 146–148.

52. Ibid., 151.

53. Ibid. 163.

54. Montesquieu, *Considerations*, 196, 198.

55. Lowenthal, "The Design of Montesquieu's *Considerations*," 165.

56. Lefort, *Le travail de l'oeuvre Machiavel*, 304. Our translation.

57. Montesquieu, *Consideration*, 42.

58. Lowenthal, "The Design of Montesquieu's *Considerations*," 149, 150.

59. Note that his translation, which first appeared in 1965, was published in a paperback edition in 1968 and reissued in 1999 by Hackett, a major publisher. It is the most recent English-language translation of the *Considerations* and the only one widely available.
60. Lowenthal, "Introduction," 4.
61. Ibid., 11.
62. Ibid., 12.
63. Abbé de Vertot, *An History of the Revolutions That Happened in the Government of the Roman Republic*, trans. John. Ozell (London: J. & J. Knapton et al., 1724).
64. We are indebted to the excellent but all too brief article by Henri Drei for having drawn our attention to the work of Vertot. H. Drei, "Les Romains de Vertot et de Montesquieu," in *Le temps de Montesquieu*, ed. Michel Porret and Catherine Volpilhac-Auger (Geneva: Droz, 2002), 337–343. All translations are ours.
65. Louis Desgraves, *Catalogue de la bibliothèque de Montesquieu* (Geneva: Droz, 1954), 205.
66. Drei, "Les Romains de Vertot et de Montesquieu," 338.
67. Ibid., 339.
68. Ibid., 340.
69. Ibid., 341.
70. Montesquieu, *Considerations*, 94.
71. Montesquieu published the *Considerations* in 1734, exactly fifteen years after the publication of Vertot's *History*.
72. Vico, *New Science*, 57.
73. Eugenio Garin, *Machiavel entre politique et histoire* (Paris: Allia, 2006), 35.
74. Vico, *New Science*, 28.
75. Ibid., 338–339.
76. Amilda Pons, "Vico et la 'barbarie de la réflexion,'" in *Figures italiennes de la rationalité*, ed. Christiane Menasseyre and André Tosel (Paris: Kimé, 1997), 341. All translations are ours.
77. Ibid.
78. Vico, *New Science*, 370.
79. Pons, "Vico et la 'barbarie de la réflexion,'" 343–344.
80. Vico, *New Science*, 195, 209.
81. Ibid., 210, 211, 83, 212.
82. Olivier Remaud, *Les archives de l'humanité* (Paris: Seuil, 2004), 343. All translations are ours.
83. Vico, *New Science*, 133. Italics added.
84. Frederick Vaughan, *The Political Philosophy of Giambattista Vico* (The Hague: Martinus Nijhoff, 1972), 58.
85. Vico, *New Science*, 57, 53, 54.
86. Ibid., 54.
87. Vaughan, *The Political Philosophy*, 59.
88. Vico, *New Science*, 219.
89. Ibid., 55–56.
90. Remaud, *Les archives*, 348.

91. Pons, "Vico et la 'barbarie de la réflexion,'" 336.

92. [Term used to designate the nobility or aristocracy of ancient Rome. —Trans.]

93. Vico, *New Science*, 283.

94. Pons, "Vico et la 'barbarie de la réflexion,'" 343.

95. Vico, *New Science*, 378–379.

96. Ibid., 382.

97. Ibid., 370.

98. Ibid., 386, 57.

99. Oscar Haac, "Introduction," in Pierre-Simon Ballanche, *La théodicée et la virginie romaine*, ed. Oscar Haac (Geneva: Droz, 1959), 9. All translations are ours.

100. Arthur McCalla, *A Romantic Historiosophy: The Philosophy of Pierre-Simon Ballanche* (Leiden: Brill, 1998), 127.

101. Pierre-Simon Ballanche, "Essais de palingénésie sociale. Formule générale de l'histoire de tous les peuples, appliquée à l'histoire du peuple romain," "1er fragment" *Revue de Paris* 2 (1829): 138–154; "2e fragment" *Revue de Paris* 4 (1829): 129–150; "3e fragment" *Revue de Paris* 6 (1829): 70–98. All translations are ours.

102. Haac, "Introduction," 12.

103. Pierre-Simon Ballanche, *Oeuvres complètes* (Geneva: Slatkine, 1967), 417–550. Note that this (incomplete) edition of Ballanche's collected works is a reprint of P.-S. Ballanche, *Oeuvres*, 6 vols. in 12 (Paris: Bureau de l'Encylopédie des connaissances utiles, 1833). All translations are ours.

104. Ballanche, "Essais."

105. Pierre-Simon Ballanche, *La ville des expiations*, ed. Amand Rastoul (Paris: Bibliothèque romantique, 1926); P.-S. Ballanche, *La vision d'Hébal*, ed. Allan J. L. Busst (Geneva: Droz, 1969). All translations are ours.

106. Haac, "Introduction," 45.

107. Ballanche, *Oeuvres complètes*, 302.

108. Paul Bénichou, "Le grand oeuvre de P.-S. Ballanche. Chronologie et inachèvement," *Revue d'Histoire Littéraire de la France* (1975): 736.

109. The decisive influence of Vico on Ballanche's thinking must nevertheless be stressed, especially with respect to the question of the plebs, even though history for Ballanche is linear and not cyclical. See Arthur McCalla, "P.-S. Ballanche as a Reader of Vico," *New Vico Studies* 9 (1991): 43–59; and Haac, "Introduction," 28.

110. Ballanche, *Oeuvres complètes*, 342–352.

111. Ballanche, "Formule générale."

112. Ballanche, *La théodicée*, 75–137.

113. Ibid., 68–71.

114. Ballanche, "Formule générale," vol. 4, 131, 134, 140, 143.

115. Ibid., vol. 6, 72, 78.

116. Ibid., 90, 91, 96.

117. Haac, "Introduction," 61.

118. Ballanche, *La théodicée*, 106, 108.

119. Ibid., 125, 133, 134.

120. Ibid., 134–135.

121. Haac, "Introduction," 68.

122. Allan Busst, "Introduction," in Ballanche, *La vision*, 25.

123. Ballanche, *La vision*, 173.

124. Ballanche, *Oeuvres completes*, 319, 399, 419.

125. Ibid., 408, 344.

126. Georges Navet, "De l'Aventin à la Croix-Rousse. Pierre-Simon Ballanche et le héros plébéien," in *Les Cahiers du Collège International de Philosophie* 5 (1988): 39. All translations are ours.

127. Ballanche, *Oeuvres complètes*, 367.

128. Agnès Kettler, *Lettres de P.-S. Ballanche à Madame Récamier 1812–1845* (Paris: Champion, 1996), 590–594. All translations are ours.

129. Navet, "De l'Aventin," 40.

130. Kettler, "Lettres," 591.

131. Ballanche, *Oeuvres complètes*, 569.

132. Lloyd Glen Seretan, *Daniel De Leon: The Odyssey of an American Marxist* (Cambridge, Mass.: Harvard University Press, 1979), 2.

133. Ibid., 5–21.

134. Aileen S. Kraditor, *The Radical Persuasion, 1890–1917: Aspects of the Intellectual History and the Historiography of Three American Radical Organizations* (Baton Rouge: Louisiana State University Press, 1981), 19.

135. Seretan, *The Odyssey*, 82.

136. Kraditor, *The Radical Persuasion*, 10.

137. Marc Karson, *American Labor Unions and Politics, 1900–1918* (Carbondale: Southern Illinois University Press, 1958), 23.

138. See Serge Denis, *Un syndicalisme pur et simple* (Montreal: Boréal, 1985). Our translation.

139. Kraditor, *The Radical Persuasion*, 10–11.

140. Karson, *American Labor*, 23.

141. See Mike Lepore, "De Leon: A Sketch of His Socialist Career," http://slp.org/De_Leon .htm#anchor345364.

142. It is worth noting that Lenin wanted to have *Two Pages* translated into Russian and even proposed to write the introduction. Though never realized, this project aptly illustrates the theoretical importance of De Leon's work. See Seretan, *The Odyssey*, 223n3.

143. Daniel De Leon, *Two Pages from Roman History* (New York City: New York Labor News Company, 1903), 5, 7.

144. Karl Marx, *The Eighteenth Brumaire of Louis Bonaparte* (New York: International Publishers, 2004).

145. De Leon, *Two Pages*, 9.

146. Ibid., 9.

147. Ibid., 14.

148. Ibid., 19.

149. Ibid., 24.

150. Ibid., 31.

151. Ibid., 46–47.

152. Jonathan Rée, *Proletarian Philosophers: Problems in Socialist Culture in Britain, 1900–1940* (Oxford: Oxford University Press, 1980), 13.

153. Stuart Macintyre, *A Proletarian Science: Marxism in Britain, 1917–1933* (Cambridge: Cambridge University Press, 1980), 78.

154. Rée, *Proletarian Philosophers*, 22.

155. Michel Foucault, "Nietzsche, Genealogy, History," in *Essential Works of Foucault 1954–1984: Aesthetics, Method, and Epistemology*, ed. J. D. Faubion, trans. D. F. Brouchard and S. Simon (New York: The New Press, 1998), 2:369–391. Michel Foucault et al., "Table Ronde" *Esprit* 413, "Normalisation et contôle social (Pourquoi le travail social?)" (April/May 1972): 678–703; reprinted in Michel Foucault, *Dits et écrits* (Paris: Gallimard, 2001), 1:1184–1207. Michel Foucault, "Pouvoir et stratégies" (discussion with Jacques Rancière et al.), *Les Révoltes Logiques* 4 (Winter 1977): 89–97; reprinted in Foucault, *Dits et écrits*, 2:418–428. All translations are ours. These are not the only texts in which Foucault discusses the plebs. But we believe that his contribution to "plebeian thought" is particularly well articulated in these three. The plebs is also at issue in, for example, "Sur la justice populaire. Débat avec les maos," *Les Temps Modernes* 310 bis (June 1971): 355–366; reprinted in Foucault, *Dits et écrits*, 1:1208–1237.

156. Foucault, "Nietzsche, Genealogy, History," 2:369.

157. Ibid., 371–373, 377–378.

158. Ibid., 382.

159. Ibid., 382–383.

160. Ibid., 383.

161. Ibid., 384.

162. Ibid. Italics added.

163. Ibid., 376.

164. Foucault et al., "Table Ronde," 1:1200, 1202.

165. Ibid, 1202, 1204.

166. Foucault, "Pouvoir et stratégies," 2:418.

167. Ibid., 420, 421.

168. Ibid, 421.

169. Mika Ojakangas, "Sovereign and Plebs: Michel Foucault Meets Carl Schmidt," *Telos* 119 (Spring 2001): 39.

170. Foucault, "Pouvoir et stratégies," 2:421.

171. Ibid. 421–422.

172. Ibid., p. 428.

173. Alain Brossat, "La plèbe. Des infâmes et des anonymes. Foucault libertaire," *Réfraction* 12 (Spring 2004): 112. All translations are ours.

174. Michel Foucault, "The Subject and Power," in *Essential Works of Michel Foucault 1954–1984: Power*, ed. J. D. Faubion (New York: The New Press, 2000), 3:326–348.

175. John Ransom, "Chapter V: 'The Plebeian Aspect,'" in *Foucault's Discipline: The Politics of Subjectivity* (Durham, N.C.: Duke University Press, 1997), 101–102.

176. Foucault, "The Subject and Power," 341.

177. Charles Taylor, "Foucault on Freedom and Truth," in *Philosophy and the Human Sciences: Philosophical Papers II* (Cambridge: Cambridge University Press, 1985), 175–176.

178. Foucault, "The Subject and Power," 343.

179. On the dangers of "catastrophism," see Miguel Abensour, "Pour une philosophie politique critique?" *Tumultes* 17–18 (2002): 249–250.
180. Foucault, "The Subject and Power," 342.
181. Ransom, "The 'Plebeian Aspect,'" 127.
182. Brossat, "La plèbe," 111–112.
183. Ibid. 112–113.
184. Ibid., 114, 115.
185. Ibid., 120, 121.
186. Ibid., 113.
187. Foucault, "Table Ronde," 1:1202.
188. Foucault, "Pouvoir et stratégies," 2:421.
189. Jacques Rancière, *Disagreement: Politics and Philosophy*, trans. J. Rose (Minneapolis: University of Minnesota Press, 1999), 28. Foucault is not the only influence acknowledged by Rancière; others include Claude Lefort and Alain Badiou.
190. Jacques Rancière, *The Nights of Labor: The Workers' Dream in Nineteenth-Century France*, trans. J. Drury (Philadelphia: Temple University Press, 1989).
191. Jacques Rancière, ed., *Gabriel Gauny. Le philosophe plébéien* (Paris: La Découverte/ Presses universitaires de Vincennes, 1983), 89. All translations are ours.
192. "Quelle mémoire aurons-nous?" *Les Révoltes Logiques* 1 (Winter 1975): inside back cover. Our translation.
193. Rancière, "Les gros mots," in *Les scènes du peuple* (Lyon: Éd. Horlieu, 2003), 9. Our translation.
194. "Quelle mémoire aurons-nous?"
195. Rancière, "Les gros mots," 11.
196. Rancière provides insight into the nature of his research project in *Les scènes du peuple*, published in 2003. See "Les gros mots," 14–15.
197. Jacques Rancière and Alain Faure, *La parole ouvrière* (Paris: UGE, 1976).
198. Jacques Rancière, "Le prolétaire et son double ou Le philosophe inconnu," *Les Révoltes Logiques* 13 (Winter 1980–1981): 4–5. Note that this text is the transcription of his thesis defense.
199. This enterprise also developed in the wake of Rancière's break with the Marxism of Louis Althusser. See Jacques Rancière, *La leçon d'Althusser* (Paris: Gallimard, 1974).
200. Rancière and Faure, *La parole*, 10.
201. Ibid.
202. Jacques Rancière, "La bergère au Goulag (sur *La cuisinière et le mangeur d'hommes*, d'André Glucksmann)," *Les Révoltes Logiques* 1 (Winter 1975): 97–111. Reprinted in Rancière, *Les scènes*, 311–332.
203. Rancière, "Les gros mots," 8–9, 15.
204. Rancière, "Introduction," in Rancière, ed., *Gabriel Gauny*, 7, 6.
205. Rancière, *Disagreement*, 23.
206. Ibid., 24.
207. Ibid.
208. Jacques Rancière, *The Ignorant Schoolmaster: Five Lessons in Intellectual Emancipation*, trans. K. Ross (Stanford, Calif.: Stanford University Press, 1991), 98.

209. Ballanche, quoted by Rancière, ibid.

210. Rancière, *Disagreement*, 26–27.

211. Jacques Rancière, "Savoirs hérétiques et émancipation du pauvre," in *Les sauvages dans la cité. Auto-émancipation du peuple et instruction des prolétaires du XIXe siècle*, ed. Jean Borreil (Seyssel: Champs Vallon, 1985), 37. Our translation.

212. Jacques Rancière, "Politics, Identification, and Subjectivization," in *The Identity in Question*, ed. John Rajchman (New York: Routledge, 1995), 63.

213. Rancière, *Disagreement*, 29.

214. Rancière, "Politics, Identification, Subjectivization," 64.

215. Rancière, *Disagreement*, 22.

216. By "distribution of the sensible," Rancière means "the system of self-evident facts of sense perception that simultaneously discloses the existence of something in common and the delimitations that define the respective parts and positions within it." See Jacques Rancière, *The Politics of Aesthetics: The Distribution of the Sensible*, trans. G. Rockhill (New York: Continuum, 2004), 12.

217. Rancière, "Politics, Identification, Subjectivization," 64.

218. Ibid., 64–65.

219. Jacques Rancière, "Le dissensus citoyen," *Carrefour* 19, no. 2 (1997): 21. Our translation.

220. Rancière acknowledges his indebtedness to Lefort in Jacques Rancière, *On the Shores of Politics*, trans. L. Heron (New York: Verso, 2007), 37n9.

221. Rancière, "Politics, Identification, Subjectivization," 66.

222. Rancière, *Disagreement*, 36. [Note that J. Rose's translation of *Disagreement* renders the French term *subjectivization* with "subjectification" rather than its synonym "subjectivization." —Trans.]

223. Quoted in Rancière, "Politics, Identification, Subjectivization," 66.

224. Ibid., 67.

225. Ibid., 68.

226. Ibid.

227. Rancière, *Disagreement*, 39.

228. Rancière, "Savoirs hérétiques," 37. Our translation.

229. Étienne de La Boétie, "The Discourse of Voluntary Servitude," in E. de La Boétie and P. Bonnefon, *The Politics of Obedience and Étienne de La Boétie*, trans H. Kurz (Montreal: Black Rose, 2007), 112.

230. Georges Lavau, *À quoi sert le Parti communiste français?* (Paris: Fayard, 1981), 356n32. Our translation.

231. Joseph Déjacque, *À bas les chefs!* (Paris: Éd. Champ Libre, 1971), 219–220. All translations are ours.

232. Ibid., 212.

233. Déjacque writes, "So many midgets . . . who would like nothing better than to have official stilts, a title, appointments, any sort of representation that would take them out of the pothole in which ordinary people flounder, and parade as giants!" Ibid., 214.

234. Ibid., 219. Italics added.

235. Ibid., 218.

236. Ibid.

237. Pierre-Joseph Proudhon, *Oeuvres completes III. De la capacité politique des classes ouvrières* (Geneva: Slatkine, 1982). All translations are ours.

238. Ibid., 219. Italics added.

239. See Rée, *Proletarian Philosophers*, 13.

PART II PROLOGUE: ON THE DOMINANT POLITICAL CONFIGURATION OF MODERNITY

1. That is why, according to Jürgen Habermas, this "historical constellation that attained dominance . . . leaves aside the *plebeian* public sphere as a variant that in a sense was suppressed in the historical process." Jürgen Habermas, *The Structural Transformation of the Public Sphere*, trans. Thomas Burger (Cambridge, Mass.: MIT Press, 1991), xvii.

2. Francis Dupuis-Déri, "L'esprit antidémocratique des fondateurs de la 'démocratie' moderne," *Agone* 22: 64. Our translation.

3. Jean-Jacques Rousseau, *The Social Contract*, trans. Maurice Cranston (London: Penguin, 1968), 141.

4. Quoted in Alexander Hamilton, John Madison, and John Jay, *The Federalist Papers* (New York: New American Library, 1961), 82.

5. Bernard Manin, *Principles of Representative Government* (Cambridge: Cambridge University Press, 1997), 3.

6. Raymond Carré de Malberg, *Contributions à la théorie générale de l'état* (Paris: Dalloz, 2003), 2:205, 207, 208. All translations are ours.

7. Manin, *Principles of Representative Government*, 94.

8. Moisey Ostrogorski, *Democracy and the Organization of Political Parties*, trans. F. Clarke (London: MacMillan, 1902), 1:3.

9. Manin, *Principles of Representative Government*, 207.

10. Robert Michels, *Political Parties* (New York: Dover, 1959), 235–329.

11. Ostrogorski, *Democracy*, 161.

12. Moisey Ostrogorski, *La démocratie et les partis politiques*, ed. Pierre Rosanvallon (Paris: Seuil, 1979), 46. Our translation.

13. The idea of the party as "machine" is already found in the work of Michelet, who regarded the "Jacobin club" during the French Revolution as a sort of machine. See Jules Michelet, *History of the French Revolution*, trans. Charles Cocks (Chicago: University of Chicago Press, 1967).

14. The question of the "omnibus" character of parties is central to the author's argument in favor of ad hoc groupings (around specific political issues), which would make it possible to expand the democratization of the public sphere by encouraging freedom of opinion and greater citizen engagement in political matters. See Ostrogorski, *La démocratie*, 209–235.

15. Pierre Rosanvallon, "Lire Ostrogorski," in Ostrogorski, *La démocratie*, 17.

16. Marcel Gauchet, *The Disenchantment of the World: A Political History of Religion*, trans. Oscar Burge (Princeton, N.J.: Princeton University Press, 1997), 181.

17. Claude Lefort, *The Political Forms of Modern Society: Bureaucracy, Democracy, Totalitarianism*, ed. John B. Thompson (Cambridge, Mass.: MIT Press, 1986), 113. Italics added.

18. Ibid., 114.

19. Ibid., 118, 119.

20. Here one must no doubt distinguish among the different periods of Lefort's work. In his "first interpretation" of totalitarianism, Lefort asserts that the development of the Soviet regime as "state capitalism will go hand in hand with the rise of a bureaucracy as a new dominant social class." Lefort's passage from Marx to Machiavelli prompts him to reject the Marxist notion of "class" because it tends to deny the autonomy of the political field, which is marked more especially by a constitutive division between the Grandees' desire to dominate and the people's desire not to be subjected to that domination (Machiavelli) than by the struggle between socioeconomic classes. The quotation is drawn from Miguel Abensour, "Les deux interprétations du totalitarisme chez Claude Lefort," in *La démocratie à l'oeuvre*, ed. Claude Habib and Claude Mouchard (Paris: Édition Esprit, 1993), 86. Our translation.

21. Lefort, *The Political Forms of Modern Society*, 113.

22. Ibid., 118.

3.   SECTIONAL SOCIETIES AND THE SANS-CULOTTES OF PARIS

1. Claude Mazauric, "Sans-culottes/Sans-culotterie/Sans-culottisme," in *Dictionnaire historique de la Revolution française*, ed. Albert Soboul (Paris: PUF, 1989), 957. Our translation.

2. Patrice Higonnet, in *A Critical Dictionary of the French Revolution*, ed. François Furet and Mona Ozouf, trans. Arthur Goldhammer (Cambridge, Mass.: The Belknap Press of Harvard University Press, 1989), 393.

3. Daniel Guérin, *Class Struggle in the First French Republic: Bourgeois and Bras Nus, 1793-1795*, trans. I. Patterson (London: Pluto, 1977). Note that for interpretive reasons Guérin borrows Michelet's term *bras nus* (bare arms) to differentiate the petit-bourgeois elements from the other sans-culottes (artisans, workers, etc.). He does, however, use the term sans-culottes, but in a restricted sense that, conversely, excludes the petit bourgeois from the ranks of the sans-culottes. On this subject, see D. Guérin, *La lutte de classes sous la première république, bourgeois et "bras nus" (1793–1797)* (Gallimard: Paris, 1946), 1:26–27. [Ian Patterson's translation is an abridged version of Daniel Guérin's original. Therefore, whenever the quoted passage is not included in the English translation, the reference is to our own translation of the French original. All other references are to Patterson's English version. —Trans.]

4. Robert Rose, *The Making of the Sans-Culottes* (Manchester: Manchester University Press, 1984), 3.

5. Together with the peasants, of course.

6. Albert Soboul, *Les sans-culottes parisiens en l'an II* (Paris: Librairie Clavreuil, 1962), 10. [English translation: *The Sans-Culottes: The Popular Movement and Revolutionary Government, 1793–1794*, trans. Remy Inglis Hall (New York: Anchor, 1972), xxvii–xxviii.] See also D. Guérin, *La lutte de classes*, 1:31–36. [Remy Inglis Hall's translation is an abridged version of Albert Soboul's original. Therefore, whenever the quoted passage is not included in the English translation, the reference is to our own translation of the French original. All other references are to Hall's English version. —Trans.]

7. Kåre Tønnesson, *La défaite des sans-culotte* (Oslo: Presses Universitaires d'Oslo, 1978), xviii.

8. A document originally published by the sans-culottes, "Réponse à l'impertinente question: Mais qu'est-ce qu'un Sans-Culotte?" and reproduced by Markov and Soboul attests to the socioeconomic status of the majority of the sans-culottes. See Walter Markov and Albert Soboul, *Die Sansculotten von Paris* (East Berlin: Akademie-verlag, 1957). Note that this is a bilingual (French-German) edition.

9. Higonnet, in Furet and Ozouf, eds., *A Critical Dictionary*, 395.

10. Guérin, *La lutte de classes*, 1:44.

11. Higonnet, in Furet and Ozouf, eds., *A Critical Dictionary*, 395.

12. Soboul, *The Sans-Culottes*, 2.

13. Mazauric, "Sans-culottes/Sans-culotterie/Sans-culottisme," 961.

14. Soboul, *The Sans-Culottes*, 95.

15. Mazauric, "Sans-culottes/Sans-culotterie/Sans-culottisme," 961.

16. Ibid.

17. Michel Vovelle, "Préface," in Maurice Genty, *Paris 1789–1795. L'apprentissage de la citoyenneté* (Paris: Messidor/Éditions sociales, 1987), 8. All translations are ours.

18. Soboul, *The Sans-Culottes*, 136.

19. Ibid.

20. For a reconstitution of the political circumstances surrounding the emergence of this phase of the political history of liberty in Paris during the Revolution, see Genty, *Paris 1789–1795*.

21. Morris Slavin provides a thorough analysis of this takeover in *The Making of an Insurrection* (Cambridge, Mass.: Harvard University Press, 1986). We will return to it below.

22. Soboul, *The Sans-Culottes*, 120–122.

23. Ibid., 122.

24. Soboul, *Les sans-culottes*, 31.

25. Ibid., 178.

26. Mazauric, "Sans-culottes/Sans-culotterie/Sans-culottisme," 962.

27. Slavin, *The Making of an Insurrection*, 159.

28. Vovelle, "Préface," 8.

29. Soboul, *Les sans-culottes*, 178.

30. Ibid., 187.

31. Genty, *Paris 1789–1795*, 222.

32. Genty, however, highlights the fact that the sans-culottes returned to the political approach of 1790 when the popular societies were created in order to prepare for the district-level general assemblies. See ibid., 223.

33. Soboul, *Les sans-culottes*, 192.

34. Soboul, *The Sans-Culottes*, 123.

35. Ibid., 207.

36. Soboul, *Les sans-culottes*, 194.

37. Ibid., 196. We will return to the political meaning of this practice.

38. Ibid., 207.

39. Ibid., 238. [The term "overall maximum" refers to a price ceiling. —Trans.]

40. Ibid., 239.

41. The reference here, of course, is to the liquidation of the Enragés, who for a time were the sans-culottes' spokespeople and whose removal by the Jacobins aptly demonstrated the desire to control the popular movement. We will come back shortly to the Enragés as a "laboratory" of plebeian politics. Ibid., 268. See also Guérin, *La lutte de classes*, 258–278.

42. Soboul, *Les sans-culottes*, 272.

43. Ibid., 274.

44. Genty, *Paris 1789–1795*, 225.

45. Soboul, *Les sans-culottes*, 276.

46. Guérin, *La lutte de classes*, 207.

47. Genty, *Paris 1789–1795*, 226.

48. See Frédéric Braesch, *La commune du 10 août 1792* (Paris: Hachette, 1911).

49. Soboul, *Les sans-culottes*, 280.

50. Ibid., 320.

51. Ibid., 324.

52. Ibid., 361–362.

53. Ibid.

54. Ibid., 361.

55. Guérin, *La lutte de classes*, 295.

56. Genty, *Paris 1789–1795*, 229–230.

57. Soboul, *Les sans-culottes*, 915.

58. Ibid., 916.

59. Ibid., 917–1024. The insurrection of Prairial Year III can arguably be seen as a further stage in the sans-culottes' struggle against the revolutionary bourgeoisie. We will come back to this below. See Philippe Riviale, *L'impatience du bonheur: apologie de Gracchus Babeuf* (Paris: Payot, 2001).

60. Alexis de Tocqueville, *The Old Regime and the Revolution*, trans. Alan S. Kahan (Chicago: University of Chicago Press, 1998), 118–124.

61. Guérin, *La lutte de classes*, 2:8.

62. Ibid.

63. Michelet, *History of the French Revolution*, 439.

64. Guérin, *La lutte de classes*, 2:8. Guérin bases himself on the analyses of Jean Jaurès, *Histoire socialiste de la Révolution française*, vol. 1 (Paris: Éditions Sociales, 1969).

65. Vovelle, "Préface," 8.

66. Soboul, *Les sans-culottes*, 375.

67. Guérin, *La lutte de classes*, 2:67.

68. Ibid., 377.

69. Soboul, *The Sans-Culottes*, 160.

70. Ibid., 159.

71. Ibid., 160.

72. Ibid., 162.

73. Such as François A. Mignet, *History of the French Revolution from 1789 to 1814*, trans. Anonymous (London: George Bell & Sons, 1906).

74. Furet "Terror," in Furet and Ozouf, eds., *A Critical Dictionary*, 146, 147–148.

75. Jacques Rancière, "Politics, Identification, and Subjectivization," in *The Identity in Question*, ed. J. Rajchman (New York: Routledge, 1995), 63.

76. Jacques Rancière, *Dis-agreement: Politics and Philosophy*, trans. Julie Rose (Minneapolis: University of Minnesota Press, 1999), 24.

77. Robert Cobb, *The Police and the People: French Popular Protest, 1789–1820* (Oxford: Oxford University Press, 1970), 186–189.

78. Niccolò Machiavelli, *Discourses on Livy*, trans. H. C. Mansfield and N. Tarcov (Chicago: University of Chicago Press, 1996), 16–17.

79. Miguel Abensour, *Democracy Against the State*, trans. Max Blechman and Martin Breaugh (Cambridge: Polity, 2001), xxxv.

80. Guérin, *Class Struggle*, 155.

81. Ibid.

82. Ibid., 156.

83. This revolt, closely associated with the Girondins, occurred in the wake of their political ouster in favor of the Jacobins, who, as mentioned earlier, had taken power with the help of the sans-culottes.

84. Guérin, *La lutte de classes*, 390–392.

85. Ibid., 396.

86. Ibid.

87. See Christian Meier, *The Greek Discovery of Politics*, trans. David McLintock (Cambridge, Mass.: Harvard University Press, 1990).

88. Hannah Arendt, "Labour, Work, Action," Speeches and Writings File, Hannah Arendt Papers, Manuscript Division, Library of Congress, Washington, D.C., 1967, 17.

89. Hannah Arendt, *The Human Condition* (Chicago: University of Chicago Press, 1998).

90. Guérin, *La lutte de classes*, 396. Marat, writing in *L'Ami du Peuple*, was in the forefront of popular opposition to the great specialists, who according to him were the "leaders" of the Committee for Public Safety.

91. Soboul, *The Sans-Culottes*, 128.

92. The Théâtre-Français Section, December 27, 1792. Quoted in ibid., 129.

93. Marcel Gauchet, "Annexe II: Les déclarations de 1793–1795," in *La révolution des droits de l'homme* (Paris: Gallimard, 1989), 324, 328. All translations are ours. Italics added.

94. The 1793 Constitution, however, was not enacted. Nevertheless, it legitimized the recourse to insurrection, thus testifying to the widespread acceptance of insurrection as a political practice.

95. Quoted in Frank Maloy Anderson, ed., *The Constitutions and Other Select Documents Illustrative of the History of France, 1789–1901* (Minneapolis: H. W. Wilson, 1904), http://www.columbia.edu/~iw6/docs/dec1793.html. Italics added.

96. Gauchet, "Annexe II," 335–337.

97. Soboul, *The Sans-Culottes*, 129.

98. Quoted in ibid.

99. Slavin, *The Making of an Insurrection*, 177. According to Slavin, the expression can be ascribed to Louis-Marie Lulier (or Lhullier), the state prosecutor and syndic of Paris. See 177n143. [Note that Slavin uses the French expression. —Trans.]

100. Jules Michelet, *Histoire de la Révolution française* (Paris: Gallimard, 1939), 2:360. [Charles Cocks's translation is an abridged version of Michelet's original. Therefore, whenever the quoted passage is not included in the English translation, the reference is to our own translation of the French original. All other references are to Cocks's English version. —Trans.]
101. Peter Kropotkin, *The Great French Revolution* (Montreal: Black Rose, 1989), 404.
102. Soboul, *The Sans-Culottes*, 130.
103. Quoted in ibid., 131.
104. Ibid.
105. Abensour, *Democracy Against the State*, xli. Italics added.
106. Slavin, *The Making of an Insurrection*, 144–155.
107. Guérin, *Class Struggle*, 62.
108. Ibid.
109. See Morris Slavin, "Jean Varlet as Defender of Direct Democracy," *Journal of Modern History* 39 (December 1967): 387–404.
110. Morris Slavin, *The Making of an Insurrection*, 127. Note that the author uses the French expression. In connection with this project, see also R. Rose, *The Enragés: Socialists of the French Revolution?* (Sydney: Sydney University Press, 1965), 18.
111. Guérin, *Class Struggle*, 73.
112. Slavin, *The Making of an Insurrection*, 4.
113. Ibid.; Guérin, *Class Struggle*, 75–76.
114. Guérin, *Class Struggle*, 77–79.
115. Guérin, *La lutte de classes*, 131.
116. Guérin, *Class Struggle*, 82.
117. Guérin, *La lutte de classes*, 130.
118. Slavin, *The Making of an Insurrection*, 21–22.
119. Kropotkin, *The Great French Revolution*, 398.
120. Richet, "Revolutionary Journées," in Furet and Ozouf, eds., *A Critical Dictionary*, 131.
121. Rose, *The Enragés*, 25.
122. Richet, "Revolutionary Journées," 132.
123. Guérin, *Class Struggle*, 86.
124. Slavin, *The Making of an Insurrection*, 127–128. On the topic of social issues and the Enragés, see also Guérin, *Class Struggle*, 87.
125. On the opposition between the two revolutions, see Miguel Abensour, "Lire Saint-Just," in Saint-Just, *Oeuvres complètes* (Paris: Gallimard, 2004), 12–13. Our translation.
126. Richet, "Revolutionary Journées," 132.
127. Guérin argues that the enragés were indeed "leaders" but "deficient leaders." He qualifies his position somewhat, adding that they "were not so much guides as spokespersons, mirrors more than magnetic poles." *La lutte de classes*, 103.
128. Tønnesson, *La défaite*, ix.
129. Ibid., xi, 10.
130. Ibid.
131. Ibid., 349.
132. Ibid., 97–116, 113.

133. Quoted by Richet in Furet and Ozouf, eds., *A Critical Dictionary*, 134.

134. Tønnesson, *La défaite*, 134.

135. Ibid., 223, 237.

136. Ibid., 250. Our translation.

137. Quoted in Guérin, *La lutte de classes*, 2:368–369.

138. "Insurrection du Peuple," quoted by Tønnesson, *La défaite*, 251.

139. Riviale, *L'impatience*, 72. Our translation.

140. Guérin, *La lutte de classes*, 2:368.

141. Might this be a distinctive feature of the plebeian public sphere? To answer this question we must attend to the blending of social and political demands by the English Jacobins and the Communards of Paris. On the existence of an oppositional public space, see Oskar Negt and Alexander Kluge, *Public Sphere and Experience: Toward an Analysis of the Bourgeois and Proletarian Public Sphere*, trans. Peter Labanyi et al. (Minneapolis: University of Minnesota Press, 1993).

142. Tønnesson, *La défaite*, 254.

143. Richet "Revolutionary journées," 135.

144. Tønnesson, *La défaite*, 272, 274.

145. Richet, "Revolutionary journées," 135.

146. Ibid. Italics added.

147. Guérin, *La lutte de classes*, 376.

148. For a thorough analysis of the repression, see Tønnesson, *La défaite*, 324–344.

149. Guérin, *La lutte de classes*, 377.

150. Riviale, *L'impatience*, 74. Our translation.

151. Edward P. Thompson, *The Making of the English Working Class* (1963; London: Penguin, 1991).

152. Gwyn A. Williams, *Artisans and Sans-Culottes* (London: Edward Arnold, 1968), 113. Italics added.

4. THE LONDON CORRESPONDING SOCIETY AND THE ENGLISH JACOBINS

1. Miguel Abensour, "Présentation: la passion d'Edward P. Thompson," in E. P. Thompson, *La formation de la classe ouvrière anglaise*, trans. Gilles Dauvé et al. (Paris: Hautes Études-Gallimard-Le Seuil, 1988), xv. Our translation. Patrick Fridenson goes so far as to affirm that this is "a book that has not yet fully expressed its potential for renewal." See Patrick Fridenson, "E. P. Thompson. La formation de la classe ouvrière anglaise," *Le Débat* 3 (July/August 1980): 176. Our translation.

2. Marilyn Morris, *The British Monarchy and the French Revolution* (New Haven, Conn.: Yale University Press, 1998), 84.

3. E. P. Thompson, "Patrician Society and Plebeian Culture," *Journal of Social History* 7, no. 4 (1974): 382–405. This article appears in modified form as the second chapter of E. P. Thompson, *Customs in Common: Studies in Traditional Popular Culture* (New York: The New Press, 1993). The page references here are to the 1974 article, with those to the 1993 book shown in parentheses except when it offers a new development, in which case the later work is referenced directly.

4. Thompson, "Patrician Society and Plebeian Culture," 395 (57).

5. Here Thompson acknowledges, in the form of a question, that there is a kind of acceptance of social division: "There is a sense in which rulers and crowds needed each other, watched each other, performed theatre and counter-theatre in each other's auditorium, moderated each other's political behavior. Intolerant of the insubordination of free labor, nevertheless the rulers of England showed in practice a surprising degree of licence towards the turbulence of the crowd. *Is there some deeply embedded, 'structural' reciprocity here?*" Ibid., 402 (71). Italics added.

6. Ibid., 395 (57), 397 (64), 398 (65–66).

7. Ibid., 399 (66–67), 400 (67–68), 402 (71).

8. Thompson, *Customs in Common*, 73.

9. Thompson, *The Making*, 171–172.

10. Ibid., 172.

11. Ibid.

12. Günther Lottes, "Radicalism, Revolution, and Political Culture: An Anglo-French comparison," in *The French Revolution and British Popular Politics*, ed. M. Philp (Cambridge: Cambridge University Press, 1991), 84n2.

13. Thompson, *The Making*, 174, 200.

14. Abensour, "Présentation," x, xi. Our translation.

15. J. Ann Hone, *For the Cause of the Truth: Radicalism in London, 1796–1821* (Oxford: Clarendon, 1982), 362.

16. For the sake of thoroughness it should be noted that Thompson approaches the issue of English Jacobinism's continuity with the preceding century from two additional angles: (1) "the tradition of Dissent, and its modification by the Methodist revival," and (2) "the ambiguous tradition of the 18th–century 'Mob.'" So as not to stray from the specifically political focus of our study, I have chosen to concentrate on the more explicitly political traditions. Concerning the two above-mentioned traditions, see Thompson, *The Making*, 27–83.

17. Thompson describes these attitudes as subpolitical because they were instinctive rather than conscious and did not make up a political doctrine able to nurture sustained political action.

18. Thompson, *The Making*, 85–87.

19. "It (radicalism) was even read back into the seventeenth century, although there was no real continuity of discourses behind the apparent similarities between the mid-seventeenth-century levellers and late eighteenth-century Jacobins." See G. Lottes, "Radicalism, Revolution, and Political Culture," 79.

20. Thompson, *The Making*, 87.

21. Philippe Riviale, *L'impatience du bonheur* (Paris: Payot, 2001), 27–106. See also chapter 3, above. Our translation.

22. Thompson, *The Making*, 89.

23. Ibid., 90–91.

24. Ibid., 92, 96.

25. Ibid., 97.

26. For a Marxist analysis of Burke's thought, see Crawford B. Macpherson, *Edmund Burke* (Oxford: Oxford University Press, 1980).

27. Thompson, *The Making*, 99.

28. Ibid. Quoted by Thompson. The original passage is found in Thomas Paine, *Rights of Man* (Hertfordshire: Woodsworth, 1996), 126.

29. Ibid., 101.

30. Ibid. Quoted by Thompson. The original passage is found in Paine, *Rights of Man*, 122.

31. Thompson, *The Making*, 102, 104.

32. Thompson writes, "We can almost say that Paine established a new framework within which Radicalism was confined for nearly 100 years, as clear and as well defined as the constitutionalism which it replaced." Ibid., 103.

33. Williams, *Artisans*, 17.

34. Thompson, *The Making*, 110.

35. Ibid., 111.

36. Ibid., 19.

37. Ibid. Quoted by Thompson and drawn from Thomas Hardy, *Memoir of Thomas Hardy Written by Himself* (Great Britain: Tilling, 1832), 16.

38. Carl B. Cone, *The English Jacobins* (New York: Scribner, 1968), 120.

39. For an analysis of these three centers of radical political agitation, see Albert Goodwin, *The Friends of Liberty* (London: Hutchinson, 1979), 136–170.

40. Thompson, *The Making*, 22.

41. Ibid., 23.

42. Ibid., 23–24. We will return to this facet of the society.

43. Goodwin, *The Friends*, 192–193.

44. Thompson, *The Making*, 167.

45. Goodwin, *The Friends*, 196.

46. Thompson, *The Making*, 167.

47. Cone, *The English Jacobins*, 122.

48. Thompson, *The Making*, 169.

49. Ibid., 170. Quoted by Thompson.

50. Abensour, "Présentation," in E. P. Thompson, *La formation de la classe ouvrière*, xiv. Our translation.

51. Cone, *The English Jacobins*, 136–137.

52. Mary Thale, ed., *Selections from the Papers of the London Corresponding Society, 1792–1799* (Cambridge: Cambridge University Press, 1983), 10.

53. Cone, *The English Jacobins*, 201.

54. Lottes, "Radicalism, Revolution, and Political Culture," 88.

55. Michael Scrivener, "John Thelwall's Political Ambivalence: Reform and Revolution," in *Radicalism and Revolution in Britain, 1775–1848*, ed. Michael T. Davis (London: Macmillan, 2000), 69.

56. Thelwall affirms, for example, "For if you treat us only like beasts of burthen, what wonder if we sometimes break to yoke and become beasts of prey! If you wish the people to be humanized restore them to the privileges of humanity—restore to every individual that liberty without which he may sometimes be a spaniel and sometimes a tyger, but never can be a man." See John Thelwall, *The Politics of English Jacobinism: Writings of John Thelwall*, ed. Gregory Claeys (University Park: Pennsylvania State University Press, 1995), 13.

57. Thompson, *The Making*, 117.

58. G. A. Williams, *Artisans and Sans-Culottes* (London: Edward Arnold, 1968), 18.

59. Thompson, *The Making*, 117, 121.

60. Cone, *The English*, 148.

61. Thompson, *The Making*, 122.

62. Ibid., 123.

63. Ibid., 125.

64. Ibid., 133, 134.

65. Ibid., 134.

66. Thompson points out that none of these representatives of English Jacobinism could truly claim to be a national leader. With respect to leadership issues, English Jacobinism was unable to comply with the model of a "revolution from above." This was not necessarily an issue, especially with regards to the democratic nature of the forms of political organization.

67. Ibid., 134.

68. Ibid., 136.

69. Cone, *The English Jacobins*, 175.

70. Thompson, *The Making*, 138.

71. Goodwin, *The Friends*, 303.

72. Cone, *The English Jacobins*, 182.

73. Thompson, *The Making*, 141.

74. Ibid., 142.

75. Cone, *The English Jacobins*, 197.

76. Thompson, *The Making*, 145.

77. Ibid. Quoted by Thompson. The passage is drawn from Frances D. Cartwright, *Life and Correspondence of Major Cartwright* (1826), 1:312.

78. Ibid., 146.

79. Ibid., 148.

80. Williams, *Artisans and Sans-Culottes*, 96.

81. Goodwin, *The Friends of Liberty*, 363–364.

82. Thompson, *The Making*, 151.

83. Cone, *The English Jacobins*, 215.

84. Goodwin, *The Friends of Liberty*, 373.

85. Williams, *Artisans and Sans-Culottes*, 96.

86. Thompson, *The Making*, 155.

87. Williams, *Artisans and Sans-Culottes*, 100.

88. Quoted in Thompson, *The Making*, 158.

89. Williams, *Artisans and Sans-Culottes*, 100.

90. Goodwin, *The Friends of Liberty*, 391.

91. Ibid., 395.

92. Thompson, *The Making*, 159. Quoted by Thompson. The original passage can be found in James Greig, ed., *The Farington Diary* (London: Hutchinson & Co., 1923), 1:118–119.

93. Quoted by Thompson in *The Making*, 159.

94. Williams, *Artisans and Sans-Culottes*, 104.

95. Goodwin, *The Friends of Liberty*, 397.

96. Thompson, *The Making*, 163.

97. The LCS nonetheless persevered in 1797, organizing a series of mass meetings to advocate peace with France and political reform in England. An overwhelming number of police officers easily dispersed the reformers at the July 31 meeting, which was truly the end of the LCS, at least in the form it had assumed since its foundation in 1792. See A. Goodwin, *The Friends of Liberty*, 412–413. See also George S. Veitch, *Genesis of Parliamentary Reform* (1913; Hamden, Conn.: Archon, 1965), 335.

98. Thompson, *The Making*, 184.

99. Horne, *For the Cause*, 49.

100. Thompson, *The Making*, 194.

101. Ibid., 199.

102. Jacques Rancière. "Politics, Identification, and Subjectivization," *October* 61, "The Identity in Question" (Summer 1992): 58. See also Jacques Rancière, *Disagreement: Politics and Philosophy*, trans. Julie Rose (Minneapolis: University of Minnesota Press, 1999), 28–29.

103. Thompson, *The Making*, 24.

104. Goodwin notes that this was also a central principle of the Society for Constitutional Information, which had been founded a short time before the LCS. See Goodwin, *The Friends of Liberty*, 191n102.

105. Abensour, "Présentation," xiv. Our translation.

106. Cone, *The English Jacobins*, 214.

107. Rancière, "Politics, Identification, and Subjectivization," 59.

108. Jacques Rancière, "Le dissensus citoyen," *Carrefour* 19, no. 2 (1997): 21. Our translation.

109. Thompson, *The Making*, 24.

110. Anna Clark, *The Struggle for the Breeches: Gender and the Making of the English Working Class* (Berkeley: University of California Press, 1995), 145–147.

111. However, there remains no documentary evidence of the actual presence of such societies within the LCS.

112. Thompson, *The Making*, 201.

113. Mary Thale, ed., *Selections from the Papers of the London Corresponding Society 1792–1799* (Cambridge: Cambridge University Press, 1983), 75.

114. On the subject of universal suffrage, especially in France, see Pierre Rosanvallon, *Le sacre du citoyen* (Paris: Gallimard, 1992).

115. Mark Philp, "The Fragmented Ideology of Reform," in *The French Revolution and British Popular Politics*, ed. Mark Philp (Cambridge: Cambridge University Press, 1991), 73–74. See also Williams, *Artisans and Sans-Culottes*, 71.

116. Mary Thale, ed., *The Autobiography of Francis Place* (Cambridge: Cambridge University Press, 1972), 198–199.

117. Abensour, "Présentation," xiv. Our translation.

118. Thompson, *The Making*, 201.

119. Ibid., 56.

120. This is a paraphrase of Claude Lefort's formulation. See Claude Lefort, *Essais sur le politique* (Paris: Seuil, 1986), 29.

121. Quoted by Thompson in *The Making*, 203.

122. Thompson, *The Making*, 816.
123. Ibid., 201.
124. Bernard Manin, *Principles of Representative Government* (Cambridge: Cambridge University Press, 1997), 55–67.
125. On the "dialectic of emancipation" (our translation), see Miguel Abensour, "Le nouvel esprit utopique," *Cahiers Bernard Lazare* 128–130 (1991): 144–151.
126. Joseph Déjacque, *À bas les chefs!* (Paris: Champ libre, 1971), 218.
127. Benjamin Constant, "The Liberty of the Ancients Compared with That of the Moderns," in *Political Writings* (Cambridge: Cambridge University Press, 1988), 307–328.
128. Hannah Arendt, *Between Past and Future* (New York: Viking, 1969), 146.

5. THE PARIS COMMUNE OF 1871 AND THE COMMUNARDS

1. Bernard Noël, "Communard," in *Dictionnaire de la Commune* (Paris: Mémoire du livre, 2000), 164. All translations are ours.
2. Martin P. Johnson, *The Paradise of Association* (Ann Arbor: University of Michigan Press, 1996), 180–181, 184.
3. Jacques Rougerie, *Procès des communards* (Paris: Julliard, 1964), 134. All translations are ours.
4. Ibid., 165.
5. However, there did exist a very active "Club des prolétaires" in the eleventh arrondissement, which published four issues of a newsletter titled *Le Prolétaire* during the Paris Commune. See, among others, B. Noël, "Prolétaire (Le)," in *Dictionnaire*, 518–519.
6. André Decouflé, *La commune de Paris (1871)* (Paris: Cujas, 1969), 30.
7. Johnson, *The Paradise*, 19.
8. Ibid., 20.
9. Maximilien Rubel, "Socialism and the Commune," in *Paradigm for Revolution? The Paris Commune, 1871–1971*, ed. E. Kamenka and R. Rose (Canberra: Australian National University Press, 1972), 35.
10. Ibid., 22.
11. William Serman, *La commune de Paris (1871)* (Paris: Fayard, 1986), 115. All translations are ours.
12. Gustave Lefrançais, *Souvenir d'un révolutionnaire* (1902; Paris: Éditions de la Tête de Feuilles, 1972), 314. All translations are ours.
13. On the subject of the Central Committee, see the seminal study by Jean Dautry and Lucien Scheler, *Le comité central républicain des vingt districts de Paris* (Paris: Éditions Sociales, 1960).
14. Rougerie, *Procès*, 39.
15. K. Steven Vincent, *Between Marxism and Anarchism: Benoît Malon and French Reformist Socialism* (Berkeley: University of California Press, 1992), 24.
16. Johnson, *The Paradise*, 24.
17. Gustave Lefrançais, *Étude sur le mouvement communaliste à Paris en 1871* (1871; Coeuvres: Ressouvenances, 2001), 94. All translations are ours.
18. Johnson, *The Paradise*, 29.

19. Ibid., 30.

20. Lefrançais, *Souvenirs*, 333.

21. Bertrand Taithe, *Citizenship and Wars: France in Turmoil, 1870–1871* (London: Routledge, 2001), 34.

22. Johnson, *The Paradise*, 30.

23. On the subject of this organization, see Ray D. Wolfe, *The Origins of the Paris Commune* (Ph.D. diss., Harvard University, 1965), 330–336.

24. Johnson, *The Paradise*, 33.

25. Ibid., 34.

26. Ibid., 39.

27. Ibid., 40.

28. Serman, *La Commune*, 162.

29. It should be stressed that on this point Johnson is at odds with the dominant interpretation of the Commune, which does not acknowledge the insurrectional nature of the red poster. See Johnson, *The Paradise*, 41n79.

30. Ibid., 44.

31. Ibid., 46.

32. On this question, see ibid., 51n107.

33. Ibid., 52.

34. Ibid., 53.

35. Ibid., 61. Here Johnson quotes a "revolutionary socialist" poster published ahead of the elections of February 8, 1871. The poster is reproduced in *Les murailles politiques françaises* (Paris: Le Chevalier, 1873–1874) 1:866.

36. Johnson, *The Paradise*, 56. However, Lefrançais's *Souvenirs* reveals that, though a distinguished member of the IWA, he was surprised by the events of March 18, to the point of being unaware of their revolutionary significance.

37. Johnson, *The Paradise*, 57.

38. Ibid., 63.

39. Ibid., 83.

40. Ibid., 77.

41. Ibid., 87.

42. Serman, *La commune*, 293.

43. Johnson, *The Paradise*, 6.

44. Cited by Johnson in ibid., 19. The original statement can be found in *L'enquête parlementaire sur l'insurrection du dix-huit mars 1871* (Paris: A. Wittersheim, 1872), 343.

45. Johnson, *The Paradise*, 89.

46. Ibid., 91.

47. The term (our translation) is borrowed from J. Dautry and L. Scheler. See *Le comité central républicain*, 241n1.

48. Johnson, *The Paradise*, 100–103. This does not imply, however, that the negotiations between the Delegation and certain vigilance committees regarding a common electoral slate were trouble free.

49. Rougerie, *Procès*, 147.

50. Johnson, *The Paradise*, 166.

51. Ibid., 171.

52. Ibid., 172.

53. Serman, *La commune*, 292. Our translation.

54. Johnson, *The Paradise*, 205.

55. Ibid., 172.

56. Ibid., 203. The idea of two worlds—the old one characterized by hierarchy and the new one characterized by association—brings to mind the work of Pierre Leroux.

57. The declaration is reproduced in Rougerie, *Procès*, 152–155. Our translation.

58. Rougerie, *Procès*, 199.

59. Serman, *La commune*, 304.

60. More specifically, the decisive influence of Proudhon and Blanqui—both closely associated with positivism—comes to mind.

61. Lefrançais, *Étude sur le mouvement communaliste*, 248.

62. Johnson, *The Paradise*, 214.

63. Ibid., 222, 218.

64. Ibid., 223, 225, 226.

65. Serman, *La commune*, 305.

66. Johnson, *The Paradise*, 118.

67. Rougerie, *Procès*, 189.

68. Johnson, *The Paradise*, 196.

69. Noël, "Minority," in *Dictionnaire*, 438.

70. Prosper-Olivier Lissagaray, *History of the Commune of 1871*, trans. Eleanor Marx Aveling (London: Reeves & Turner, 1886), 241–242.

71. Quoted in Noël, "Comité de salut public," in *Dictionnaire*, 155. Our translation.

72. Rougerie, *Procès*, 158.

73. Serman, *La commune*, 91.

74. Maurice Moissonnier, "L'expérience de la commune, le marxisme et les problèmes de l'État," *La Nouvelle Critique*, "Expériences et langage de la Commune de Paris" (special issue; March 1971): 24.

75. Quoted in Lefrançais, *Étude sur le mouvement communaliste*, 303.

76. Noêl, "Majorité," in *Dictionnaire*, 414. Our translation.

77. Even Lefrançais, a key member of the minority, recognized this necessity while at the same time refuting the idea that the Committee for Public Safety could remedy the Commune's military deficiencies. See Lefrançais, *Souvenirs*, 399.

78. Johnson, *The Paradise*, 196, 262.

79. Lissagaray, *History of the Commune of 1871*, 259.

80. Johnson, *The Paradise*, 260.

81. Joseph Déjacque, "Down with the Bosses" [1859], trans. Shawn P. Wilbur, 4, 6. http://theanarchistlibrary.org.

82. Lefrançais, *Étude sur le mouvement communaliste*, 278.

83. Karl Marx, *The Civil War in France*, in Karl Marx and Frederick Engels, *Selected Works* (New York: International Publishers, 1968), 272 .

84. The question of the Commune as an example of a "proletarian dictatorship" is not at issue here. Our goal, more modestly, is to grasp how and to what extent the

Commune can be regarded as a properly modern moment of political freedom. It is in this connection, notwithstanding Marxist debates on the Commune, that Marx's analysis provides a "fruitful"—antistate—approach supporting our position.

85. Marx, *The Civil War in France*, 289, 290.
86. Ibid., 290, 291.
87. Ibid., 291.
88. Ibid.
89. Ibid., 292.
90. Ibid., 293.
91. Ibid., 294, 292, 293.
92. Ibid., 294.
93. Ibid., 307.
94. Lefrançais, *Étude sur le mouvement communaliste*, 279.
95. Ibid., 368.
96. Rougerie, *Procès*, 180.
97. The Latin root of "govern" is *gubernare*, which refers to a person who directs or steers a vessel. We use the related term "gubernator" to indicate the "directed," indeed authoritarian, nature of a government engendered by the "state" form.
98. Karl Marx, *Toward a Critique of Hegel's Philosophy of Right*, ed. Joseph O'Malley, trans. Annette Jolin and Joseph O'Malley (Cambridge: Cambridge University Press, 1970), 31.
99. Miguel Abensour, *Democracy Against the State: Marx and the Machiavellian Moment*, trans. Martin Breaugh and Max Blechman (Cambridge: Polity, 2011), 88.
100. Lefrançais, *Souvenirs*, 447. Our translation.
101. Jürgen Habermas, *The Theory of Communicative Action*, vol. 2: *Lifeworld and System: A Critique of Functionalist Reason*, trans. Thomas McCarthy (Boston: Beacon, 1987).
102. Lefrançais, *Étude sur le mouvement communaliste*, 368.

PART III PROLOGUE: SOCIAL BOND, POLITICAL BOND, AND MODERNITY

1. Francis Farrugia, *La crise du lien social. Essai de sociologie critique* (Paris: L'Harmattan, 1993), 20.
2. Maria E. Leandro, "Le lien social dans la pensée sociologique classique," in *Le lien social et l'inachèvement de la modernité*, ed. Jean Pavageau et al. (Paris: L'Harmattan: 1997), 42.
3. Ferdinand Tönnies, *Community and Society*, trans. Charles P. Loomis (1887; Mineola, N.Y.: Dover, 2002).
4. Emile Durkheim, "Communauté et société selon Tönnies," in *Éléments d'une théorie sociale* (1889; Paris: Minuit, 1975), 387–388. On Durkheim's agreement with Tönnies, see Farrugia, *La crise du lien social*, 26, 98–99.
5. Jean Lawruszenko, "De la nécessité d'un nouveau lien social," *DESS. La Revue des Sciences Économiques et Sociales* 113 (October 1998): 79. Our translation.
6. See Patrick Cingolani, "La communauté et son dehors. Pour une critique des représentations du lien fondées sur l'individualisme ou le sociologisme," *Lien Social et Politique* 39 (Spring 1998): 47–57.

7. The works of Pierre Clastres confirm that even the state of war where "all [are] against all" involves a form of human sociability. See Pierre Clastres, *Recherches d'anthropologie politique* (Paris: Seuil, 1980).

8. Concerning the question of the "human bond," it should be specified that the world of Nazi concentration camps involves the creation of a nonhuman "community." There can be no "human bond" in such an environment. The destruction of the bond among individuals is clearly brought out in Primo Levi's narrative *If This Is a Man* (London: Vintage, 1996). The effects of totalitarian domination on the social and political bond are discussed below.

9. Miguel Abensour, "D'une mésinterprétation du totalitarisme et de ses effets," *Tumultes* 8 (1996): 11–44.

10. Hannah Arendt, *The Promise of Politics* (New York: Schocken, 2005), 95.

11. Miguel Abensour, *De la compacité. Architecture et régimes totalitaires* (Paris: Sens & Tonka, 1997), 23, 37. All translations are ours.

12. Ibid., 38. Abensour quotes Elias Canetti, *Crowds and Power*, trans. Carol Stewart (New York: Seabury, 1978), 18.

13. Abensour, *De la compacité*, 59, 69.

14. The totalitarian destruction of the social and political bond from the point of view of the German resistance is effectively illustrated in Hans Fallada's *Alone in Berlin*, trans. Michael Hofmann (London: Penguin, 2009).

6. The Sans-Culottes: A Political Bond of Fraternity

1. Philippe Riviale, *L'impatience du bonheur* (Paris: Payot, 2001), 110.

2. Albert Soboul, *Les sans-culottes Parisiens en l'an II* (Paris: Librairie Claveuil, 1962), 874. All translations are ours. Note that only an abridged English translation of this work exists: A. Soboul, *The Sans-Culottes: The Popular Movement and Revolutionary Government, 1793–1794*, trans. Rémy Inglis Hall (1972; Princeton, N.J.: Princeton University Press, 1980).

3. For a discussion of the theological and revolutionary origins of this concept, see Catherine Chalier, *La fraternité, un espoir en clair-obscur* (Paris: Buchet Chastel, 2004).

4. Kåre Tønnesson, *La défaite des sans-culottes* (Oslo: Presses Universitaires d'Oslo, 1978), xvii. Our translation.

5. Soboul, *Les sans-culottes*, 454.

6. Mona Ozouf, "Fraternity," in *A Critical Dictionary of the French Revolution*, ed. François Furet and Mona Ozouf, trans. Arthur Goldhammer (Cambridge, Mass.: Belknap Press of Harvard University Press, 1989), 694.

7. Gérald Antoine, *Liberté, égalité, fraternité ou les fluctuations d'une devise* (Paris: UNESCO, 1989), 134.

8. Ozouf, "Fraternity," 696.

9. The Jacobins also referred to the notion of fraternity, but their use of it was more ideological than practical. See Marcel David, *Fraternité et révolution française* (Paris: Aubier, 1987), 107–108. All translations are ours.

10. Ozouf, "Fraternity," 697.

11. Soboul, *Les sans-culottes*, 570.
12. It should be pointed out, as David does, that Soboul's use of the term "mass" to describe the actions of the sans-culottes is problematical. For it seems difficult to apply "mass" to the actions of a restricted group of sans-culottes. On the other hand, however, Soboul's equivocal recourse to the notion of "mass" can be seen as a legitimate way to underscore the collective nature of the sans-culottes' action and their rudimentary anti-individualism. See David, *Fraternité et révolution*, 150.
13. [Italics added. —Trans.]
14. Ibid., 144–145.
15. Soboul, *Les sans-culottes*, 576. Italics added.
16. Ibid., 409.
17. Ibid., 655.
18. David, *Fraternité et révolution*, 162.
19. Fraternity among *men*, it must be specified. Because the use of *tu* encountered one of the blind spots of the sans-culottes' political practice: the question of women. Indeed, the sans-culottes seemed to be divided as to the appropriateness of addressing women using *tu*. As women were not considered equal to men, the use of *tu* seemed jarring for a certain number of sans-culottes. See David, *Fraternité et révolution*, 162.
20. Soboul, *Les sans-culottes*, 36.
21. Ibid., 178.
22. Ibid., 575.
23. Ozouf, "Fraternity," 697.
24. Chalier, *La fraternité*, 77.
25. Soboul, *Les sans-culottes*, 549–550.
26. Ozouf, "Fraternity," 699.
27. David, *Fraternité et révolution*, 146.
28. For an in-depth analysis of this expression, see ibid., 166–175.
29. Ibid., 160.
30. Jean-Paul Sartre, *Critique of Dialectical Reason*, trans. A. Sheridan-Smith (London: Verso, 1982), 438.
31. Éric Négrel, "Le journaliste-orateur: rhétorique et politique sans-culottes dans Le publiciste de la République française de Jacques Roux (juillet-octobre 1793)," in *Enlightenment, Revolution, and the Periodical Press*, ed. Hans-Jurgen Lüsebrink and Jeremy Popkin (Oxford: Voltaire Foundation, 2004), 174.
32. Soboul, *Les sans-culottes*, 578.
33. Albert Soboul, "Violence collective et rapports sociaux: Les foules révolutionnaires (1789–1795)," in *La révolution française* (1984; Paris: Gallimard, 1987), 576–582. Our translation.
34. Tønnesson, *La défaite*, 270, 277–278.
35. Soboul, *Les sans-culottes*, 361.
36. David, *Fraternité et révolution*, 152.
37. Arendt, *The Promise*, 93.
38. But, though it was decisive, Rousseau's influence was not exclusive. The sans-culottes' social practices also played a role in the idea of fraternity. Yet it seems plau-

sible to identify Rousseau's thought as the primary source of fraternity among the sans-culottes.

39. Bernard Groethuysen, *Philosophie de la révolution française* (Paris: Gallimard, 1956), 171–215.

40. Jean-Jacques Rousseau, "The Civil Religion," in *The Social Contract*, trans. M. Cranston (New York: Penguin, 2006), 154–168.

41. Lucien Jaume, "Robespierre," in *Dictionnaire des oeuvres politiques* (Paris: PUF, 1986), 687. Our translation.

42. Groethuysen, *Philosophie de la révolution*, 193. Our translation.

43. Daniel Guérin, *La lutte de classes sous la première république* (Paris: Gallimard, 1968), 1:44.

44. Claude Lefort masterfully elucidates this phenomenon in *Machiavelli in the Making*, trans. Michael B. Smith (Evanston, Ill.: Northwestern University Press, 2012), 61–77.

45. Albert Soboul, "L'audience des lumières sous la révolution. Jean-Jacques Rousseau et les classes populaires," in *Utopie et institutions au XVIIIe siècle*, ed. Pierre Francastel (Paris: Mouton et Co., 1963), 291.

46. Ibid., 294–303, 299.

47. Ibid., 300. Our translation.

48. Ibid., 303.

49. Ibid.

50. David, *Fraternité et révolution*, 27, 29, 30.

51. Chalier, *La fraternité*, 71–74.

52. Rousseau, *The Social Contract*, book 4, chap. 8, 164.

53. Chalier, *La fraternité*, 74.

54. Soboul, "L'audience des lumières," 301.

55. Rousseau, *The Social Contract*, book 1, chap. 8, 21; book 1, chap. 9, 25; book 4, chap. 2, 125.

56. Soboul, "L'audience des lumières," 303. Italics added.

57. Ozouf, "Fraternity," 698.

58. Hannah Arendt, *Men in Dark Times* (New York: Harcourt, Brace & World, 1968), 12–17.

59. Chalier, *La fraternité*, 85.

7. THE ENGLISH JACOBINS: A POLITICAL BOND OF PLURALITY

1. Karl Polanyi, *The Great Transformation* (1944; Boston: Beacon, 2001), 42–43.

2. Hannah Arendt, *The Human Condition* (Chicago: University of Chicago Press, 1998), 178.

3. Frank Huggett, *Factory Life and Work* (London: Harrap, 1973), 1, 10–12.

4. Polanyi, *The Great Transformation*, 164.

5. Edward P. Thompson, *The Making of the English Working Class* (1963; London: Penguin, 1968), 208.

6. Robert Owen quoted in ibid., 208.

7. On the question of the "barbarians," see Pierre Michel, *Un mythe romantique, les barbares (1785–1848)* (Lyon: Presses universitaires de Lyon, 1981).

8. This brings to mind Louis Chevalier's "classic" study, *Laboring Classes and Dangerous Classes in Paris During the First Half of the Nineteenth Century*, trans. Frank Jellinek (New York: H. Fertig, 1973).

9. Thompson, *The Making*, 211.

10. Ibid., 213.

11. Karl Marx, *Capital*, vol. 1 (1867; London: Penguin, 1990); Arnold Toynbee, *The Industrial Revolution* (1884; Boston: Beacon, 1956); John Laurence Hammond and Barbara Hammond, *The Rise of Modern Industry* (London: Methuen & Co., 1925).

12. Thompson is referring to the economists T. S. Ashton and A. Redford, among others. See T. S. Ashton, *The Industrial Revolution* (1948; London: Oxford University Press, 1950); A. Redford, *The Economic History of England* (1931; London: Longmans, 1960). Thompson, *The Making*, 214n2.

13. Thompson, *The Making*, 214.

14. Pierre Sansot, *Les gens de peu* (Paris: PUF, 1991), 7.

15. Ibid., 230.

16. Karl Polyani is equally critical of economists who deny the catastrophic nature of the industrial revolution. See Polyani, *The Great Transformation*, 168–169.

17. Thompson, *The Making*, 231.

18. Polanyi, *The Great Transformation*, 35.

19. Thompson, *The Making*, 218–222.

20. Ibid., 348.

21. This portrayal of the way of life of English workers during the Industrial Revolution corresponds quite closely to Thomas Hobbes's encapsulation of the lives of human beings in the state of nature: "solitary, poor, nasty, brutish and short." T. Hobbes, *Leviathan* (1651; Cambridge: Cambridge University Press, 1992), part 1, chap. 13, 89.

22. Thompson, *The Making*, 441.

23. On the destruction of peasant villages in England, see Hammond and Hammond, *The Rise*, 81–96.

24. Thompson, *The Making*, 442.

25. Ibid., 444.

26. Ibid., 448.

27. Robert Montgomery Martin, quoted in ibid., 487.

28. Polanyi, *The Great Transformation*, 44, 164.

29. Thompson, *The Making*, 449.

30. Arendt, *The Human Condition*, 176.

31. We will come back shortly to the English Jacobins' attempt to transform the workplace into a political space.

32. Arendt, *The Human Condition*, 134.

33. Quoted by Thompson, *The Making*, 203. The original is taken from John Thelwall, *The rights of nature against the usurpations of the establishments: a series of letters to the people of Britain on the state of public affairs and the recent effusions of the Right Honourable Edmund Burke* (Norwich: H. D. Symonds & J. March, 1796), 21, 24.

34. Jürgen Habermas, *The Structural Transformation of the Public Sphere: An Inquiry Into a Category of Bourgeois Society*, trans. Thomas Burger (Cambridge, Mass.: MIT Press, 1991).

35. Kevin Gilmartin, "Introduction: Locating a Plebeian Counterpublic Sphere," in *Print Politics* (Cambridge: Cambridge University Press, 1996), 4.

36. Gunther Lottes, *Politische Aufklärung und plebejisches Publikum* (Munich: R. Oldenburg Verlag, 1979), 14.

37. For Oscar Negt and Alexander Kluge, the political action of the lower classes in early nineteenth-century England represents the constitution not of a "plebeian" but of a "proletarian" public sphere. The choice of a Marxist term is not insignificant in light of the authors' wish to save Marxism from the crisis that it is has been grappling with since the beginning of the twentieth century; they therefore propose an analysis apt to lead it out of this impasse. Oscar Negt and Alexander Kluge, *Erfahrung und Öffentlichkeit* (Frankfort: Suhrkamp Verlag, 1972), 313–333. English translation: *The Public Sphere and Experience: Towards an Analysis of the Bourgeois and Proletarian Public Sphere*, trans. Peter Labanyi et al. (Minneapolis: University of Minnesota Press, 1993). For a general study of this work, see Eberhard Knödler-Bunte, "The Proletarian Public Sphere and Political Organisation: An Analysis of Oskar Negt and Alexander Kluge's *The Public Sphere and Experience*," *New German Critique* 4 (Winter 1975): 51–75.

38. Thompson, *The Making*, 19, 26.

39. Arendt, *The Human Condition*, 178.

40. Thompson, *The Making*, 170, 172.

41. Ibid., 150–151.

42. Ibid., 109.

43. Ibid.

44. Polanyi, *The Great Transformation*, 175–182. See also Dorothy Thompson, *The Chartists* (New York: Pantheon, 1984), 106–150.

8. THE COMMUNARDS: A POLITICAL BOND OF ASSOCIATION

1. Pierre Leroux, "Lettre au Docteur Deville," in Miguel Abensour, *Le procès des maîtres rêveurs* (Arles: Sulliver, 2000), 147. On the subject of association and the year 1830, see Bruno Viard, "Pierre Leroux et le socialisme associatif de 1830 à 1848," *Revue du MAUSS* 16 (second semester, 2000): 265–276.

2. Karl Marx, *The Civil War in France*, in K. Marx and F. Engels, *Selected Works* (New York: International Publishers, 1968), 290.

3. Bernard Noël, *Dictionnaire de la commune* (Paris: Mémoire du Livre, 2001), 253. All translations are ours.

4. Philippe Riviale, *Sur la commune. Cerises de sang* (Paris: L'Harmattan, 2003), 32–34.

5. Maurice Moissonnier, "Des origines à 1871," in *La France ouvrière*, ed. Claude Willard (Paris: Éditions de l'Atelier, 1995), 1:169.

6. As evidence of the ferment of those years, Proudhon's *De la capacité politique de la classe ouvrière* was published posthumously in 1865.

7. Riviale, *Sur la commune*, 39. Our translation.

8. Michel Winock and Jean-Pierre Azéma, *Les communards* (Paris: Seuil, 1964), 20. All translations are ours.

9. Jean Ellenstein, *Réflexions sur la commune de 1871* (Paris: Julliard, 1971), 47–48.

10. Jacques Rougerie, *La commune de Paris de 1871* (Paris: PUF, 1992), 19. All translations are ours.

11. Winock and Azéma, *Les communards*, 22.

12. Noël, *Dictionnaire*, 322.

13. Rougerie, *La commune de Paris*, 28–29.

14. Elleinstein, *Réflexions*, 60–61.

15. Prosper-Olivier Lissagaray, *History of the Commune of 1871*, trans. Eleanor Marx Aveling (London: Reeves & Turner, 1886), 40–41.

16. Riviale, *Sur la commune*, 123.

17. William Serman, *La commune de Paris* (Paris: Fayard, 1986), 191.

18. Noël, *Dictionnaire*, 202.

19. Marx, *The Civil War in France*, 283–284.

20. Charles Rihs, *La commune de Paris 1871. Sa structure et ses doctrines* (Paris: Seuil, 1973), 11. All translations are ours.

21. Lissagaray, *History of the Commune*, 40.

22. Martin P. Johnson, *The Paradise of Association* (Ann Arbor: University of Michigan Press, 1996), 4. Although Johnson omits to mention the central role of Pierre Leroux in propagating the idea of "association," he explicitly recognizes Leroux's decisive influence in the framing of the principle of association. See Johnson, *The Paradise of Association*, 133.

23. Ibid., 4.

24. Others included Charles Fourier and Auguste Blanqui. See Gustave Lefrançais, *Étude sur le mouvement communaliste à Paris, en 1871* (1871; Coeuvres: Ressouvenances, 2001), 247.

25. Pierre Leroux, *Aux philosophes, aux artistes, aux politiques* (Paris: Payot, 1994), 194. All translations are ours.

26. Miguel Abensour, "Postface: comment une philosophie de l'humanité peut-elle être une philosophie politique moderne?" in ibid., 311. Our translation.

27. Leroux, *Aux philosophes*, 199, 202.

28. Pierre Leroux, *De l'humanité* (1840; Paris: Fayard, 1985).

29. Abensour, "Postface," 316. Our translation.

30. Pierre-Joseph Proudhon, *Oeuvres complètes III. De la capacité politique de la classe ouvrière* (1865; Geneva: Slatkine, 1982), 120–126.

31. Pierre Ansart, "Proudhon, De la capacité politique de la classe ouvrière," in *Dictionnaire des oeuvres politiques*, ed. F. Châtelet et al. (Paris: PUF, 1986), 658. Our translation.

32. Pierre Leroux, "Réponse à Proudhon," *La République* (November 10, 1849).

33. Leroux quotes Proudhon. Ibid.

34. Ibid.

35. Fawzia Tobgui, "De l'anarchisme au fédéralisme. Articulation entre droit et État dans le système politique de Proudhon," *Réfractions* 6 (Fall 2000): 14. Our translation.

36. Stunning illustrations of the fraternization episode can be found in the first volume of *Le cri du peuple*, the excellent graphic novel about the Paris Commune of 1871 adapted by the artist Tardi from the novel by Jean Vautrin. See Jacques Tardi and Jean Vautrin, *Le cri du peuple. Les canons du 18 mars* (Paris: Casterman, 2001), 1:32–41.

37. Lefrançais, *Étude sur le mouvement communaliste*, 272.

38. Serman, *La commune*, 367.

39. Moissonnier, "Des origines à 1871," in Willard, ed., *La France*, 216.

40. Noël, *Dictionnaire*, 61.

41. Johnson, *The Paradise of Association*, 147–148.

42. Ibid., 156.

43. Ibid., 153.

44. Serman contends, however, that the imperative mandate in fact was not respected by the Commune. Nevertheless, our aim here is simply to demonstrate that the principle of association guided the political intentions of the elected members of the Commune. See Serman, *La commune*, 317–319.

45. Johnson, *The Paradise of Association*, 153.

46. Arthur Arnould, quoted by Noël, *Dictionnaire*, 249. The original text can be found in Arthur Arnould, *Histoire populaire et parlementaire de la commune de Paris* (1878; Lyon: Jacques-Maris Laffont, 1981). Our translation.

47. Johnson, *The Paradise of Association*, 153.

48. Noël, *Dictionnaire*, 414, 437.

CONCLUSION

1. Jacques Rancière, *Hatred of Democracy*, trans. Steven Corcoran (London: Verso, 2006), 73.

2. Boris Porchnev, *Les soulèvements populaires en France au XVIIe siècle* (Paris: Flammarion, 1972), 290.

3. See David Worall, *Radical Culture: Discourse, Resistance, and Surveillance, 1790–1820* (Detroit, Mich.: Wayne State University Press, 1992), 23.

4. Pierre Lévêque and Pierre Vidal-Naquet, *Cleisthenes the Athenian*, trans. David Ames Curtis (Atlantic Highlands, N.J.: Humanities Press, 1996).

BIBLIOGRAPHY

THE PLEBS

Abensour, Miguel. "Ça se passe bien! Pour François Châtelet." *La Mazarine*, special issue (March 1988): 11–15.

———. *Democracy Against the State: Marx and the Machiavellian Moment*. Trans. Max Blechman and Martin Breaugh. London: Polity, 2011.

———. "De l'intraitable." In *Jean-François Lyotard. L'exercice du différend*, ed. Dolorès Lyotard and Gérald Sfez, 241–260. Paris: Presses Universitaires de France, 2001.

———. "Pour une philosophie politique critique?" *Tumultes* 17–18 (2002): 207–257.

———. "Préface à la seconde édition. De la démocratie insurgeante." In *La démocratie contre l'état. Marx et le moment machiavélien*, 5–19. Paris: Félin, 2004.

Anweiler, Oskar. *The Soviets: The Russian Workers, Peasants, and Soldiers Councils, 1905–1921*. Trans. Ruth Hein. New York: Pantheon, 1975.

Arendt, Hannah. *The Human Condition*. Chicago: University of Chicago Press, 1998.

———. "Labour, Work, Action." Speeches and Writings File, Hannah Arendt Papers, Manuscript Division, Library of Congress, Washington, D.C., 1967.

Bakhtin, Mikhail. *Rabelais and His World*. Trans. Helene Iswolsky. Bloomington: Indiana University Press, 1984.

Ballanche, Pierre-Simon. "Essais de Palingénésie Sociale. Formule générale de l'histoire de tous les peuples, appliquée à l'histoire du peuple romain. 1er fragment." *Revue de Paris* 2 (1829): 138–154.

———. "Essais de Palingénésie Sociale. Formule générale de l'histoire de tous les peuples, appliquée à l'histoire du peuple romain. 2e fragment." *Revue de Paris* 4 (1829): 129–150.

———. "Essais de Palingénésie Sociale. Formule générale de l'histoire de tous les peuples, appliquée à l'histoire du peuple romain. 3e fragment." *Revue de Paris* 6 (1829): 70–98.

———. *Oeuvres.* 6 vols. Paris: Bureau de l'Encyclopédie des Connaissances Utiles, 1833.

———. *Oeuvres complètes.* Geneva: Slatkine Reprints, 1967.

———. *La théodicée et la virginie romaine.* Ed. Oscar Haac. Genève: Droz, 1959.

———. *La ville des expiations.* Ed. Amand Rastoul. Paris: Bibliothèque Romantique, 1926.

———. *La vision d'Hébal.* Ed. Allan J. L. Busst. Geneva: Droz, 1969.

Barbéris, Pierre. "Mal du siècle, ou d'un romantisme de droite à un romantisme de gauche." In *Romantisme et politique, 1815–1851,* 164–182. Paris: Collins, 1969.

———. "Le romantisme plébéien." In *Histoire littéraire de la France,* 4:512–514. Paris.

Barchou de Penhoën, Auguste. "Essai d'une formule générale de l'histoire d'humanité, d'après les idées de M. Ballanche." *Revue des Deux Mondes* 1–2 (1831): 526–560.

Barrow, Logie. "Socialism in Eternity: Plebeian Spiritualists, 1853–1913." *History Workshop* 9 (May 1980): 37–69.

Barrows, Sussana. *Distorting Mirrors: Visions of the Crowd in Late Nineteenth-Century France.* New Haven, Conn.: Yale University Press, 1981.

Bayet, Jean. "Appendice." In Tite-Live, *Histoire romaine,* vol. 3, book 3, 115–153. Paris: Les Belles Lettres, 1969.

Belchem, John C. "Radical Language and Ideology in Early Nineteenth-Century England: The Challenge of the Platform." *Albion* 20 (1988): 251.

Bénichou, Paul. "Le grand oeuvre de Ballanche. Chronologie et inachèvement." *Revue d'Histoire Littéraire de la France* 75 (1975): 736–748.

———. *Le temps des prophètes.* Paris: Gallimard, 1977.

Bercé, Yves-Marie. *Fêtes et révoltes. Des mentalités populaires du XVIe au XVIIIe siècle.* Paris: Hachette, 1976.

Borreil, Jean, ed. *Les sauvages dans la cité. Auto-émancipation du peuple et instruction des prolétaires au XIXe siècle.* Seyssel: Champs Vallon, 1985.

Bristol, Michael. *Carnival and Theater: Plebeian Culture and the Structure of Authority in Renaissance England.* New York: Methuen, 1985.

Brossat, Alain. "La plèbe. Des infâmes et des anonymes. Foucault libertaire." *Réfractions* 12 (Spring 2004): 111–123.

———. *Le serviteur et son maître. Essai sur le sentiment plébéien.* Paris: Éditions Léo Scheer, 2003.

Burke, Peter. "The Virgin of Carmine and the Revolt of Masaniello." *Past and Present* 99 (1983): 3–21.

Busst, Allan J. L. "Ballanche and Saint-Simonism." *Australian Journal of French Studies* 9 (1972): 290–307.

———. *La théorie du langage de Pierre-Simon Ballanche.* Lewinston: Edwin Mellen, 2000.

Calhoun, Craig, ed. *Habermas and the Public Sphere.* Cambridge, Mass.: MIT Press, 1992.

Castoriadis, Cornelius. *L'expérience du mouvement ouvrier I. Comment lutter.* Paris: UGE 10–18, 1974.

Centre Aixois d'études et de recherches sur le dix-huitième siècle. *Images du peuple au XVIIIe siècle. Actes du colloque d'Aix-en-Provence 25–26 octobre 1969.* Paris: Armand Collin, 1973.

Châtelet, François, Gilles Lapouge, and Olivier Revault d'Allonnes. *La révolution sans modèle*. Paris: Mouton, 1975.

Chevalier, Louis. *Laboring Classes and Dangerous Classes in Paris During the First Half of the Nineteenth Century*. Trans. Frank Jellinek. New York: H. Fertig, 1973.

Chisick, Harvey. *The Limits of Reform in the Enlightenment: Attitudes Toward the Education of the Lower Classes in Eighteenth-Century France*. Princeton, N.J.: Princeton University Press, 1981.

Christmas, William J. *The Lab'ring Muses: Work, Writing, and the Social Order in English Plebeian Poetry, 1730–1830*. Newark: University of Delaware Press, 2001.

Cingolani, Patrick. "Modernité, démocratie, hérésie." *Critique* 601–602 (June/July 1997): 446–460.

Coates, Alfred William. "Contrary Moralities: Plebs, Paternalists, and Political Economists." *Past and Present* 54 (February 1972): 130–133.

Cogniot, Georges. "Qu'est-ce que 'le peuple' pour Michelet et pour nous?" *Europe* 535–536 (November/December 1973): 43–51.

Crampe-Casnabet, Michèle. "Le peuple en démocratie. Une illusion ou une espérance rationnelle?" *Cahiers pour l'Analyse Concrète* 48 (2001): 3–11.

Crapez, Marc. *La gauche réactionnaire. Mythes de la plèbe et de la race dans le sillage des Lumières*. Paris: Berg, 1997.

Curry, Patrick. *Prophecy and Power: Astrology in Early Modern England*. Princeton, N.J.: Princeton University Press, 1989.

Dahl, Robert. *Who Governs? Democracy and Power in an American City*. New Haven, Conn.: Yale University Press, 1961.

Dahlgren, Peter, and Collin Sparks, eds. *Communication and Citizenship: Journalism and the Public Sphere in the New Media Age*. London: Routledge, 1991.

Davis, Nathalie Z. *Les cultures du peuple. Rituels, savoirs et résistances au XVIe siècle*. Paris: Aubier-Montagne, 1979.

Déjacque, Joseph. *À bas les chefs!* [1859]. Paris: Éditions Champ Libre, 1970.

———. "Down with the Bosses!" Trans. Shawn P. Wilbur. 2011. http://theanarchistlibrary .org/library/joseph-dejacque-down-with-the-bosses.

Delacampagne, Christian. *Le philosophe et le tyran*. Paris: Presses Universitaires de France, 2000.

De Leon, Daniel. "Two Pages from Roman History, Address delivered in Manhattan Lyceum, New York, April 2 & 16 1902, Section Greater New York, Socialist Labor Party." http://www.slp.org/pdf/two_pages.pdf.

Denis, Serge. *Un syndicalisme pur et simple*. Montréal: Boréal, 1985.

Deranty, Jean-Phillipe. "Jacques Rancière's Contribution to the Ethics of Recognition." *Political Theory* 31, no. 1 (February 2003): 136–156.

Desgraves, Louis. *Catalogue de la bibliothèque de Montesquieu*. Genève: Droz, 1954.

Drei, Henri. "Les Romains de Vertot et de Montesquieu." In *Le temps de Montesquieu*, ed. M. Porret et al., 337–343. Genève: Droz, 2002.

Dupuis-Deri, Francis. "Révolte au coeur de l'Empire: pourquoi? L'esprit radical du mouvement 'altermondialisation.'" *Argument* 5, no. 2 (Spring/Summer 2003): 115–130.

Dupuy, Roger. *La politique du peuple*. Paris: Albin Michel, 2002.

Durkheim, Émile. "La plèbe romaine." In *Textes 3. Fonctions sociales et institutions*, 297–298. Paris: Minuit, 1975.

Duvignaud, Jean. *L'anomie, hérésie et subversion*. Paris: Anthropos, 1973.

———. *Hérésie et subversion*. Paris: La Découverte, 1986.

———. *Le langage perdu*. Paris: Presses Universitaires de France, 1973.

Epstein, James. *Radical Expression: Political Language, Ritual, and Symbol in England, 1790–1850*. New York: Oxford University Press, 1994.

Farge, Arlette. *La vie fragile. Violence, pouvoir et solidarités à Paris au XVIIIe siècle*. Paris: Hachette, 1986.

Fink, Wolfgang. *Le peuple, la populace et le prolétariat. L'émergence du personnage de l'ouvrier dans le roman allemand 1780–1848*. Paris: Maison des sciences de l'homme, 2002.

Fishman, William J. *The Insurrectionnists*. London: Methuen, 1970.

Foucault, Michel. *Discipline and Punish: The Birth of the Prison*. Trans. Alan Sheridan. New York: Vintage, 1995.

———. *Essential Works of Foucault, 1954–1984*. Vol. 1: *Ethics: Subjectivity and Truth*. Trans. Robert Hurley et al., ed. James D. Faubion. New York: The New Press, 1998.

———. *Essential Works of Foucault, 1954–1984*. Vol. 2: *Aesthetics, Method, and Epistemology*. Trans. Robert Hurley et al., ed. James D. Faubion. New York: The New Press, 1998.

———. *Essential Works of Michel Foucault 1954–1984*. Vol. 3: *Power*. Trans. Robert Hurley et al., ed. James D. Faubion. New York: The New Press, 2000.

———. *Power/Knowledge*. New York: Pantheon, 1980.

Fustel de Coulanges, Numa Denis. *The Ancient City: A Study on the Religion, Laws, and Institutions of Greece and Rome* [1874].Trans. Willard Small. New York: Doubleday Anchor, 1955.

Gagé, Jean. *Les classes sociales dans l'Empire romain*. Paris: Payot, 1964.

Garin, Eugenio. *Machiavel entre politique et histoire*. Paris: Allia, 2006.

Garnot, Benoît. *Le peuple au siècle des Lumières*. Paris: Imago, 1990.

Garrigou, Alain. *Histoire sociale du suffrage universel en France, 1848–2000*. Paris: Seuil, 2002.

Gilmartin, Kevin. *Print Politics: The Press and Radical Opposition in Early Nineteenth-Century England*. Cambridge: Cambridge University Press, 1996.

Giovannini, Adelberto, ed. *Nourrir la plèbe*. Busel: Friedrich Reinhardt Verlag, 1991.

Girard, Louis. *Les libéraux français, 1814–1875*. Paris: Aubier, 1985.

Gramsci, Antonio. *Selections from the Prison Notebooks*. New York: International Publishers, 1971.

Grass, Günter. *The Plebeians Rehearse the Uprising: A German Tragedy*. Trans. Ralph Manheim. New York City: Harcourt, Brace & World, 1966.

Greenblatt, Stephen, ed. *The Power of Forms in the English Renaissance*. Norman, Ok.: Pilgrim, 1982.

Gret, Marion, and Yves Sintomer. *Porto Alegre. L'espoir d'une autre démocratie*. Paris: La Découverte, 2002.

Gutierrez, Gustavo. *The Power of the Poor in History*. Maryknoll, N.Y.: Orbis, 1983.

Habermas, Jürgen. *The Structural Transformation of the Public Sphere: An Inquiry Into a Category of Bourgeois Society.* Trans. Thomas Burger. Cambridge, Mass.: MIT Press, 1991.

———. *The Theory of Communicative Action.* 2 vols. Trans. T. McCarthy. Boston: Beacon, 1984–1987.

Hardt, Michael, and Antonio Negri. *Empire.* Cambridge, Mass.: Harvard University Press, 2000.

———. *Multitude: War and Democracy in the Age of Empire.* New York: Penguin, 2004.

Hoggart, Richard. *The Uses of Literacy: Aspects of Working-Class Life.* London: Penguin, 2009.

Holstun, James. *Ehud's Dagger: Class Struggle in the English Revolution.* London: Verso, 2000.

Howe, Irving. *The Critical Point.* New York: Horizon, 1973.

Humbert, Michel. *Institutions politiques et sociales de l'Antiquité.* Paris: Dalloz, 2003.

Inchausti, Robert. *The Ignorant Perfection of Ordinary People.* Albany, N.Y.: SUNY Press, 1991.

Jones, Gareth Stedman. *Languages of Class: Studies in English Working-Class History, 1832–1982.* Cambridge: Cambridge University Press, 1983.

Joyce, Patrick. *Visions of the People.* Cambridge: Cambridge University Press, 1991.

Kahn, Victoria. "Reduction and the Praise of Disunion in Machiavelli's *Discourses.*" *Journal of Medieval and Renaissance Studies* 18, no. 1 (Spring 1988): 1–19.

Karson, Marc. *American Labor Unions and Politics, 1900–1918.* Carbondale: Southern Illinois University Press, 1958.

Kaye, Harvey J., and Kate McClelland, eds. *E. P. Thompson: Critical Perspectives.* Cambridge: Cambridge University Press, 1990.

Keen, Paul. *The Crises of Literature in the 1790s: Print Culture and the Public Sphere.* Cambridge: Cambridge University Press, 1999.

Kettler, Agnès. *Lettres de Ballanche à Madame de Récamier, 1812–1845.* Paris: Honoré Champion, 1996.

Kervégan, Jean-François. "Démocratie." In *Dictionnaire de philosophie politique,* ed. Philippe Raynaud and Stéphane Rials, 127–133. Paris: Presses Universitaires de France, 1996.

———. "Peuple." In *Dictionnaire de philosophie politique,* ed. Philippe Raynaud and Stéphane Rials, 461–463. Paris: Presses Universitaires de France, 1996.

Klancher, Jon. *The Making of the English Reading Audiences, 1790–1832.* Madison: University of Wisconsin Press, 1987.

Knödler-Brunte, Eberhard. "The Proletarian Public Sphere and Political Organization: An Analysis of O. Negt's and A. Kluge's *The Public Sphere and Experience.*" *New German Critique* 4 (1975): 51–75.

Kraditor, Aileen S. *The Radical Persuasion 1890–1917: Aspects of the Intellectual History and the Historiography of Three American Radical Organizations.* Baton Rouge: Louisiana State University Press, 1981.

Krantz, Frederick, ed. *History from Below: Studies in Popular Protest and Ideology in Honour of George Rudé.* Oxford: Oxford University Press, 1988.

Labelle, Gilles. "Maurice Merleau-Ponty et la genèse de la philosophie politique de Claude Lefort." *Politique et sociétés* 22, no. 3 (2003): 9–44.

Lafue, Pierre. *Histoire du peuple français, de la Régence aux trois révolutions, 1715–1848.* Paris: Nouvelle Librairie de France, 1952.

Lavau, Georges. *À quoi sert le Parti Communiste Français?* Paris: Fayard, 1981.

Lefort, Claude. *Les formes de l'histoire.* Paris: Gallimard, 2000.

———. *Un homme en trop.* Paris: Seuil, 1976.

———. *L'invention démocratique. Les limites de la domination totalitaire.* Paris: Fayard, 1994.

———. *Machiavelli in the Making.* Trans. Michael B. Smith. Evanston, Ill.: Northwestern University Press, 2012.

———. "Le nom d'Un." In *Le discours de la servitude volontaire*, by Étienne de La Boétie. Paris: Payot, 1976.

———. "Préface." In *Discours sur la première décade de Tite-Live*, by Niccolo Machiavelli, 9–19. Paris: Champs-Flammarion, 1985.

———. *Sur une colonne absente. Écrits autour de Merleau-Ponty.* Paris: Gallimard, 1978.

———. *Le travail de l'oeuvre. Machiavel.* Paris: Gallimard, 2005.

Lefort, Claude, and Marcel Gauchet. "Sur la démocratie. Le politique et l'institution du social." *Textures* 2, no. 3 (1971): 7–78.

Leibovici, Martine. "From Fight to Debate: Machiavelli and the Revolt of the Ciompi." *Philosophy and Social Criticism* 28, no. 6: 647–660.

Leinwand, Theodore. "Spongy Plebs, Mighty Lords, and the Dynamics of the Alehouse." *Journal of Medieval and Renaissance Studies* 19, no. 2 (Fall 1989): 159.

Lepore, Mike. "A Short Review of the Life and Work of Daniel De Leon." April 22, 1996. http://www.deleonism.org/deleon.htm.

Le Roy Ladurie, Emmanuel. *Carnival in Romans.* Trans. M. Feeney. New York: Braziller, 1979.

Lewis, Gwynne, and Colin Lucas. *Beyond the Terror.* Cambridge: Cambridge University Press, 1983.

Lewis, Oscar. *A Study of Slum Culture.* New York: Random House, 1968.

Livy. *Early History of Rome.* Trans. Aubrey de Sélincourt and R. Ogilvie. New York: Penguin, 2005.

———. *A History of Rome: Selections.* Trans. Moses Hadas and Joe Poe. New York: Random House, 1962.

Lottes, Günther. *Politische Aufklärung und Plebejisches Publikum.* Munich: R. Oldenbourg Verlag, 1979.

Lowenthal, David. "The Design of Montesquieu's *Considerations on the Causes of the Greatness of the Romans and their Decline.*" *Interpretation* 1, no. 2 (Winter 1970): 144–168.

———. Introduction to Montesquieu, *Considerations on the Causes of the Greatness of the Romans and Their Decline.* Ithaca: Cornell University Press, 1965.

Löwy, Michael, and Robert Sayre. *L'insurrection des Misérables. Romantisme et révolution en Juin 1832.* Paris: Éd. Minard, 1992.

———. *Révolte et mélancolie. Le romantisme à contre-courant de la modernité.* Paris: Payot, 1992.

Lyotard, Jean-François. *Rudiments païens. Genre dissertatif.* Paris: Union générale d'éditions, 1977.

Machiavelli, Niccolo. *Discourses on Livy.* Trans. Harvey C. Mansfield and Nathan Tarcov. Chicago: University of Chicago Press, 1996.

——. *Florentine Histories.* Trans. Laura F. Banfield and Harvey C. Mansfield. Princeton, N.J.: Princeton University Press, 1988.

——. *The Prince.* Trans. Harvey C. Mansfield. Chicago: University of Chicago Press, 1998.

MacGuigan, Jim. *Culture and the Public Sphere.* London: Routledge, 1996.

Macintyre, Stuart. *A Proletarian Science: Marxism in Britain, 1917–1933.* Cambridge: Cambridge University Press, 1980.

Maillard, Alain. *La communauté des égaux.* Paris: Kimé, 1999.

Mandrou, Robert. "Pourquoi 'relire' 'Le peuple'?" *L'Arc* 52 (1973): 50–53.

Manent, Pierre. *Naissances de la politique moderne. Machiavel, Hobbes, Rousseau.* Paris: Payot, 1977.

——. "Vers l'oeuvre et vers le monde. Le *Machiavel* de Claude Lefort." In *La démocratie à l'oeuvre. Autour de Claude Lefort,* ed. Claude Habib and Claude Mouchard, 169–190. Paris: Éditions Esprit, 1993.

Mansfield, Harvey C. *Machiavelli's New Modes and Orders: A Study on the Discourses on Livy.* Ithaca: Cornell University Press, 1979.

——. *Machiavelli's Virtue.* Chicago: University of Chicago Press, 1996.

Marx, Karl. *The Eighteenth Brumaire of Louis Bonaparte.* Whitefish, Mt.: Kessinger, 2010.

——. *Toward a Critique of Hegel's Philosophy of Right,* ed. Joseph O'Malley, trans. Annette Jolin and Joseph O'Malley. Cambridge: Cambridge University Press, 1970.

Marx, Karl, and Friedrich Engels. *The German Ideology.* Amherst, N.Y.: Prometheus, 1998.

McCalla, Arthur. "P.-S. Ballanche as Reader of Vico." *New Vico Studies* 9 (1991): 43–59.

——. *A Romantic Historiosophy: The Philosophy of Pierre-Simon Ballanche.* Leiden: Brill, 1998.

McCalman, Iain. *Radical Underworld: Prophets, Revolutionaries, and Pornographers in London, 1795–1840.* Cambridge: Cambridge University Press, 1988.

Medick, Hans. "Plebeian Culture and the Plebeian Public: On Some Forms of Preproletarian Behavior and Consciousness. Some Reflections on the Economy of Plebeian Culture in the Transition to Capitalism." Seventh Round Table in Social History, University of Konstanz, June 24–25, 1977.

——. "Plebeian Culture in the Transition to Capitalism." In *Culture, Ideology and Politics,* ed. Gareth Stedman Jones and Raphael Samuel, 84–113. London: Routledge, 1982.

Mee, John. *Dangerous Enthusiasm: William Blake and the Culture of Radicalism in the 1790s.* Oxford: Clarendon, 1992.

Mercier-Josa, Solange. *Entre Hegel et Marx.* Paris: L'Harmattan, 1999.

——. "La plèbe et la naissance des sciences sociales." In *Histoire et histoires des sciences sociales,* 1:7–51. Nancy: Presses Universitaires de Nancy, 1986.

——. *Théorie allemande et pratique française de la liberté.* Paris: L'Harmattan, 1993.

Merleau-Ponty, Maurice. *Phenomenology of Perception.* Trans. Colin Smith. London: Routledge, 1958.

———. *The Visible and the Invisible*. Trans. Alfonso Lingis. Evanston, Ill.: Northwestern University Press, 1968.

Michaud, Yves. "Les pauvres et leur philosophe." *Critique* 601–602 (June/July 1997): 421–445.

Michel, Pierre. *Un mythe romantique, les barbares (1785–1848)*. Lyon: Presses Universitaires de Lyon, 1981.

Miles, Andy. "Workers Education: The Communist Party and the Plebs League in the 1920s." *History Workshop* 18 (Autumn 1984): 102–114.

Miller, Fergus. *The Crowd in Rome in the Late Republic*. Ann Arbor: University of Michigan Press, 1998.

Mirabaud, Albert. *Théâtre de la rue*. Paris: Chamuel, 1898.

Mitchell, Richard. *Patricians and Plebeians*. Ithaca, N.Y.: Cornell University Press, 1990.

Montesquieu. *Considerations on the Causes of the Greatness of the Romans and Their Decline*. Trans. David Lowenthal. New York: The Free Press, 1965.

———. *The Spirit of the Laws*. Trans. Anne M. Cohler et al. Cambridge: Cambridge University Press, 1989.

Morris, Lydia. *Dangerous Classes: The Underclass and Social Citizenship*. London: Routledge, 1994.

Mouritsen, Henrik. *Plebs and Politics in the Late Roman Empire*. Cambridge: Cambridge University Press, 2001.

Mulhmann, Géraldine. *Journalism for Democracy*. Trans. Jean Birrell. London: Polity, 2011.

Murphy, Paul. *Toward a Working-Class Canon: Literary Criticism in British Working-Class Periodicals, 1816–1858*. Columbus: Ohio State University Press, 1994.

Nadeau, Christian, "Machiavel. Domination et liberté politique." *Philosophiques* 30, no. 2 (Fall 2003): 321–351.

Nattrass, Leonara. *William Cobbett: The Politics of Style*. Cambridge: Cambridge University Press, 1995.

Navet, Georges. "De l'Aventin à la Croix-Rousse: P-S. Ballanche et le héros plébéien." *Les cahiers du Collège international de philosophie* 5 (1988): 29–41.

Negt, Oskar. *L'espace public oppositionnel*. Paris: Payot, 2007.

———. *The Public Sphere and Experience: Toward an Analysis of the Bourgeois and Proletarian Public Sphere*. Minneapolis: University of Minnesota Press, 1993.

Negt, Oskar, and Alexander Kluge. *Erfahrung und Öffentlichkeit*. Frankfurt: Suhrkamp Verlag, 1972.

Nicolas, Jean. *La rébellion française*. Paris: Seuil, 2002.

Nicolet, Claude, ed. *Demokratia et aristokratia*. Paris: Publications de la Sorbonne, 1983.

Ojakangas, Mika. "Sovereign and Plebs: Michel Foucault meets Carl Schmitt." *Telos* 119 (Spring 2001): 32–40.

Parel, Anthony J. *The Machiavellian Cosmos*. New Haven, Conn.: Yale University Press, 1992.

Payne, Harry C. *The Philosophes and the People*. New Haven, Conn.: Yale University Press, 1976.

Pessin, Alain. *Le mythe du peuple et la société française du XIXe siècle*. Paris: Presses Universitaires de France, 1992.

Pezzani, André. *Exposé d'un nouveau système philosophique*. Lyon, 1847.

Phillips, Anne, and Tim Putnam. "Education for Emancipation: The Movement for Independent Working Class Education, 1908–1928." *Capital and Class* 10 (Spring 1980): 18–42.

Pillorget, René. *Les mouvements insurrectionnels de Provence entre 1596 et 1715.* Paris: Éditions A. Pedone, 1975.

Pocock, John G. A. *The Machiavellian Moment: Florentine Political Thought and the Atlantic Republican Tradition.* Princeton, N.J.: Princeton University Press, 1975.

Pons, Alain. "Vico et la « barbarie de la réflexion »." In *Figures italiennes de la rationalité,* ed. Christianne Menasseyre and André Tosel, 335–358. Paris: Kimé, 1997.

Porchnev, Boris. *Les soulèvements populaires en France au XVIIe siècle.* Paris: Flammarion, 1972.

Poulet, Robert. *Contre la plèbe.* Paris: Denoël, 1967.

Proudhon, Pierre-Joseph. *Oeuvres complètes III. De la capacité politique des classes ouvrières.* Genève: Slatkine, 1982.

Prudhomme, Sieur L. M. "De l'urgence d'une constitution." *Révolution de Paris* 197 (April 13–20, 1793).

"Quelle mémoire aurons-nous?" *Les révoltes logiques* 1 (Winter 1975): inside covers.

Quinet, Edgar. *La révolution.* Paris: Belin, 1987.

——. *Les révolutions d'Italie.* Bruxelles: Imprimerie et Lith. de Ch. Vanderauwera, 1853.

Rancière, Jacques. *Althusser's Lesson.* Trans. Emiliano Battista. New York: Continuum, 2011.

——. *Disagreement: Politics and Philosophy.* Trans. Julie Rose. Minneapolis: University of Minnesota Press, 1999.

——. "Le dissensus citoyen." *Carrefour* 19, no. 2 (1997): 21–36.

——. *The Ignorant Schoolmaster: Five Lessons in Intellectual Emancipation.* Trans. Kristin Ross. Stanford, Calif.: Stanford University Press, 1991.

——. *On the Shores of Politics.* Trans. Liz Heron. New York: Verso, 1995.

——. *The Philosopher and His Poor.* Trans. John Drury et al. Durham, N.C.: Duke University Press, 2004.

——. *La politique des poètes.* Paris: Albin Michel, 1992.

——. "Le prolétaire et son double ou Le philosophe inconnu." *Les Révoltes Logiques* 13 (Winter 1980–1981): 4–12.

——. *Proletarian Nights: The Workers' Dream in Nineteenth-Century France.* Trans. John Drury. New York: Verso, 2012.

——. "La représentation de l'ouvrier ou la classe impossible." In *Le retrait du politique,* ed. Phillipe Lacoue-Labarthe and Jean-Luc Nancy. Paris: Galilée, 1983.

——. "Savoirs hérétiques et émancipation du pauvre." In *Les sauvages dans la cité. Auto-émancipation du peuple et instruction des prolétaires au XIXe siècle,* ed. Jean Borreil, 34–53. Seyssel: Champs Vallon, 1985.

——. *Les scènes du people.* Lyon: Horlieu, 2003.

——. *Staging the People: The Proletarian and His Double.* Trans. David Fernbach. London: Verso, 2011.

Rancière, Jacques, ed. *Gabriel Gauny. Le philosophe plébéien.* Paris: La Découverte/Presses Universitaires de Vincennes, 1983.

Rancière, Jacques, and Alain Faure. *La parole ouvrière.* Paris: UGE, 1976.

Ransom, John S. *Foucault's Discipline: The Politics of Subjectivity*. Durham, N.C.: Duke University Press, 1997.

Rauschning, Herman. *The Revolution of Nihilism: Warning to the West*. Trans. E. W. Dickes. New York: Arno, 1972.

Rée, Jonathan. *Proletarian Philosophers: Problems in Socialist Culture in Britain, 1900–1940*. Oxford: Oxford University Press, 1984.

Remaud, Olivier. *Les archives de l'humanité*. Paris: Seuil, 2004.

Richard, Jean-Claude. *Les origines de la plèbe romaine. Essai sur la formation du dualisme partricio-plébéien*. Paris/Rome: BEFAR, 1978.

Richer, Jacques. "La régénération sociale et l'avenir de l'homme selon P.-S. Ballanche." In *Régénération et reconstruction sociale entre 1780 et 1848*. Paris: Vrin, 1978.

Richter, Melvyn. *The Political Theory of Montesquieu*. Cambridge: Cambridge University Press, 1977.

Rioux, Jean-Pierre, ed. "Les populismes" *Vingtième siècle* 56 (1997).

Robert, Jean-Louis, and Danielle Tartakowsky. *Paris le peuple XVIIIe-XXe siècles*. Paris: Publications de la Sorbonne, 1999.

Roche, Daniel. *France in the Enlightenment*. Trans. Arthur Goldhammer. Cambridge, Mass.: Harvard University Press, 1998.

———. *Le peuple de Paris. Essai sur la culture populaire au XVIIIe siècle*. Paris: Fayard, 1998.

———. "La violence vue d'en-bas. Réflexions sur les moyens de la politique en période révolutionnaire." *Annales ESC* 1 (1989): 47–66.

Rosanvallon. Pierre. *Le peuple introuvable*. Paris: Gallimard, 1998.

Sacks, David Harris. "Searching for 'Culture' in the English Renaissance." *Shakespeare Quarterly* 39, no. 4 (Winter 1988): 465–488.

Saint-Victor, Paul de. *Barbares et bandits. La Prusse et la commune*. Paris: Lévy Frères, 1871.

Samuels, Raphael, and Gareth Stedman Jones, eds. *Culture, Ideology, and Politics*. London: Routledge, 1982.

Scrivener, Michael, ed. *Poetry and Reform: Periodical Verse from the English Democratic Press, 1792–1824*. Detroit, Mich.: Wayne State University Press, 1992.

Seretan, Glen L. *Daniel De Leon: The Odyssey of an American Marxist*. Cambridge, Mass.: Harvard University Press, 1979.

Sfez, Gérald. "Machiavel: la raison des humeurs." *Rue Descartes* 12–13 (May 1995): 11–37.

Sfez, Gérald, and Michel Senellart, eds. *L'enjeu Machiavel*. Paris: Presses Universitaires de France, 2001.

Simard, Augustin. "Les formes politiques de la modernité: signification et portée de la démocratie dans la pensée de Claude Lefort." Master's thesis, Laval University, 2000.

Skinner, Quentin. *Liberty Before Liberalism*. Cambridge: Cambridge University Press, 1998.

Sorel, Georges. *Matériaux pour une théorie du proletariat*. Paris, Marcel Rivière, 1921.

Steinberg, Mark. *Proletarian Imagination: Self, Modernity, and the Sacred in Russia, 1910–1925*. Ithaca, N.Y.: Cornell University Press, 2002.

Stella, Allesandro. *La révolte des Ciompi*. Paris: Éditions de l'EHESS, 1993.

Sullivan, Vickie. *Machiavelli's Three Romes: Religion, Human Liberty, and Politics Reformed*. DeKalb: Northern Illinois University Press, 1996.

Strauss, Leo. *Thoughts on Machiavelli*. Chicago: University of Chicago Press, 1995.

———. *What Is Political Philosophy?* Westport, Conn.: Greenwood, 1959.

Taylor, Charles. *Philosophy and the Human Sciences: Philosophical Papers II.* Cambridge: Cambridge University Press, 1985.

Thériault, Joseph-Yvon. "Sur les traces de la démocratie avec Claude Lefort." *Conjonctures* 20–21 (Fall 1994): 125–144.

Thompson, Edward P. *Customs in Common: Studies in Traditional Popular Culture.* New York: The New Press, 1993.

———. "The Moral Economy of the English Crowd in the Eighteenth Century." *Past and Present* 50 (February 1971): 76–136.

———. "Patrician Society, Plebeian Culture." *Journal of Social History* 7, no. 4 (1974): 382–405.

———. *Plebejische Kultur und moralische Ökonomie.* Frankfurt am Main: Ullstein, 1980.

Turquin, Norbert. *Mémoires et aventures d'un prolétaire à travers la Révolution.* Paris: Maspero, 1977.

Underdown, David. *Revel, Riot, and Rebellion: Popular Politics and Culture in England, 1603–1660.* Oxford: Clarendon, 1985.

Vargas, Yves, ed. *De la puissance du peuple II. La démocratie chez les penseurs révolutionnaires.* Paris: Le Temps des Cerises, 2000.

Vatter, Miguel. *Between Form and Events: Machiavelli's Theory of Political Freedom.* London: Kluwer, 2000.

Vaughan, Frederick. *The Political Philosophy of Giambattista Vico.* The Hague: Martinus Nijhoff, 1972.

Venault, Phillipe, Phillipe Blon, and Joël Farges. *Un soulèvement populaire—Romans 1580.* Paris: Albatros, 1979.

Vernes, Pierre-Marc. "Hegel: libération formelle et inégalité dans la société civile bourgeoise." *Dialogue* 37, no. 4 (Fall 1998): 393–702.

Verret, Michel. *La culture ouvrière.* Paris: L'Harmattan, 1996.

———. "Figures culturelles de l'ouvrier." *Utinam* 24 (January 1998): 97–108.

Vertot, René (Abbé). *Histoire des révolutions arrivées dans le gouvernement de la République romaine.* 3 vols. Paris: François Barois, 1719.

———. *An History of the Revolutions That Happened in the Government of the Roman Republic.* Trans. John Ozell. London: J. J. Knapton et al., 1724.

Vico, Giambattista. *The New Science of Giambattista Vico.* Trans. Thomas Goddard Bergin and Max H. Fisch. Ithaca, N.Y.: Cornell University Press, 1984.

Villari, Rosario. "Masaniello: Contemporary and Recent Interpretations." *Past and Present* 108 (1985): 117–132.

Virno, Paolo. *A Grammar of the Multitude.* New York: Semiotext[e], 2004.

Walsh, Mary. "Machiavelli, Politics, and the Public Realm." Paper presented to the British Political Studies Association Annual Conference, April 5–7, 2002, University of Aberdeen (Scotland).

Weber, Eugen. *Peasants Into Frenchmen.* Stanford, Calif.: Stanford University Press, 1976.

Weber, Max. *The Agrarian Sociology of Ancient Civilizations.* Trans. R. I. Frank. London: NLB, 1976.

Weil, Simone. *Simone Weil, Selected Essays: 1934–1943.* Trans. Richard Rees London: Oxford University Press, 1962.

Wells, Roger. *Insurrection: The British Experience, 1795–1803*. Gloucester: Alan Sutton, 1983.

Whale, John, ed. *Edmund Burke's Reflections on Revolution in France: New Interdisciplinary Essays*. Manchester: Manchester University Press, 2000.

Williams, Raymond. *Culture and Society*. Garden City, N.Y.: Doubleday, 1958.

———. *Keywords: A Vocabulary of Culture and Society*. London: Fontana, 1976.

Wirszubski, Chaïm. *Libertas as a Political Idea in Rome*. Cambridge: Cambridge University Press, 1950.

Wolff, Philippe, and Michel Mollat. *The Popular Revolutions of the Late Middle Ages*. Trans. Arthur Lytton-Sells. London: Allen & Unwin, 1973.

Wood, Marcus. *Radical Satire and Print Culture, 1790–1822*. Oxford: Clarendon, 1994.

Worrall, David. *Radical Culture: Discourse, Resistance, and Surveillance, 1790–1820*. Detroit, Mich.: Wayne State University Press, 1992.

Yavetz, Zvi. *Plebs and Princeps*. Oxford: Clarendon, 1969.

THE SANS-CULOTTES

Braesch, Frédéric. *Papiers de Chaumette*. Paris: Librairie Édouard Cornély et cie, 1908.

———. *1789 L'année cruciale*. Paris: Gallimard, 1941.

Bouthier, Jean, and Philippe Boutry. "Les sociétés politiques en France de 1789 à l'an III: une machine?" *Revue d'Histoire Moderne et Contemporaine* 36 (Winter 1989): 29–67.

Bossut, Nicole. *Chaumette, porte-parole des sans-culottes*. Paris: Éditions du Comité des travaux historiques et scientifiques, 1998.

Cobb, Richard C. *The Police and the People: French Popular Protest, 1789–1820*. Oxford: Clarendon, 1970.

Dommaget, Maurice. *Enragés et curés rouges en 1793. Jacques Roux et Pierre Dolivier*. Paris: Spartacus, 1993.

Furet, François, and Mona Ozouf. *A Critical Dictionary of the French Revolution*. Trans. A. Goldhammer. Cambridge, Mass.: The Belknap Press of Harvard University Press, 1989.

Gauchet, Marcel. *La révolution des droits de l'homme*. Paris: Gallimard, 1989.

Gentry, Maurice. *Paris 1789–1795. L'apprentissage de la citoyenneté*. Paris: Messidor, 1987.

Guérin, Daniel. *Class Struggle in the First French Republic: Bourgeois and Bras Nus, 1793–1795*. London: Pluto, 1977.

———. *La lutte des classes sous la Première République*. 2 vols. Paris, Gallimard, 1968.

Guilhaumou, Jacques. "Espace public et Révolution française. Autour d'Habermas." *Raisons pratiques* 3 (1992): 275–390.

———. "Prises de parole démocratiques et pouvoirs intermédiaires pendant la Révolution française." *Politix* 26 (May 1994): 86–107.

Jaurès, Jean. *Histoire socialiste de la Révolution française*. Vol. 1. Paris: Éditions Sociales, 1969.

Kropotkin, Pierre. *The Great French Revolution*. Montreal: Black Rose, 1989.

Mathiez, Albert. *Le club des Cordeliers pendant la crise de Varennes et le massacre du Champ de Mars*. Paris: Librairie Ancienne H. Champion, 1910.

Michelet, Jules. *History of the French Revolution.* Trans. Charles Cocks. Chicago: University of Chicago Press, 1967.

Mignet, François-Auguste. *History of the French Revolution from 1789 to 1814.* London: George Bell & Sons, 1906.

Nathans, Benjamin. "Habermas's 'Public Sphere' in the Era of the French Revolution." *French Historical Studies* 16, no. 3 (1990): 620–644.

Négrel, Eric. "Le journaliste-orateur: rhétorique et politique sans-culottes dans *Le Publiciste de la République Française* de Jacques Roux (juillet–octobre 1793)." In *Enlightenment, Revolution, and the Periodical Press,* ed. Hans-Jürgen Lüsebrink and Jeremy Popkin, 158–177. Oxford: Voltaire Foundation, 2004.

Resnick, Phillip. "Des sans-culottes à la démocratie participative. La démocratie directe peut-elle coexister avec l'État moderne ?" In *Les formes modernes de la démocratie,* ed. Gérard Boismenu et al., 245–261. Montréal/Paris: Presses Universitaires de Montréal and L'Harmattan, 1992.

Riviale, Philippe. *L'impatience du bonheur. Apologie de Gracchus Babeuf.* Paris: Payot, 2001.

Rose, Robert Barrie. *The Enragés: Socialists of the French Revolution.* Victoria: Melbourne University Press, 1965.

———. *The Making of the Sans-Culotte: Democratic Ideas and Institutions in Paris, 1789–92.* Manchester: Manchester University Press, 1983.

Rudé, Georges. *The Crowd in the French Revolution.* Oxford: Oxford University Press, 1959.

Slavin, Morris. "Jean Varlet as Defender of Direct Democracy." *Journal of Modern History* 39 (December 1967): 387–404.

———. *The Making of an Insurrection. Parisian Sections and the Gironde.* Cambridge, Mass.: Harvard University Press, 1986.

Soboul, Albert. "L'audience des Lumières sous la Révolution. Jean-Jacques Rousseau et les classes populaires." In *Utopie et institutions au XVIIIe siècle,* ed. Pierre Francastel, 289–303. Paris: Mouton, 1963.

———. *Comprendre la Révolution. Problèmes politiques de la Révolution française.* Paris: Maspero, 1981.

———. "De l'an II à la Commune de 1871. La double tradition révolutionnaire française." *Annales historiques de la Révolution française* 4 (1971): 535–553.

———. "Démocratie représentative ou démocratie directe: l'exemple de la démocratie populaire en l'An II." *Raison Présente* 49 (January–March 1979): 15.

———. *Les papiers des sections de Paris (1790–an IV). Répertoire sommaire.* Paris: Commission de recherche et de publication des documents relatifs à la vie économique de la Révolution française et Société des études robespierristes, 1950.

———. "Recherche sur la Révolution française. Sans-culottes et Gouvernement révolutionnaire." *L'information historique* (March 1955).

———. *Les sans-culottes.* Paris: Seuil, 1968.

———. *Les sans-culottes parisiens en l'An II.* Paris: Librairie Clavreuil, 1962.

———. *The Sans-Culottes: The Popular Movement and Revolutionary Government, 1793–1794.* Trans. Rémy Inglis Hall. New York: Anchor, 1972.

———. *La Révolution française.* Paris: Gallimard, 1984.

Soboul, Albert, ed. *Dictionnaire historique de la Révolution française*. Paris: Presses Universitaires de France, 1989.

Soboul, Albert, and Walter Markov, *Die Sansculotten von Paris. Dokumente zur Geschichte der Volksbewegung. 1793–1794*. Berlin: Akademie-Verlag, 1957.

Tocqueville, Alexis de. *The Old Regime and the Revolution*. Trans. Alan Kahan. Chicago: University of Chicago Press, 1998.

Tønnesson, Kåre. *La défaite des sans-culottes*. Oslo: Presses universitaires d'Oslo, 1978.

The English Jacobins

Abensour, Miguel, "Présentation: la passion d'Edward P. Thompson." In *La formation de la classe ouvrière anglaise*, by Edward P. Thompson, i–xvi. Paris: Hautes-Études-Gallimard-Seuil, 1988.

Birley, Robin. *The English Jacobins from 1785–1802*. Oxford: Oxford University Press, 1924.

Calhoun, Craig. *The Question of Class Struggle: Social Foundations of Popular Radicalism During the Industrial Revolution*. Chicago: University of Chicago Press, 1982.

Cartwright, Frances Dorothy, ed. *Life and Correspondence of Major Cartwright*, vol. 1. London: Henry Colbrun, 1826.

Clark, Anna. *The Struggle for the Breeches: Gender and the Making of the British Working Class*. Berkeley: University of California Press, 1995.

Clark, Peter. *The English Alehouse: A Social History, 1200–1830*. London: Longman, 1983.

Cone, Carl B. *The English Jacobins*. New York: Charles Scribner's Sons, 1968.

Dickinson, Harry Thomas. *British Radicalism and the French Revolution*. Oxford: Blackwell, 1985.

Fridenson, Patrick. "E. P. Thompson: la formation de la classe ouvrière anglaise (livre-montage)." *Le Débat* 3 (July/August 1980): 175–188.

Goodwin, Albert. *The Friends of Liberty*. London: Hutchinson, 1979.

Greig, James, ed. *The Farington Diary*. London: Hutchinson, 1923.

Hardy, Thomas. *Memoir of Thomas Hardy . . . Written by Himself*. London, 1832.

Hone, J. Ann. *For the Cause of the Truth: Radicalism in London 1796–1821*. Oxford: Clarendon, 1982.

Lottes, Günther. "Radicalism, Revolution, and Political Culture: An Anglo-French Comparison." In *The French Revolution and British Popular Politics*, ed. Mark Philp, 78–98. Cambridge: Cambridge University Press, 1991.

Morris, Marilyn. *The British Monarchy and the French Revolution*. New Haven, Conn.: Yale University Press, 1998.

Paine, Thomas. *Rights of Man*. Hertfordshire: Wordsworth, 1996

Palmer, Bryan D. *The Making of E. P. Thompson*. Toronto: New Hogtown, 1981.

Palmer, Robert Roswell. *The Age of Democratic Revolution*. 2 vols. Princeton, N.J.: Princeton University Press, 1964.

Philp, Mark. "The Fragmented Ideology of Reform." In *The French Revolution and British Popular Politics*, ed. Mark Philp, 25–78. Cambridge: Cambridge University Press, 1991.

Polanyi, Karl. *The Great Transformation*. Boston: Beacon, 2001.

Prothero, Iorwerth J. *Artisans and Politics in Early Nineteenth-Century England.* Baton Rouge: Louisiana State University Press, 1979.

Scrivener, Michael. "John Thelwall's Political Ambivalence: Reform and Revolution." In *Radicalism and Revolution in Britain, 1775–1848*, ed. Michael T. Davis, 69–83. London: Macmillan, 2000.

Smith, Olivia, *The Politics of Language.* Oxford: Clarendon, 1984.

Thale, Mary. *The Autobiography of Francis Place.* Cambridge: Cambridge University Press, 1972.

———, ed. *Selections from the Papers of the London Corresponding Society, 1792–1799.* Cambridge: Cambridge University Press, 1983.

Thelwall, John. *The Politics of English Jacobinism: Writings of John Thelwall.* Ed. Gregory Claeys. University Park: Pennsylvania State University Press, 1995.

Thompson, Edward P. *The Making of the English Working Class.* London: Penguin, 1991.

Veitch, George Stead. *Genesis of Parliamentary Reform.* Hamden: Archon, 1965.

Williams, Gwyn A. *Artisans and Sans-Culottes.* London: Libris, 1989.

The Paris Commune of 1871

Andrieu, Jules. *Notes pour servir à l'histoire de la Commune de Paris de 1871.* Ed. Maximilien Rubel and Louis Janover. Paris: Spartacus, 1984.

Arnould, Arthur. *Histoire populaire et parlementaire de la Commune de Paris.* Lyon: Jacques-Marie Laffont, 1981.

Dautry, Jean, and Lucien Scheler. *Le Comité Central Républicain des vingt arrondissements de Paris.* Paris: Éditions sociales, 1960.

Decouflé, André. *La commune de Paris (1871).* Paris: Cujas, 1969.

Dommanget, Maurice. *Blanqui, la guerre de 1870–71 et la commune.* Paris: Domat, 1947.

———. *La commune.* Paris: La Taupe, 1971.

Elleinstein, Jean. *Réflexions sur la commune de 1871.* Paris: Julliard, 1971.

L'Enquête parlementaire sur l'Insurrection du Dix-Huit mars 1871. Paris: A. Wittersheim, 1872.

Johnson, Martin Phillip. *The Paradise of Association.* Ann Arbor: University of Michigan Press, 1996.

Lefebvre, Henri. *La proclamation de la commune.* Paris: Gallimard, 1965.

Lefrançais, Gustave. *Souvenirs d'un révolutionnaire.* Ed. J. Cerny. Paris: Éditions de la Tête de Feuilles, 1972.

———. *Étude sur le mouvement communaliste à Paris, en 1871.* Coeuvres: Ressouvenances, 2001.

Le Quillec, Robert. *La commune de Paris. Bibliographie critique 1871–1997.* Paris: La Boutique de l'histoire éditions, 1997.

Loraux, Nicole. "Corcyre 427, Paris 1871. La 'guerre civile grecque' en deux temps." *Les Temps Modernes* 569 (December 1993): 82–119.

Malon, Benoît. *La troisième défaite du prolétariat français.* Neuchâtel: G. Guillaume fils, 1871.

Marx, Karl. *The Paris Commune, 1871.* London: Sidgwick & Jackson, 1971.

Marx, Karl, and Frederick Engels. *Selected Works*. New York: International, 1968.

Moissonnier, Maurice. "L'expérience de la commune, le marxisme et les problèmes de l'État." *La Nouvelle Critique*, special issue (1971): 21–28.

———. "Des origines à 1871." In *La France ouvrière*, ed. Claude Willard, 1:11–220. Paris: Éditions de l'Atelier, 1995.

Les murailles politiques françaises. Vol. 1. Paris: Le Chevalier, 1873–1874.

Noël, Bernard. *Dictionnaire de la commune*. Paris: Mémoire du Livre, 2000.

Lissagaray, Prosper-Oliver. *History of the Commune of 1871*. New York: Monthly Review Press, 1967.

Petit-Dutaillis, Charles. *Les communes françaises*. Paris: Albin Michel, 1947.

Reclus, Élisé. *Correspondance*. 3 vols. Schleicher, 1911.

Rihs, Charles. *La commune de Paris 1871. Sa structure et ses doctrines*. Paris: Seuil, 1973.

Riviale, Philippe. *Sur la commune. Cerises de sang*. Paris: L'Harmattan, 2003.

Rougerie, Jacques. *La commune de Paris de 1871*. Paris: Presses Universitaires de France, 1992).

———. *Paris libre: 1871*. Paris: Seuil, 1971.

———. *Procès des communards*. Paris: Julliard, 1964.

———. "Quelques documents nouveaux pour l'histoire du Comité Central Républicain des Vingt Arrondissements." *Le mouvement social* 37 (1961): 3–29.

Rubel, Maximilien. *Marx critique du marxisme*. Paris: Payot, 2000.

———. "Socialism and the Commune." In *Paridigm for Revolution? The Paris Commune 1871–1971*, ed. Eugene Kamenka and Robert B. Rose, 272–289. Canberra: Australian National University Press, 1972.

Serman, William. *La commune de Paris (1871)*. Paris: Fayard, 1986.

Taithe, Bertrand. *Citizenship and Wars: France in Turmoil, 1870–1871*. London: Routledge, 2001.

Tardi, Jacques, and Jean Vautrin. *Le cri du peuple. Les canons du 18 mars*. Vol. 1. Paris: Casterman, 2001.

Viard, Bruno. "Pierre Leroux et le socialisme associatif de 1830 à 1848." *Revue du MAUSS* 16 (2000): 265–280.

Vincent, Steven K. *Between Marxism and Anarchism: Benoît Malon and French Reformist Socialism*. Berkeley: University of California Press, 1992.

Winock, Michel, and Jean-Pierre Azéma. *Les communards*. Paris: Seuil, 1964.

Wolfe, Robert D. *The Origins of the Paris Commune*. PhD. diss., Harvard University, 1965.

General References

Abensour, Miguel. "Appendix: 'Savage Democracy' and the 'Principle of Anarchy.'" In *Democracy Against the State: Marx and the Machiavellian Moment*, trans. M. Blechman and M. Breaugh, 102–125. London: Polity, 2011.

———. *De la compacité. Architecture et régimes totalitaires*. Paris: Sens & Tonka, 1997.

———. "Les deux interprétations du totalitarisme chez Claude Lefort." In *La démocratie à l'oeuvre*, ed. Claude Habib and Claude Mouchard, 79–136. Paris: Éditions Esprit, 1993.

———. "Lire Saint-Just." In *Oeuvres complètes*, by Antoine-Louis de Saint-Just, 9–100. Paris: Gallimard-Folio, 2004.

———. "Postface: comment une philosophie de l'humanité peut-elle être une philosophie politique moderne?" In *Aux philosophes, aux artistes, aux politique*, by Pierre Leroux, 295–320. Paris: Payot, 1994.

———. "D'une mésinterprétation du totalitarisme et de ses effets." *Tumultes* 8 (1996): 11–44.

———. "Utopie et démocratie." In *L'utopie en questions*, ed. Michèle Riot-Sarcey, 245–256. Saint-Denis: Presses Universitaires de Vincennes, 2001.

Ansart, Pierre. "Proudhon, *De la capacité politique de la classe ouvrière*." In *Dictionnaire des oeuvres politiques*, ed. François Châtelet et al., 652–659. Paris: Presses Universitaires de France, 1986.

Arendt, Hannah. *Between Past and Future: Eight Exercises in Political Thought*. New York: Penguin, 2006.

———. *The Life of the Mind*. New York: HBJ, 1981.

———. *Men in Dark Times*. London: Cape, 1970.

Aristotle. *The Athenian Constitution*. Trans. P. J. Rhodes. New York: Penguin, 1984.

Bataille, Georges. *Inner Experience*. Trans. L. Anne Boldt. Albany, N.Y.: SUNY Press, 1988.

———. *Visions of Excess: Selected Writings, 1927–1939*. Trans. Allan Stoekl et al. Minneapolis: University of Minnesota Press, 1985.

Canetti, Elias. *Crowds and Power*. Trans. Carol Stewart. New York: Farrar Straus Giroux, 1984.

Carré de Malberg, Raymond. *Contribution à la théorie générale de l'État*. Paris: Dalloz, 2004.

Chalier, Catherine. *La fraternité, un espoir en clair-obscur*. Paris: Buchet Chastel, 2003.

De La Boétie, Étienne. "The Discourse of Voluntary Servitude." In *The Politics of Obedience and Étienne de la Boétie*, by Étienne de La Boétie and Paul Bonnefon, trans. Harry Kurz. Montreal: Black Rose, 2007.

Deleuze, Gilles. *Negotiations, 1972–1990*. Trans. Martin Joughin. New York: Columbia University Press, 1995.

Derrida, Jacques. *Politics of Friendship*. Trans. George Collins. London: Verso, 1997.

Dupuis-Déri, Francis. "L'esprit antidémocratique des fondateurs de la 'démocratie' moderne." *Agone* 22 (1999): 95–113.

———. "The Political Power of Words: The Birth of Prodemocratic Discourse in the Nineteenth Century in the United States and France." *Political Studies* 52 (March 2004): 118–134.

Durkheim, Émile. *The Division of Labor in Society*. Trans. W. D. Halls. New York: The Free Press, 1984.

Fallada, Hans. *Alone in Berlin*. Trans. Michael Hofmann. London: Penguin, 2009.

Farrugia, Francis. *La crise du lien social*. Paris: L'Harmattan, 1993.

Gauchet, Marcel. *The Disenchantment of the World: A Political History of Religion*. Trans. Oscar Burge. Princeton, N.J.: Princeton University Press, 1997.

———. *La révolution des pouvoirs*. Paris: Gallimard, 1995.

Hamilton, Alexander, James Madison, and John Jay. *The Federalist Papers*. New York: New American Library, 1961.

Lawruszenko, Jean. "De la nécessité d'un nouveau lien social." *DESS: La Revue des Sciences Économiques et Sociales* 113 (October 1998): 73–79.

Lefort, Claude. *Éléments d'une critique de la bureaucratie*. Paris: Gallimard, 1979.

Leroux, Pierre. *Aux philosophes, aux artistes, aux politiques*. Paris: Payot, 1994.

———. *De l'humanité*. Paris: Fayard, 1985.

———. "Lettre au Docteur Deville." In *Le procès des maîtres rêveurs*, by Miguel Abensour, 119–167. Arles: Sulliver, 2000.

———. "Réponse à Proudhon." *La République* (November 10, 1849).

Lévêque, Pierre, and Pierre Vidal-Naquet. *Cleisthenes, the Athenian*. Trans. David Ames Curtis. Atlantic Highlands, N.J.: Humanities Press, 1996.

Manin, Bernard. *The Principles of Representative Government*. Cambridge: Cambridge University Press, 1997.

Michels, Robert. *Political Parties*. New York: Dover, 1959.

Michelet, Jules. *History of the French Revolution*. Trans. Charles Cocks. Chicago: University of Chicago Press, 1967.

Orwell, Georges. *Homage to Catalonia*. London: Penguin, 2003.

Ostrogorski, Moisey. *Democracy and the Organization of Political Parties*. Trans. F. Clarke. New York: Haskell House, 1970.

———. *La démocratie et les partis politiques*. Ed. Pierre Ronsanvallon. Paris: Seuil, 1979.

Rubel, Maximilien. "Socialism and the Commune." In *Paridigm for Revolution? The Paris Commune 1871–1971*, ed. Eugene Kamenka and Robert Barrie Rose, 272–289. Canberra: Australian National University Press, 1972.

Rousseau, Jean-Jacques. *Discourse on the Origins of Inequality*. Trans. Gordon D. H. Cole. New York: Barnes & Noble, 2008.

———. "Que l'état de guerre naît de l'état social." In *Oeuvres complètes*, 3:601–602. Paris: Gallimard-Pléiade, 1969.

———. *The Social Contract*. Trans. Maurice Cranston. New York: Penguin, 2006.

Sartre, Jean-Paul. *Critique of the Dialectical Reason I*. Trans. Quintin Hoare. New York: Verso, 2010.

Thériault, Joseph-Yvon. "Sur les traces de la démocratie avec Claude Lefort." *Conjonctures* 20–21 (Fall 1994): 125–144.

Tobgui, Fawzia. "De l'anarchisme au fédéralisme. Articulation entre droit et État dans le système politique de Proudhon." *Réfractions* 6. http://refractions.plusloin.org/textes/refractions6/tobgui_anarchisme_federalisme.htm.

Tonnies, Ferdinand. *Communauté et société. Catégories fondamentales de la sociologie pure*. Paris: Presses Universitaires de France, 1944.

Vachet, André. *L'idéologie libérale. L'individu et sa propriété*. Ottawa: Presses de l'Université d'Ottawa, 1988.

INDEX

À bas les chefs! (Déjacque), 100–102
Abensour, Miguel, 36–37, 203–4
action. *See* political action
active citizenship, 170–72
AFL. *See* American Federation of Labor
age of gods, 61–62
age of heroes, 61–62
age of men, 61, 62–66
ages of humanity, 60–66
agoraphilia, xiii, xxii, 129–30, 164–72, 191–97
agoraphilic tradition, xxii, 241
agoraphobia, xxii, 105
Agrippa, Menenius, xx–xxii, 9–10, 11, 69, 93, 94
Alabres, 32–33
Althusser, Louis, 258n199
American Federation of Labor (AFL), xii, 74, 79
American War of Independence, 152
ammonizone (proscriptions), 13–14
ancien régime, 59–60, 112–13, 121, 128

animal laborans, xv, 10–11, 166, 224, 226
"Anthology of Rousseau's Most Beautiful Thoughts," 214
Anweiler, Oskar, xxii
Arab Spring, xiii
architecture, 203–4
Arendt, Hannah, xv, xxiii, xxiv, 130, 203, 217, 218, 226
aristocracy, 110
aristocrats, xviii
Arnould, Arthur, 238
artisans and indigent (*popolani minuti*), 12, 13, 219
Asiatic despotism, 54
assassination, 22–23, 34, 41
association, xiii, 230, 234–40, 280n22, 281n44
Association for Preserving Liberty and Property Against Republicans and Levellers, 155–56
Athens, Greece, xviii, 243

Aventine Hill, xi, 126; Ballanche on, 68–69; camp at, xix–xx, 9–10, 11, 40, 42; communalist tradition at, xxi–xxii; issue at stake in, xx–xxi; Machiavelli on, 50; political nature of insurrection at, xx; Rancière on, 93–94, 95, 98

Babeuf, Gracchus, 205
Bakhtin, Mikhail, 18, 19–20, 40, 73–74
balia. See councils
Ballanche, Pierre-Simon, xii, xx–xxi, 3, 45, 66–73, 92, 93–94, 112, 255n109
barbarians, 72–73
barbarism, 61, 64
Barère. *See* Vieuzac, Barère de
base curiosity, 83
Bataille, Georges, xv–xvi, 43
Battle of Sedan, 232
belly and parts, xx, 9–10, 94
Bin Laden, Osama, 89, 90
biopolitics, 242–43
Blanqui, Auguste, 96–97, 175, 273n60
Blanquistes, 178
Bloody Week, 188–89, 196
Bloom, Allan, 57–58
Bourbon Restoration, 66–67
bourgeoisie: ancien régime's struggle with, 112–13; artisans and indigent's political power limited by, 13; definition of, 12; fear harbored by, 84, 90; under French Empire, 191; nobles' reconciliation with, 16; plebeian, 77–79
bras nus, 261n3
British Socialist Labour Party (BSLP), 79–80, 102
Brossat, Alain, 88–89, 90
brutal insurrection, 131–32
Brutus, 69
BSLP. *See* British Socialist Labour Party
bureaucracy, 108–10, 128
Burke, Edmund, 148–49

Caesarism, 234
Cambon, 127, 128

Candlemas, 22
Canetti, Élias, 203
carnival, xi, 18–25, 30, 31, 40–41, 42, 43
Carnot, 127
Cartwright (major), 160
Catholic Church, 185–86, 192
caucus, 108
Central Committee (Paris Commune), 175, 176, 178–79
Central Committee of the National Guard, 180–81, 183
centralization, 121–23, 125–27
Central Labour College, 80
Chalier, Catherine, 210, 215–16, 217
Chaumette, 120
Cheateaubriand, François-René de, 66
child labor, 221–22
children, 184–85, 221–22
Christianity, 54–57, 215
Ciompi: council causing dissatisfaction of, 15–16; council elected by, 15, 42; Minor Arts' alliance with, 15; motivation of, 14; revolt of, xi, 11–18, 39, 40, 51–52; riots of, 14–15; on trade guilds, 14; voluntary servitude with, 42
circle of plebeian, 88–89
Citizen (*Citoyen*), 208
Citizen Groves, 160
citizens, 207
citizenship, 96, 170–72
Citoyen (Citizen), 208
civil religion, 213, 215–16
Civil War in France, The (Marx), 191–94, 196
civitas, 5, 6
Clark, Anna, 166–67
class divisions, 77–79
Clastres, Pierre, 275n7
Claudius, Appius, 69–70
clergy, 185–86, 192
clientela (clients), 6–7, 9
Club central, 177
Club de la solidarité, 177–78
Club des prolétaires, 271n5

Comité central de la garde nationale. *See* Central Committee of the National Guard
Comité central républicain. *See* Central Committee
Comité de l'Évêché, 134, 135
Comité de salut public (French Revolution), 118, 122, 124, 128–29
Comité de sûreté générale, 119
Comité insurrectionnel, 134
Commission of Work, Industry, and Exchange, 236–37
Committee for Public Safety (Paris Commune), 188–90, 273n77
commons, 36
Communal Constitution, 193
Communal Council, 119, 120, 188–89, 190, 240
communalism, 129–30
communalist clubs and associations (Paris Commune), 181
communalist forces (Paris Commune), 174–75, 183, 185–86
communalist movement (Paris Commune), 174–82, 183
communalist revolution, xxii
communalist traditions, xxi–xxii, 191–97, 241
communard, 173–74
Communards, 242; association advanced by, 234–36; clergy as enemy of, 185–86; dividedness among, 239–40; equality and, 187–88; French Revolution influencing, 189–90; Hôtel de Ville taken by, 182; human bond rebuilt by, 234–36; political cohesion of, 174; revolutionary justice motivating, 186; social makeup of, 174; undividedness among, 239–40; violence resorted to by, 186–87
Commune of Paris. *See* Paris Commune
communities: concentration camps creating nonhuman, 275n8; English Jacobins encouraging participation in, 165–66; Industrial Revolution influenc-ing traditional, 222–24; originary division of social structuring, 50; political, 52, 60, 61, 66; political freedom coming to, 3–4; universal makeup of, 49–50; working-class, 219
Community and Society (Tönnies), 202
Comte, Auguste, 202
concentration camps, 275n8
conflicts: artisans and indigent mediating, 12; Ballanche's theory of, 73; Comité de salut public opposed by, 124; democracy's thriving caused by, 28; equality tied to, 97; in Florence, 12; freedom and, 46–52; freedom's broadening enabled by, xvii, 28, 126–27; as good laws' root, xvii, 26–27, 50; as liberty's motor force, 27, 53–54; monarchs ending, 59; between patricians and plebs, 7–11, 20, 22–25, 61–65, 71; plebeians and, 46–52; plebs as agents of, 65; political union resulting from absence of, 54; of politics, 95; in Roman Republic, xix–xxii, 4, 5, 7–11, 77–79; in Rome, xvi–xvii, 4, 5, 7–11, 77–79; sectional societies opposed by, 124; wrong bringing to light, 126
Conservative Party, xi
Considerations on the Causes of the Greatness of the Romans and Their Decline (Montesquieu), 45, 52–60
Constant, Benjamin, 172
Constitutional Act of June 24, 1793, 131
constitutionalism, 147, 157
Constitution of 1791, 122
Constitution of Year II, 131
consuls, 8
Convention, 132, 134, 139
Copenhagen House, 161, 162, 167
Coriolanus (Shakespeare), 76
corresponding societies, 152–53
Coulanges, Fustel de, 6–7
councilist tradition. *See* communalist tradition
councils (*balia*), 15–16, 42, 74–75

Courbet, Gustave, 188–89
creditors, 7–8
Critique of Dialectical Reason (Sartre),
    211–12
Crowds and Power (Canetti), 203
Crustumerium, 69–70

David, Marcel, 215, 276n12
debtors, 8
debts, 7–9
dechristianization, 37–38
Declaration of the Rights of Man, 130–31
"Declaration to the French People" (Paris
    Commune), 185–86
decrees, 116, 118, 122–23
Déjacque, Joseph, 100–102, 259n233
De la capacité politique de la classe ouvrière
    (Proudhon), 235, 279n6
De la compacité (Abensour), 203
Delegation of the Twenty Districts, 178,
    179, 180, 181, 183, 184, 272n48
De Leon, Daniel, xii, 45–46, 73–80, 99,
    102, 256n142
Delescluze, Charles, 180
Deleuze, Gilles, 45, 105
democracy, 28, 47, 64, 105–7. *See also* direct
    democracy
demos, xviii, 96
depoliticizing mobilization, 204
Dé-sans-cullotisation, 137
Desmarets, 214–15
Dictionnaire de philosophie politique
    (Kervégan), 44
dignity, 208
Dionysius of Halicarnassus, 6–7
direct democracy, 114, 133, 154
Directoire, 140
Disagreement: Politics and Philosophy
    (Rancière), 93–94
Discourse on the Origins of Inequality
    (Rousseau), 215
Discourse on Voluntary Servitude, The (La
    Boétie), xvii–xviii
Discourses on Livy (Machiavelli), xvi,
    26–27, 46–52

"Dissentions That Always Existed in the
    City, The" (Montesquieu), 53–54
distribution of sensible, 95, 259n216
division of humors, xvi, 26–31, 47–52,
    126–27, 145
divisions: in Central Committee, 176; class,
    77–79; among Communards, 239–40;
    of Florence, 12–13; freedom influenced
    by, xvi–xvii; Montesquieu praising,
    52–60; in Paris Commune, 239–40;
    political bond of, 227–29; of Roman
    society, 4–5; totalitarianism quelling,
    28. *See also* originary division of
    social
doctrinal fragmentation, 239
Domenach, J.-M., 83–84
domestics and servants (*famuli*), 61–62
domination: Agrippa ruining order of,
    xxi; gap fracturing, xxiii; gap of, 171;
    grandees' desire for, 126–27; nobles'
    desire for, xvii, 26, 50–51; origins of,
    xvii–xviii; patricians' desire for, 30;
    plebs expressing opposition to, xvii, 26;
    of sans-culottes, 113; totalitarian, 28,
    242. *See also* political domination
Dominicans, 33
Dream of John Ball, A (Morris), 241
Drei, Henri, 58
dual power, 21
duke of Arcos, 32, 33, 34, 35, 38, 41
Duprat, G., 44
Dupuis-Déri, Francis, xxii
Durkheim, Émile, 202
Duval, Georges, 138
dynasties, 12

Eaton, Daniel, 159
economic domination, 13
Edinburgh Convention, 158–59
education, 79–80; Catholic Church losing,
    192; for emancipation, 102, 171, 225;
    LCS counting on, 171; LCS's activity in,
    153–54, 225; Paris Commune reform-
    ing, 237–38; sectional societies promot-
    ing, 117; state losing, 192

Éducation nouvelle, 237
effective history, 82
Eighteenth Brumaire of Louis Bonaparte, The (Marx), 76
Eight Saints of the People of God, 42
elections, 107, 183–84, 272n48
emancipation, 63–64; definition of, 95; dialectic of, 171; education for, 102, 171, 225; enactment of, 96; leader as responsible for, 100; police's encounter with, 95; Proudhon's strivings for, 101–2; as self-emancipation, 166
England, 146–51, 155–56, 157, 162, 163, 164, 165–67
English Chartism, 229
English Constitution, 146–47, 148, 149, 150, 157
English Jacobinism: active citizenship and, 171–72; continuity of, 267n16; internationalism tradition bequeathed by, 168–69; leader problem circumvented by, 171; national leader of, 157–58, 269n66; as oppositional Jacobinism, 146; Paine's influence on, 150–51; political heritage of, 164–72; political spaces heritage of, 169–70; Thompson on, 146–51, 267n16
English Jacobins, xiii, 141, 242; accusations against, 159–60; active citizenship conception presented by, 170–72; agoraphilia contributions of, 164–72; bond of division of, 228–29; community participation encouraged by, 165–66; components of, 145; division of humors of, 145; equality before law believed in by, 148; human bond of, 218; Ireland's relationships with, 228; Jacobins' differences with, 144–46; many respected by, 165–66; originary division of social of, 145; otherness attitude of, 168–69; persecution of, 158, 164; political organization of, 154; political spaces used by, 169–70; radical democratic bodies created by, 167; sans-culottes resembling, 144, 172; Thelwall on, 145–46;

Thompson on, 144–45; trials dealing heavy blow to, 160–61
Enragés, 123, 132–33, 134, 135–36, 263n41
equality: Communards and, 187–88; conflict tied to, 97; enactment of, 96; English Jacobins' belief in legal, 148; police inflicting wrong on, 95, 126; radical, xx; sans-culottes defending, 113–14; verification of, 96–97, 98, 166; of women, 237–38
Esprit, 83–84
Euripides, 3
Europe, 83
events of May 1968, xiii
experience, xv–xvi

fable of belly and parts, xx
fairs, 222–23
families. *See* patrician families
famuli (domestics and servants), 61–62
Farrugia, Francis, 202
Favre, Jules, 232
feast days, 222–23
federalism, 236–37
Féraud, 212
festival, 19, 20, 31
few, xx
First International. *See* International Workingmen's Association
First Republic, 207
fiscal inequality, 12
Florence, Italy, xi, 11–18, 39, 40, 46–47, 51–52
Florentine Histories (Machiavelli), 14, 17, 47, 51
foodstuffs, 187
"Formule générale de l'histoire de tous les peuples, appliquée à l'histoire du peuple Romain" (Ballanche), 67, 68–72
Foucault, Michel, xii, xiii, 46, 81–91, 257n155
France, 122, 231–33
Franco-Prussian War, 175–80, 231–33
Frankel, Léo, 236–37
fraternal bond, 213

fraternity, 205, 206–9, 211–17, 227–28, 275n9, 276n19, 276n38

fraternization, 115–16, 124, 209–11, 236

free-born Englishmen, 147–48, 221, 223, 224

freedom: conflict and, 46–52; conflict enabling broadening of, xvii, 28, 126–27; Constitution granting, 146–47; division influencing, xvi–xvii; gap represented by, 66; guard of, 51; leadership problem encountered by desire for, 40–43; plebs and, 46–52; plebs as incapable of assuming, 65–66; plebs' desire for, xvi, 30, 99–100; as politics' *raison d'être*, 172; power and, 87–88; regime of, 27–28; representative government limiting, 106; of Roman Republic, 47, 59; totalitarianism causing perishing of, 28

French Empire, 191–92, 231–32

French Jacobins. *See* Jacobins

French Revolution: beautiful, 135; Committee for Public Safety as product of, 189–90; Communards influenced by, 189–90; dechristianization campaign in, 37–38; England and, 146–51; English response to, 148–49; hideous, 135–36; insurrection as point of no return for, 135–36; LCS's contact with, 146–48; Rousseau influencing, 213–17. *See also* sans-culottes

Fructidor 5 Constitution of Year III, 139–40

Furet, François, 124

"Futility in Revolution" (Lyotard), 37–38

gabella (tax), 32

Gabriel Gauny—le philosophe plébéien (Rancière), 91–92

gap: at carnival, 19; definition of, xxiii; of domination, 171; domination fractured by, xxiii; freedom experience representing, 66; plebeian experience, as temporality specific to, 241; plebeian secession as result of, 7; political

freedom's history explained by, xxiii; as political subject's place, 97

Gauchet, Marcel, 25, 28–29, 30

Gauny, Gabriel, 91, 92–93

genealogy, 81–82

General Committee, 153

General Safety Committee. *See* Comité de sûreté générale

general will, 216

Genty, Maurice, 262n32

George III (king), 161–62

Germinal insurrection, 136–37, 138

Gerrald, Joseph, 157–59

Ghibellines, 12, 13–14

Girondin Convention, 114–15

Girondins, 114–15, 122, 128, 132–36, 209, 264n83

Glorious Revolution, 147

Glucksmann, André, 92

Gompers, Samuel, xii, 74, 79

gonfaloniere, 14, 15, 16

good laws, xvii, 26–27, 50

Goodwin, Albert, 270n104

government, 195–96

governmental authority, 100–101

Government of National Defense, 175, 176–77, 179–80, 181, 232

grandees: acquisition craving of, 51; attack on hegemony of, 31; domination desire of, 126–27; people's split with, 11; pronouncement of, 27; rise of, 40

Great Britain, 79–80, 108, 163

great specialists, 127–30

gubernator state, 195–96, 274n97

Guelph faction, 12–14

Guérin, Antoine, 20–21, 22–23, 30, 41, 113

Guérin, Daniel, 37–38, 127–28, 133–34, 140, 214, 261n3

guillotine, 123–24

gulags, 84–85

Haac, Oscar, 66, 68

Habermas, Jürgen, 197, 260n1

Hardy, Thomas, 151, 157, 160, 161

Hébertistes, 37

hereditary principle, 149–50
hierarchy, 11
Hiero of Syracuse, 43
historian, 82, 83
historian-plebeian, 82–83
historical movements, 60–66
historical subject, 36
history: effective, 82; Foucault on, 82–83;
   ideal eternal, 45; of many, xviii–xix;
   Roman, 94; of sans-culottes, 112–13;
   theodicy of, 67–68. See also political
   history
History of Rome (Livy), xix–xx, 46
History of the Revolutions That Happened
   in the Government of the Roman Republic, An (Vertot), 58–60
Hobbes, Thomas, 61, 278n21
hoi polloi, xviii–xix
Holy Roman Empire, 12
Homage to Catalonia (Orwell), 201
Horne Tooke, John, 160
Hôtel de Ville, 176, 177, 178, 182
human bond: articulation of, xiii; Communards rebuilding, 234–36; in
   concentration camps, 275n8; definition
   of, 201–2, 202–3; fraternity influencing, 207, 208, 211; Industrial Revolution
   severing, 222–23; LCS creating, 224–26;
   of Parisians, 233; as political bond, 203,
   238; as research subject, 202; sans-
   culottes' fraternity articulating, xiii; as
   social bond, 202–3, 223–24; totalitarianism's treatment of, 203–4
human communities. See communities
humankind, 71–72, 73, 102, 139
humors (umori), xvi, xvii, 26–31, 47–52,
   126–27
"Hymn to Liberty and Equality" (Desmarets), 214–15

ideal eternal history, 45
If This Is a Man (Levi), 275n8
Ignorant Schoolmaster, The (Rancière), 94
imperative mandate, 238, 281n44
impossibilists, 79–80

indigent. See artisans and indigent
individuals, 203–4, 224
industrialization, 220–24, 225–26
Industrial Revolution, 218, 219–24, 278n21
Industrial Workers of the World (IWW),
   74
inequalities, 138
infanticide, 69–70
insurrectional ideology, 137
"Insurrection du Peuple pour obtenir du
   Pain and reconquérir ses Droits," 138
insurrection morale (moral insurrection),
   131, 134–35, 264n99
insurrections: brutal, 131–32; definition of,
   131; as French Revolution's point of no
   return, 135–36; of Germinal, 136–37,
   138; against Girondins, 114–15, 132–36;
   against Government of National
   Defense, 176–77, 179–80; Jacobins
   desiring to domesticate, 135; legality of, 130–31, 139–40, 205, 264n94;
   nonviolent modes of, 131; plebeian
   politics integrating, 114; as political
   action method, 114; practice of, 130–32;
   Prairial, 136–37, 138–40, 263n59; against
   Thermidoreans, 136–40; as ultimate
   recourse, 130; violence of, 131–32
internationalism, 168–69
International Workingmen's Association
   (IWA), 73–74, 175, 176, 231
intractable, 36–39
Iranian Revolution, 89, 90
Ireland, 164, 228
Irish rebellion of 1798, 164
isonomy, xiii, 70, 243
IWA. See International Workingmen's
   Association
IWW. See Industrial Workers of the World

Jacobinism, 145–46
Jacobins: English Jacobins' differences
   with, 144–46; fraternity referred to by,
   275n9; Girondins at odds with, 133–36,
   209, 264n83; insurrection domestication desire of, 135; offensive against

Jacobins (*continued*)
  sectional societies, 118; political
  system of, 37; revolutionary committees strengthened by, 122–23; sectional
  societies destroyed by, 121, 136, 205;
  sectional societies' discord with, 119;
  sectional societies disrupted by, 120;
  society of, 119. *See also* English Jacobins
Janiculum Hill, 70
Jesuits, 33
Jesus of Nazareth, 56
Johnson, Martin P., 174, 179, 180, 181, 184,
  272n29, 280n22
Jones, John Gale, 162
justice, 34

Kervégan, J.-F., 44
Knights of Labor, 74

La Boétie, Étienne de, xvii–xviii, 18, 41–42
*La commune de Paris 1871. Sa structure et
  ses doctrines* (Rihs), 230
La cuisinière et le mangeur d'hommes
  (Glucksmann), 92
Lando, Michele di, 15, 16, 17, 40, 43, 51–
  52, 80
*La parole ouvrié*re (Rancière), 91–92
Largius, Titus, 8–9
laughter, 19–20
La ville des expiations (Ballanche), 67
La vision d'Hébal (Ballanche), 67
Law, 27, 31
Law of the Twelve Tables, 63
Lazzari, 32–33
LCS. *See* London Corresponding Society
leaders: creation of, 77–78; De Leon and,
  74–80; designation of, 99–100; eman-
  cipation responsibility of, 100; English
  Jacobinism's national, 157–58, 269n66;
  Enragés as, 136; One and, 102; as political actors, 78–79; problem of, 17–18,
  38–39, 40–43, 171; in Roman Republic,
  77–79; servitude desire tied to, 99–100;
  solution to difficulties caused by, 102;
  union, 76, 77–78, 79

Leclerc, Theophile, 133
Le Combat, 180
Lefort, Claude, xii, 25–31, 42, 45, 47, 50, 57,
  96, 109–10, 145, 261n20
Lefrançais, Gustave, 175–76, 190, 194, 196,
  197, 238, 272n36, 273n77
legality, 186
Légion garibaldienne, 177
Lenin, Vladimir, 256n142
Le Prolétaire, 271n5
Le Réveil, 180
Leroux, Pierre, 66, 186, 230, 234–36,
  273n56, 280n22
Le Roy Ladurie, Emmanuel, 20, 23–24
Les communes françaises (Petit-Dutaillis),
  173
*Les révoltes logiques : Cahiers du centre de
  recherche des idéologies de la révolte*,
  91–92
Les révolutions d'Italie (Quinet), 17, 18
Les sans-culottes parisiens en l'an II (Soboul), 205
Le travail de l'oeuvre Machiavel (Lefort), 57
Levi, Primo, 275n8
Lex Hortensia, 70
liberals, 66–67
libertas, 5–6, 7
liberty: conflict as motor force of, 27,
  53–54; definition of, xvi; enchantment causing distancing from, xviii;
  humankind entering era of, 102; many
  desiring, 126; plebeian aspect as source
  of, 88; as plebeian principle history
  constant, 39; plebs desiring, xvii; sans-
  culottes desiring, 126–27
liberty tree, 155–64
libidinal-pagan history, 38
license (*licenzia*), 48
licenzia (license), 48
L'ignorance du peuple (Duprat), 44
Ligue républicaine de défense à outrance,
  177–78
Lissagaray, P.-O., 233
Livy, xix–xx, 7–11, 40, 46–52, 93
logos, xxi, 94

London, England, 152
London Corresponding Society (LCS),
xiii; agoraphilia contributions of,
164–72; convictions of, 146; corresponding societies compared with,
152–53; demands of, 154; direct democracy demanded by, 154; divisions of,
153; educational activity of, 153–54, 225;
education counted on by, 171; fall of,
163, 270n97; financial management of,
153; French Revolution's contact with,
146–48; General Committee of, 153;
human bond created by, 224–26; inaugural meeting of, 151; internal structure
of, 153; Irish rebellion supported by,
164; lottery used by, 172; mass meetings
organized by, 270n97; membership of,
151–55, 156–57, 161, 165, 226–27; operations of, 171; parliamentary reform and,
151–52; plebeian nature of, 152; plebeian
principle asserting itself from, 142–43;
plurality embraced by, 165; political
capacity beliefs of, 167; political spaces
used by, 169–70; rally held by, 161, 162;
res publica belief of, 167; revolutionary nature of, 152; secret executive
committee of, 160; subpolitical beliefs'
contact with, 146–48; trials of reformist
members of, 160–61; Two Acts de-
fied by, 162–63; women's position in,
166–67; zoon politikon transformation
of members of, 152
London Reforming Society, 161
lottery, 172
Lottes, Günther, 154
Lowenthal, David, 54–58
loyalist committees, 160
Lulier, Louis-Marie, 264n99
Luxemburg, Rosa, 24
lynching, 212
Lyotard, Jean-François, xii, 36–38

Machiavelli, Niccolò, xii, xvi–xvii, 14, 17,
26–27, 40, 43, 45, 46–52, 54–55, 56–57,
60, 126–27, 261n20

Machiavelli in the Making (Lefort), 25
Madison, James, 105–6
magistrates, 53
magnati. See nobles
Making of the English Working Class, The
(Thompson), 142–43, 218, 220
Malberg, Carré de, 106–7
Malon, Benoît, 176
Manin, Bernard, 171
many, the: carnival influencing, 18;
direct action of, xxii; dual history of,
xviii–xix; English Jacobins' respect
for, 165–66; few's distinction with, xx;
history of, xviii–xix; liberty desired by,
126; patrician politics neutralizing political expression of, 105; plebs rejecting
few's distinction with, xx; political
capacities of, 24, 35–36, 167, 197; politics
returned to by, 125
Marat, Jean-Paul, 128–29
Mardi Gras, 22
Margarot, Maurice, 157, 158–59
marriage, 63–64, 69–70
Marx, Karl, xii, xiii, 45, 73–74, 76, 190,
191–94, 196, 197, 261n20, 273n84
Marylebone Fields, 162, 167
Masaniello, xi, 31–36, 38–40, 41, 42–43, 242
masked civil war (French Revolution), 115
massacre, 22, 23
May 1968, xiii
Medici, Salvestro de', 14
Médicis, Catherine de, 21
Merleau-Ponty, Maurice, 25–26, 29–30
Methodism, 222–24
Metz, France, 231–32
Michelet, Jules, 122, 261n3
Michels, Robert, 107
Minor Arts, 15
Mitchell, Andrew, xi, xiv
moderates, 116, 128, 209–10
modern disciplinary archipelago, 84,
88–89, 242
monarchists, 181, 232
monarchs, 59, 100
monarchy, 64–65, 66, 100

moneylenders, 9

Montagnards, 114, 118

Montagne, 114–15, 135, 209

Montesquieu (baron), xii, 45, 52–60, 106–7

moral insurrection (*insurrection morale*),
    131, 134–35, 264n99

Morris, William, 241

Mouritsen, H., 6

Muir, Thomas, 158

multitude, xviii–xix

mutualism, 235

Naples, Italy, xi, 31–36, 41, 42–43, 242

Napoleon III (emperor), 175, 231, 234

National Assembly, 233

National Guard, 181, 182, 232, 233, 236

naval mutinies, 163

Navet, Georges, 71

Nazi concentration camps, 275n8

Negt, Oskar, xxiii, 279n37

New Science, The (Vico), 60–66

Nietzsche, Friedrich, 81–83

"Nietzsche, Genealogy, History" (Fou-
    cault), 81–83, 88

Nietzschean perspectivism, 81–82

Nights of Labor, The (Rancière), 91–92

9/11 attacks, 90

nobles (*magnati*): bourgeoisie's reconcili-
    ation with, 16; commoners' division
    with, 12; domination desire of, xvii, 26,
    50–51; plebeians' tumults with, xvi–
    xvii, 26–27; plebs as superior to, 63;
    political domination desire of, xvi

noise (*phoné*), xxi, 94

notables, 20, 23–24

Occident, 71–72

Oeuvres complètes (Ballanche), 112

"Of the Civil Principality" (Machiavelli),
    26, 52

One, the: desire for, 42, 64–65, 100, 173,
    217, 228; effects of attraction of, 115;
    leader and, 102; monarchy as, 64–65,
    100; Paris Commune succumbing to,
    190; tyrant image and, 28

On the Social Contract (Rousseau), 215

ontology of social, 29–30

openness, 114

Orient, 71

originary division of social, 25–31, 50, 145

Orphée (Ballanche), 67

Orwell, George, 201

Ostrogorski, Moisey, 108

otherness, 168–69

Owen, Robert, 219, 229

Ozouf, Mona, 206

paganism, 37–38

Paine, Thomas, 145, 148, 149–51, 155, 156,
    166, 268n32

Palmer, T. F., 158

Paris Commune, xiii, 137, 281n44; ago-
    raphile traditions contributed to by,
    191–97; as antihierarchical, 239–40;
    association developing during, 236–39;
    clergy impugned by, 185–86, 192; Com-
    mittee for Public Safety remedying
    military deficiencies of, 273n77; com-
    munalist tradition contribution of, 191–
    97; council, 119, 120, 188–89, 190, 240;
    as decentralized, 239–40; declaration
    adopted by, 185–86; democratic nature
    of, 185; division in, 239–40; doctrinal
    fragmentation of, 239; education re-
    formed by, 237–38; election of support-
    ers of, 183–84, 272n48; establishment
    of, 176–77, 178, 180–82, 192–93, 230,
    233; France's political situation before,
    231–33; as French Empire's antithesis,
    192; Lefrançais on, 196; local politi-
    cal bodies' relationship with, 238–39;
    majority/minority split within council
    of, 240; Marx on, 191–94, 273n84;
    One succumbed to by, 190; political
    clubs under, 182–90; political events
    marking, 230; political form of, 192–94,
    196–97; sectional societies' relationship
    with, 119; as state power refutation, 173,
    192–93, 194–97; two worlds struggle
    engagement of, 185–86, 273n56

Parisians, 233

"Paris Libre 1871", 186, 230, 233

Parker, Richard, 163

parliamentary reform, 151–52

Paterculus, 69

patrician class, 13

patrician families, 12, 47

patrician politics, 105

patrician principle, 71, 72

patricians: as belly, xx; carnival as critique of, 24–25; debtors clamped down on by, 8; domination desire of, 30; Florence controlled by, 13; of Naples, 32, 33, 34, 38; plebeians' alliance with, xii; plebeians' common stage with, xxi, 93; plebeians' conflict with, 7–11, 20, 22–25, 61–65, 71; plebeians' division with, 4–5, 47; political control taken back by, 16–17; political power of, 20–21; in Romans, 20–21

Paumier. See Serve, Jean

peace, 54, 60

peasantry, 21, 23

people, 11, 50, 52, 91

People, The, 73

permanence, 107–8, 116

permanent revolution, 37–38

Petit-Dutaillis, C., 173

Phenomenology of Perception (Merleau-Ponty), 29

Philon, Publius, 63

phoné (noise), xxi, 94

Pitt, William, 145, 154, 155, 157–63

Place, Francis, 153–54, 168

Platform, 148

plebeian action, xxii–xxiii, 89

plebeian aspect, 85–86, 88

plebeian constitutionalism, 147–48

plebeian experience: agoraphilic tradition confirmed by, 241; analysis of, xxiii–xxiv; birth of, xix; communalist traditions confirmed by, 241; definition of, xvi, xvii, xviii; description of, xii–xiv, xv–xvi; founding moment of, 10–11; gap as temporality

specific to, 241; inaugural scene of, xix–xxiii, 126; overview of, 241–43; political meaning of, xx–xxi; study of, xvi; tragic nature of, 43; understanding, 110–11

plebeian insurrection. See insurrections; plebeian secessions

plebeianism, 71–72

plebeian memory, 242

plebeian movements, 241–42

plebeian organizations, 177–78

plebeian politics, 52, 89–90, 114, 132–36, 143–44

plebeian principle, xxiv, 3, 4, 39, 66–73, 140, 142–43. See also carnival; Ciompi; plebeian secessions

plebeian public sphere, 260n1, 266n141

plebeians: Ballanche's attitude toward, 72–73; bourgeoisie, 77–79; Brossat on, 88–89, 90; conflict and, 46–52; as conflicts' agent, 65; definition of, 5, 76, 98–102, 143–44; domination opposed by, xvii, 26; emergence of, 5–11; Foucault on, 82–90; freedom and, 46–52; freedom assumption incapability of, 65–66; freedom desire of, xvi, 30, 99–100; heterogeneity of, 5; hierarchy rejected by, 11; liberty desired by, xvii; Machiavelli as partial to, 50–51; monarch's rest sought by, 100; as nobles' superior, 63; nobles' tumults with, xvi–xvii, 26–27; as parts, xx; patricians' alliance with, xii; patricians' common stage with, xxi, 93; patricians' conflict with, 7–11, 20, 22–25, 61–65, 71; patricians' division with, 4–5, 47; peace rejected by, 60; as political actors, 5, 60, 99–100, 148; political history of, 88; as political subjects, xvii, xx, xxi–xxii, 5, 10–11, 64, 89–90; in power, 124; Rancière on, 91–98; reason for term of, xviii–xix; in Roman Senate, 77–78; terms for, xviii–xix; Thompson on, 143–44; Vico's idea of, 64–66; working class transformation of, 144 plebeian secessions: Ballanche on, 68–70; first, xix–xxii, 4–11, 39, 40, 42, 68–69, 93–94, 95, 98, 126; gap leading to, 7; political nature of, xx; in Roman Republic, xix–xxii, 4–11, 39, 40, 42, 68–70; Roman Senate overcoming, xx; second, 69–70; third, 70

plebeian thought: authors taking part in, 44–46, 99; Ballanche's contribution to, 73; De Leon's legacy of, 79–80; Foucault's contribution to, 90, 257n155; Montesquieu's contribution to, 60; within political thought, 44; Rancière's contribution to, 98; Vico's contribution to, 66

Plebs, The, 80

plebs leaders. *See* leaders

Plebs League, 80

plurality, 165–67, 213, 218, 226–27, 228–29

Polanyi, Karl, 218, 224

police, 95, 126, 165, 166

political action: analysis of, xxiii–xxiv; effects of, xvi–xvii; in England, 162; insurrection as method for, 114; political management replacing, 130; of sans-culottes, 206, 207–8, 209–13; sans-culottes putting forward conception of, 125; sans-culotte's specificity of, 121–30; sans-culotte's will for, 114

political actors: *libertas* exploited by, 7; plebs as, 5, 60, 99–100, 148; plebs leaders as, 78–79

political bond: association as, 236–40; beginning of, xiii; definition of, 203; of division, 227–29; of fraternity, 205, 213–17, 227–28; general will as, 216; human bond as, 203, 238; of plurality, 218, 228–29; plurality as, 226–27; among sans-culottes, 211, 215–17; sans-culottes creating, 213; totalitarianism striking at, 203–4, 275n14

political capacities, 24, 35–36, 167, 197

political clubs, 182–90

political communities, 52, 60, 61, 66

political configuration, xix, 105

political domination, xvi, 13

political events, 59–60, 64

political freedom, xix, xxiii, 3–4, 43

political history, xxiv, 3–4, 88

political management, 130

political parties, 107–9, 260n14

political phenomena, xvi–xvii

political philosophy, 53, 54

political practice, 209–11, 212

political reforms, xviii

political repression, 13–14

political rights, 63–64, 114

political spaces, 169–70

political subjects: direct agency of, xxi–xxii; gap as place of, 97; plebs as, xvii, xx, xxi–xxii, 5, 10–11, 64, 89–90; radical equality among, xx

political thought, xxiv, 44

political union, 54

political upheavals, 12

politics: conflict of, 95; daily life's link with, 129; freedom as *raison d'être* of, 172; homogenization of, 129–30; many's return to, 125; as necessary, xiii; social division overcome by, xii; socioeconomic relations as reduction of, xii; of Terror, 123–24. *See also* plebeian politics

politics of many, xxi–xxiii, 126

poor, 12

popolani. See commoners

popular justice, 34

popular societies, 156, 159, 164

popular sovereignty, 116, 122–23

populus, xviii

Porshnev, Boris, xxiii, 23–24, 241–42

"Pouvoir et stratégies" (Foucault), 81, 84–88

power: of communalists, 183; definition of, 201; Foucault on, 87–88; freedom and, 87–88; patricians' political, 20–21; plebs in, 124; of sectional societies, 120–21

power relationships, 87–88

Prairial insurrection, 136–37, 138–40, 263n59

prince, 43, 48, 52

Prince, The (Machiavelli), 26, 43, 47, 51, 52
principality, 48
principle of distinction, 107
progressive principle, 67–73
proletarian, 96–97
proletarian plebeians, 77, 84
proletariat, 45, 84, 91
Promise of Politics, The (Arendt), xv
proscriptions (*ammonizone*), 13–14
Proudhon, Pierre-Joseph, 101–2, 234, 235–36, 273n60, 279n6
Prussia, 231–33
public action, 210
Public Safety Committee. *See* Comité de salut public
punishment, 7–8
purges, 117–18, 120–21, 125, 212–13
putsch, 21
Pyat, Félix, 180

Quinet, Edgar, 17, 18, 40

radical democratic bodies, 167
radical egalitarianism, 150
radical equality, xx
Rancière, Jacques, xii, xx–xxi, 46, 91–98, 126, 165, 258n199, 259n216
reason, 55
rebellion, 164
Récamier, Juliette, 72
recurrent historical movements, 60–66
red poster, 178–79, 272n29
Reeves, John, 155–56
Reflections on the Revolution in France (Burke), 149
regimes, xvi, 27–28, 48
religion, 55, 66–67, 213, 215–16
representation, 106–7
representative government, 105–7, 108–9, 133
republic, xvii, 48, 49–50, 54, 75–76
Republican League, 180
res publica, 5, 6, 50, 167
revolts: carnival and, 18–25, 30, 31; of Ciompi, xi, 11–18, 39, 40, 51–52; of

famuli, 61–62; festival interconnecting with, 20, 31; of Masaniello, 31–36, 38–40, 41, 42–43; in Roman Empire, 56
revolution: first English, 147; in Florence, 15; fraternization forming, 236; Glorious, 147; Iranian, 89, 90; 1905 Russian, 16; permanent, 37–38; political events as, 59–60; of Roman Republic, 59; of 1640–1642, 147; twofold nature of, 38; Vertot's use of, 59. *See also* French Revolution
revolutionary committees, 119, 122–23
revolutionary industrial unionism, 74–75
revolutionary justice, 186–87
revolutionary socialist movement, 181–82
Richard, Jean-Claude, 4–5
Richet, Denis, 135–36
rights, 70, 147–48, 186. *See also* political rights
Rights of Man (Paine), 149–51, 155, 166
Rights of Nature, The (Thelwall), 142
Rihs, C., 230
riots, 7–8, 14–15
Robespierre, Maximilien de, 37, 38, 128, 134–35, 136, 145, 213
Roman Empire, 56
Roman history, 94
Roman Republic, xvi–xvii; Ballanche on, 68–70; conflict in, xix–xxii, 4, 5, 7–11, 77–79; debts in, 7–9; De Leon on, 76–79; freedoms of, 47, 59; isonomy coming to, 70; leaders in, 77–79; Machiavelli on, 46–52; Montesquieu on, 52–60; plebeian secessions in, xix–xxii, 4–11, 39, 40, 42, 68–70; political events of, 59–60; revolutions of, 59; Vertot on, 58–60; veterans in, 8–9
Romans, France, xi, 18–25, 30, 31, 39, 40–41, 42, 43
Roman Senate, xx, 8–9, 70, 77–78
Rome, 39, 42; Ballanche on, 68–70; conflicts in, xvi–xvii, 4, 5, 7–11, 77–79; creditors in, 7–8; De Leon on, 76–79; division of society of, 4–5; labor shortage undermining, xix; Machiavelli on,

Rome (*continued*)
  46–52; Montesquieu on, 52–60; pagan,
  55, 56; riot in, 7–8; social division in,
  76–79; social question of, 76; triple
  victory of, 9; Vico on, 60, 62–64; Volsci
  attacking, 8
Rougerie, Jacques, 174, 195
Rousseau, Jean-Jacques, 61, 105–6, 213–17,
  228, 276n38
Roux, Jacques, 123, 132–33, 135
rural monarchists, 232
Russian Revolution of 1905, 16

Sacred Law, xx, 10
Saint-André, Jeanbon, 127
Saint Blaise's feast, 21
Saint-Marc-Girardin, 72–73
sans-culottes, 242, 261n3, 262n32; centralization struggled against by, 121–23,
  125–27; coining of, 112; Comité de
  salut public's relationship with, 118;
  decentralization focusing attention
  on, 122; defining, 112, 206; direct
  democracy as keystone for mentality of, 114; domination of, 113; English
  Jacobins resembling, 144, 172; equality
  defended by, 113–14; fraternity of, 205,
  227–28; fraternization devised by,
  115–16; fraternization used by, 209–11;
  great specialists struggled against by,
  127–30; history of, 112–13; human bond
  articulated by fraternity of, xiii; liberty
  desired by, 126–27; lynching practice
  of, 212; mass and, 276n12; moderates
  prevailed over by, 116; openness of, 114;
  political action conception put forward
  by, 125; political action of, 206, 207–8,
  209–13; political action specificity of,
  121–30; political action will of, 114;
  political behavior of, 205, 208; political bond among, 211, 215–17; political
  bond created by, 213; political rights'
  enactment influencing, 114; principles
  of, 113–14; in Romans, 24; Rousseau
  influencing, 215–17, 276n38; sectional

societies established by, 116–17; social
  composition of, 113; Terror directly
  practiced by, 123; Terror supported by,
  123–24; as title of glory, 112; undividedness among, 213–17; violence of, 123,
  210, 211–13
Sartre, Jean-Paul, 211–12
Scotland, 158
second life, 18, 19
sectional societies: action of, 115–21;
  autonomy of, 120; central committee
  of, 120; conflicts opposing, 124; control
  avoided by, 118–19; coordination of,
  117; double role of, 117; education
  promoted by, 117; establishment of,
  125–26; Jacobin government destroying, 121, 136, 205; Jacobin government
  disrupting, 120; Jacobin offensive
  against, 118; Jacobins' discord with, 119;
  multiplication of, 118; origin of, 114–16;
  Paris Commune's relationship with,
  119; plebeian nature of, 120; power of,
  120–21; purges used by, 117–18, 120–21,
  125; revolutionary committees' conflict
  with, 119; sans-culottes establishing,
  116–17; surveillance carried out by, 117
sections, 114–16, 209
Sedan, France, 232
self-emancipation, 166
Senate. *See* Roman Senate
September 11, 2001 terrorist attacks, 90
Serman, William, 179, 184, 281n44
servants and domestics (*famuli*), 61–62
Serve, Jean, 21–23, 30, 40–41, 43
Servilius, 69
servitude, 41–42, 54, 99–100. *See also*
  voluntary servitude
1793 Constitution, 131, 264n94
Severus, Septimus, 51
Shakespeare, William, 76
shoemakers, 145
siege of Metz, 231
siege of Paris, 175–80, 232
Sieyès, Emmanuel, 105–6
Simoncino, 14

singer-songwriters, 214–15
slavery, 7–8
Slavin, Morris, 134, 264n99
SLP. *See* Socialist Labor Party of America
Soboul, Albert, 24, 120, 121, 205, 206, 207–8, 214, 216–17, 276n12
social behaviors, 109
social bond, xiii, 202–3, 222–24, 275n14
social contract, 216
social division, xii, 57–58, 76–79, 267n5. *See also* originary division of social
social friction, 12
Socialist Labor Party of America (SLP), 73–75, 79
socialist republic, 75–76
Socialist Trades and Labor Alliance (STLA), 74
social palingenesis, 67–68
social question, 76
societies of gentry, 155–56
societies of magistrates, 155–56
society, 27
Society for Constitutional Information, 159, 160–61, 270n104
Society for the Suppression of Vice, 222
Society of the Friends of Liberty, 161
socioeconomic relations, xii
Socrates, 82–83
songs, 214–15
Souvenirs d'un révolutionnaire (Lefrançais), 196, 272n36
soviet, 16
speech, xxi, 93–94
Spirit of Laws, The (Montesquieu), 52–53
standard-of-life, 220–21
state, 173, 192–93, 194–97
stationary principle, 67–73
STLA. *See* Socialist Trades and Labor Alliance
Strauss, Leo, 54–55, 57–58
Structural Transformation of the Public Sphere, The (Habermas), 260n1
Struggle for the Breeches, The (Clark), 166–67
subjectivization, 96–97

Suppliants, The (Euripides), 3
"Sur la démocratie: le politique et l'institution du social" (Lefort and Gauchet), 25, 28–29, 30
surname, 93–94
surveillance, 117

"Table ronde" (Foucault), 81
tax (*gabella*), 32
Taylor, Charles, 87
Terror, 118, 123–24, 145
terrorism, 90
"That the Disunion of the Plebs and the Roman Senate Made the Republic Free and Powerful" (Machiavelli), 26, 49
Thelwall, John, 142, 145–46, 154–55, 157, 160, 161, 170, 225–26, 268n56
theodicy of history, 67–68
Thermidor, 128, 137, 138
Thermidorean Convention, 212
Thermidoreans, 136–40
Thiers, Adolphe, 181, 182, 232–33
Thompson, E. P., 24, 142–45, 146–51, 150–51, 152–53, 156–58, 159, 161, 163, 164, 165, 167, 169, 170, 171, 172, 218, 219–22, 223, 226–27, 228, 267n5, 267n16, 268n32, 269n66
Thornton (colonel), 162
Thoughts on Machiavelli (Strauss), 55
Time-Image, The (Deleuze), 105
Tocqueville, Alexis de, 121
Tønnesson, Kåre, 137, 212
Tönnies, Ferdinand, 202
torture, 7–8
totalitarian domination, 28, 242
totalitarianism: architecture of, 203–4; division quelled by, 28; freedom perishing due to, 28; human bond treatment of, 203–4; individuals' spacing abolished by, 203–4; Lefort on, 261n20; overview of, 28; political bond struck at by, 203–4, 275n14; social bond destroyed by, 275n14
Toward a Critique of Hegel's Philosophy of Right (Marx), 196

traces, xxiii, 241–42
trade guilds, 14
tradition, xi–xiv, 149, 222–24
transgression, 19
tribunes: appointment of, xx, 10, 50, 53, 62–63, 69, 78; bonitary ownership defended by, 62–63; Machiavelli on, 50
Trochu (general), 177, 180, 181, 232–33
Tullius, Servius, 62–63
Two Acts, 162–63
"Two Causes of Rome's Ruin" (Montesquieu), 53, 54
Two Pages of Roman History (De Leon), 75–80, 99, 256n142
2008 financial crisis, xiii
two worlds, 185–86, 273n56
tyrannicide, 56
tyrant, 28

ultras, 66–67
umori. See humors
Union des femmes pour la défense de Paris et les soins des blessés, 236–37
union leaders, 76, 77–78, 79
United Kingdom (UK), 168–69
unity, 210–11
uprisings. *See* insurrections; revolts
Utilitarianism, 222–24
utopian isonomia, 243

Vaillant, Édouard, 237–38
Valerius, Marius, 9
Vallès, Jules, 189
Varlet, Jean, 133, 134, 135
Varlin, Eugène, 176
Versailles, France, 233
Vertot, René-Aubert, 58–60
veterans, 8–9
Vico, Giambattista, xii, 45, 60–66, 100, 255n109

Vieuzac, Barère de, 124, 127, 128
vigilance committees, 175–76, 184
violence, 123, 131–32, 186–87, 210, 211–13
Virginia, 69–70
Visible and the Invisible, The (Merleau-Ponty), 29–30
Volsci, 8, 9
voluntary servitude, xvii–xviii, 18, 41–42, 64
von Bismarck, Otto, 176, 231–33

Walker, Thomas, 159
war, 12, 115, 175–80, 231–33, 275n7
warrior republic, 54
way-of-life, 220–22, 278n21
Weber, Max, 5, 7
Weil, Simone, 11, 14, 18, 40
West, 3, 11
"What Is Bureaucracy?" (Lefort), 109–10
"Where the Guard of Freedom May Be Settled More Securely, in the People or in the Great" (Machiavelli), 50–51
Wilkes, John, 148
Williams, G. A., 162
women, 166–67, 184–85, 236–38, 276n19
Women's Union to Defend Paris and Care for the Wounded, 236–37
workers, 219–24, 231, 237, 278n21
workers' councils, 74–75
working class, 144, 219–22
wrong, 95, 97, 126, 166
"Wrong: Politics and Police" (Rancière), 93–94

zoon politikon, 97; *animal laborans* combined with, 226; *animal laborans* metamorphosing into, xv, 10–11, 166; humans as, 139; LCS members transformed into, 152